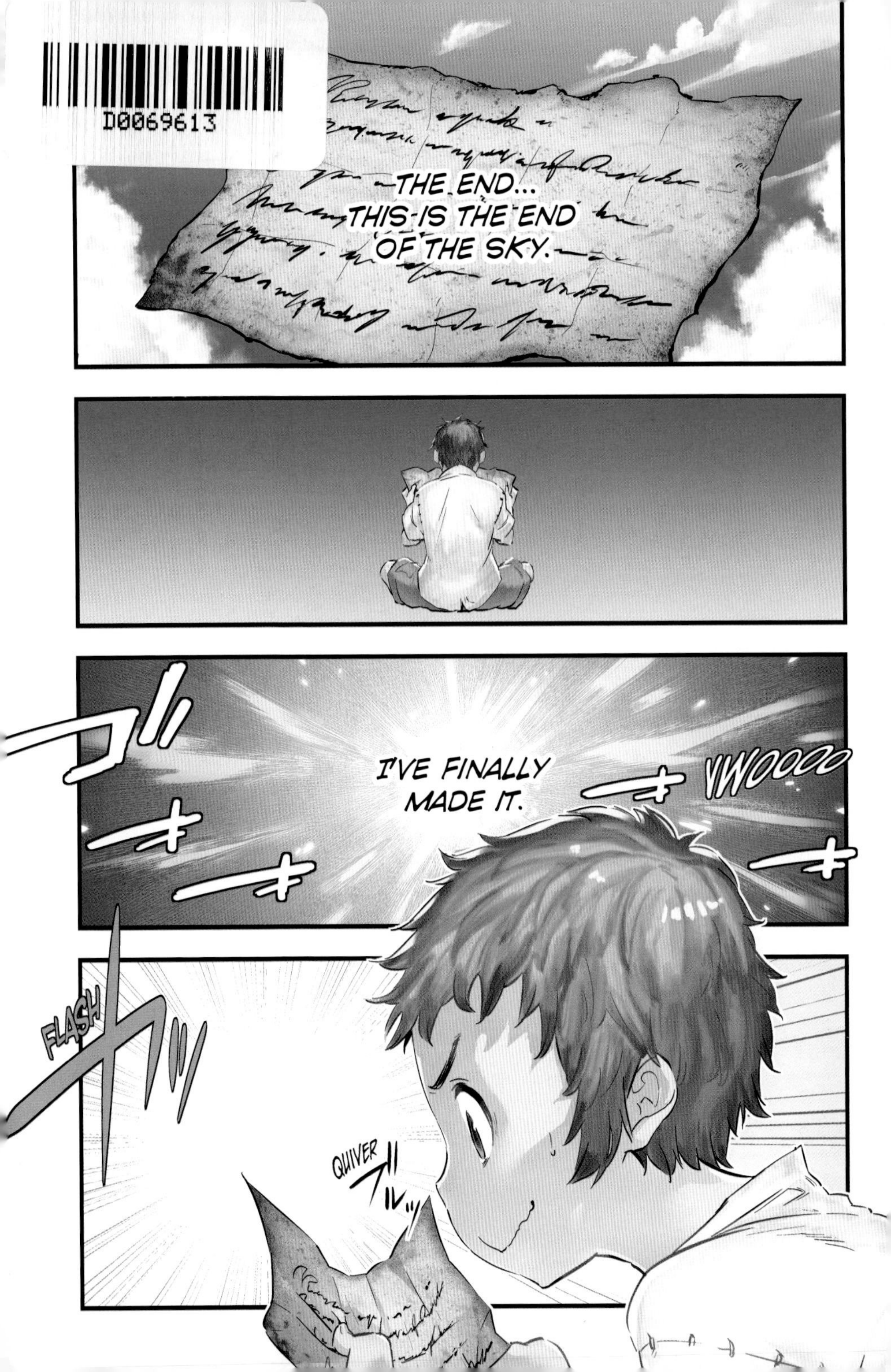
THE END...
THIS IS THE END OF THE SKY.
VWOOOO
I'VE FINALLY MADE IT.
FLASH
QUIVER

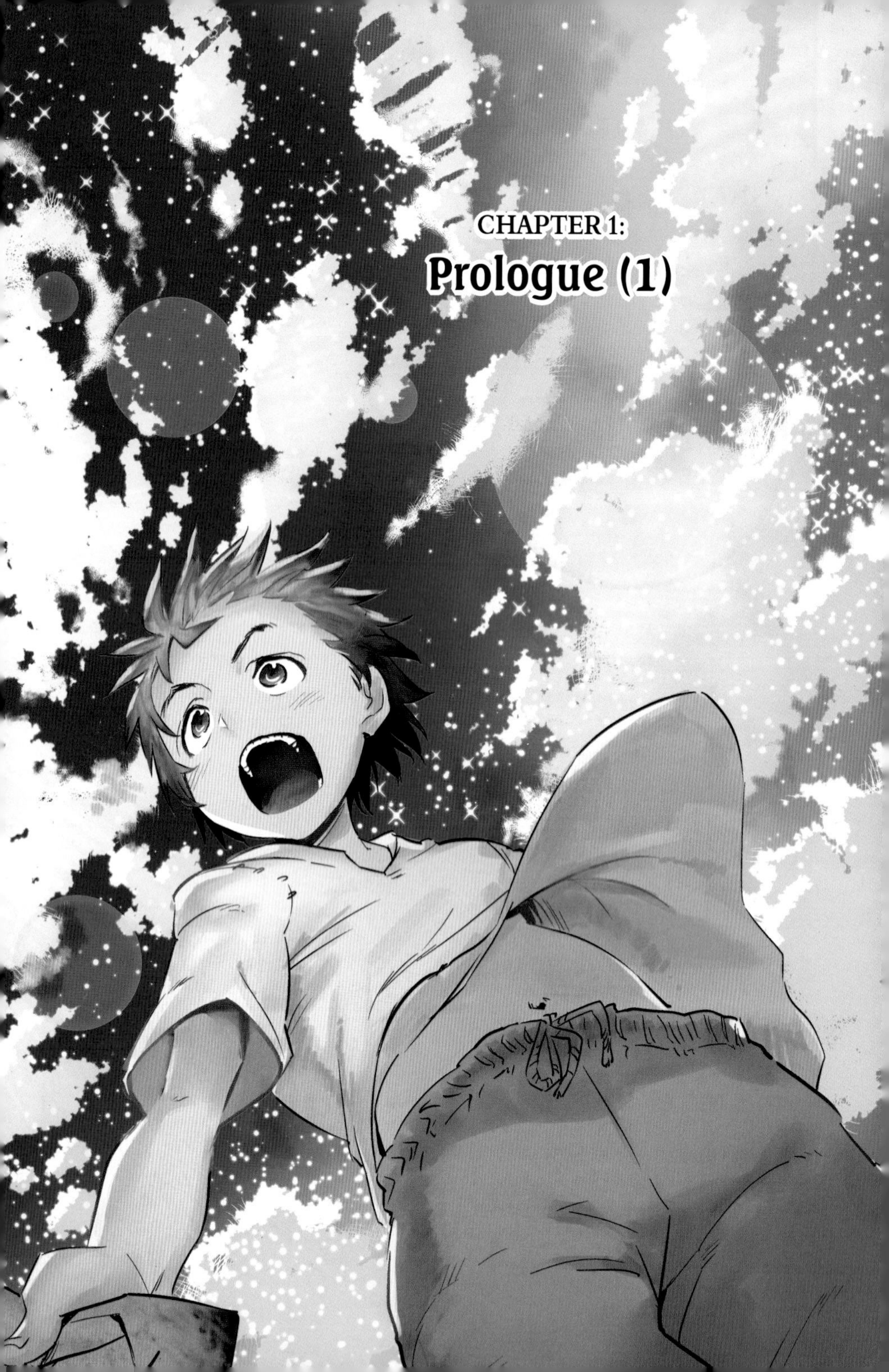
CHAPTER 1:
Prologue (1)

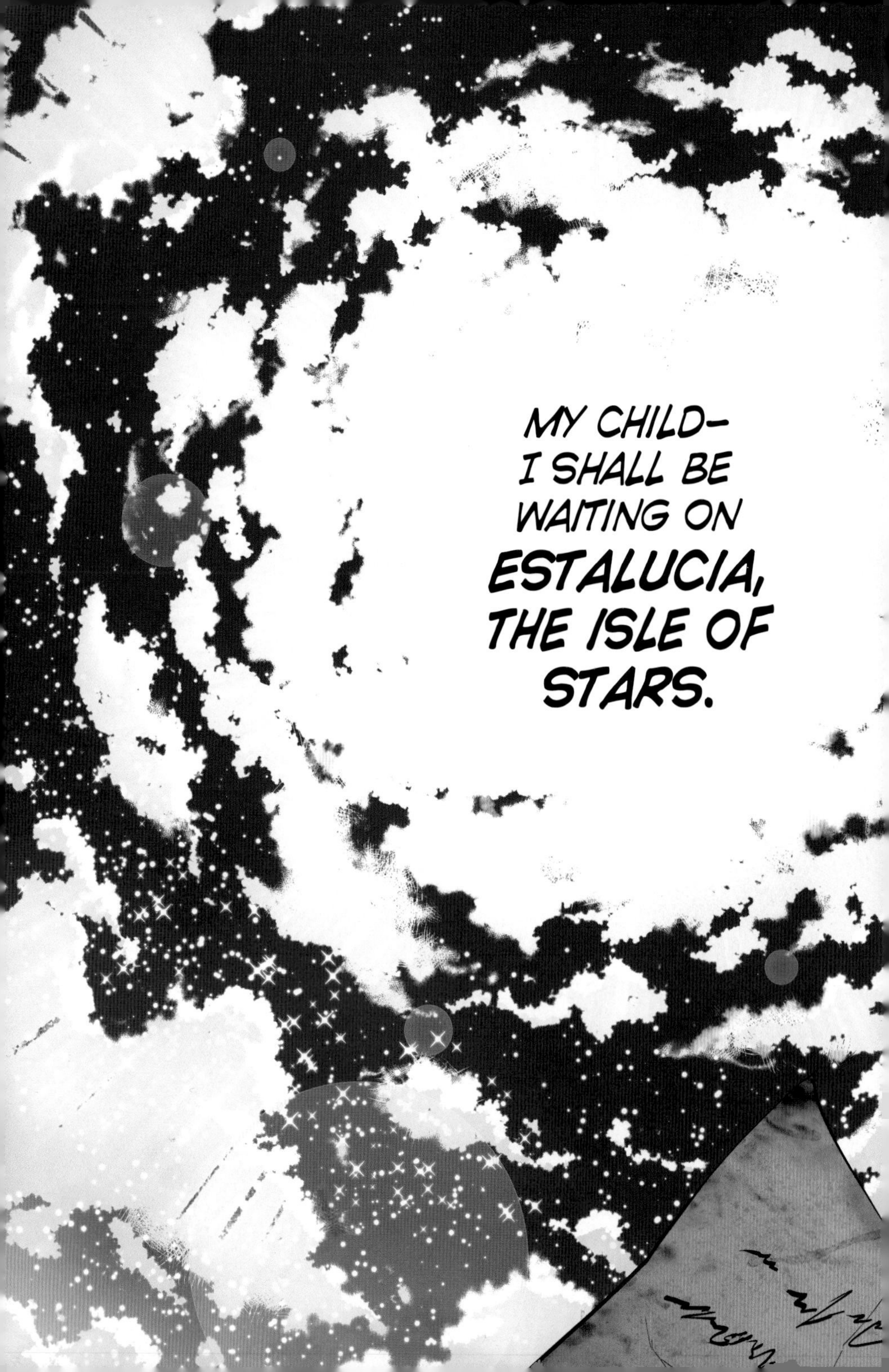
MY CHILD–
I SHALL BE
WAITING ON
ESTALUCIA,
THE ISLE OF
STARS.

CONTENTS

volume.

01

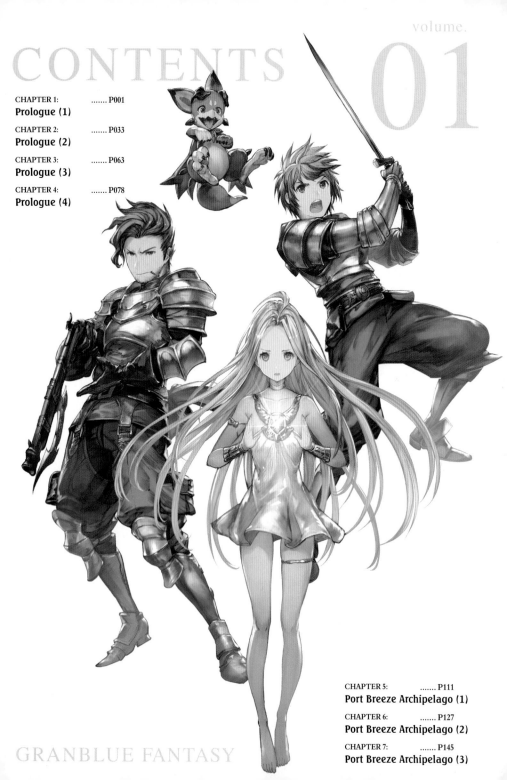

GRANBLUE FANTASY

GRANBLUE FANTASY
グランブルーファンタジー

volume.

01

original story: Cygames   art: cocho   layouts: makoto fugetsu

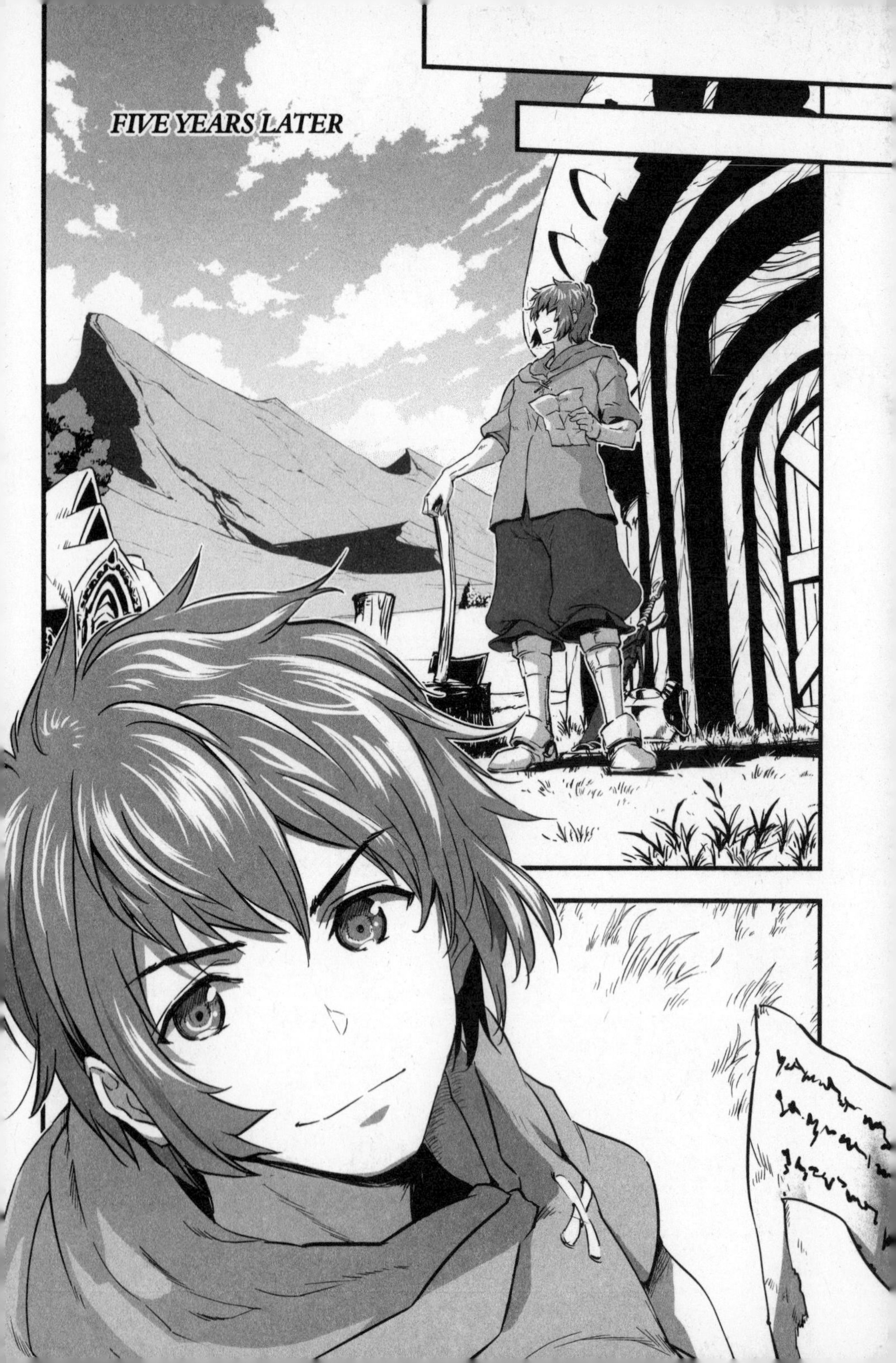
FIVE YEARS LATER

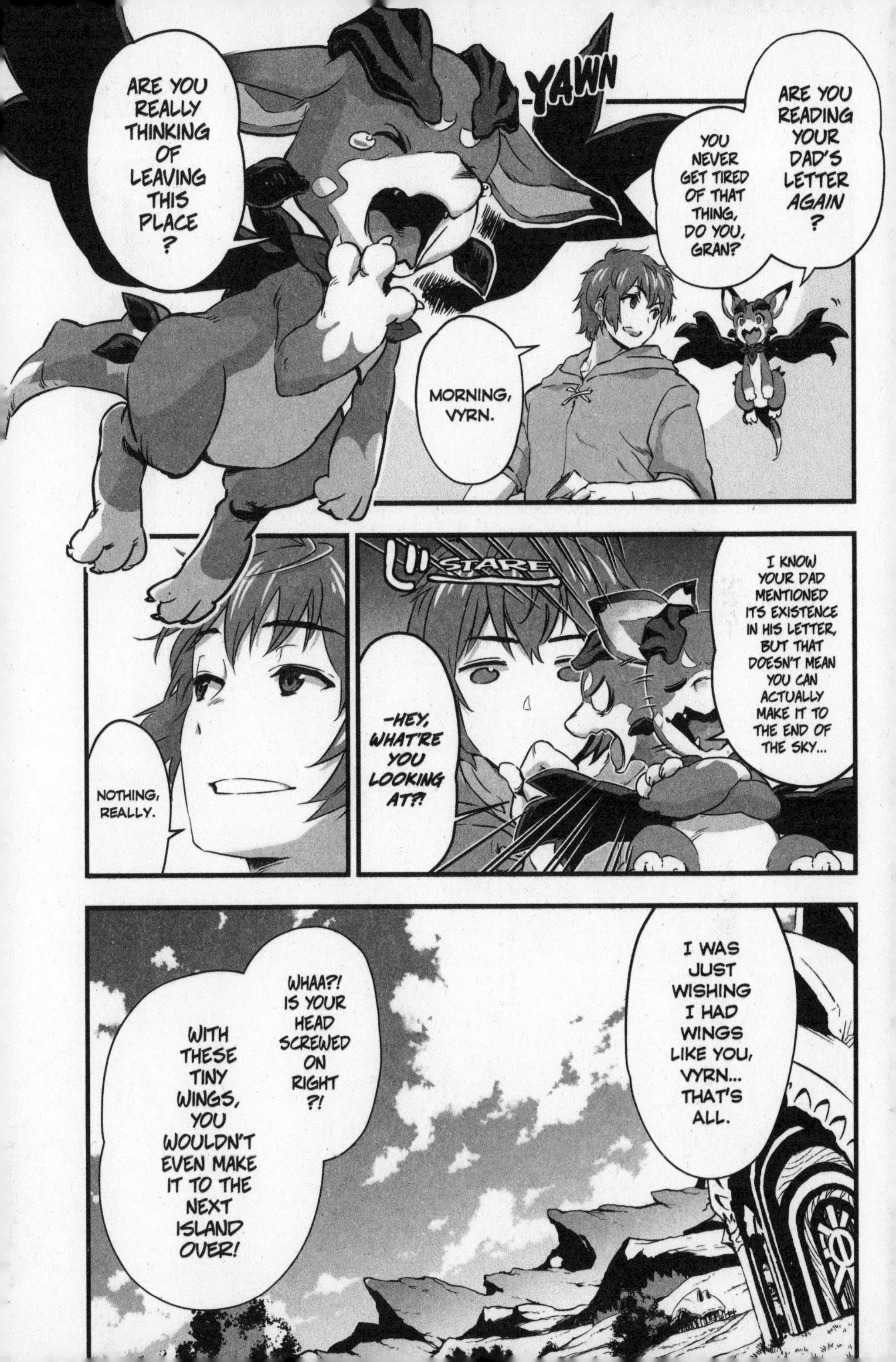
ARE YOU READING YOUR DAD'S LETTER AGAIN?
YOU NEVER GET TIRED OF THAT THING, DO YOU, GRAN?
YAWN
ARE YOU REALLY THINKING OF LEAVING THIS PLACE?
MORNING, VYRN.
I KNOW YOUR DAD MENTIONED ITS EXISTENCE IN HIS LETTER, BUT THAT DOESN'T MEAN YOU CAN ACTUALLY MAKE IT TO THE END OF THE SKY...
STARE
-HEY, WHAT'RE YOU LOOKING AT?!
NOTHING, REALLY.
I WAS JUST WISHING I HAD WINGS LIKE YOU, VYRN... THAT'S ALL.
WHAA?! IS YOUR HEAD SCREWED ON RIGHT?!
WITH THESE TINY WINGS, YOU WOULDN'T EVEN MAKE IT TO THE NEXT ISLAND OVER!

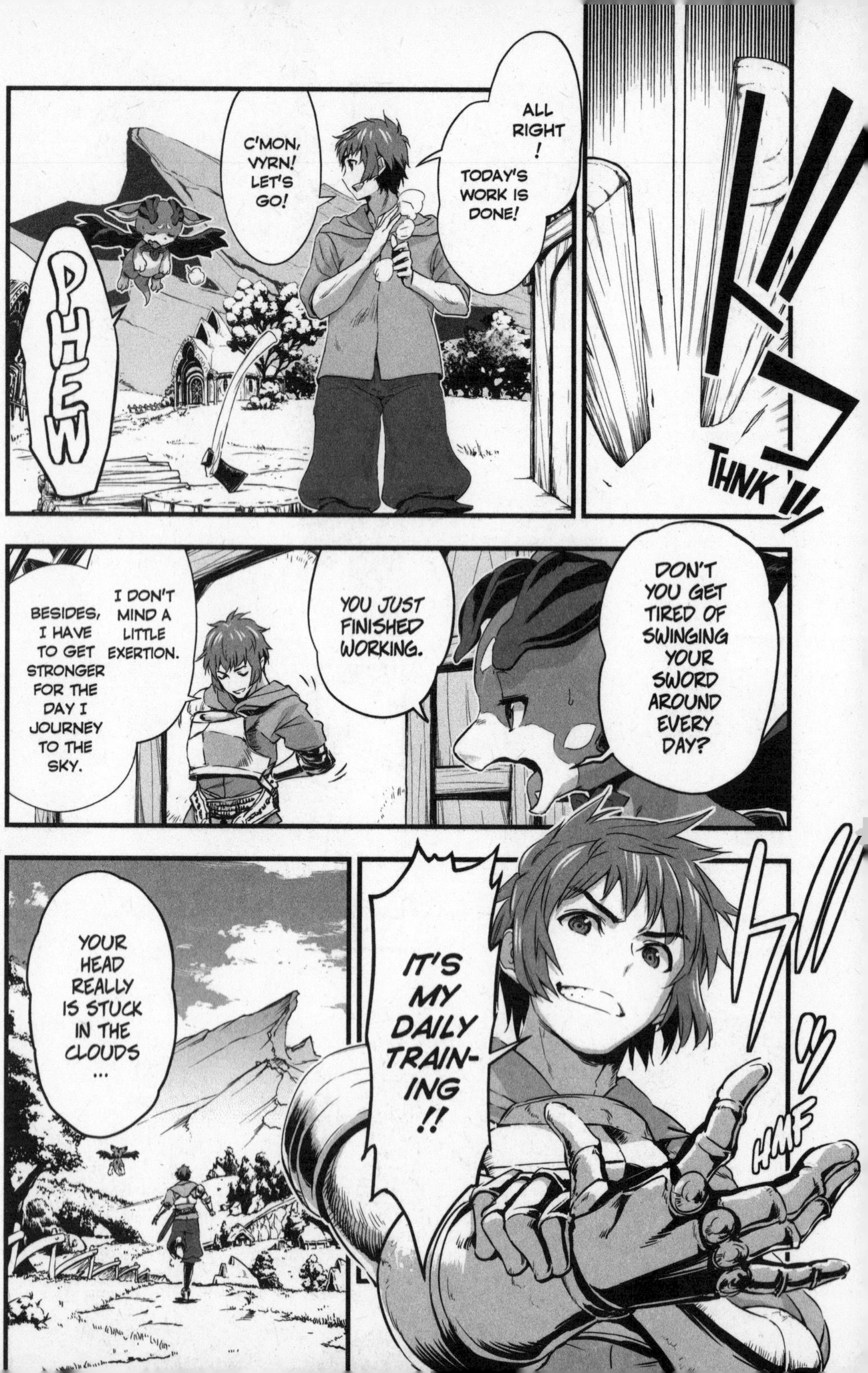
THNK!!
ALL RIGHT! TODAY'S WORK IS DONE!
C'MON, VYRN! LET'S GO!
PHEW
DON'T YOU GET TIRED OF SWINGING YOUR SWORD AROUND EVERY DAY?
YOU JUST FINISHED WORKING.
I DON'T MIND A LITTLE EXERTION.
BESIDES, I HAVE TO GET STRONGER FOR THE DAY I JOURNEY TO THE SKY.
IT'S MY DAILY TRAINING!!
HMF
YOUR HEAD REALLY IS STUCK IN THE CLOUDS...

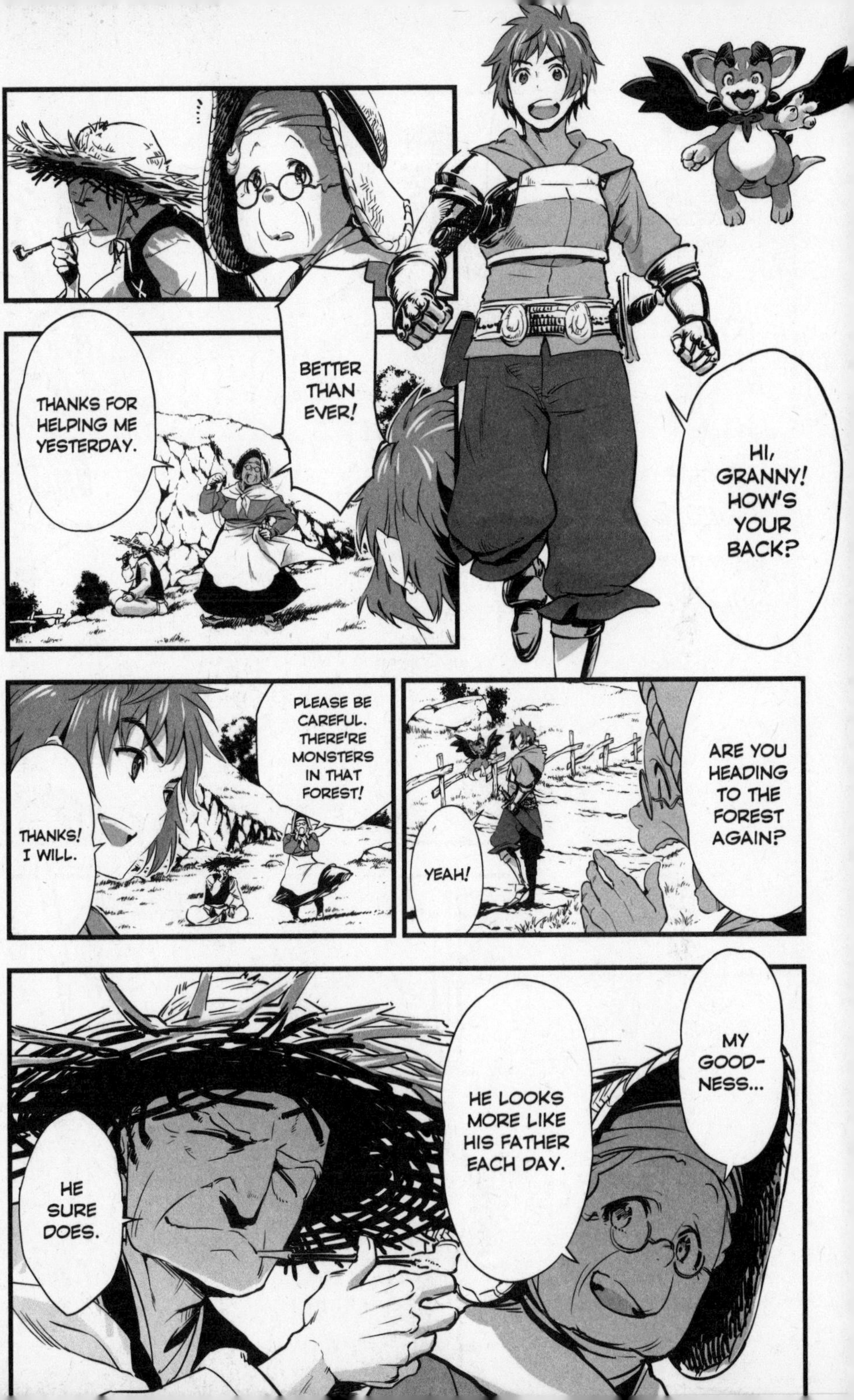
HI, GRANNY! HOW'S YOUR BACK?
...
BETTER THAN EVER!
THANKS FOR HELPING ME YESTERDAY.
ARE YOU HEADING TO THE FOREST AGAIN?
YEAH!
PLEASE BE CAREFUL. THERE'RE MONSTERS IN THAT FOREST!
THANKS! I WILL.
MY GOODNESS...
HE LOOKS MORE LIKE HIS FATHER EACH DAY.
HE SURE DOES.

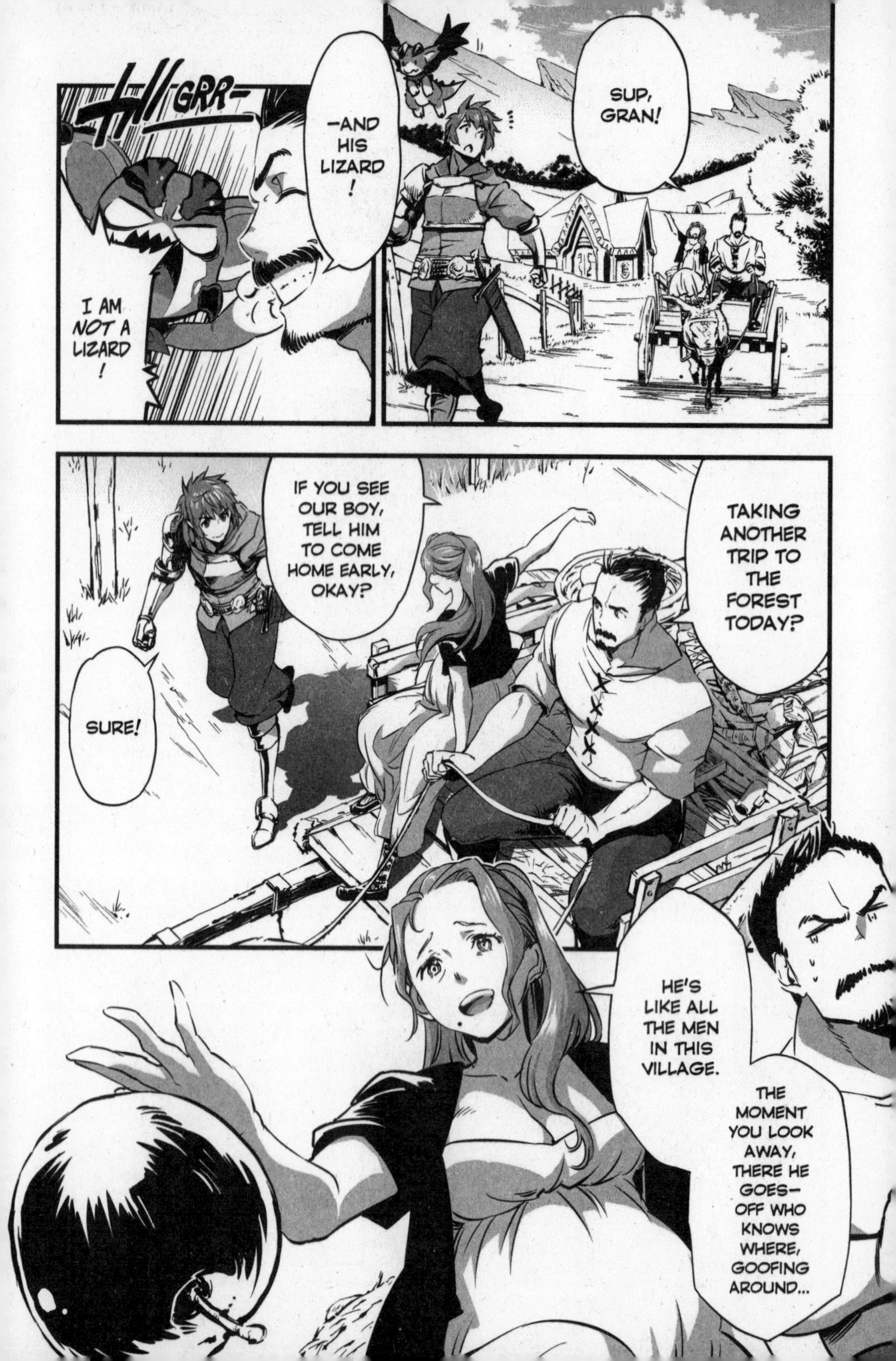
SUP, GRAN!
—AND HIS LIZARD!
GRR—
I AM NOT A LIZARD!
TAKING ANOTHER TRIP TO THE FOREST TODAY?
IF YOU SEE OUR BOY, TELL HIM TO COME HOME EARLY, OKAY?
SURE!
HE'S LIKE ALL THE MEN IN THIS VILLAGE.
THE MOMENT YOU LOOK AWAY, THERE HE GOES—OFF WHO KNOWS WHERE, GOOFING AROUND...

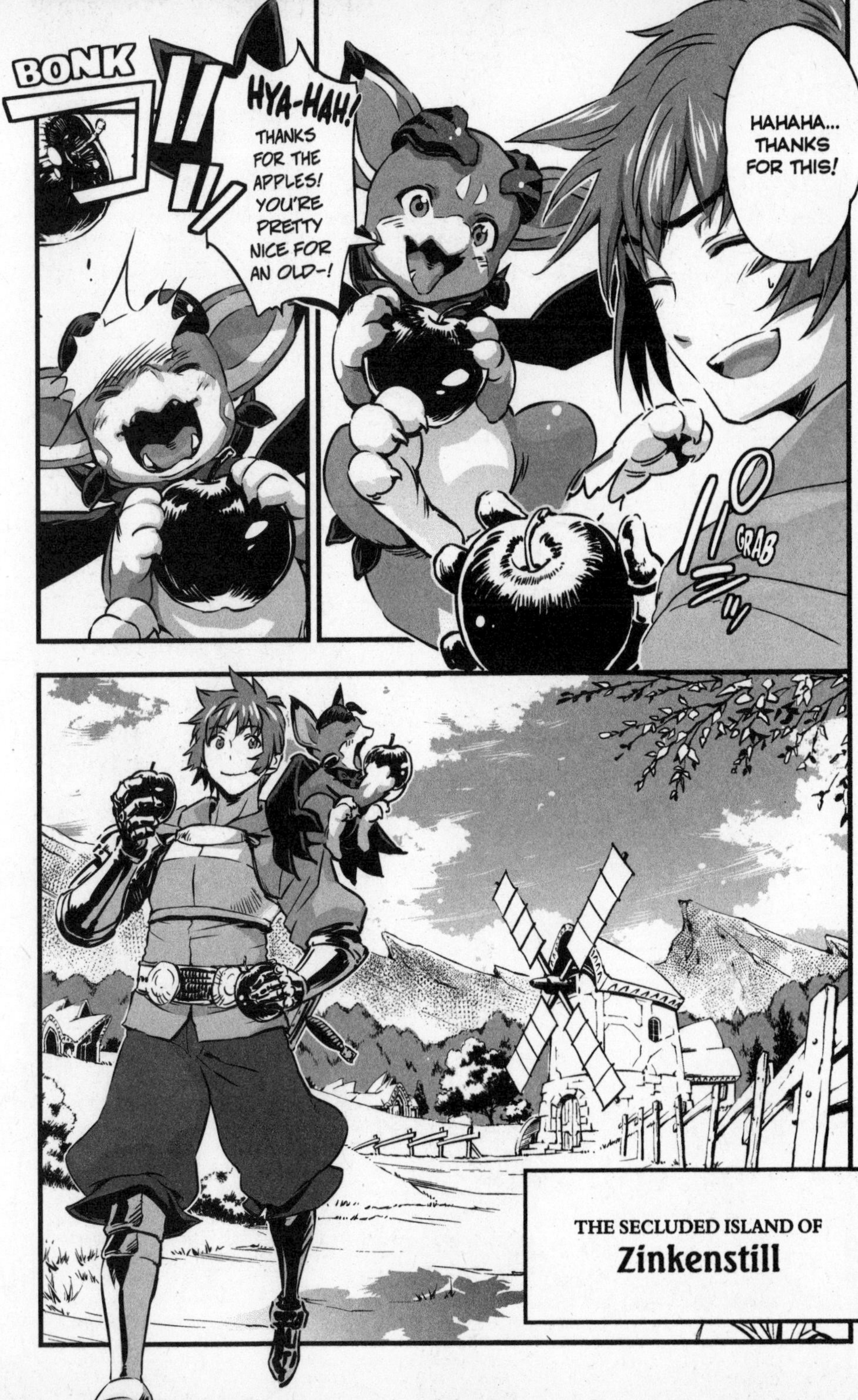
HAHAHA... THANKS FOR THIS!
GRAB
HYA-HAH! THANKS FOR THE APPLES! YOU'RE PRETTY NICE FOR AN OLD-!
BONK
THE SECLUDED ISLAND OF
Zinkenstill

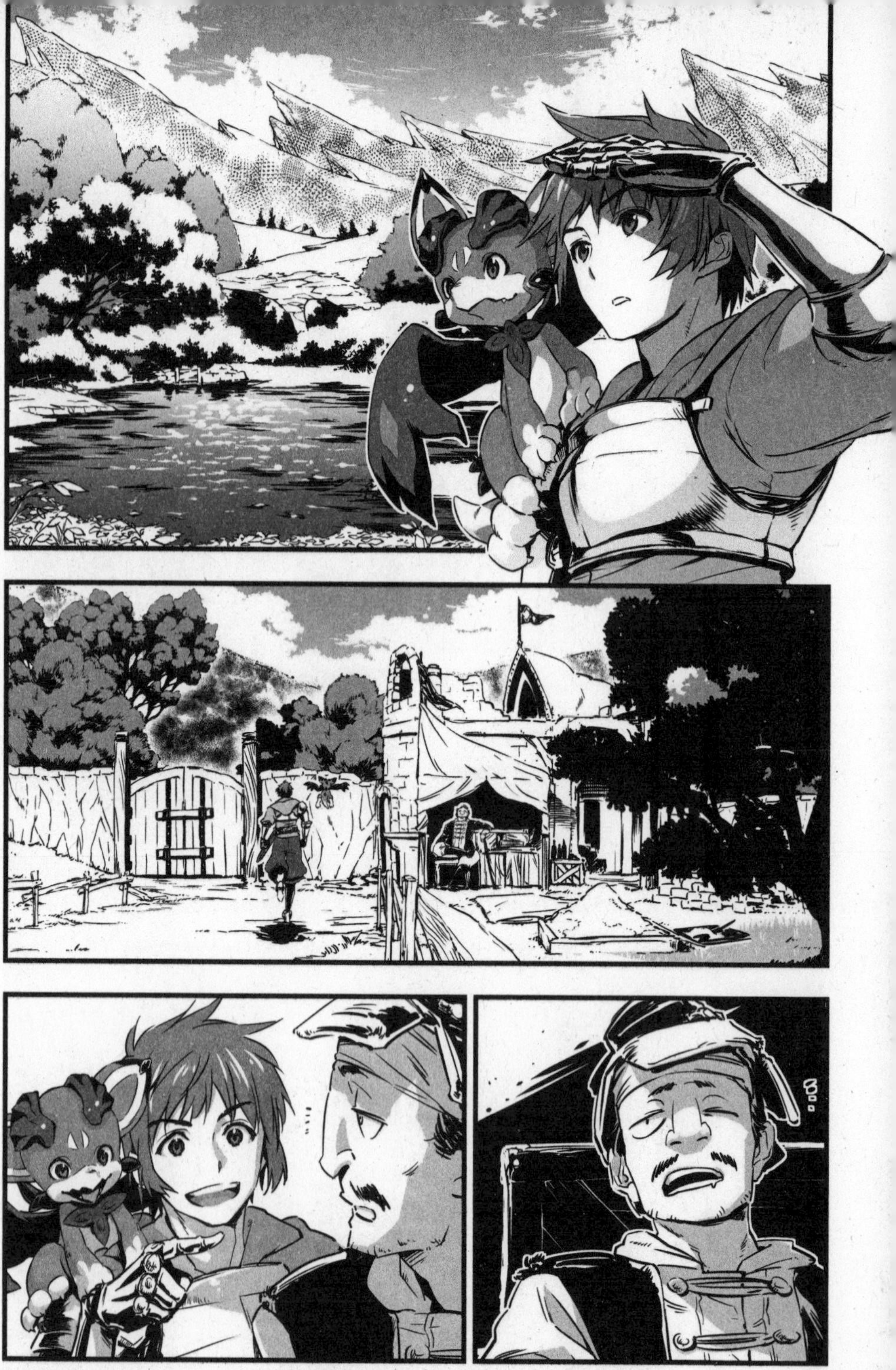

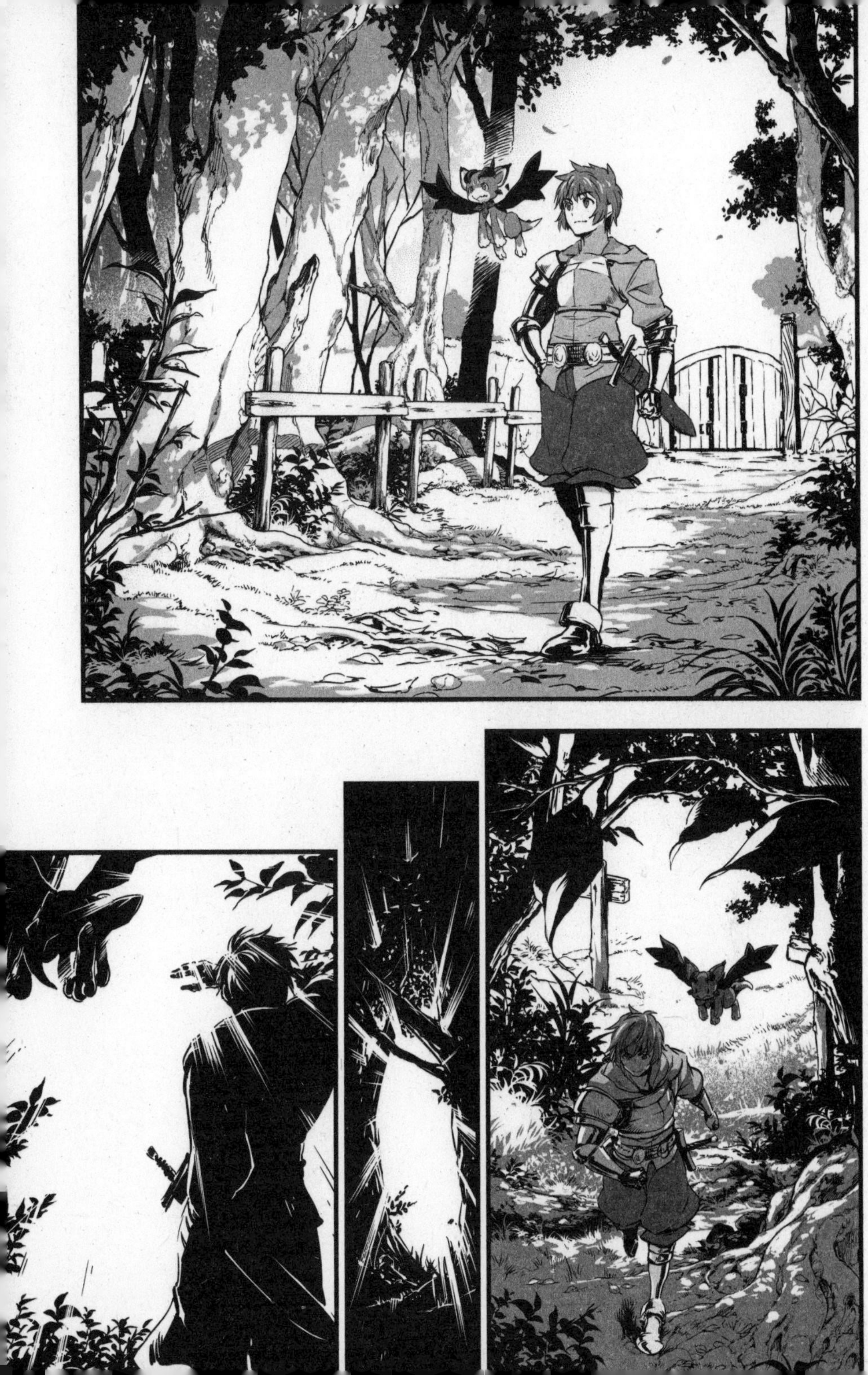

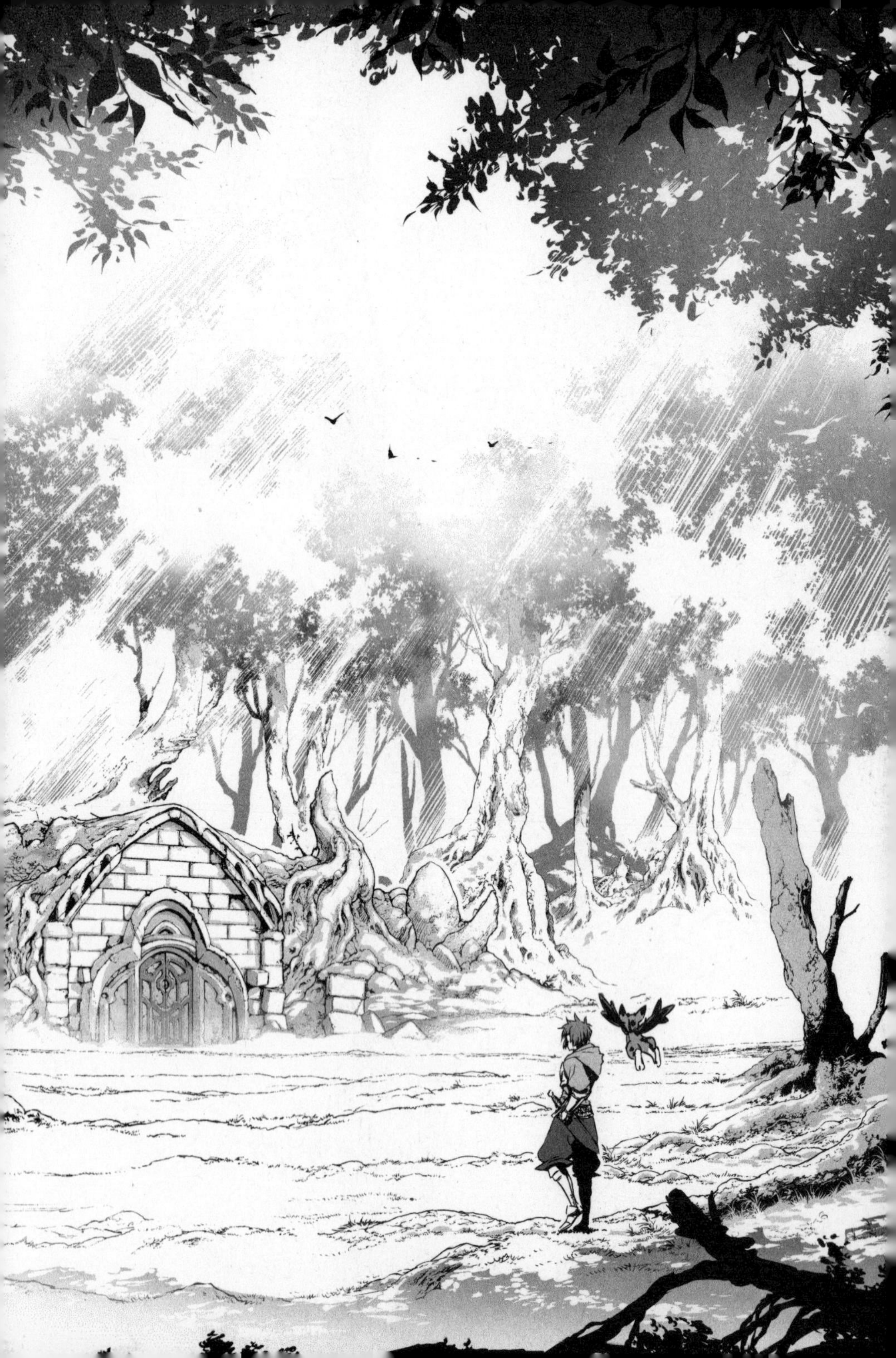

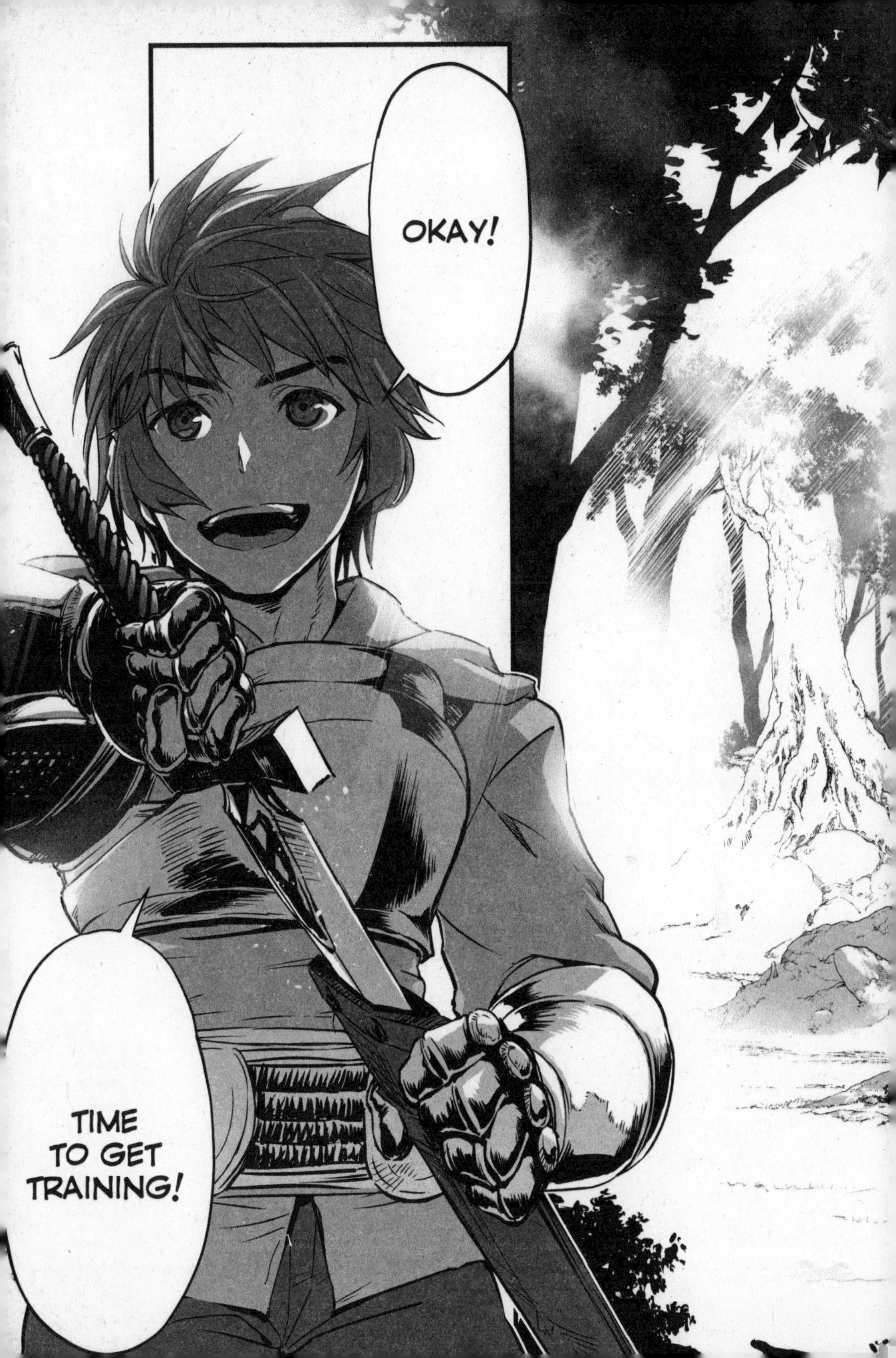
OKAY!
TIME TO GET TRAINING!

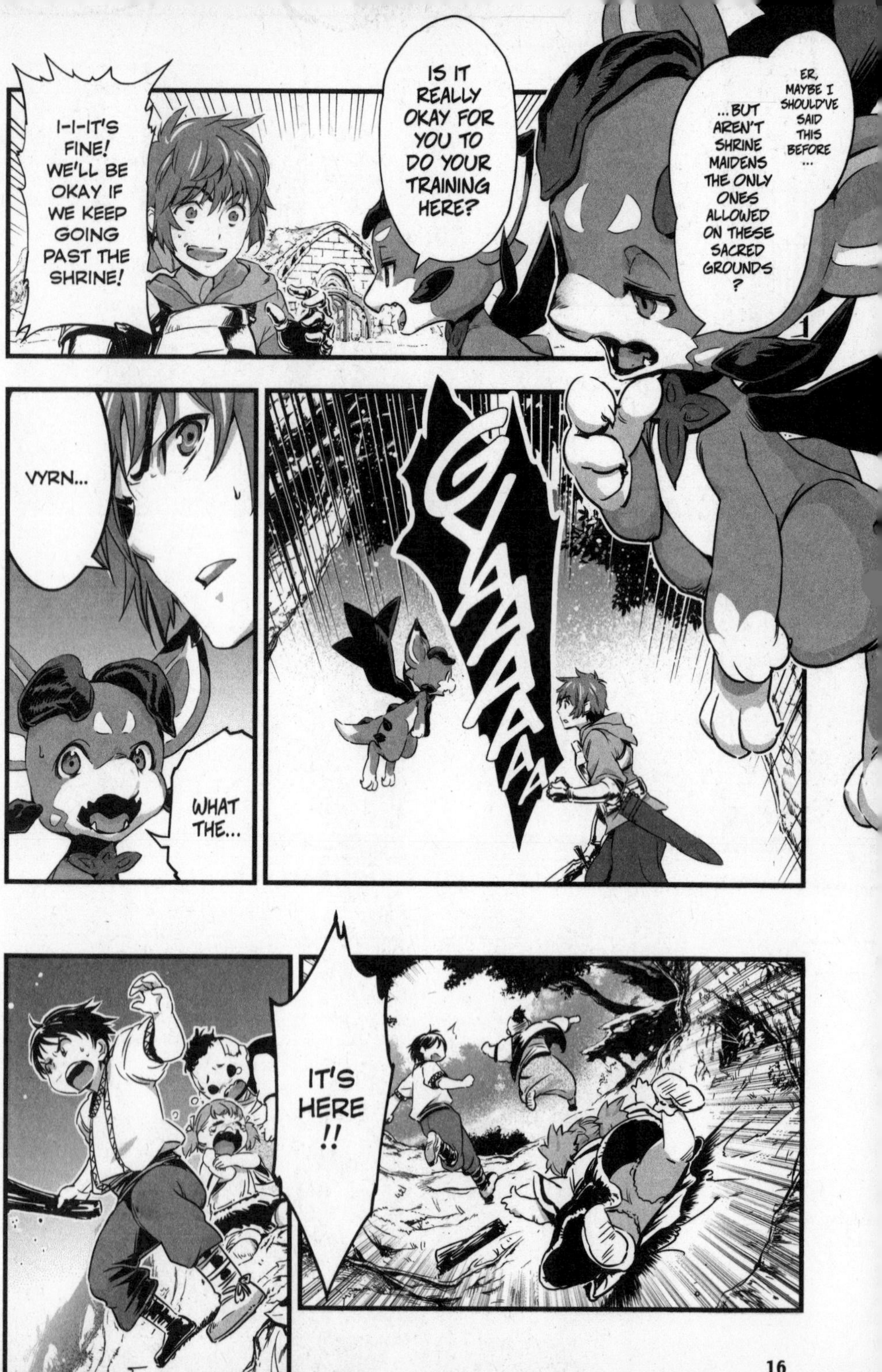
IS IT REALLY OKAY FOR YOU TO DO YOUR TRAINING HERE?
...BUT AREN'T SHRINE MAIDENS THE ONLY ONES ALLOWED ON THESE SACRED GROUNDS?
ER, MAYBE I SHOULD'VE SAID THIS BEFORE...
I-I-IT'S FINE! WE'LL BE OKAY IF WE KEEP GOING PAST THE SHRINE!
GYAAAA
VYRN...
WHAT THE...
IT'S HERE!!

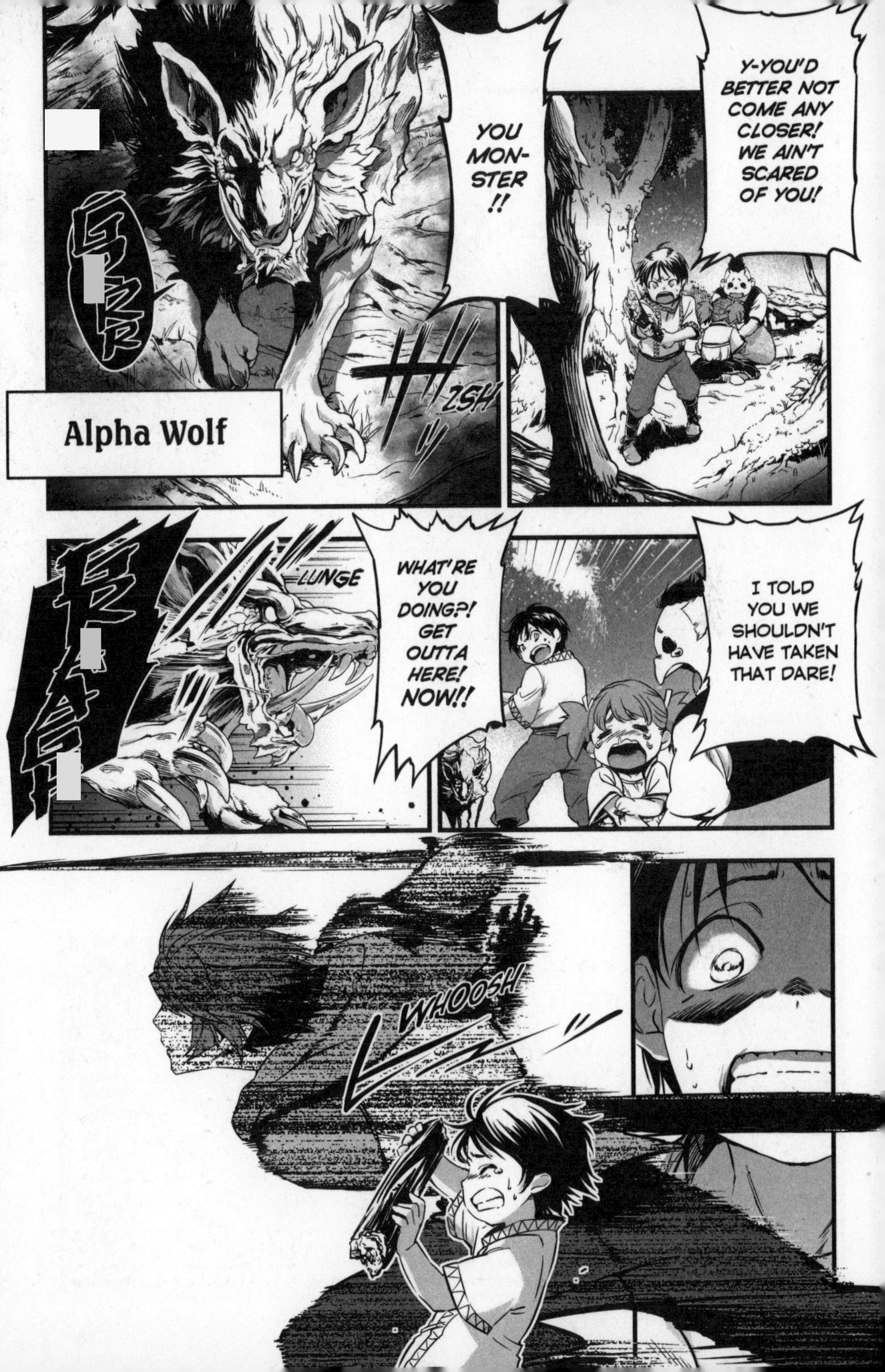
Y-YOU'D BETTER NOT COME ANY CLOSER! WE AIN'T SCARED OF YOU!
YOU MONSTER!!
ZSH
Alpha Wolf
I TOLD YOU WE SHOULDN'T HAVE TAKEN THAT DARE!
WHAT'RE YOU DOING?! GET OUTTA HERE! NOW!!
LUNGE
WHOOSH

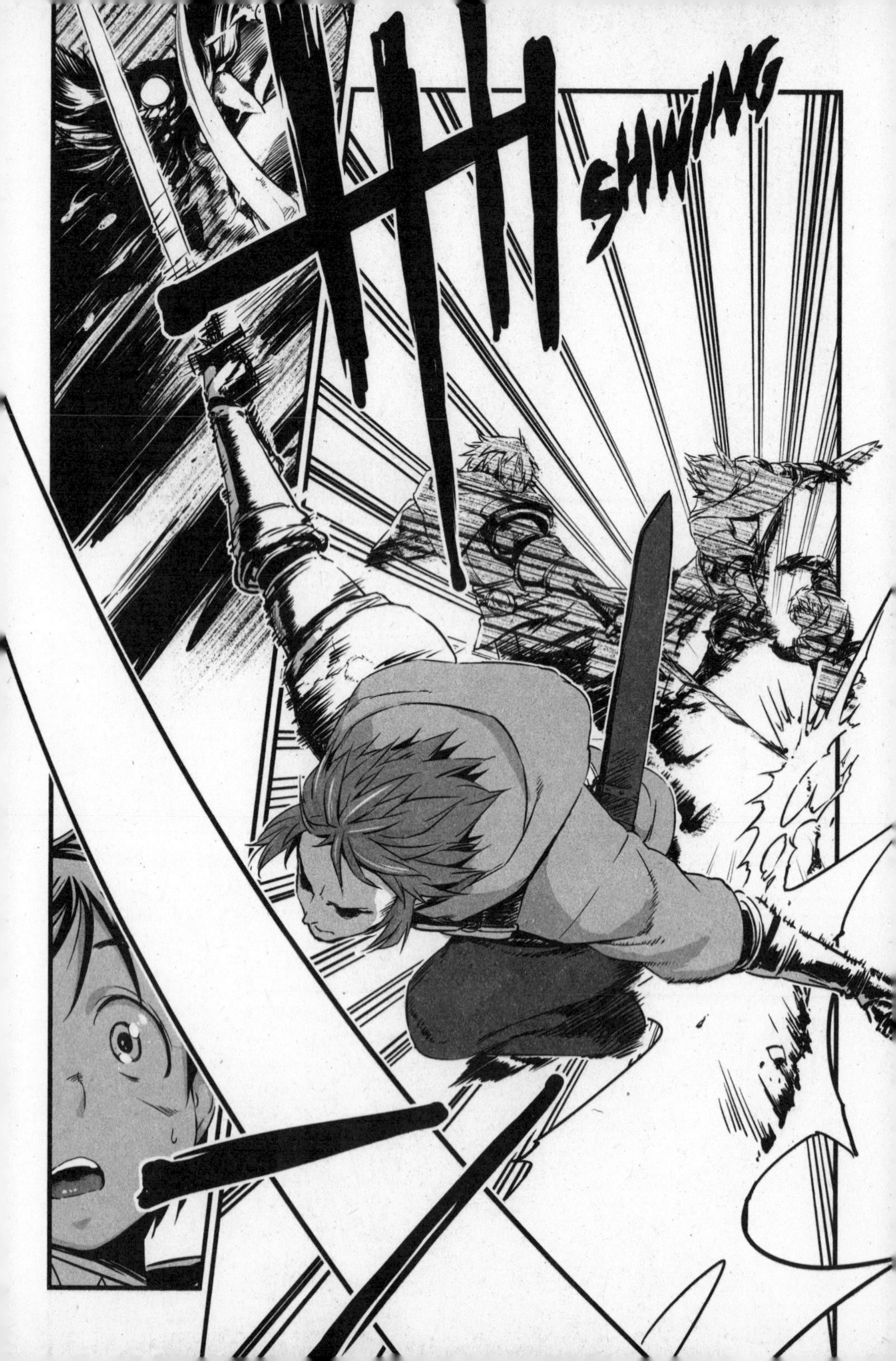
SHWING

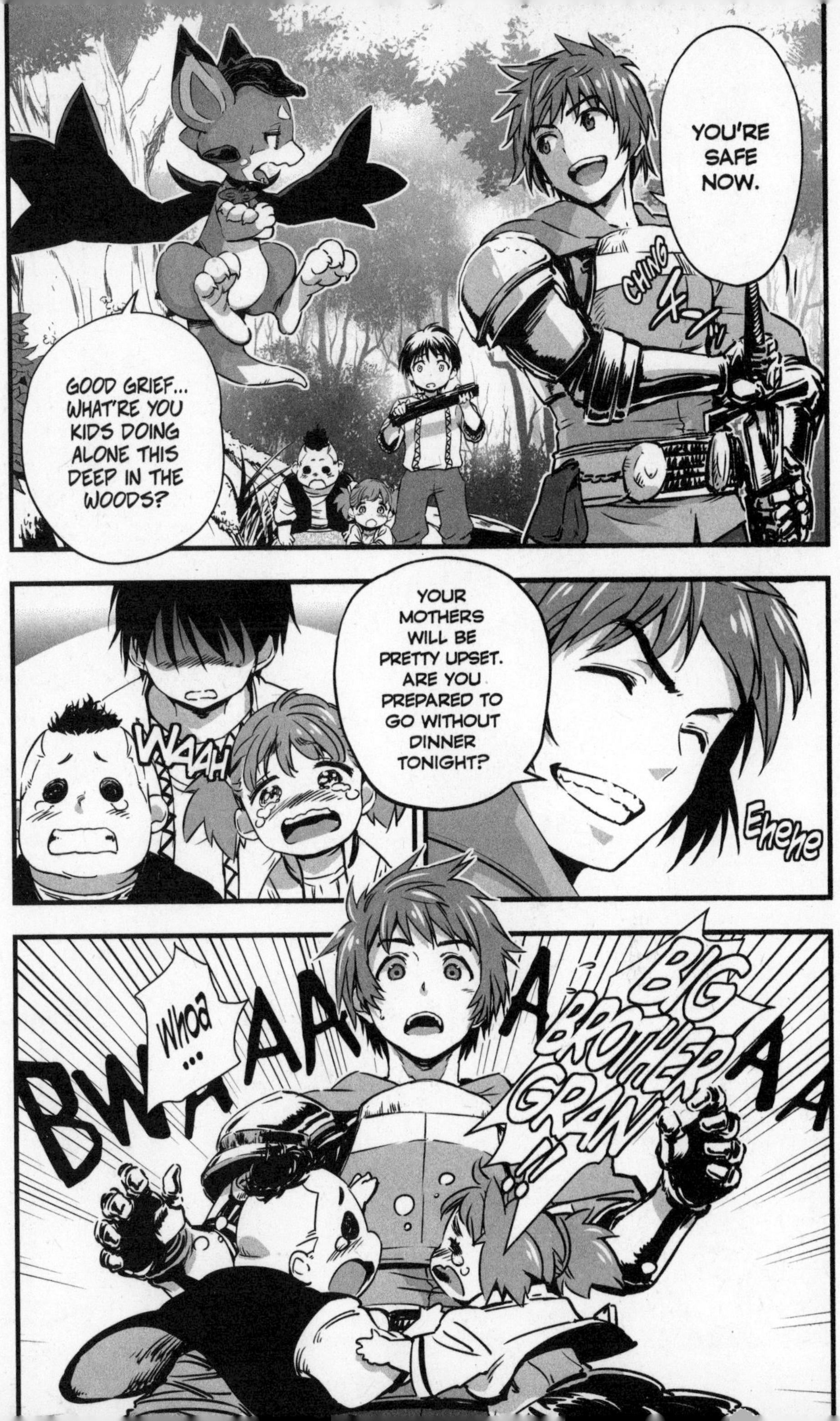
YOU'RE SAFE NOW.
CHING
GOOD GRIEF... WHAT'RE YOU KIDS DOING ALONE THIS DEEP IN THE WOODS?
YOUR MOTHERS WILL BE PRETTY UPSET. ARE YOU PREPARED TO GO WITHOUT DINNER TONIGHT?
Ehehe
WAAH
BIG BROTHER GRAN!!
BWAAAAAAA
Whoa...

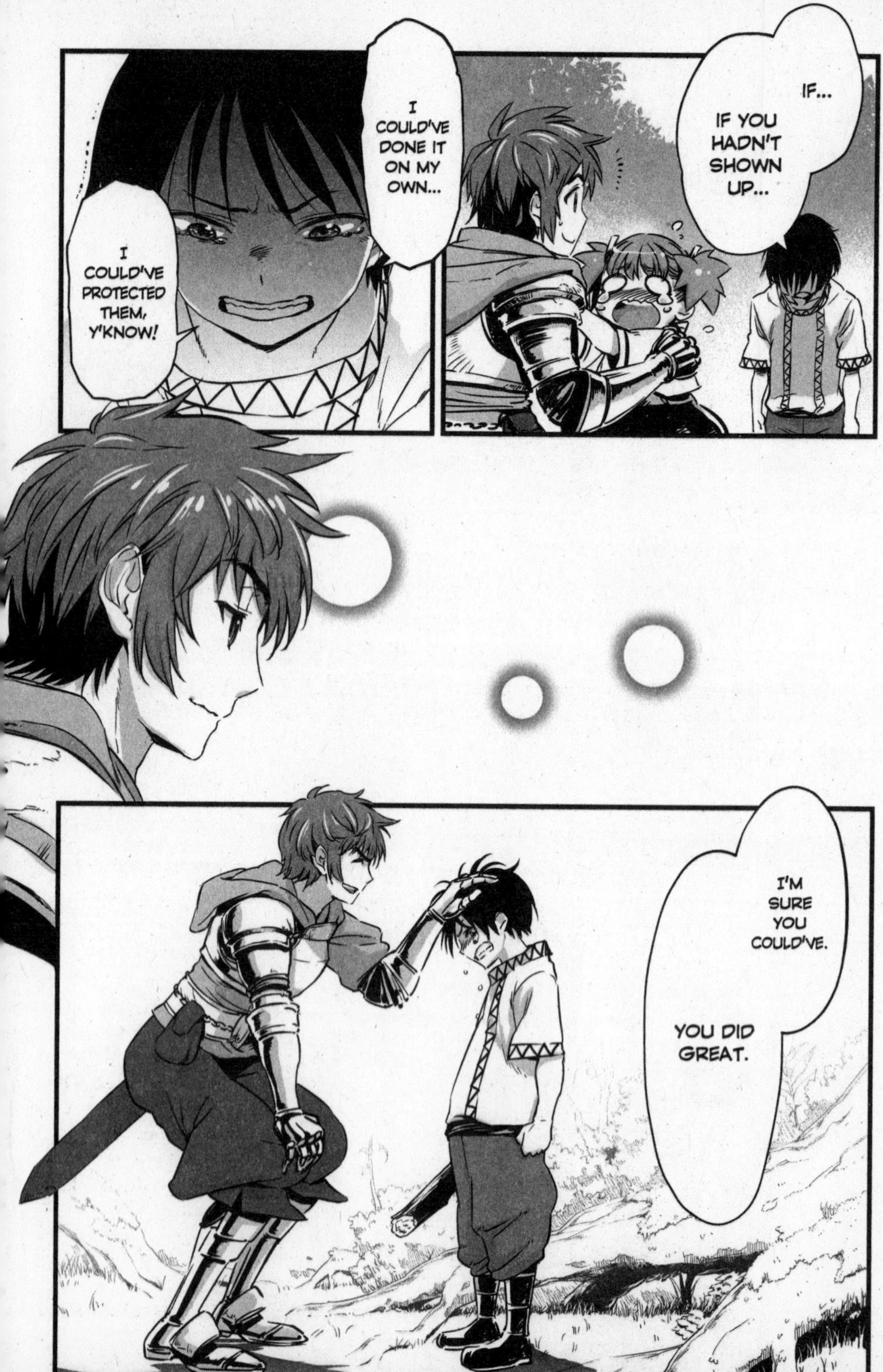
IF...
IF YOU HADN'T SHOWN UP...
I COULD'VE DONE IT ON MY OWN...
I COULD'VE PROTECTED THEM, Y'KNOW!
I'M SURE YOU COULD'VE.
YOU DID GREAT.

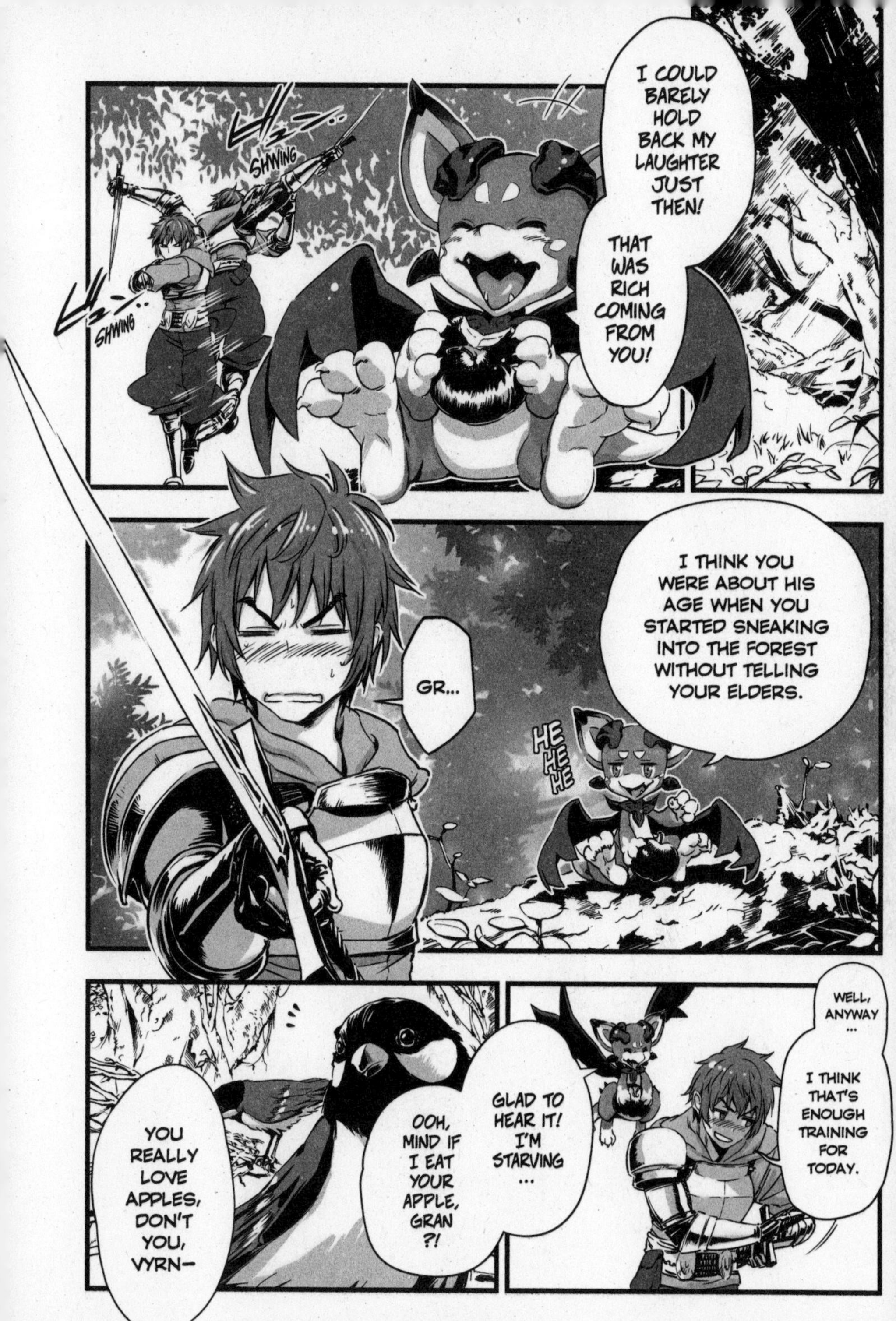

I COULD BARELY HOLD BACK MY LAUGHTER JUST THEN!
THAT WAS RICH COMING FROM YOU!
SHWING
SHWING
I THINK YOU WERE ABOUT HIS AGE WHEN YOU STARTED SNEAKING INTO THE FOREST WITHOUT TELLING YOUR ELDERS.
HE HE HE
GR...
WELL, ANYWAY...
I THINK THAT'S ENOUGH TRAINING FOR TODAY.
GLAD TO HEAR IT! I'M STARVING...
OOH, MIND IF I EAT YOUR APPLE, GRAN?!
YOU REALLY LOVE APPLES, DON'T YOU, VYRN—

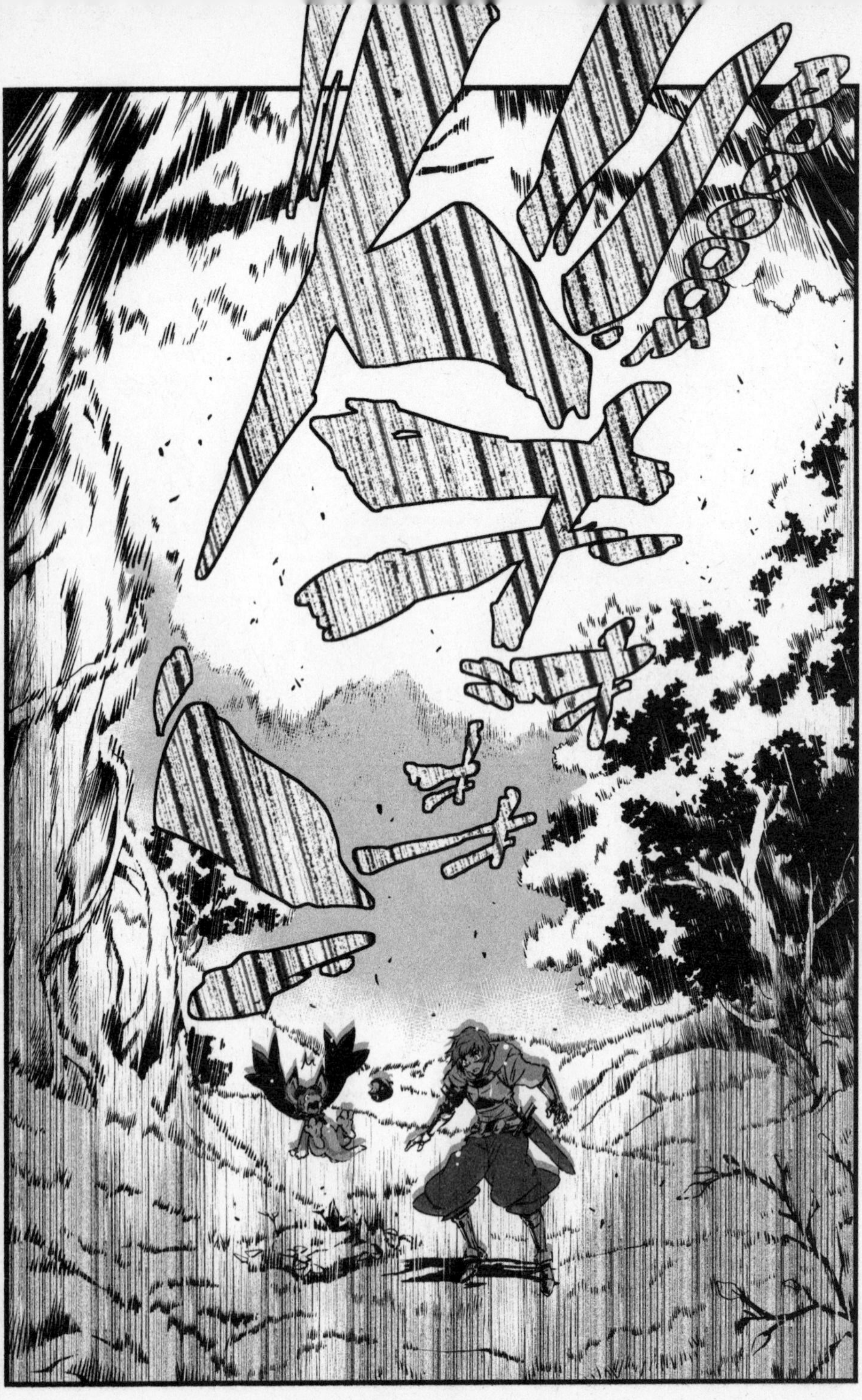
BOOOOOM

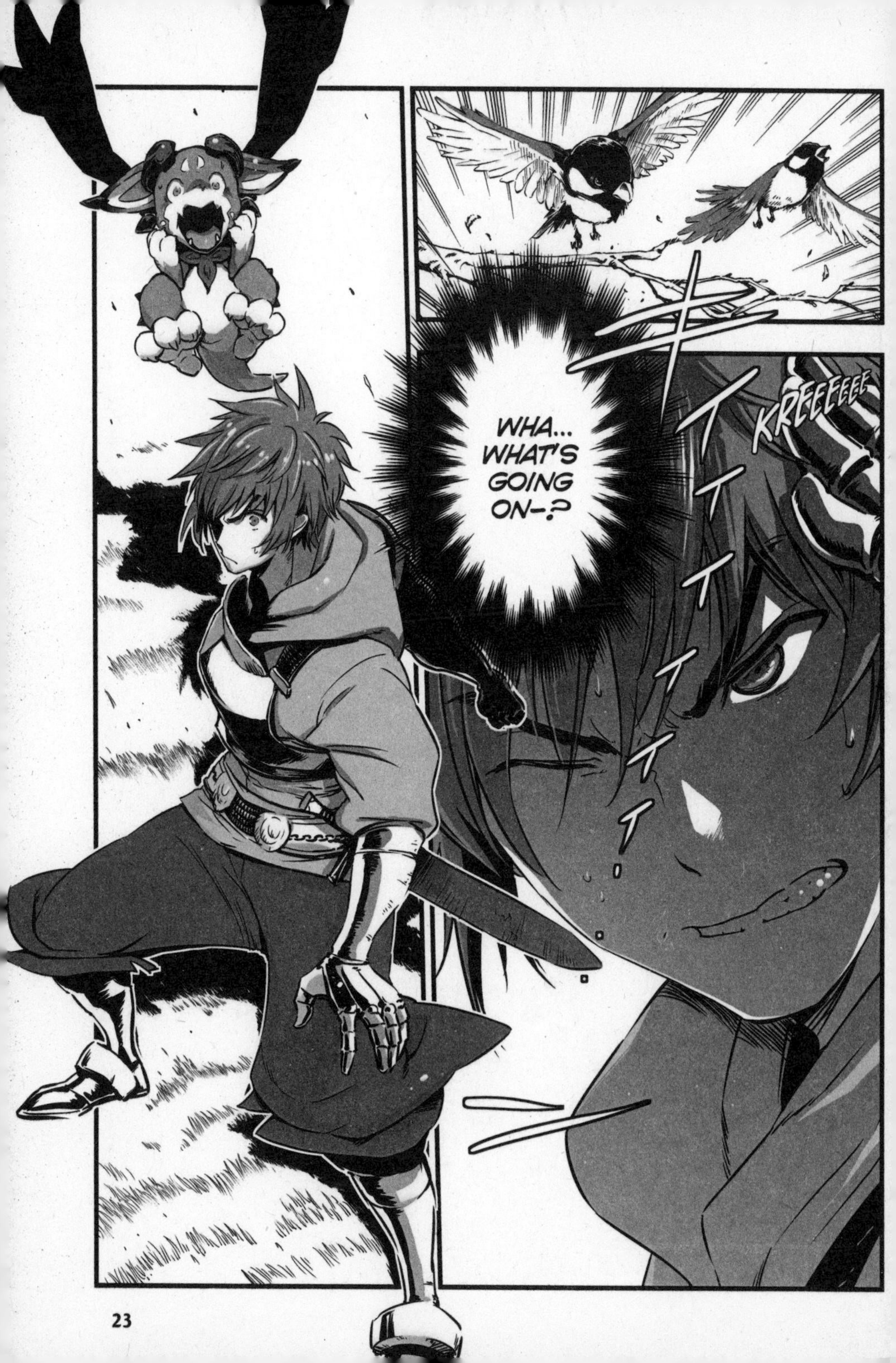
KREEEEEEE
WHA... WHAT'S GOING ON-?

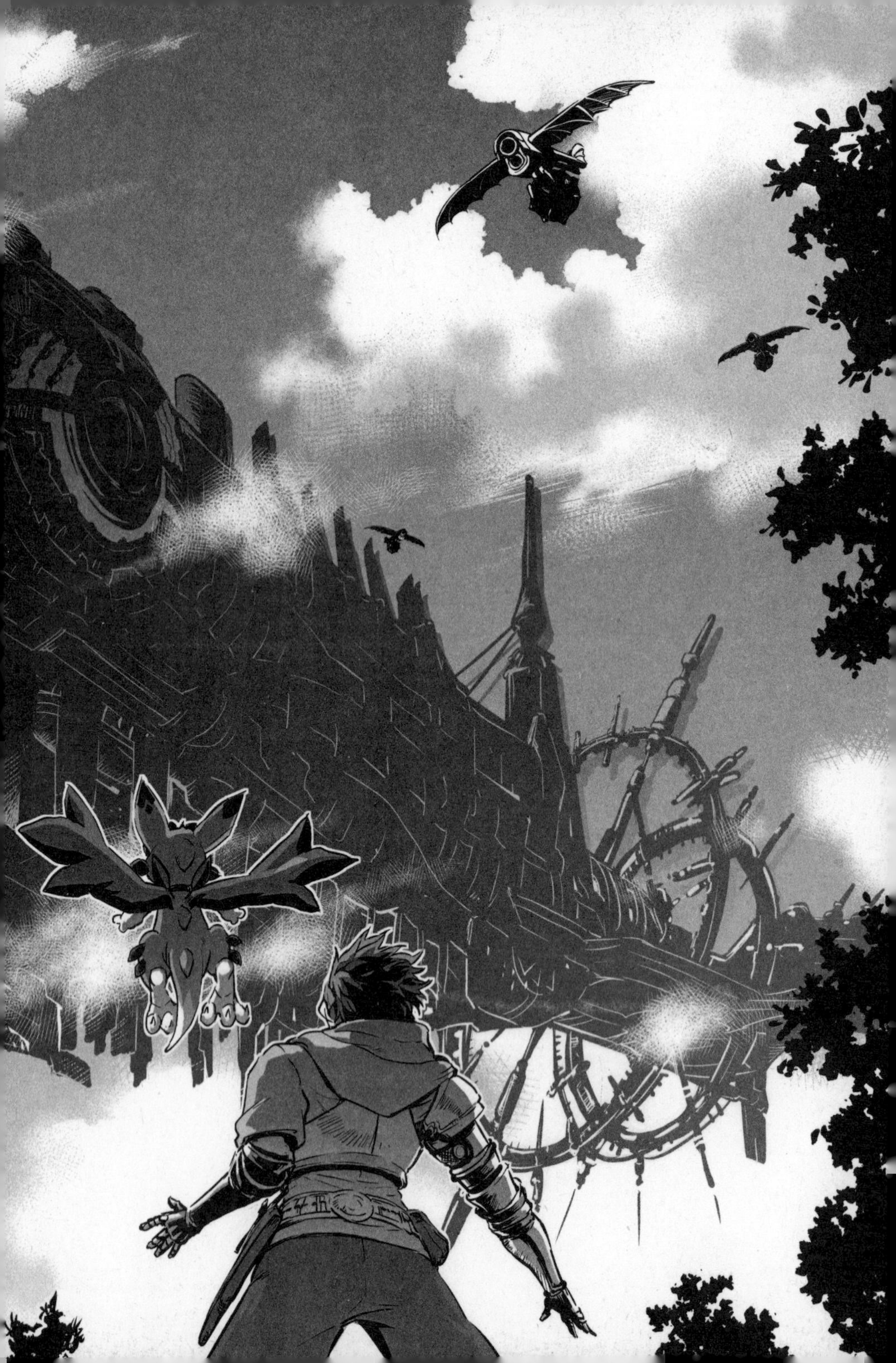

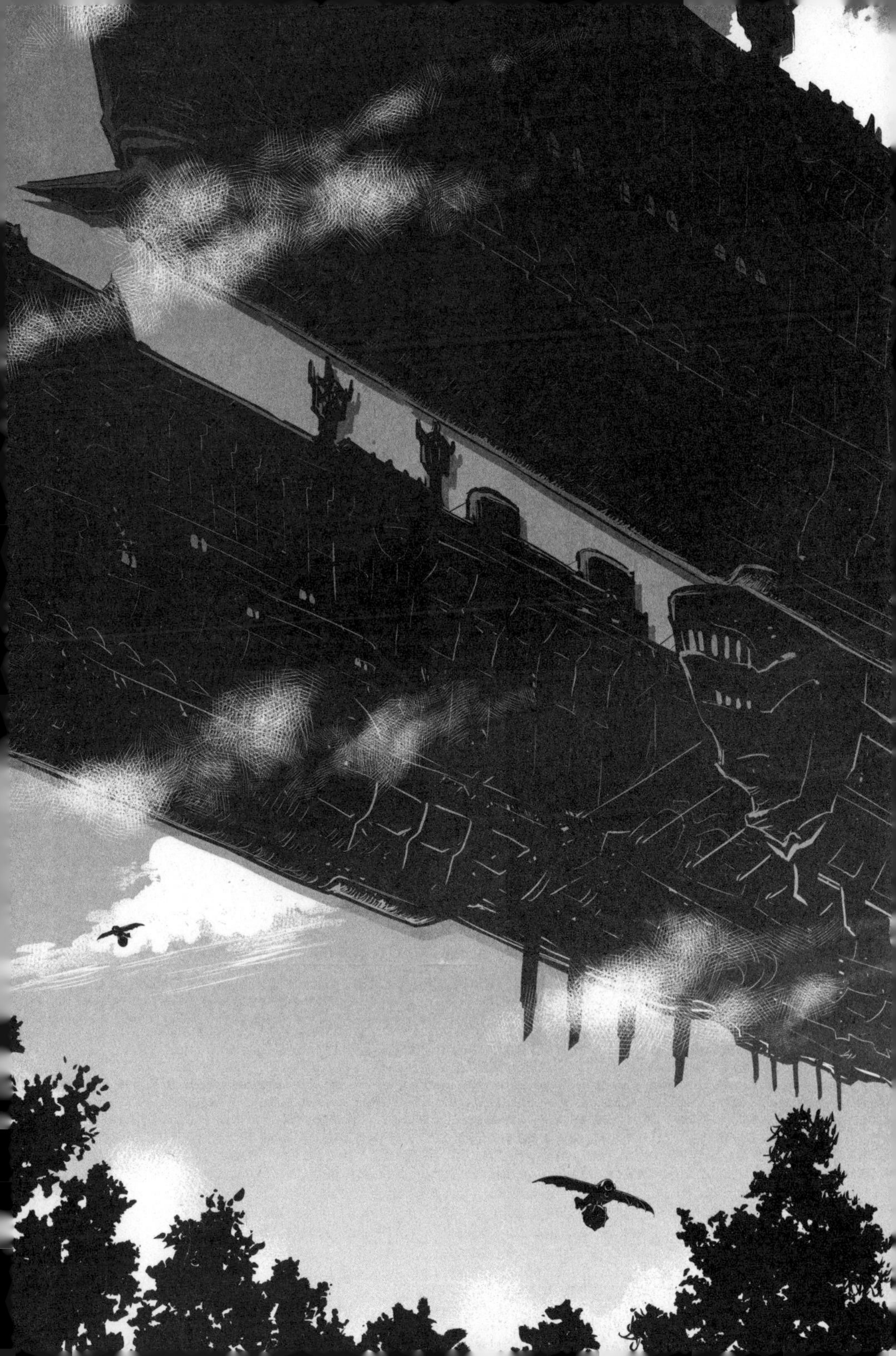

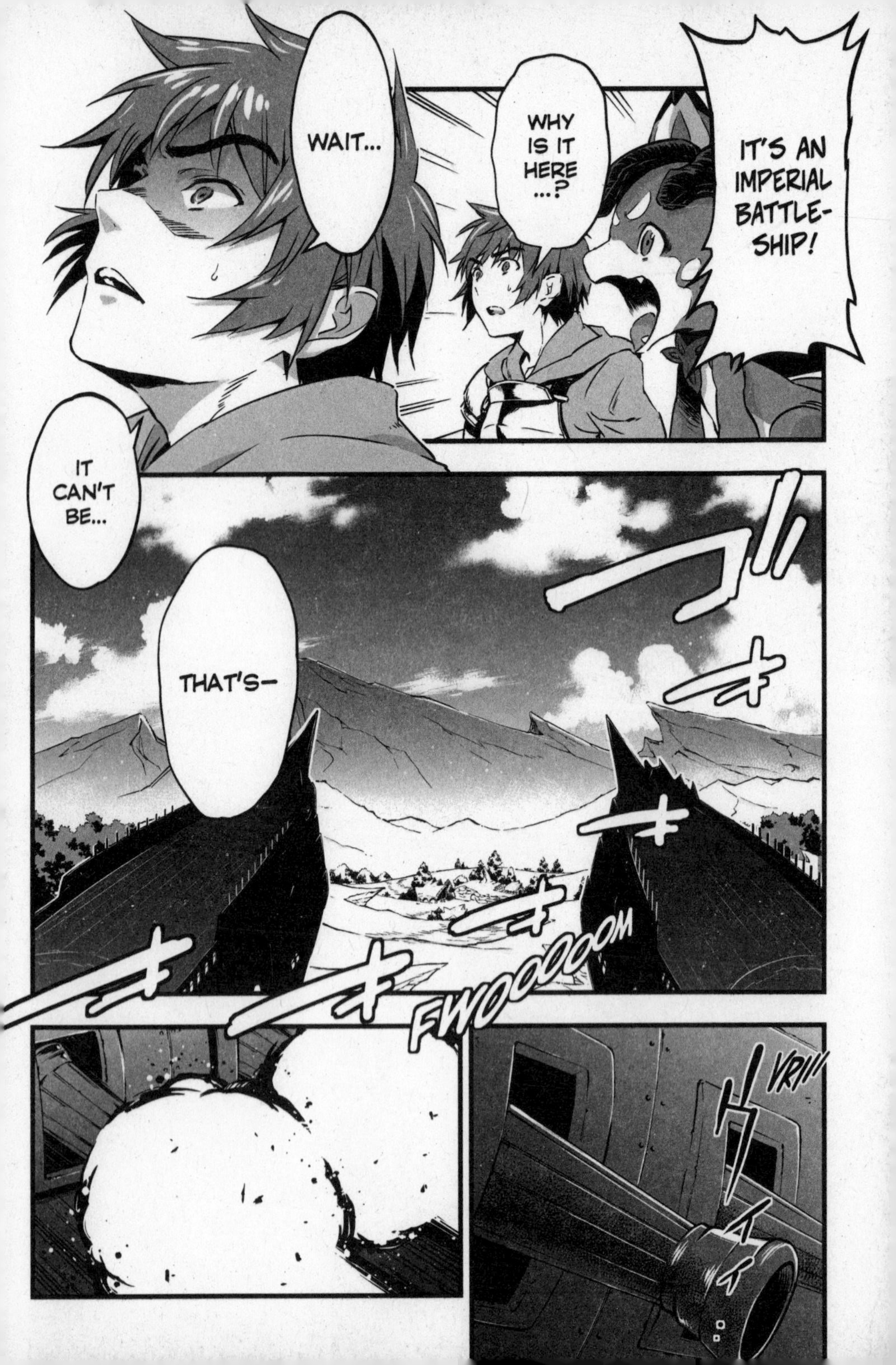
IT'S AN IMPERIAL BATTLE-SHIP!
WHY IS IT HERE ...?
WAIT...
IT CAN'T BE...
THAT'S—
FWOOOOOOM
VRII

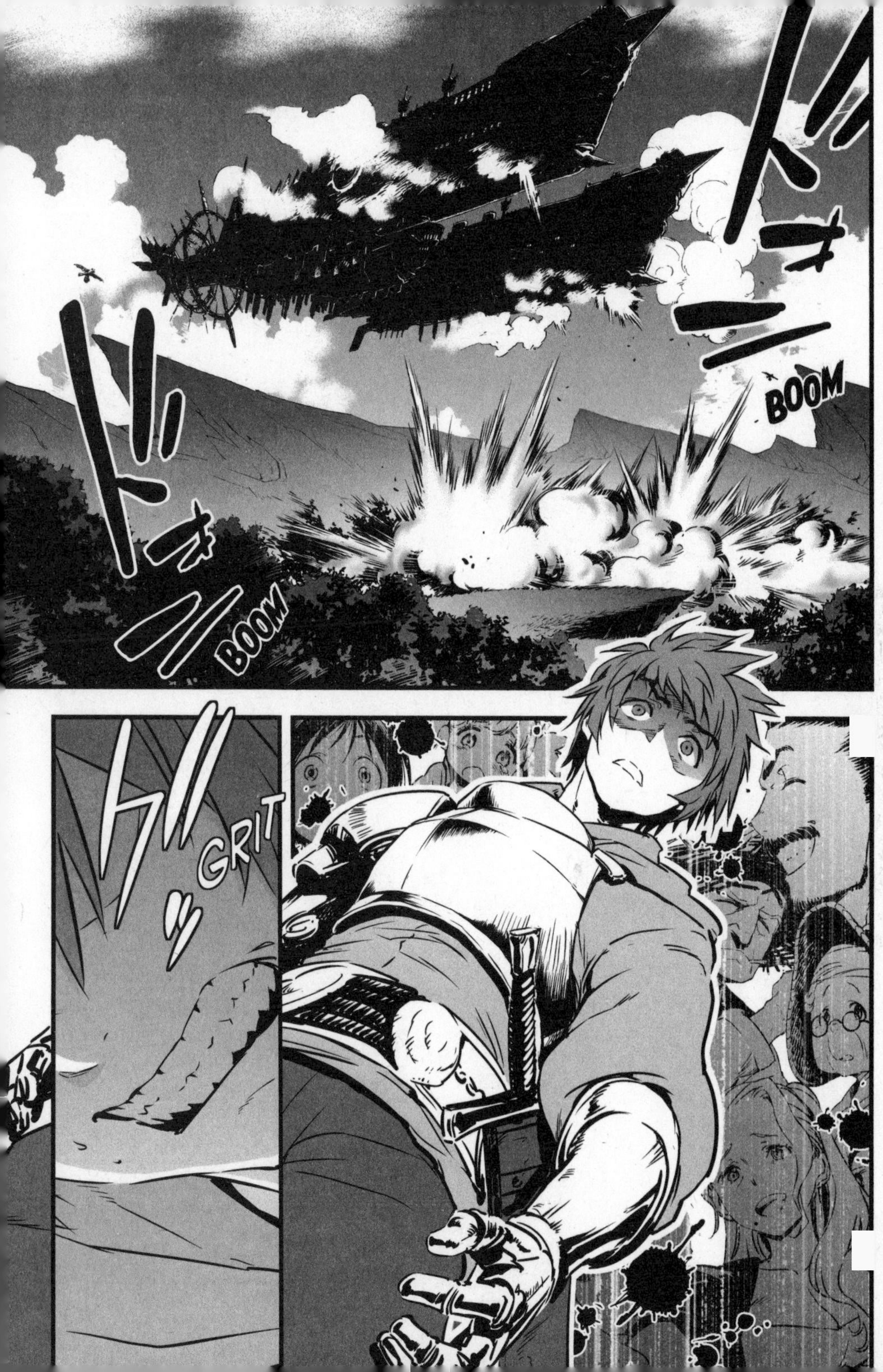
BOOM
BOOM
GRIT

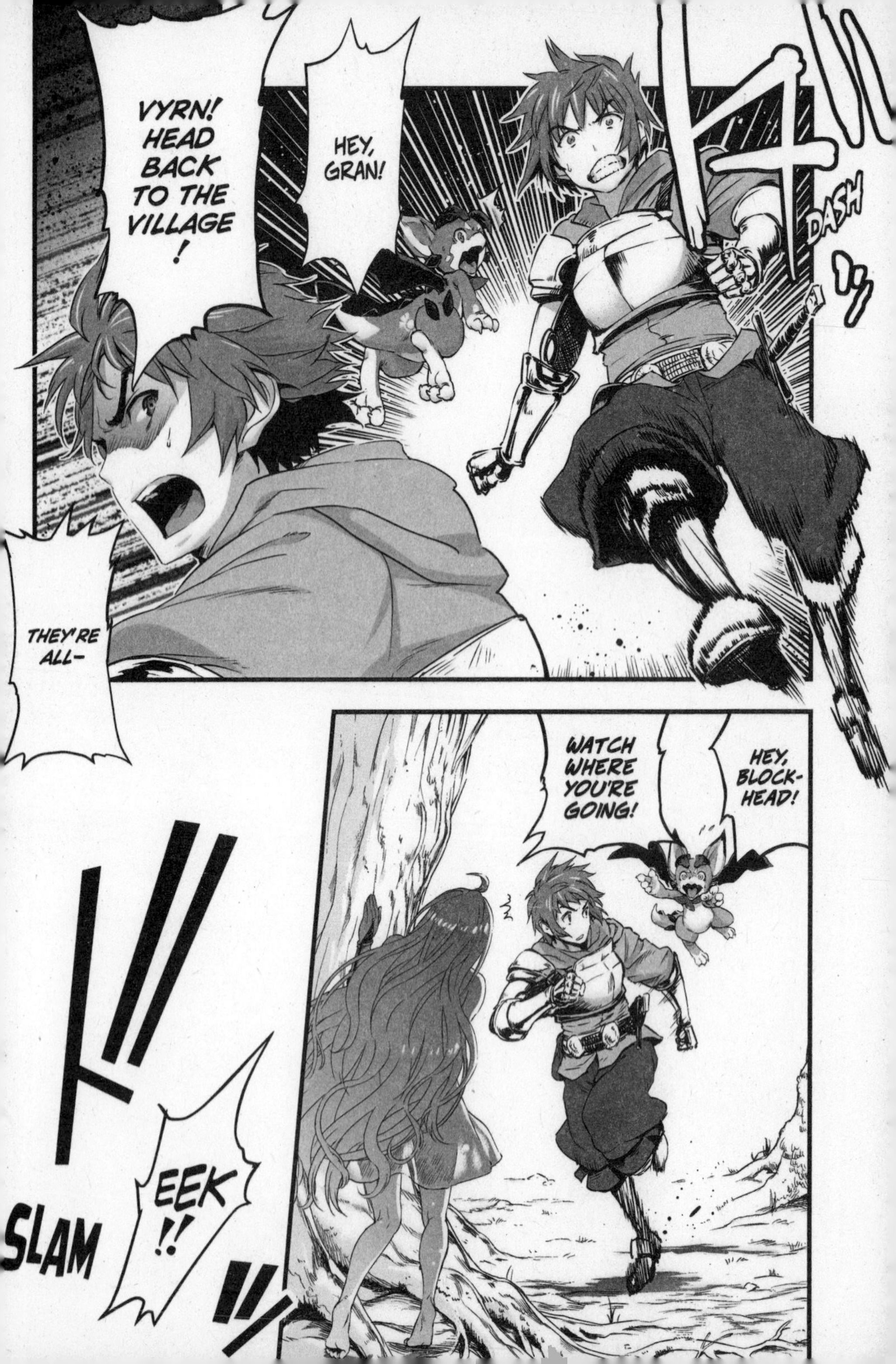
DASH
HEY, GRAN!
VYRN! HEAD BACK TO THE VILLAGE!
THEY'RE ALL—
HEY, BLOCK-HEAD!
WATCH WHERE YOU'RE GOING!
EEK!!
SLAM

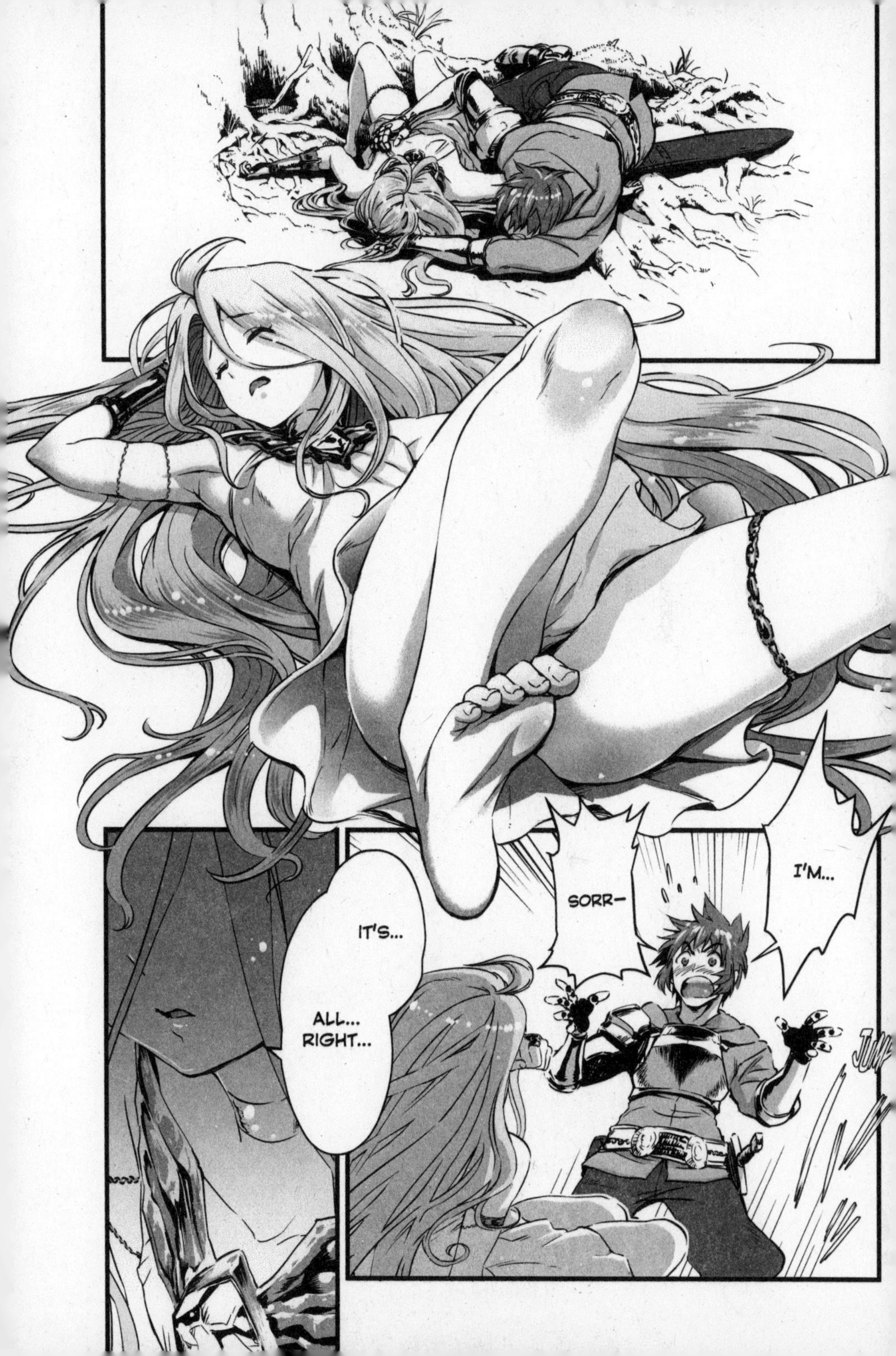
I'M...
SORR-
IT'S...
ALL... RIGHT...

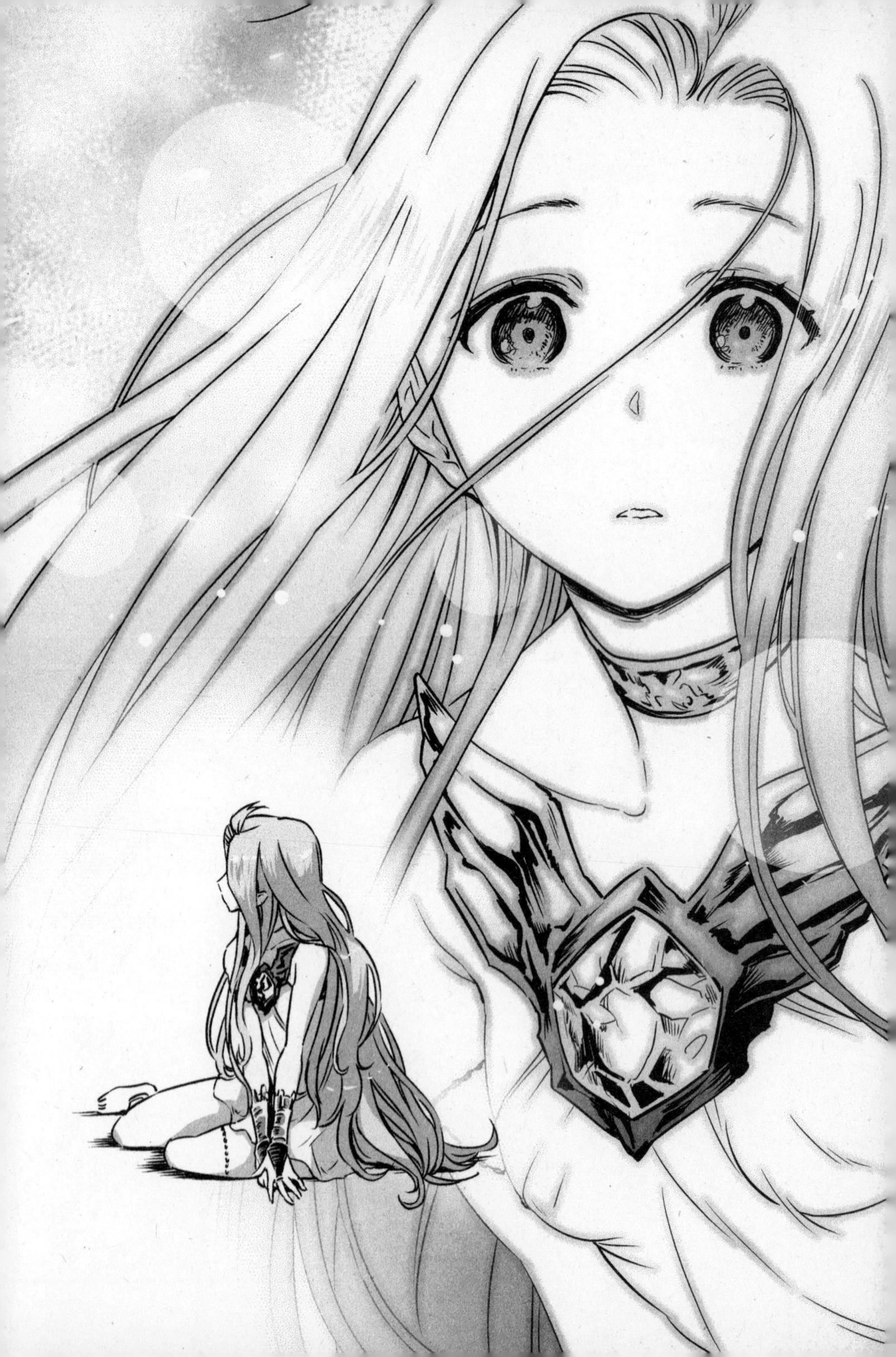

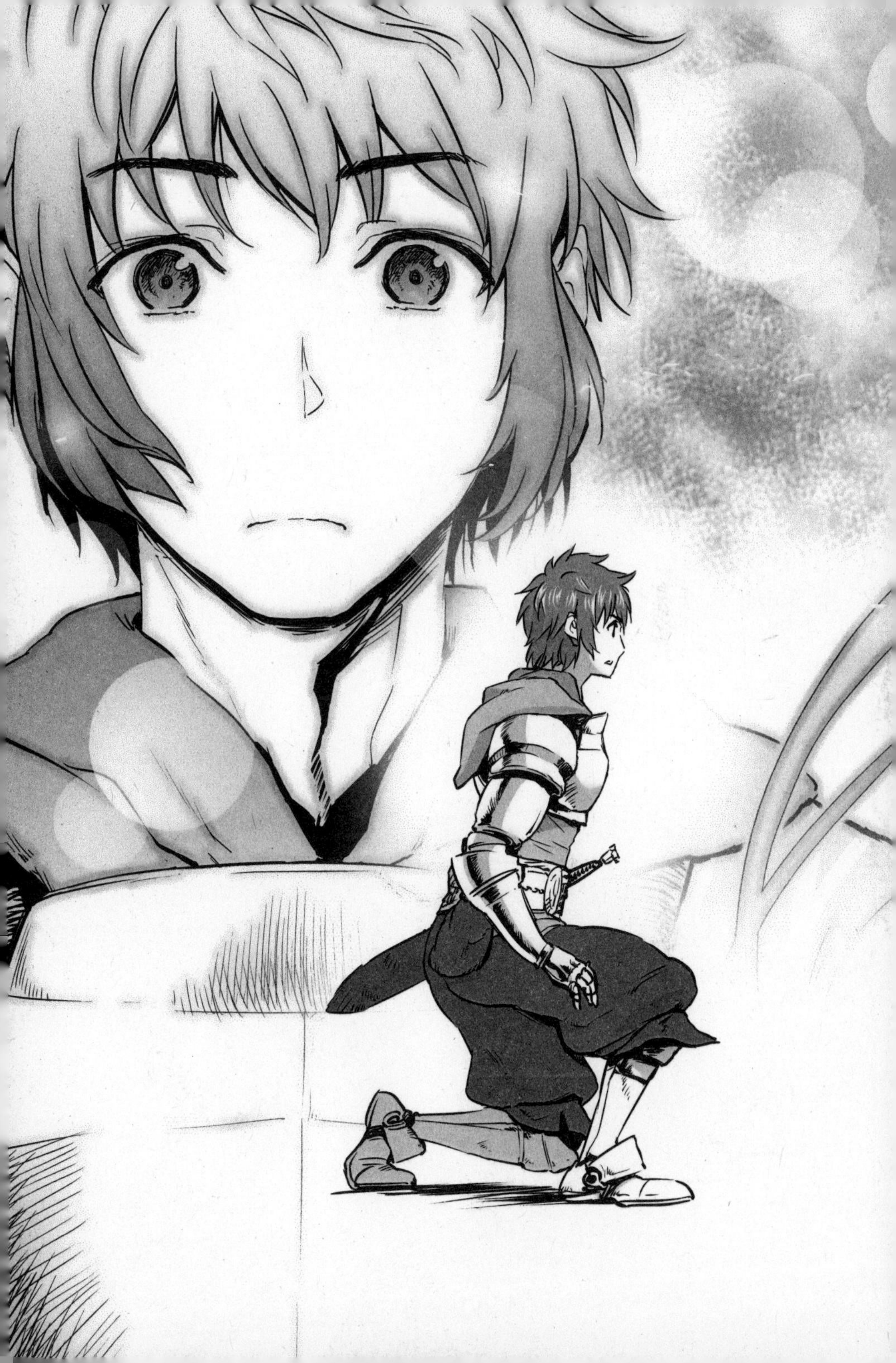

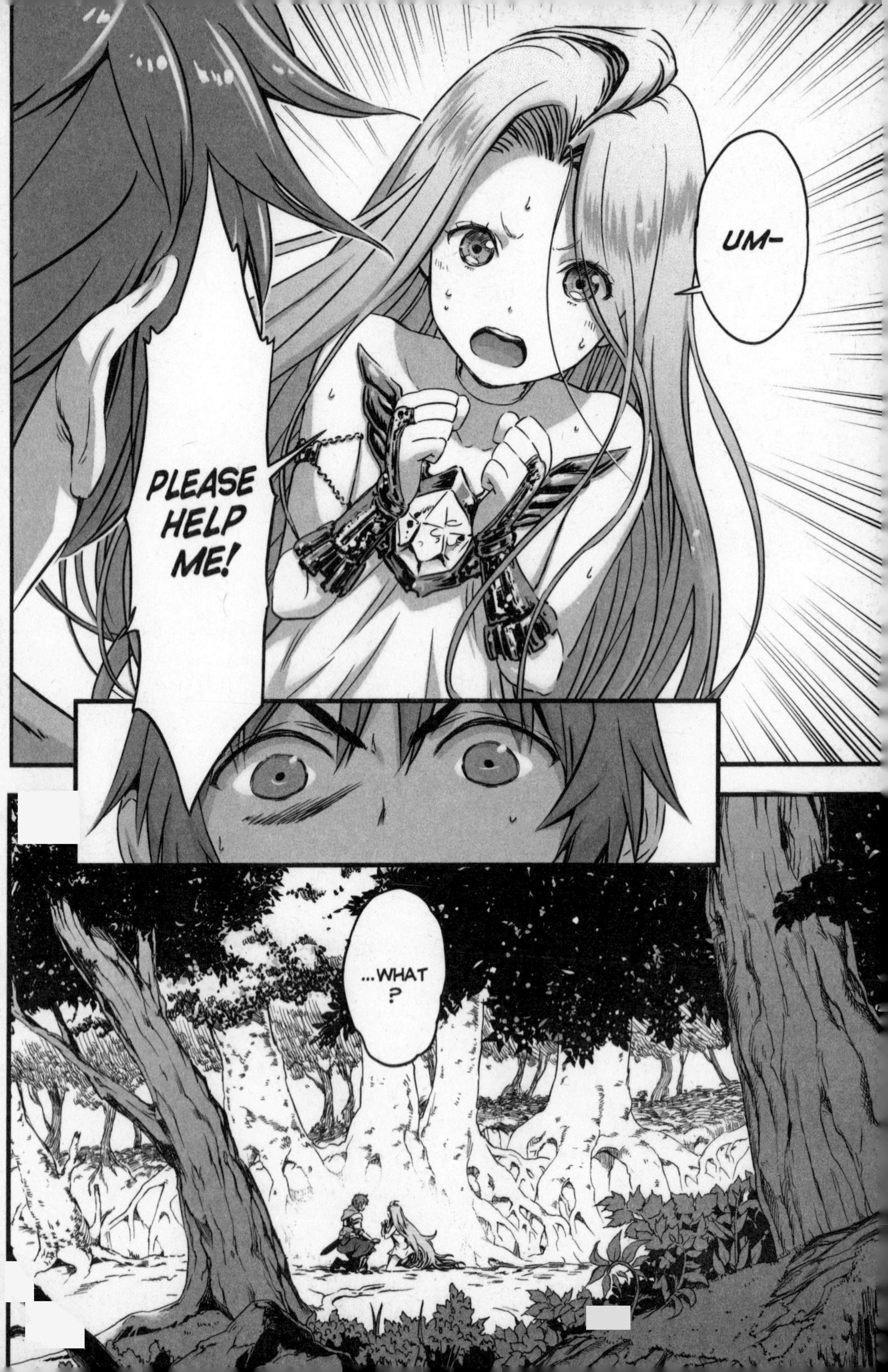
UM-
PLEASE HELP ME!
...WHAT?

CHAPTER 2: Prologue (2)

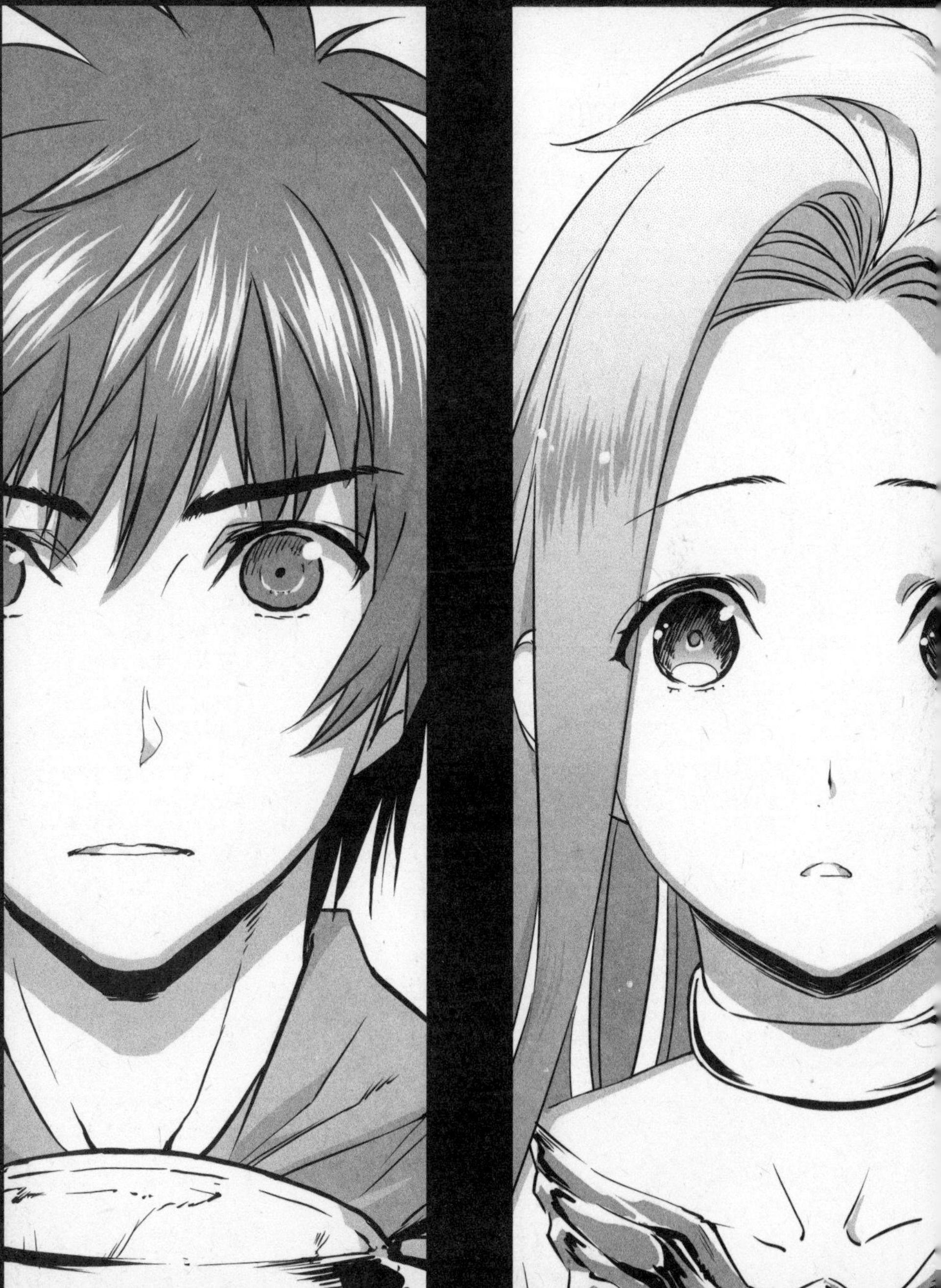

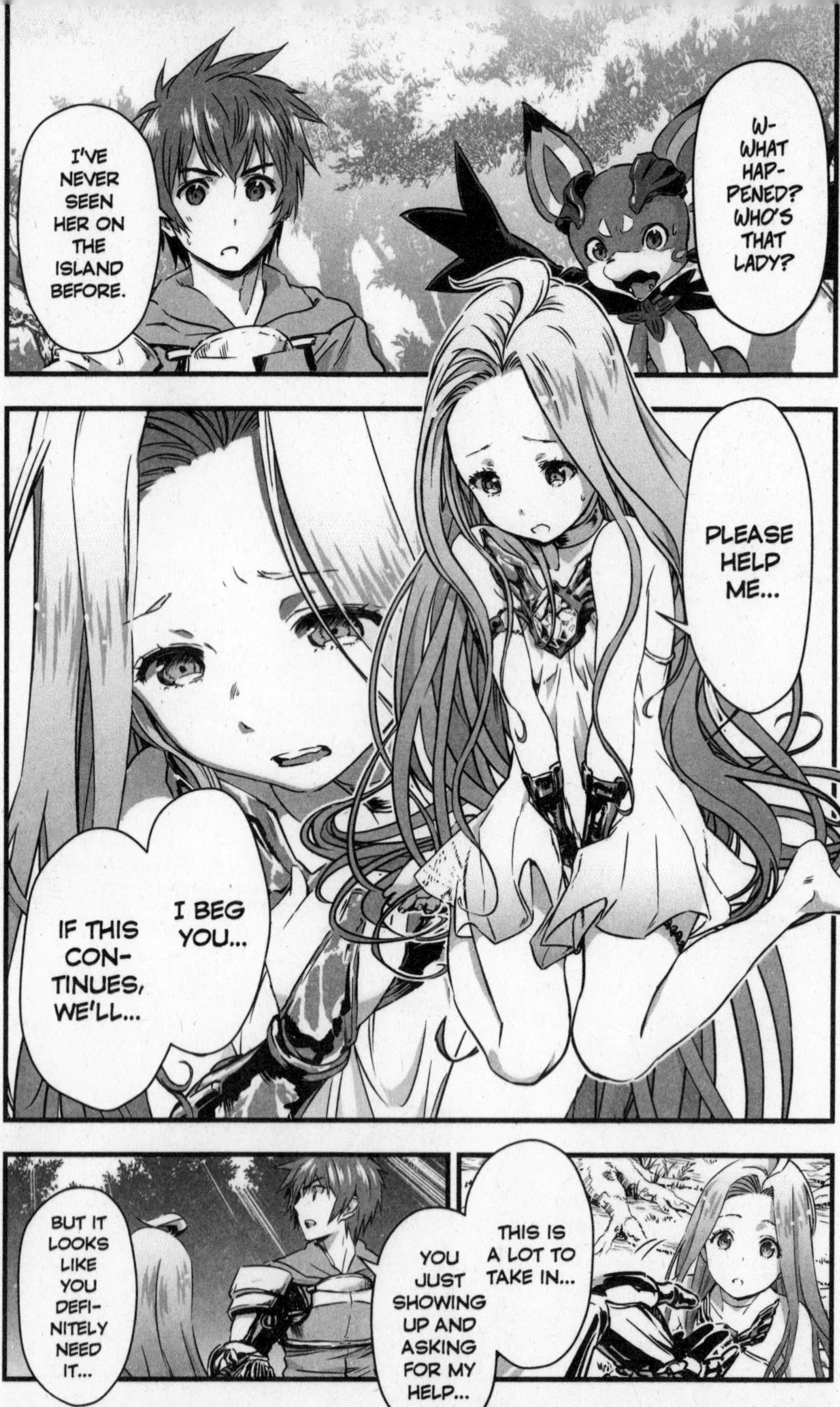
W-WHAT HAPPENED? WHO'S THAT LADY?
I'VE NEVER SEEN HER ON THE ISLAND BEFORE.
PLEASE HELP ME...
I BEG YOU...
IF THIS CONTINUES, WE'LL...
THIS IS A LOT TO TAKE IN...
YOU JUST SHOWING UP AND ASKING FOR MY HELP...
BUT IT LOOKS LIKE YOU DEFINITELY NEED IT...

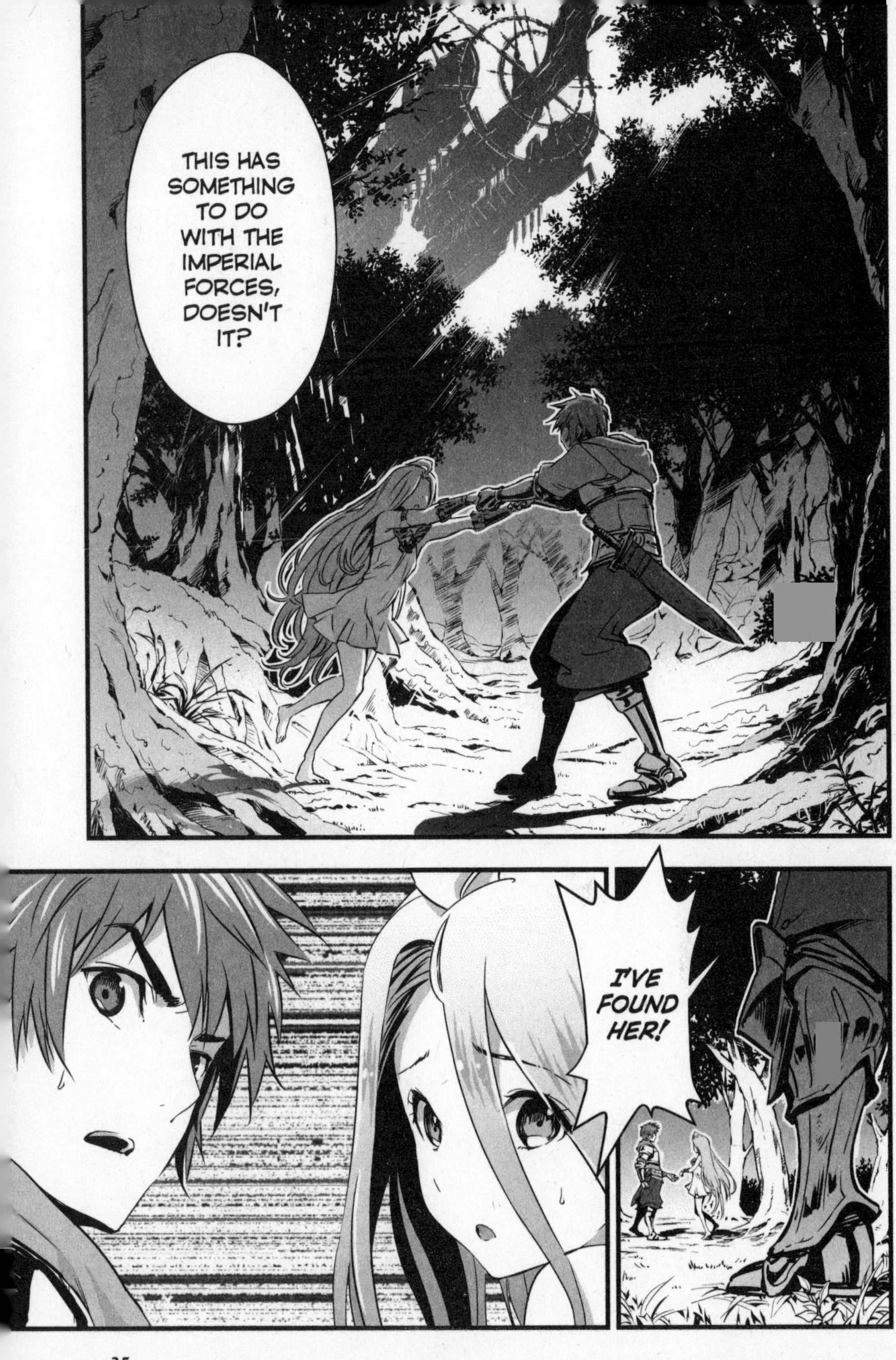
THIS HAS SOMETHING TO DO WITH THE IMPERIAL FORCES, DOESN'T IT?
I'VE FOUND HER!

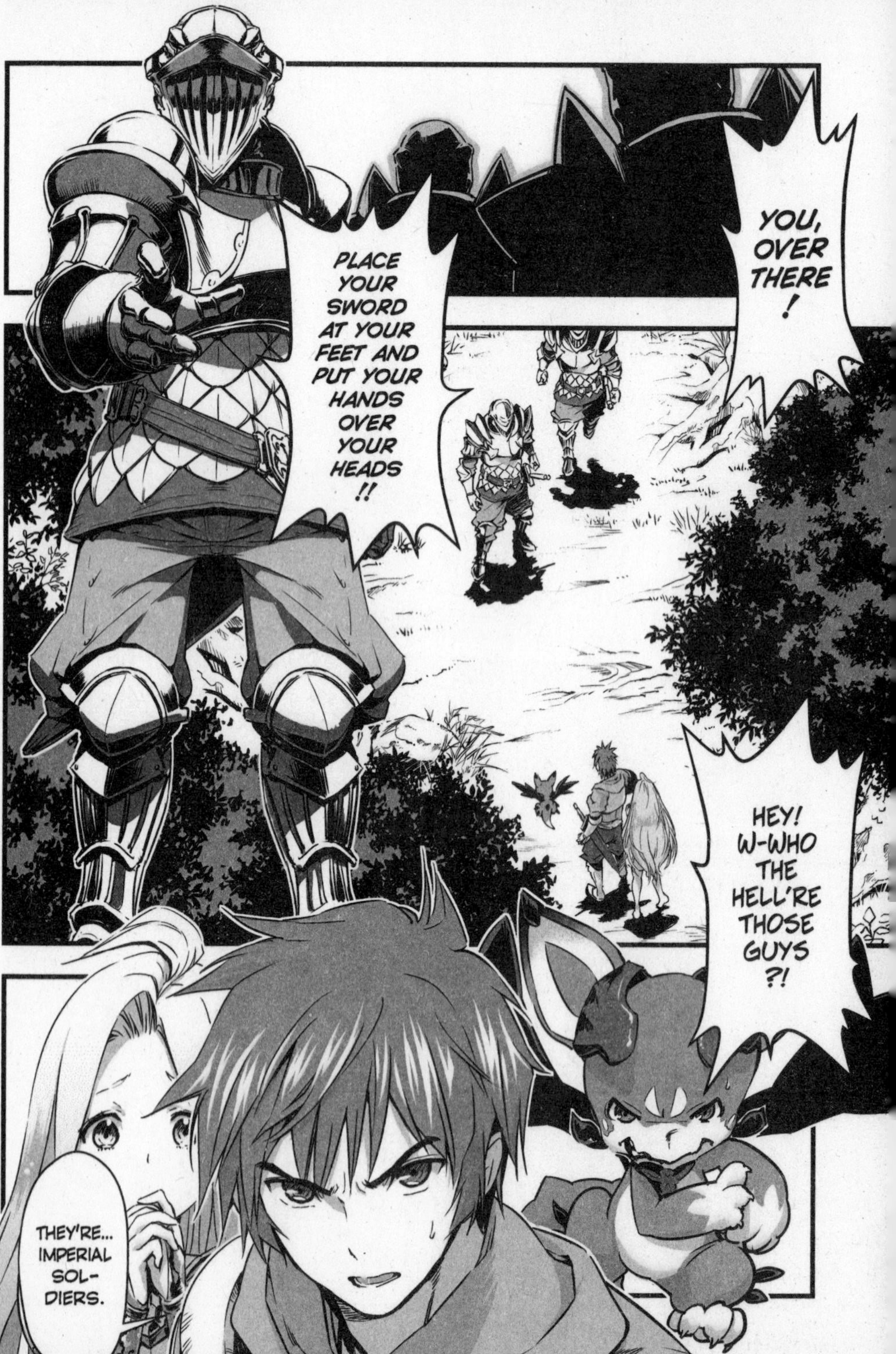
YOU, OVER THERE!
PLACE YOUR SWORD AT YOUR FEET AND PUT YOUR HANDS OVER YOUR HEADS!!
HEY! W-WHO THE HELL'RE THOSE GUYS?!
THEY'RE... IMPERIAL SOL-DIERS.

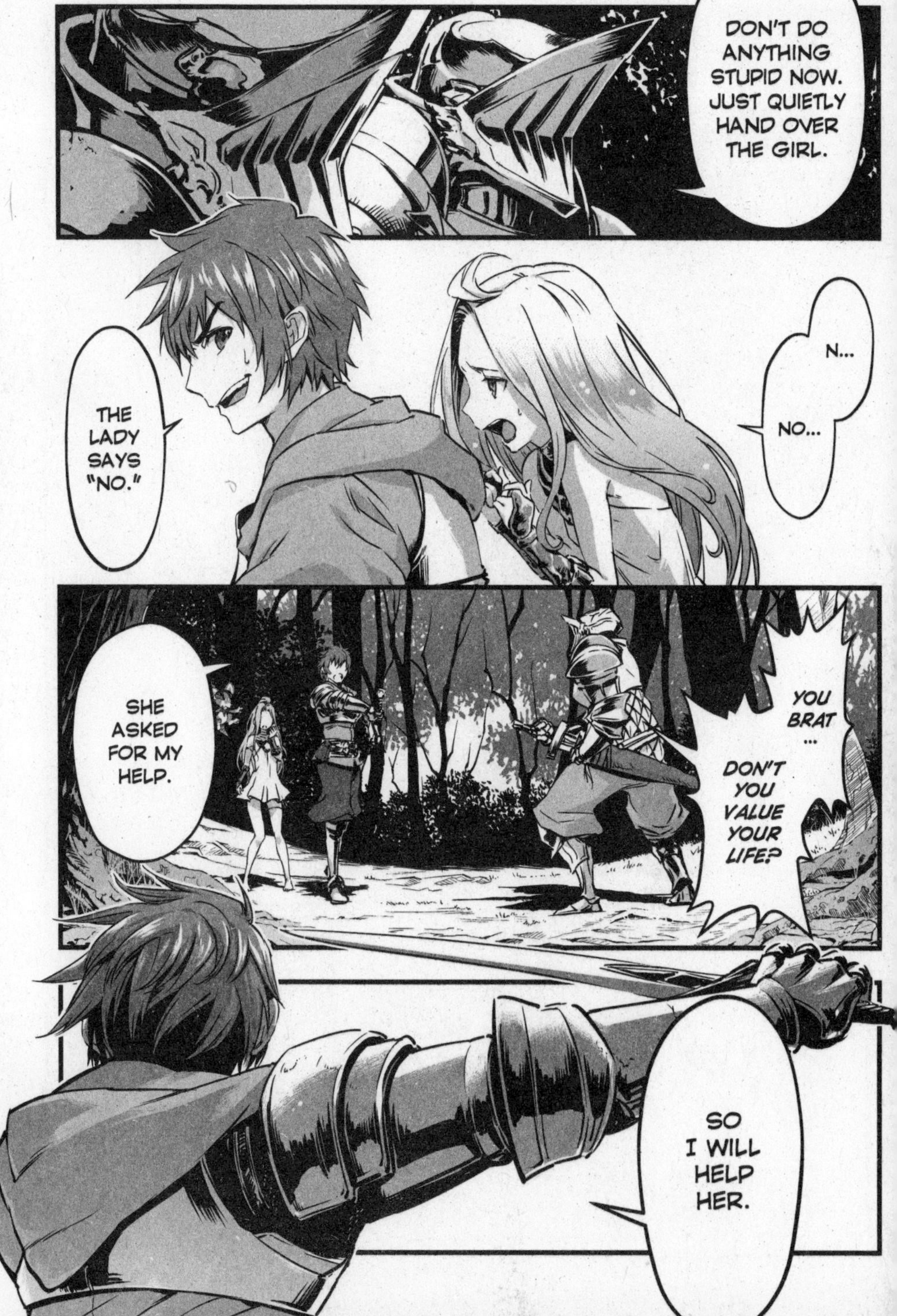
DON'T DO ANYTHING STUPID NOW. JUST QUIETLY HAND OVER THE GIRL.
N... NO...
THE LADY SAYS "NO."
YOU BRAT ... DON'T YOU VALUE YOUR LIFE?
SHE ASKED FOR MY HELP.
SO I WILL HELP HER.

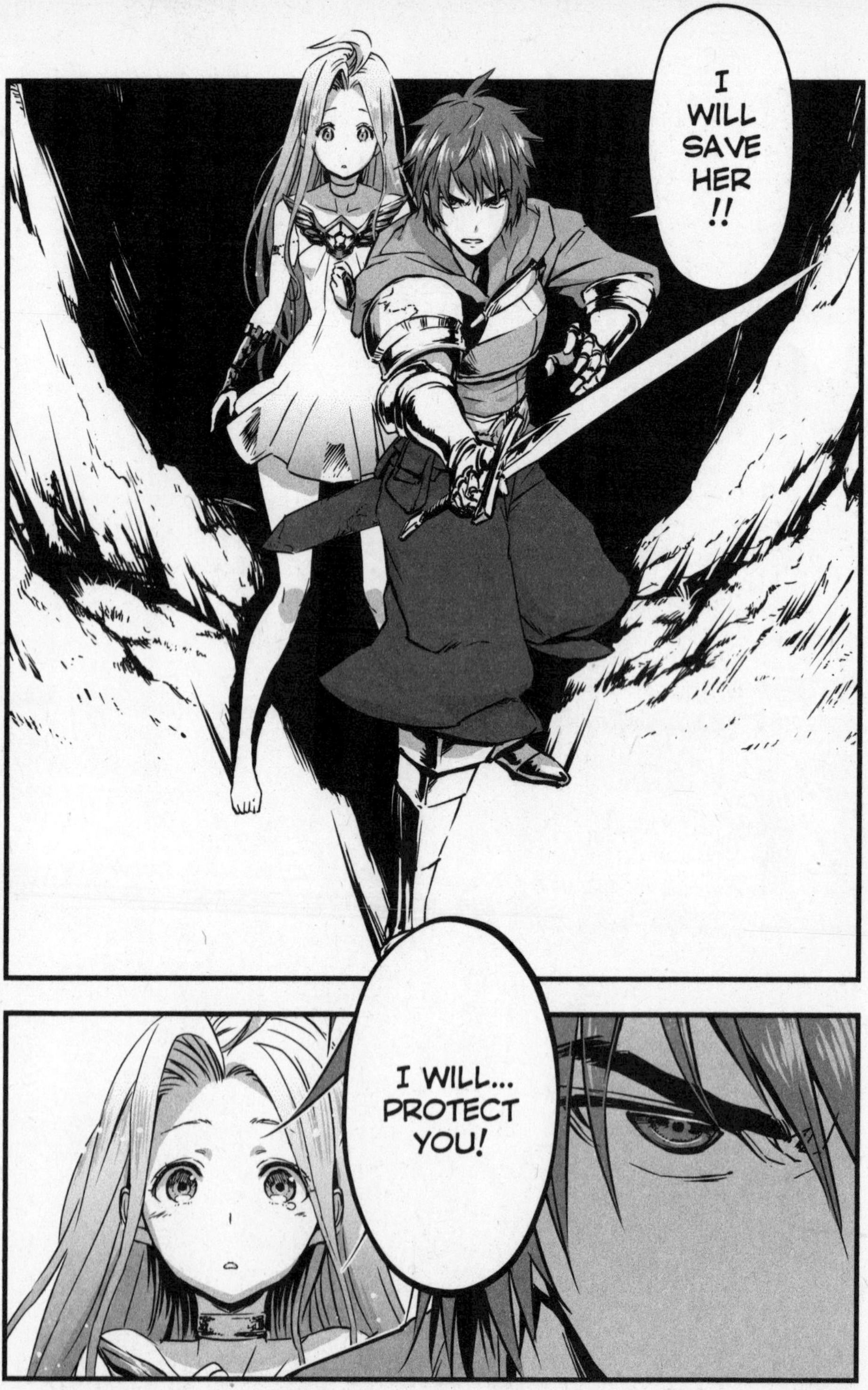
I WILL SAVE HER!!
I WILL... PROTECT YOU!

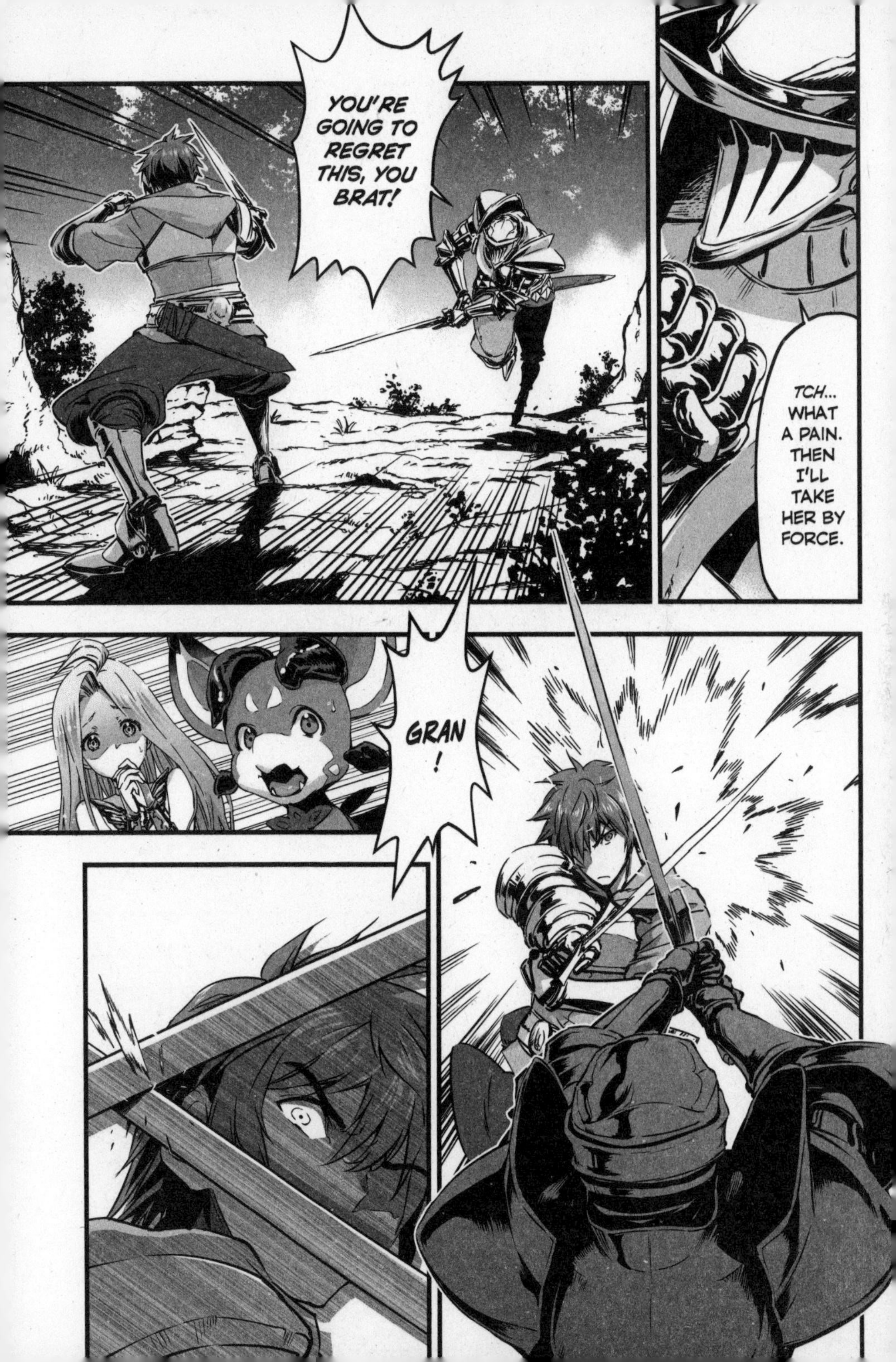
TCH... WHAT A PAIN. THEN I'LL TAKE HER BY FORCE.
YOU'RE GOING TO REGRET THIS, YOU BRAT!
GRAN!

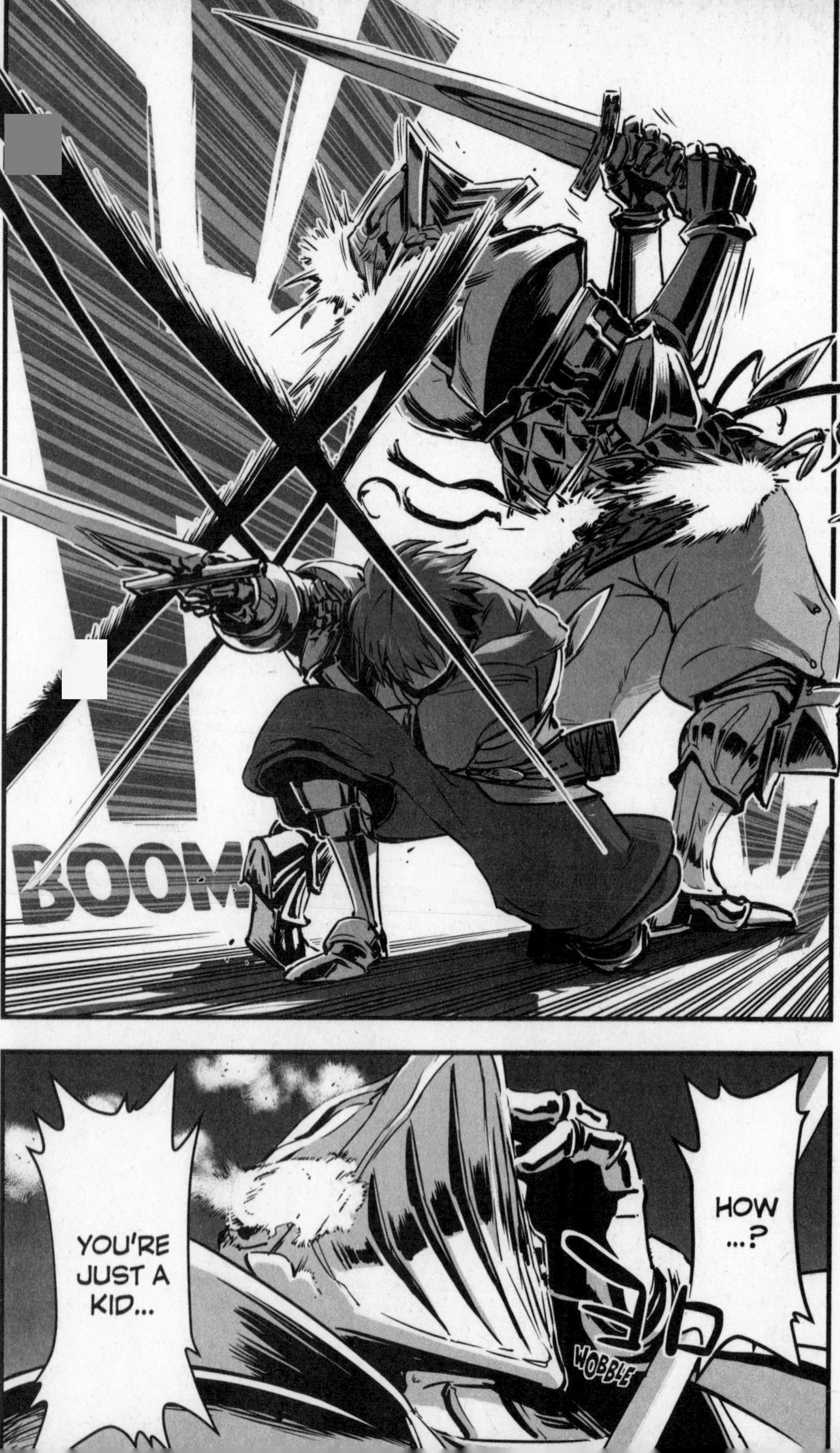
BOOM
HOW ...?
YOU'RE JUST A KID...
WOBBLE

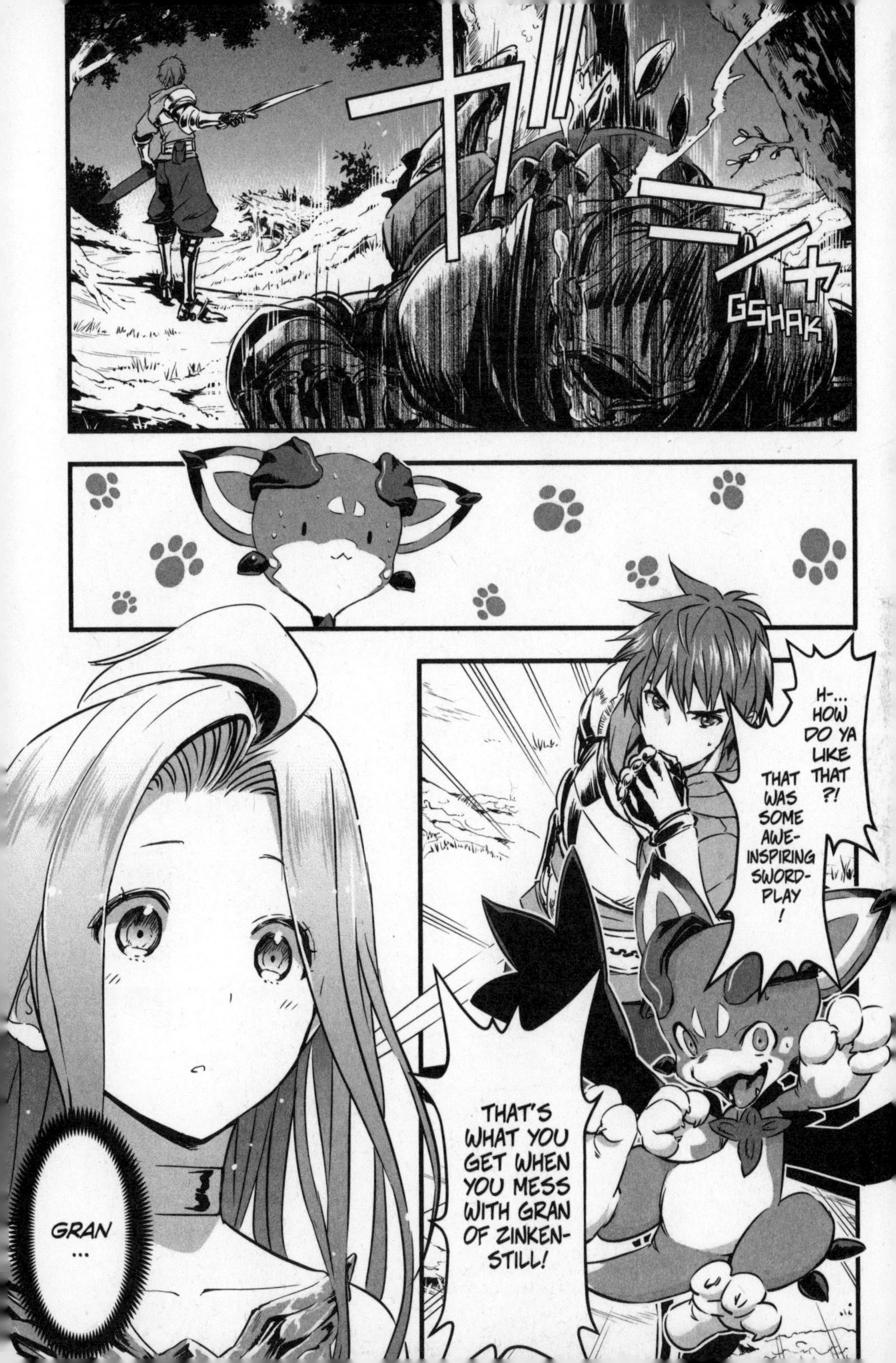
GSHAK
H-... HOW DO YA LIKE THAT?!
THAT WAS SOME AWE-INSPIRING SWORDPLAY!
THAT'S WHAT YOU GET WHEN YOU MESS WITH GRAN OF ZINKENSTILL!
GRAN...

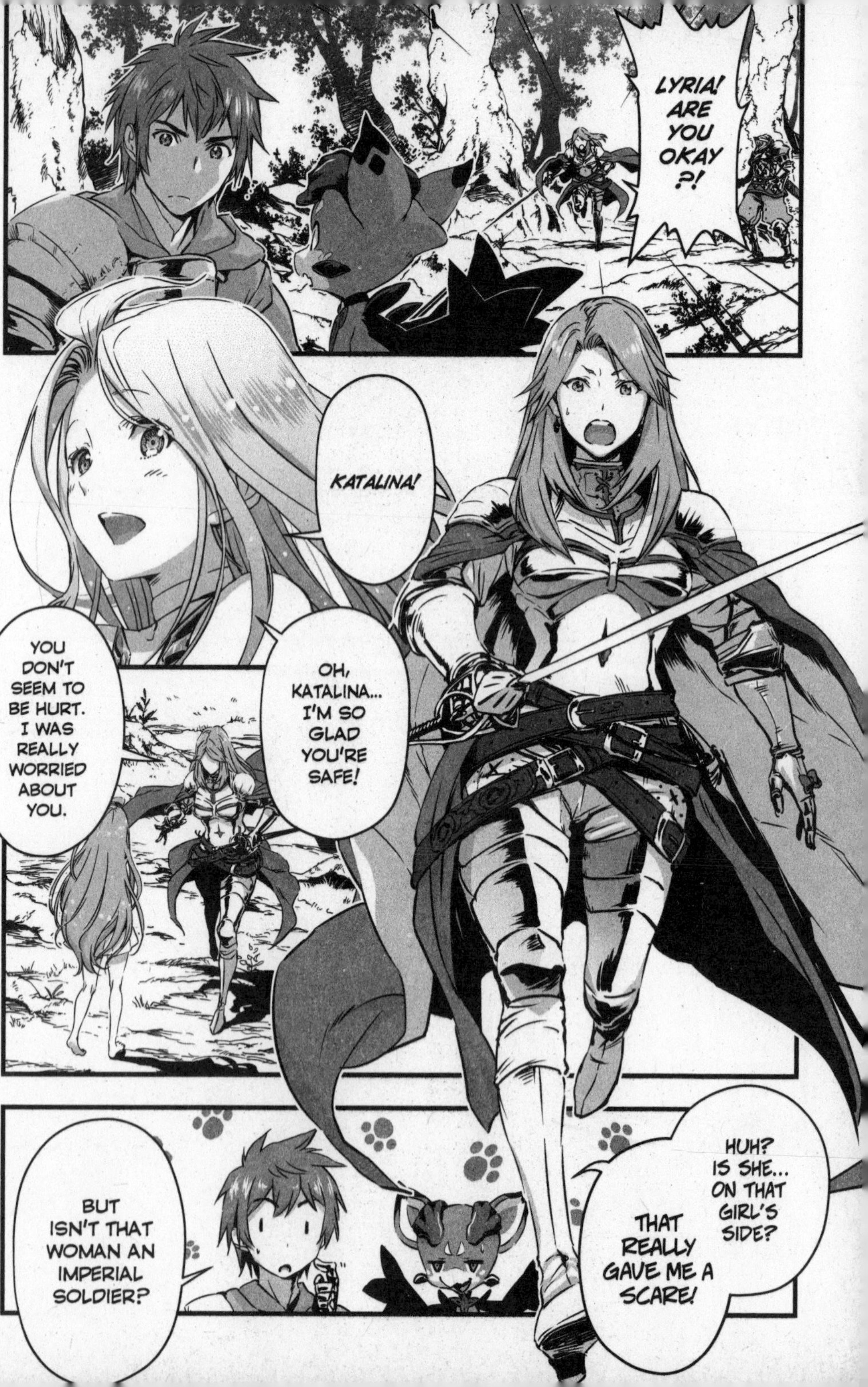

LYRIA! ARE YOU OKAY ?!
KATALINA!
OH, KATALINA... I'M SO GLAD YOU'RE SAFE!
YOU DON'T SEEM TO BE HURT. I WAS REALLY WORRIED ABOUT YOU.
HUH? IS SHE... ON THAT GIRL'S SIDE?
THAT REALLY GAVE ME A SCARE!
BUT ISN'T THAT WOMAN AN IMPERIAL SOLDIER?

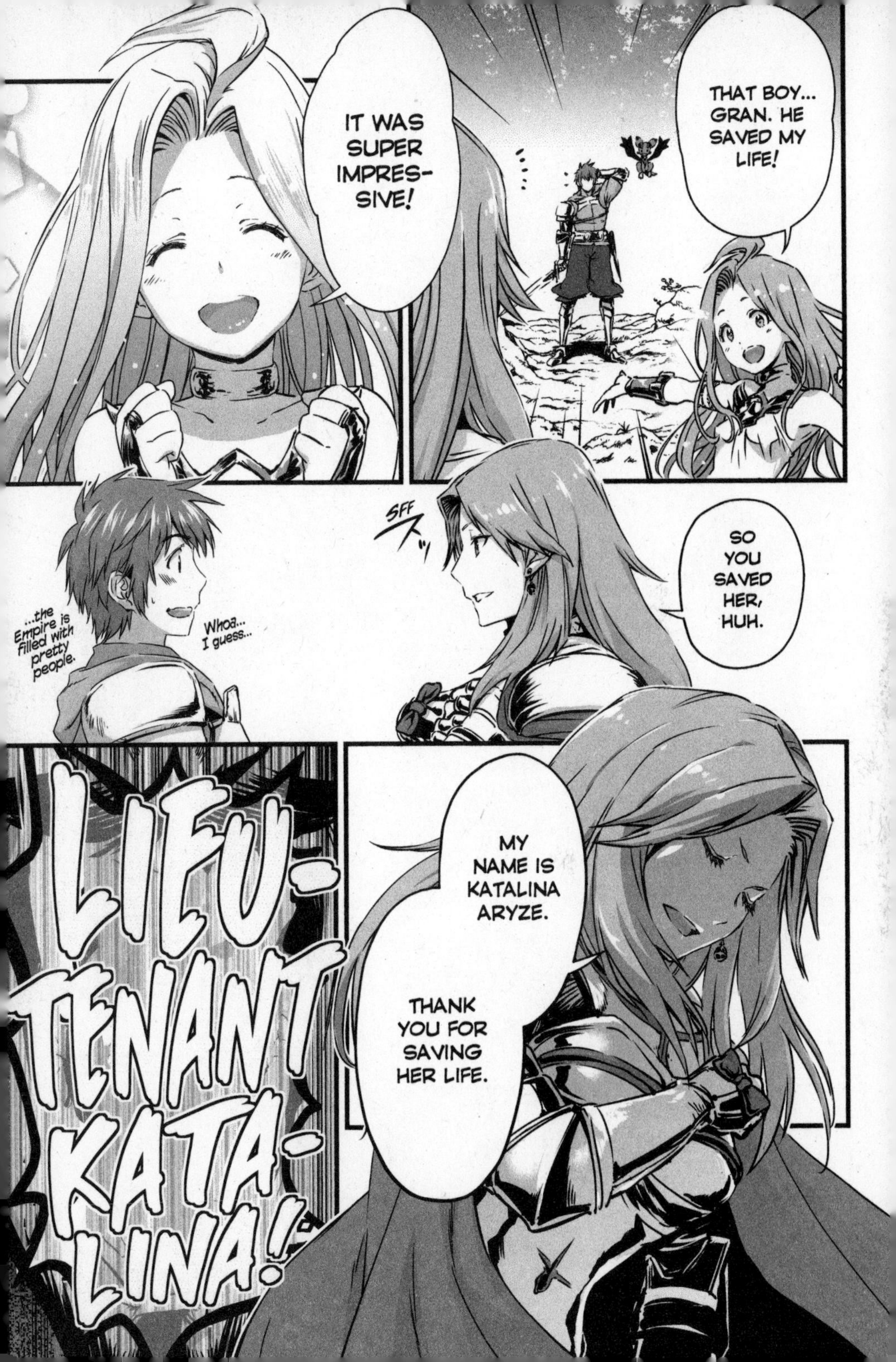
THAT BOY... GRAN. HE SAVED MY LIFE!
IT WAS SUPER IMPRES-SIVE!
SO YOU SAVED HER, HUH.
SFF
Whoa... I guess...
...the Empire is filled with pretty people.
MY NAME IS KATALINA ARYZE.
THANK YOU FOR SAVING HER LIFE.
LIEU-TENANT KATA-LINA!

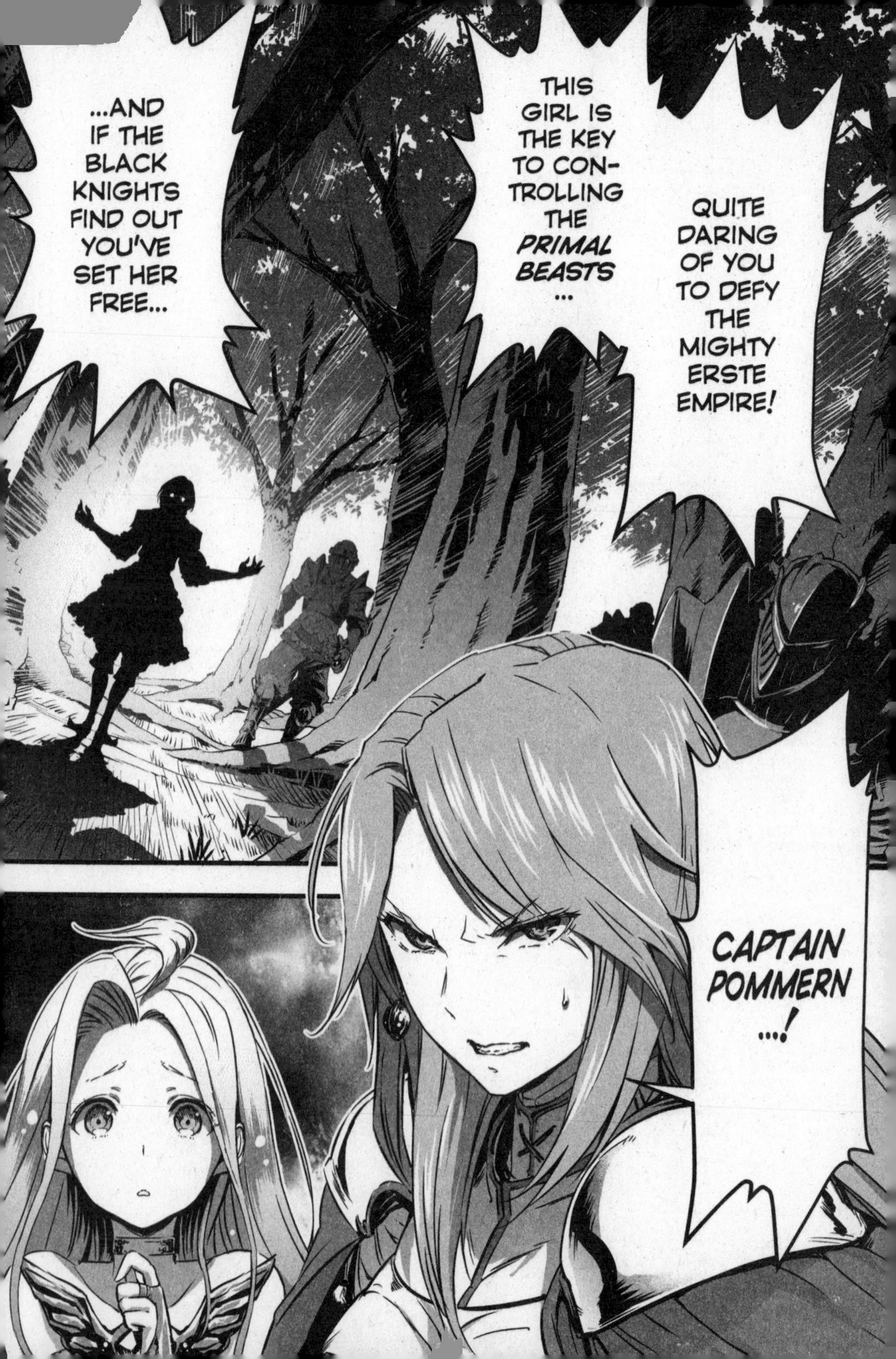
QUITE DARING OF YOU TO DEFY THE MIGHTY ERSTE EMPIRE!
THIS GIRL IS THE KEY TO CON-TROLLING THE *PRIMAL BEASTS*...
...AND IF THE BLACK KNIGHTS FIND OUT YOU'VE SET HER FREE...
CAPTAIN POMMERN...!

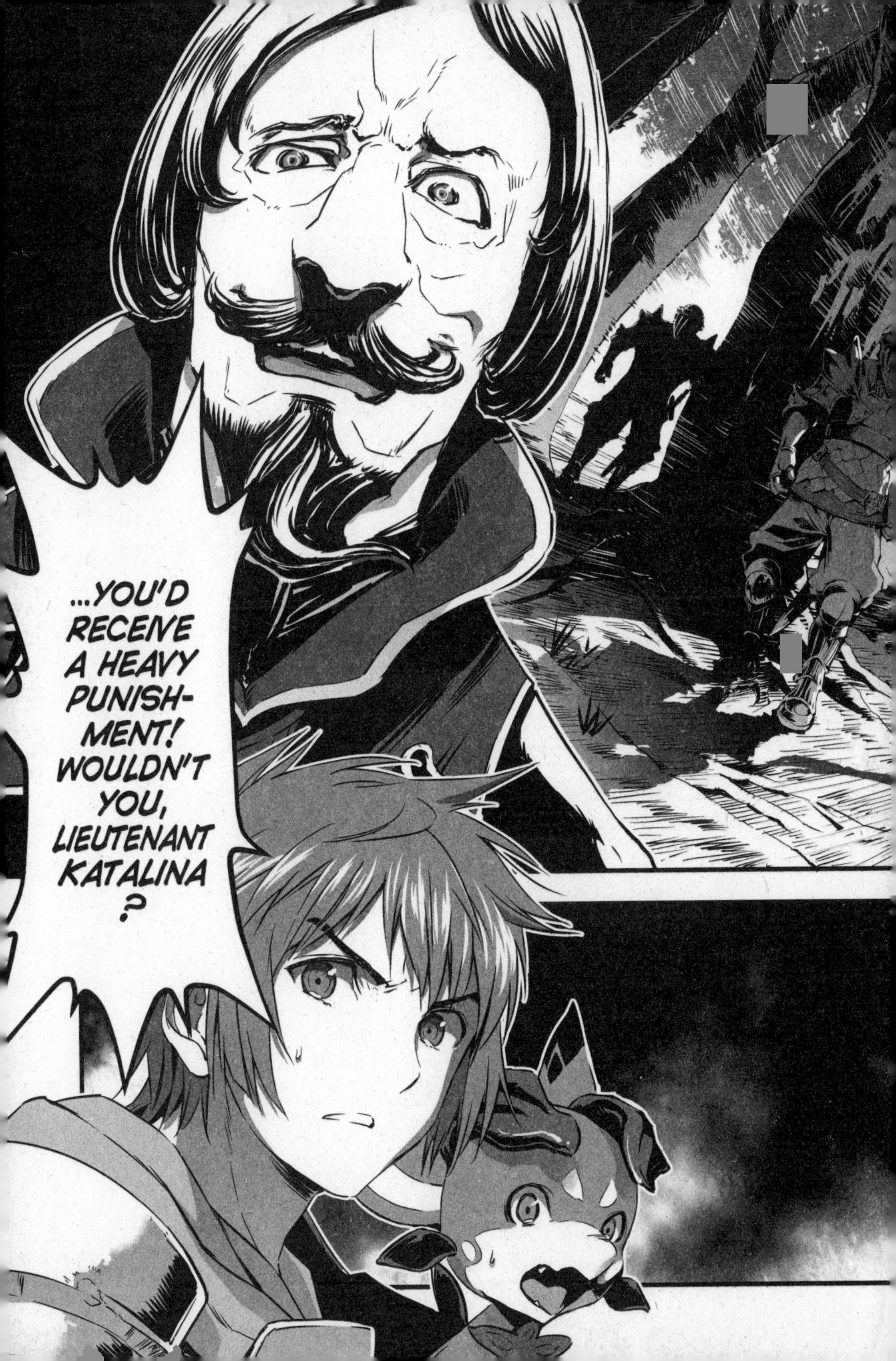
...YOU'D RECEIVE A HEAVY PUNISH-MENT! WOULDN'T YOU, LIEUTENANT KATALINA ?

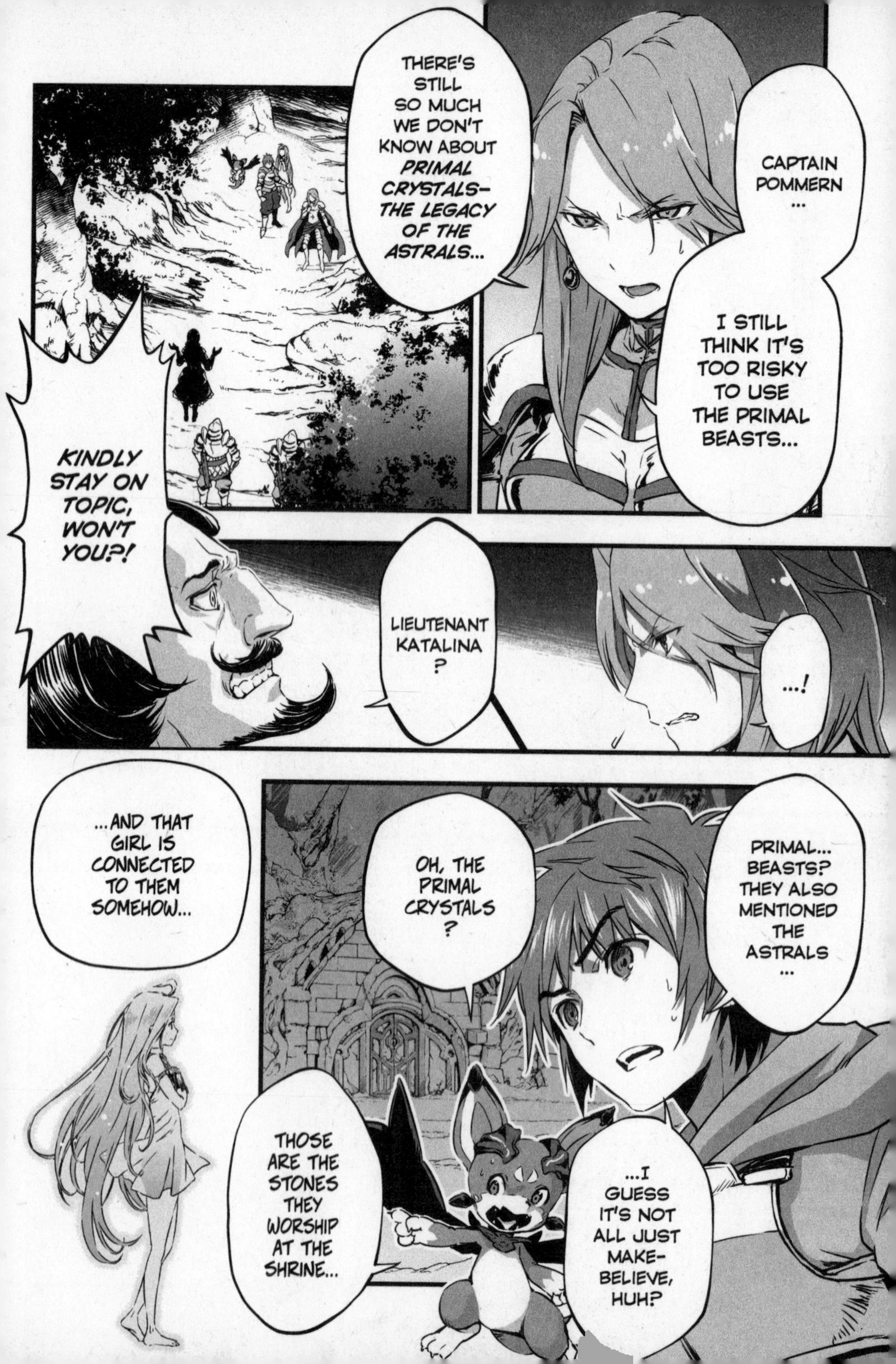
CAPTAIN POMMERN ...
I STILL THINK IT'S TOO RISKY TO USE THE PRIMAL BEASTS...
THERE'S STILL SO MUCH WE DON'T KNOW ABOUT PRIMAL CRYSTALS– THE LEGACY OF THE ASTRALS...
...!
LIEUTENANT KATALINA?
KINDLY STAY ON TOPIC, WON'T YOU?!
PRIMAL... BEASTS? THEY ALSO MENTIONED THE ASTRALS ...
OH, THE PRIMAL CRYSTALS?
...I GUESS IT'S NOT ALL JUST MAKE-BELIEVE, HUH?
THOSE ARE THE STONES THEY WORSHIP AT THE SHRINE...
...AND THAT GIRL IS CONNECTED TO THEM SOMEHOW...

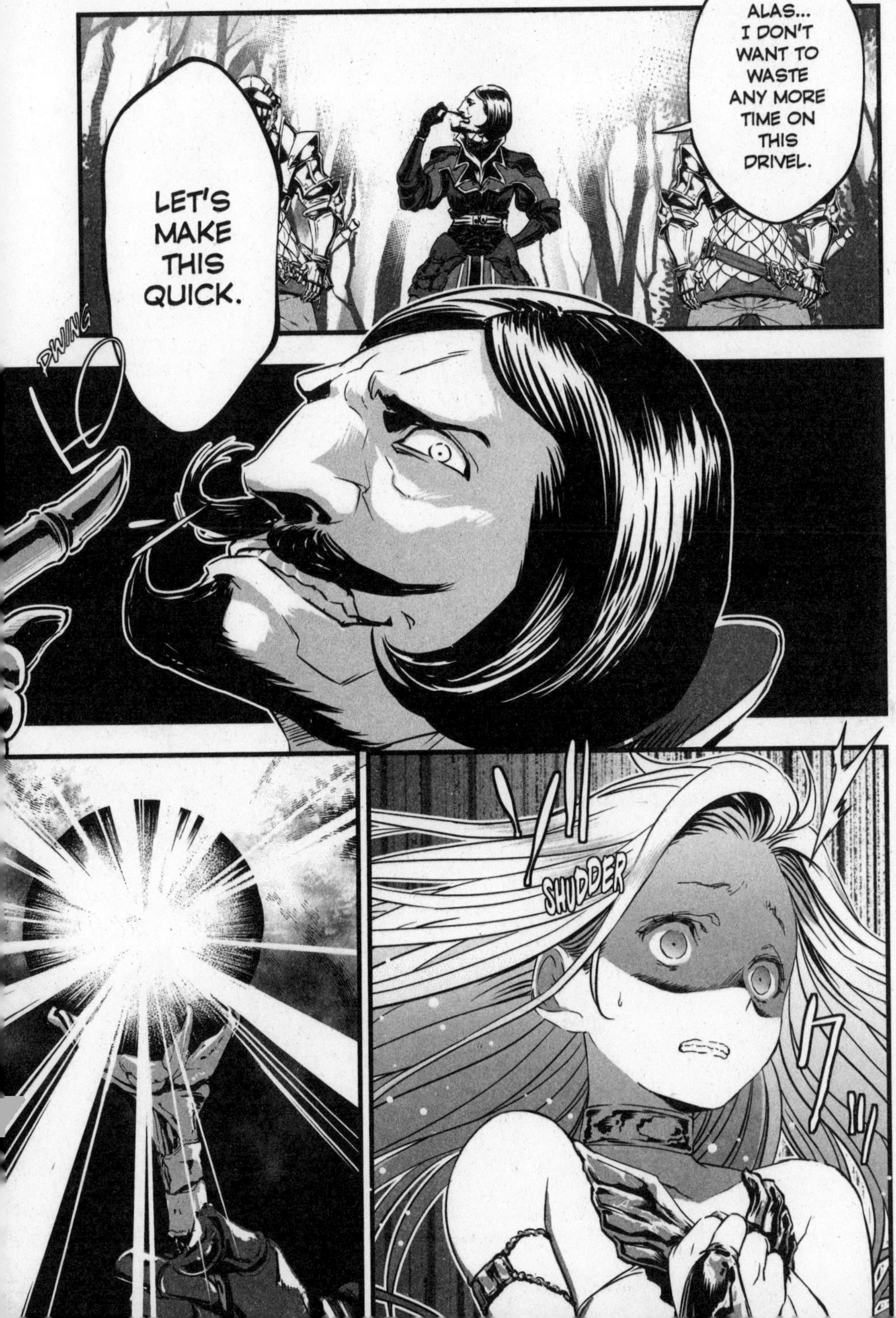
ALAS... I DON'T WANT TO WASTE ANY MORE TIME ON THIS DRIVEL.
LET'S MAKE THIS QUICK.
DWING
SHUDDER

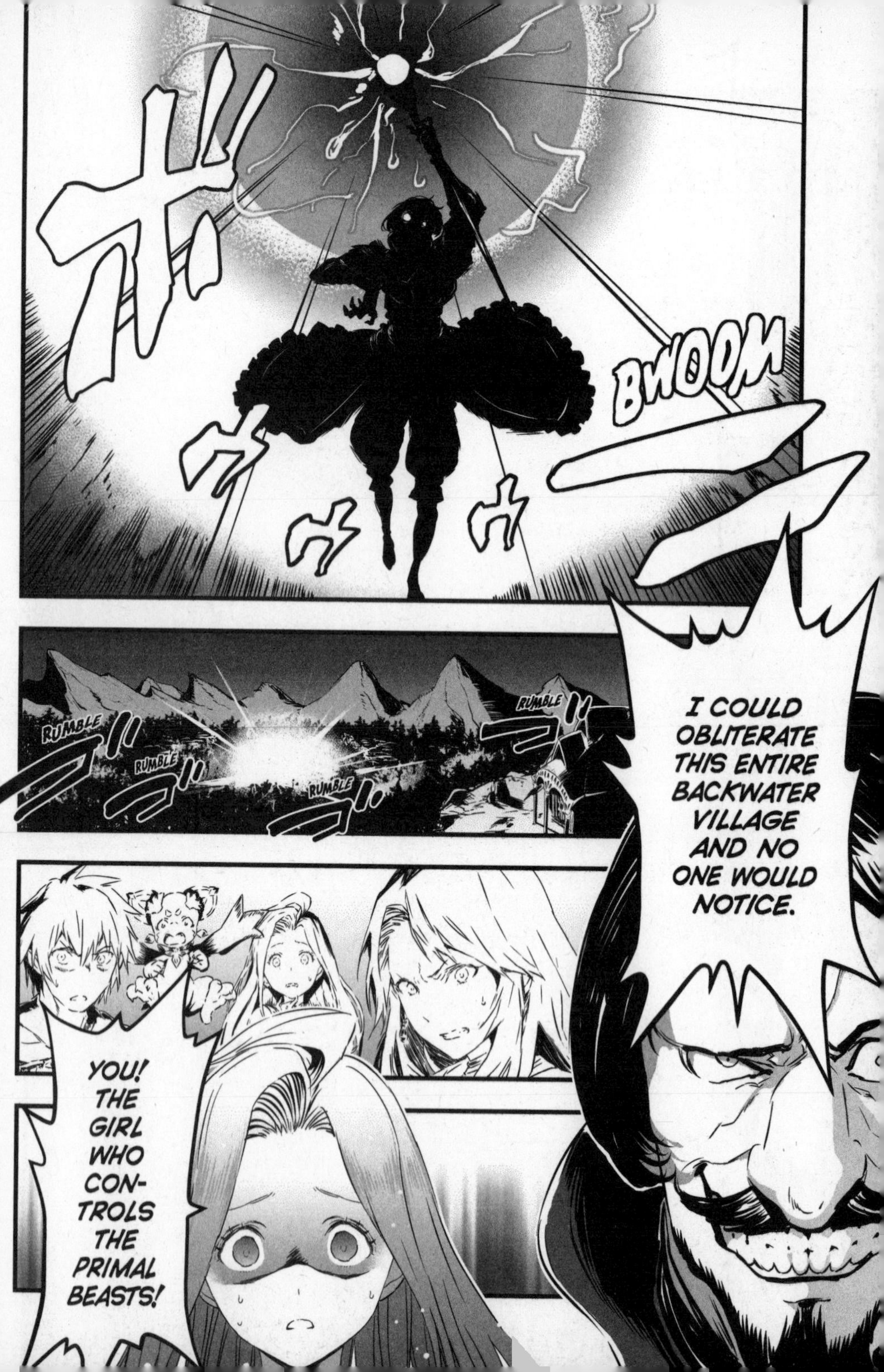
BWOOM
I COULD OBLITERATE THIS ENTIRE BACKWATER VILLAGE AND NO ONE WOULD NOTICE.
RUMBLE
RUMBLE
RUMBLE
RUMBLE
YOU! THE GIRL WHO CON-TROLS THE PRIMAL BEASTS!

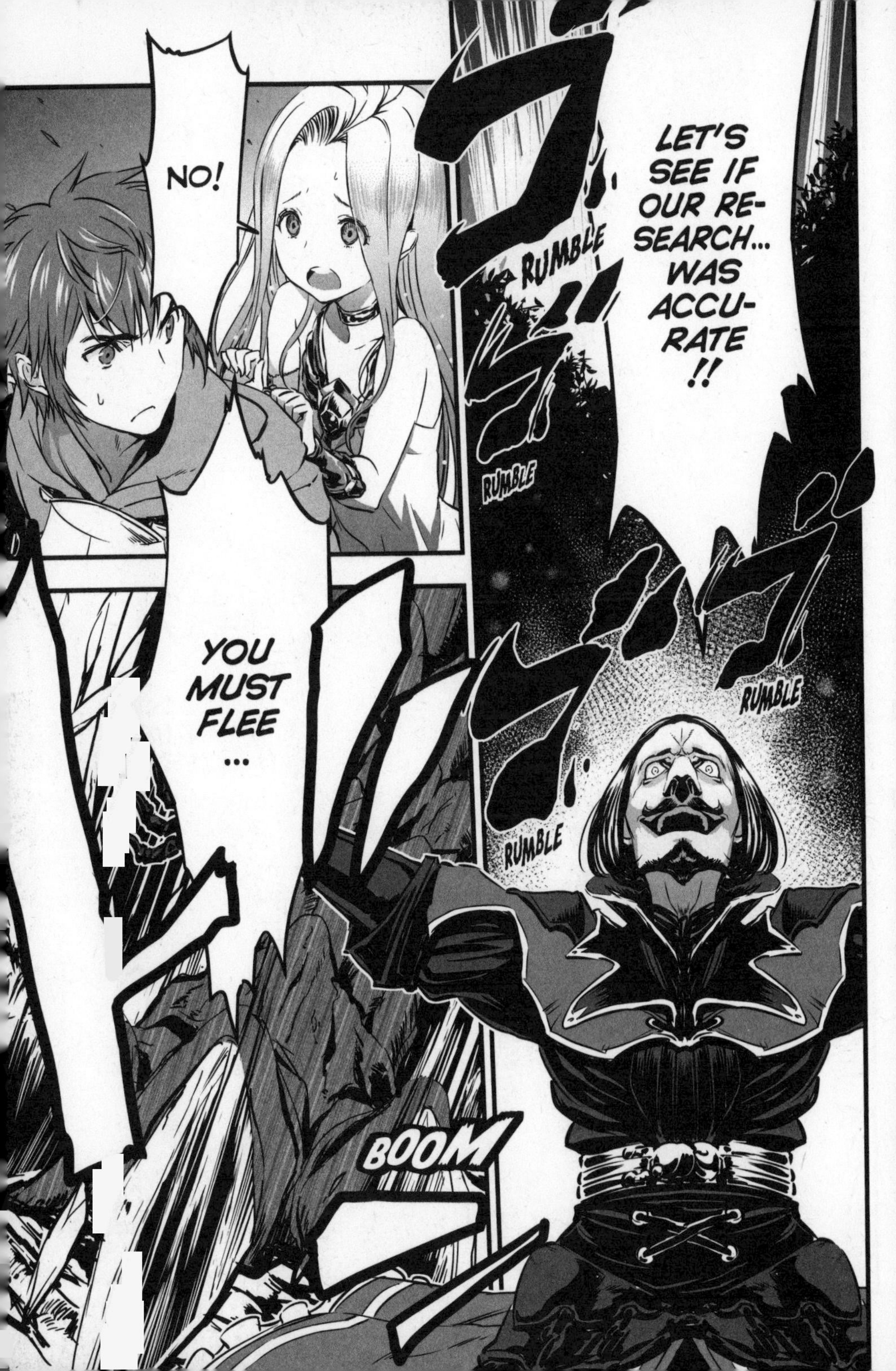
RUMBLE
LET'S SEE IF OUR RE-SEARCH... WAS ACCU-RATE!!
RUMBLE
RUMBLE
RUMBLE
NO!
YOU MUST FLEE...
BOOM

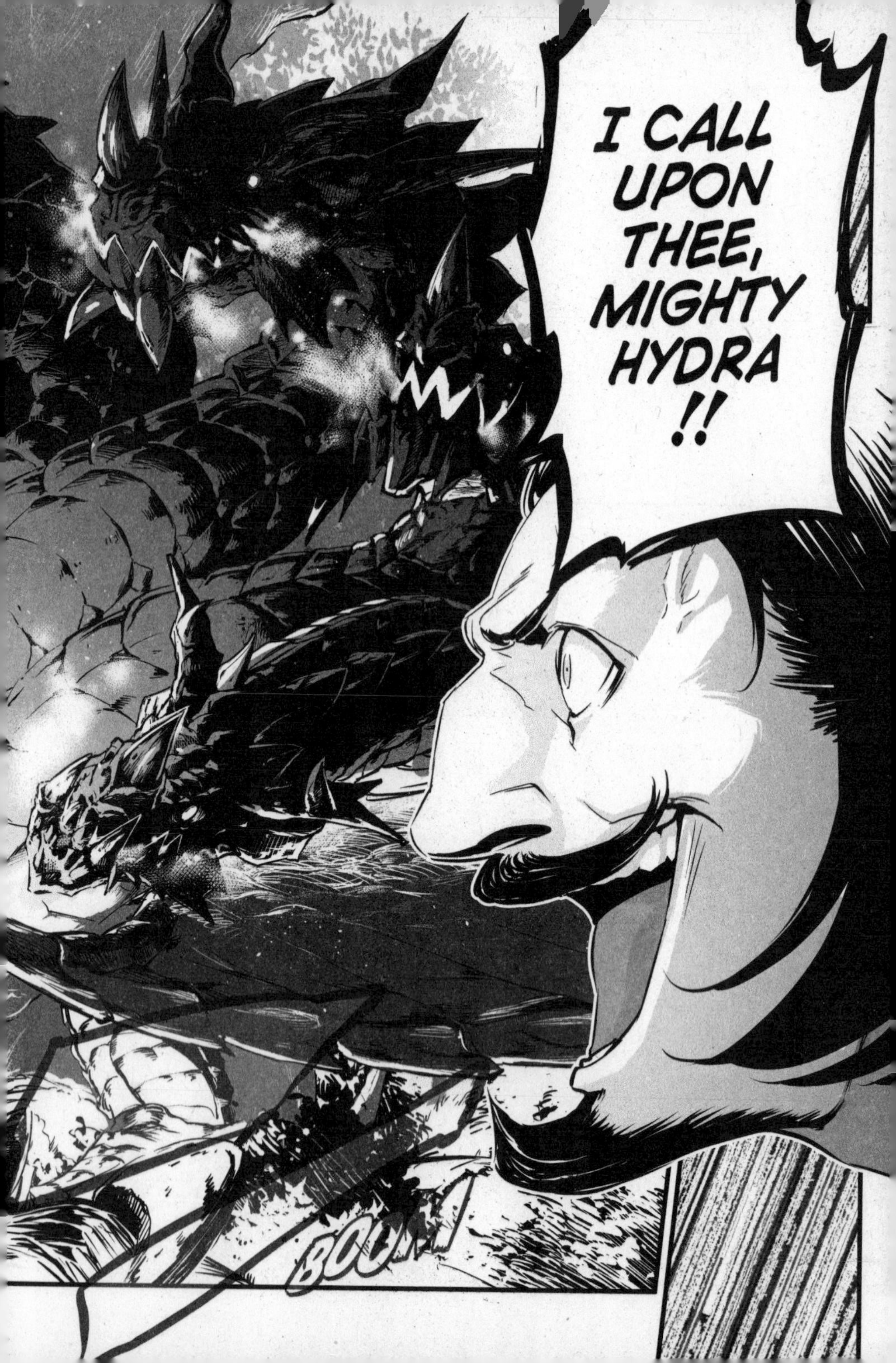
I CALL UPON THEE, MIGHTY HYDRA !!
BOOM

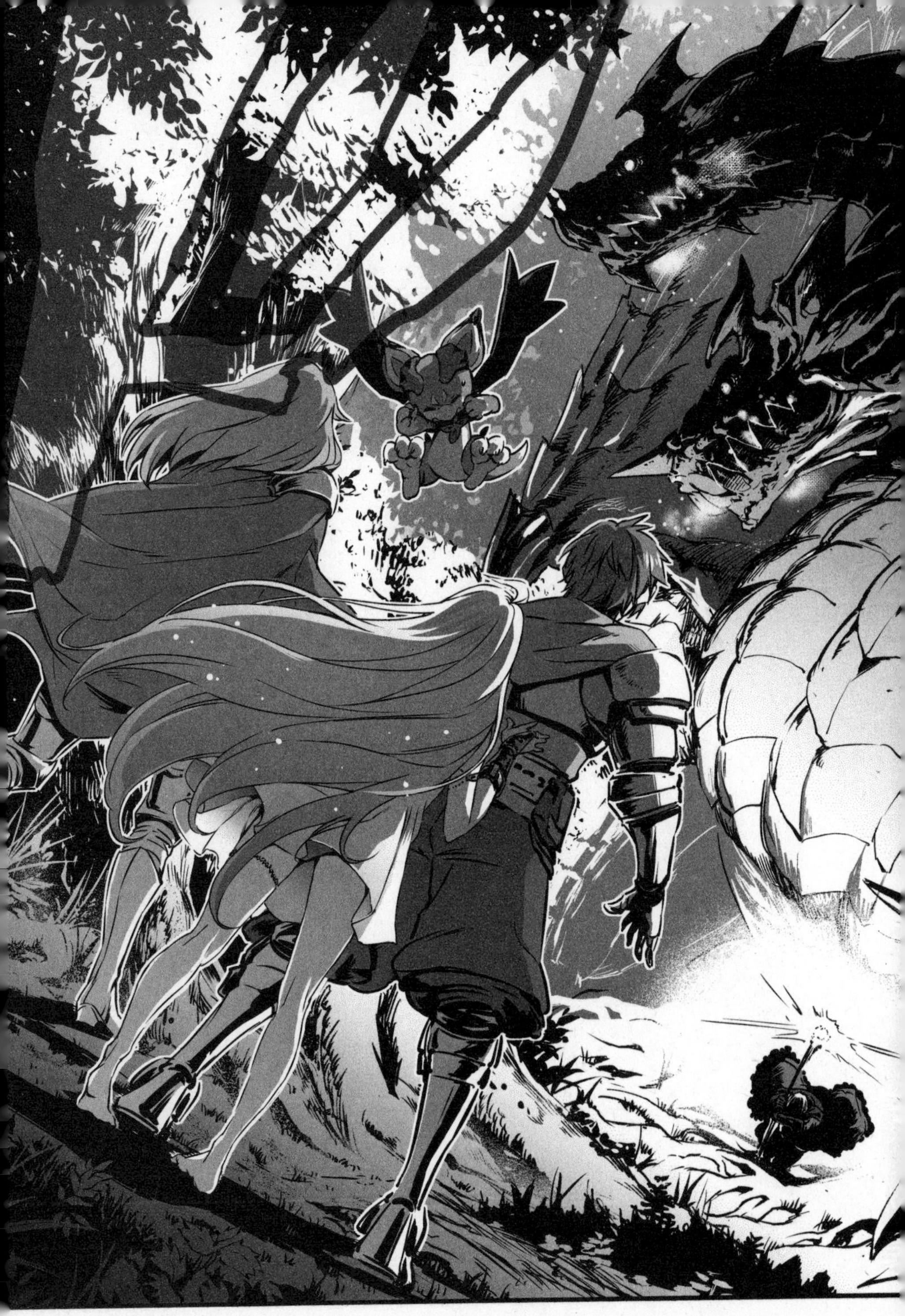

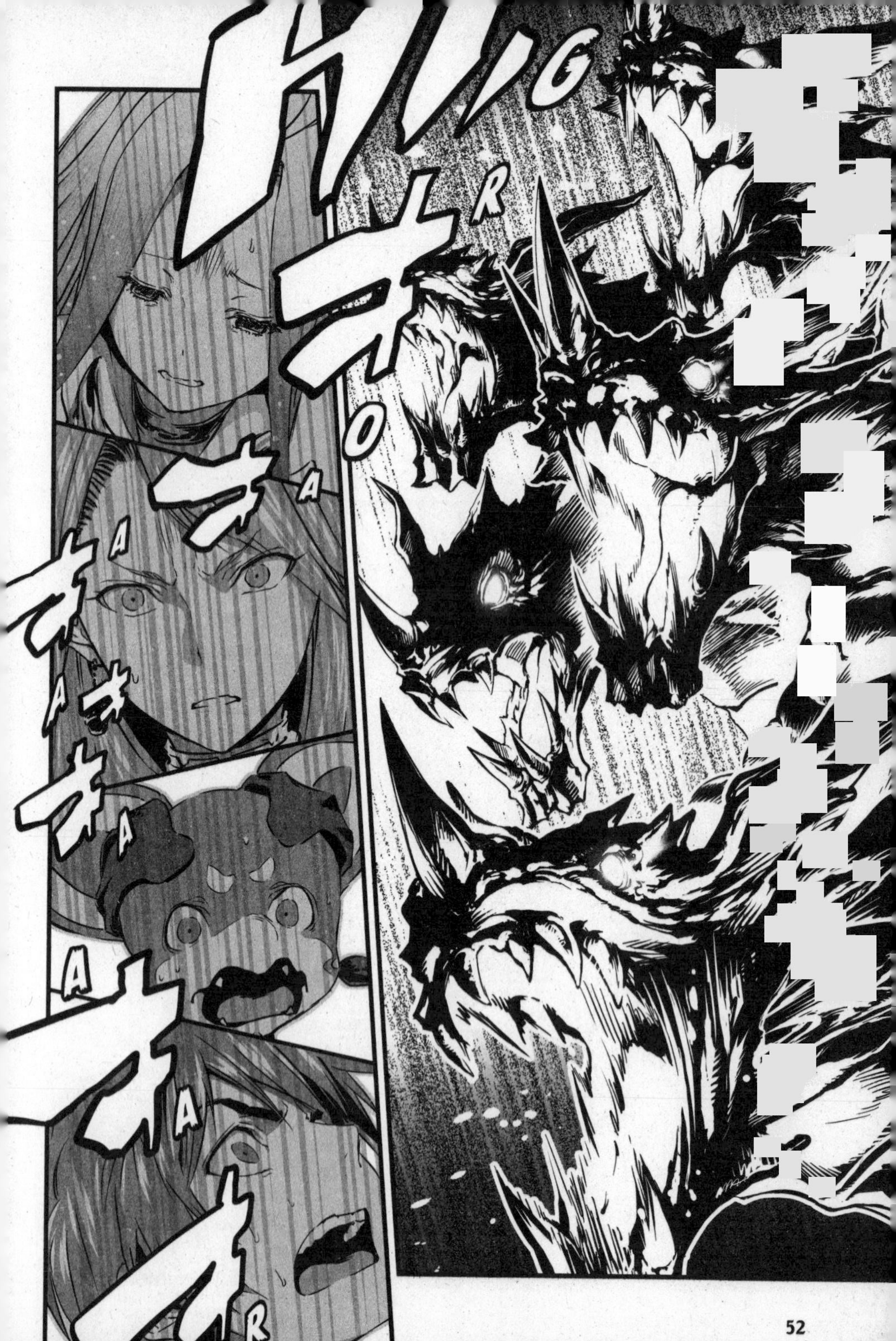
GROAAAAAAR

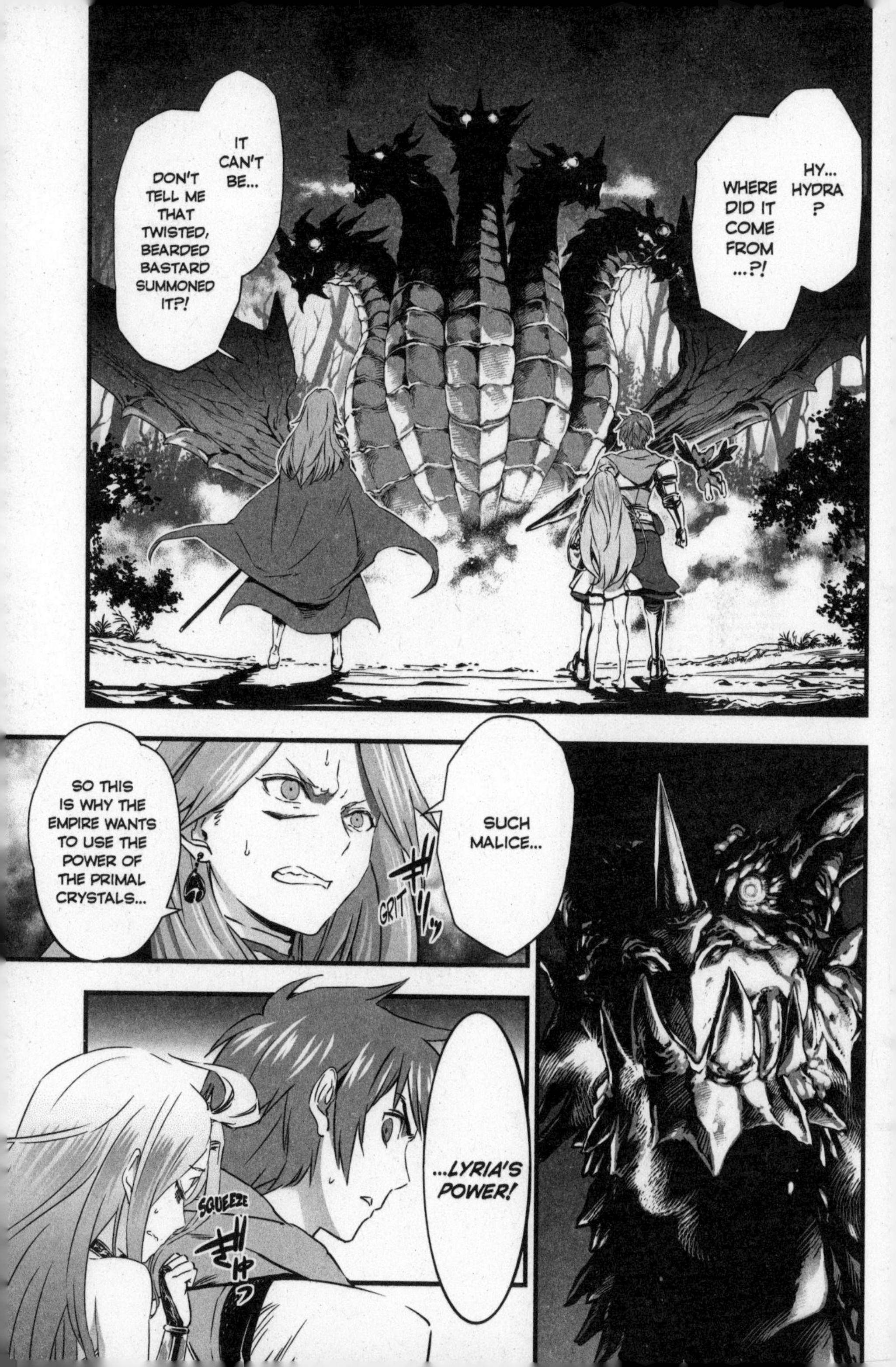
HY... HYDRA?
WHERE DID IT COME FROM ...?!
IT CAN'T BE...
DON'T TELL ME THAT TWISTED, BEARDED BASTARD SUMMONED IT?!
SUCH MALICE...
SO THIS IS WHY THE EMPIRE WANTS TO USE THE POWER OF THE PRIMAL CRYSTALS...
GRIT
...LYRIA'S POWER!
SQUEEZE

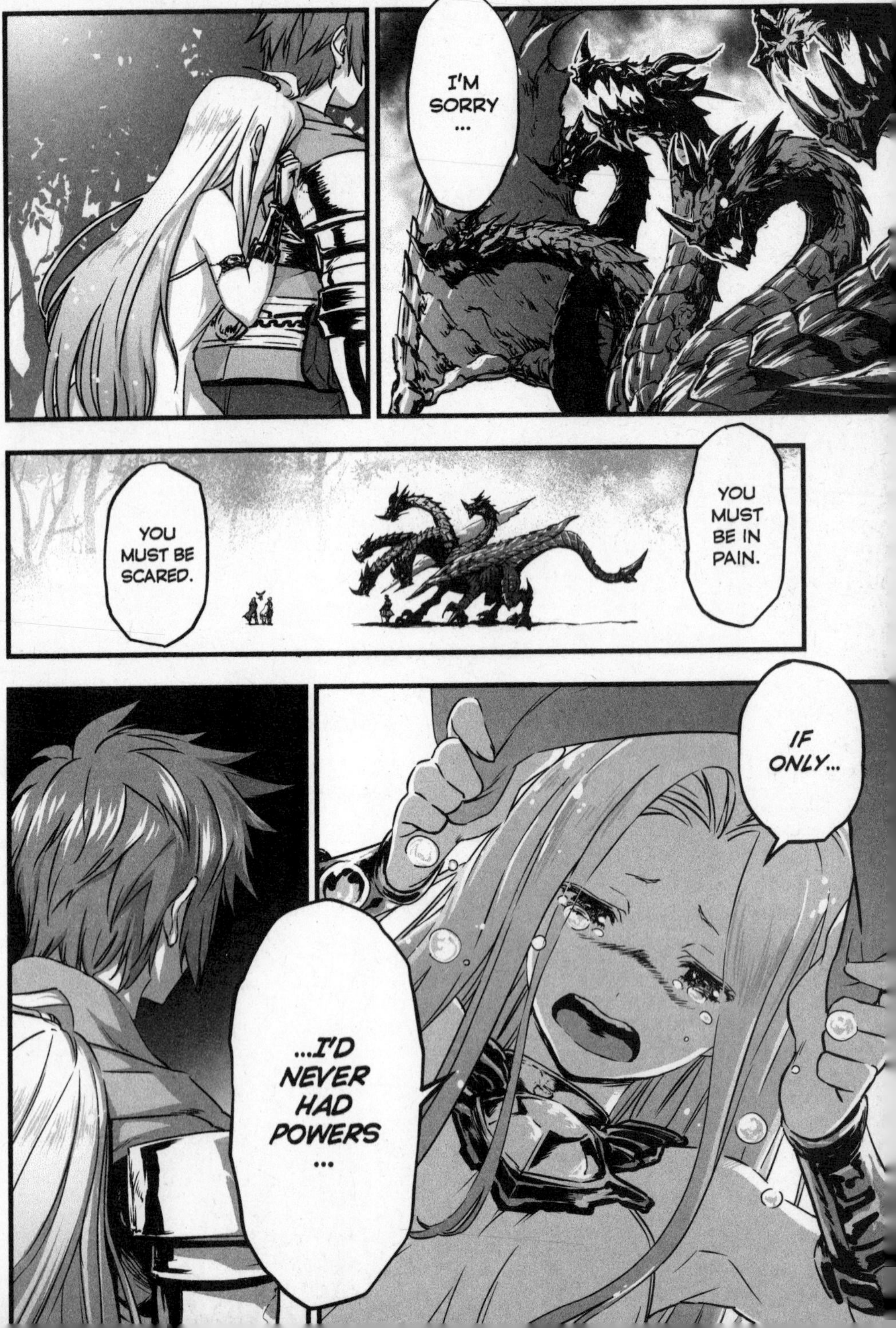
I'M SORRY ...
YOU MUST BE IN PAIN.
YOU MUST BE SCARED.
IF ONLY...
...I'D NEVER HAD POWERS ...

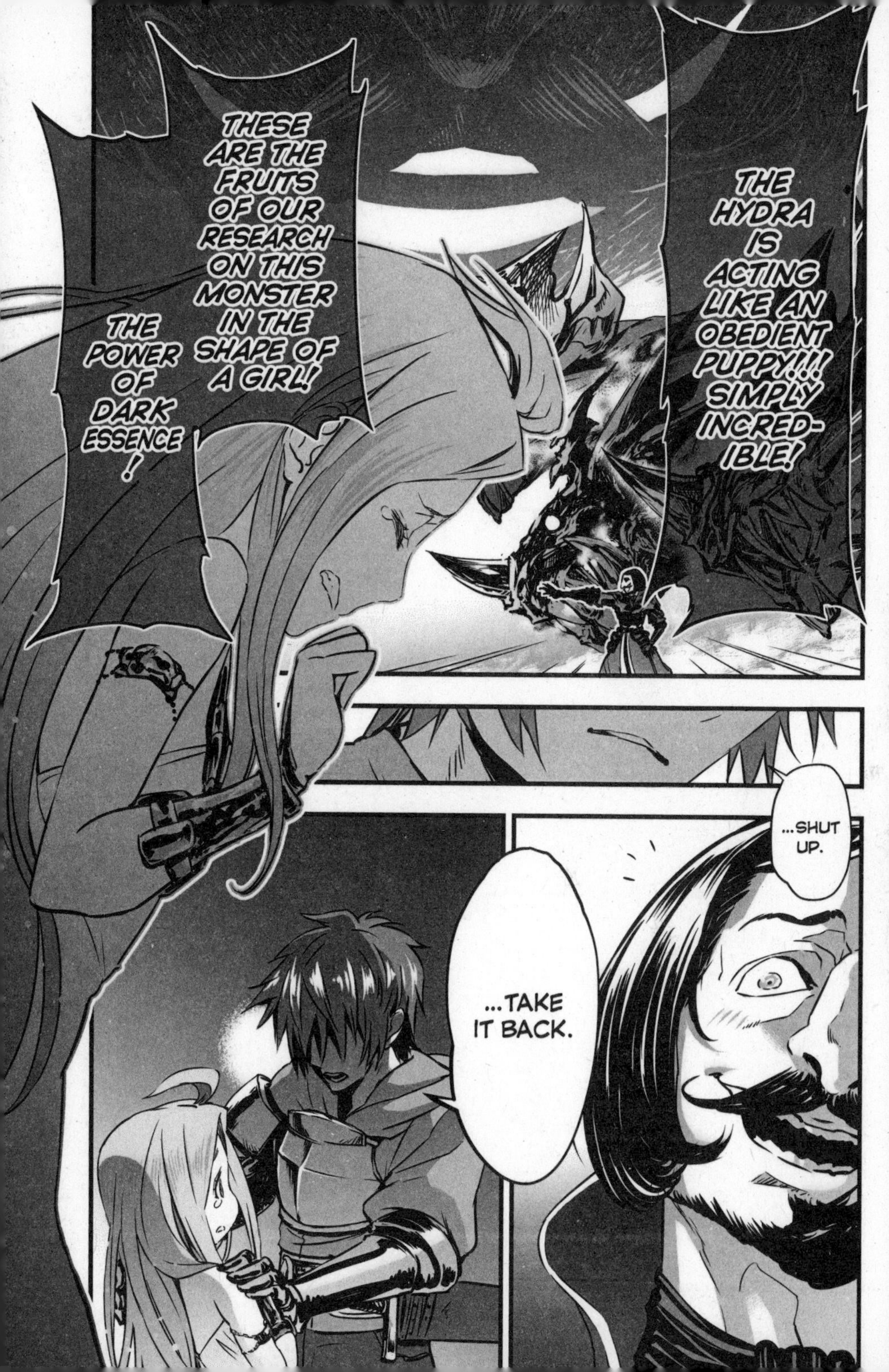
THE HYDRA IS ACTING LIKE AN OBEDIENT PUPPY!!! SIMPLY INCRED-IBLE!
THESE ARE THE FRUITS OF OUR RESEARCH ON THIS MONSTER IN THE SHAPE OF A GIRL!
THE POWER OF DARK ESSENCE!
...SHUT UP.
...TAKE IT BACK.

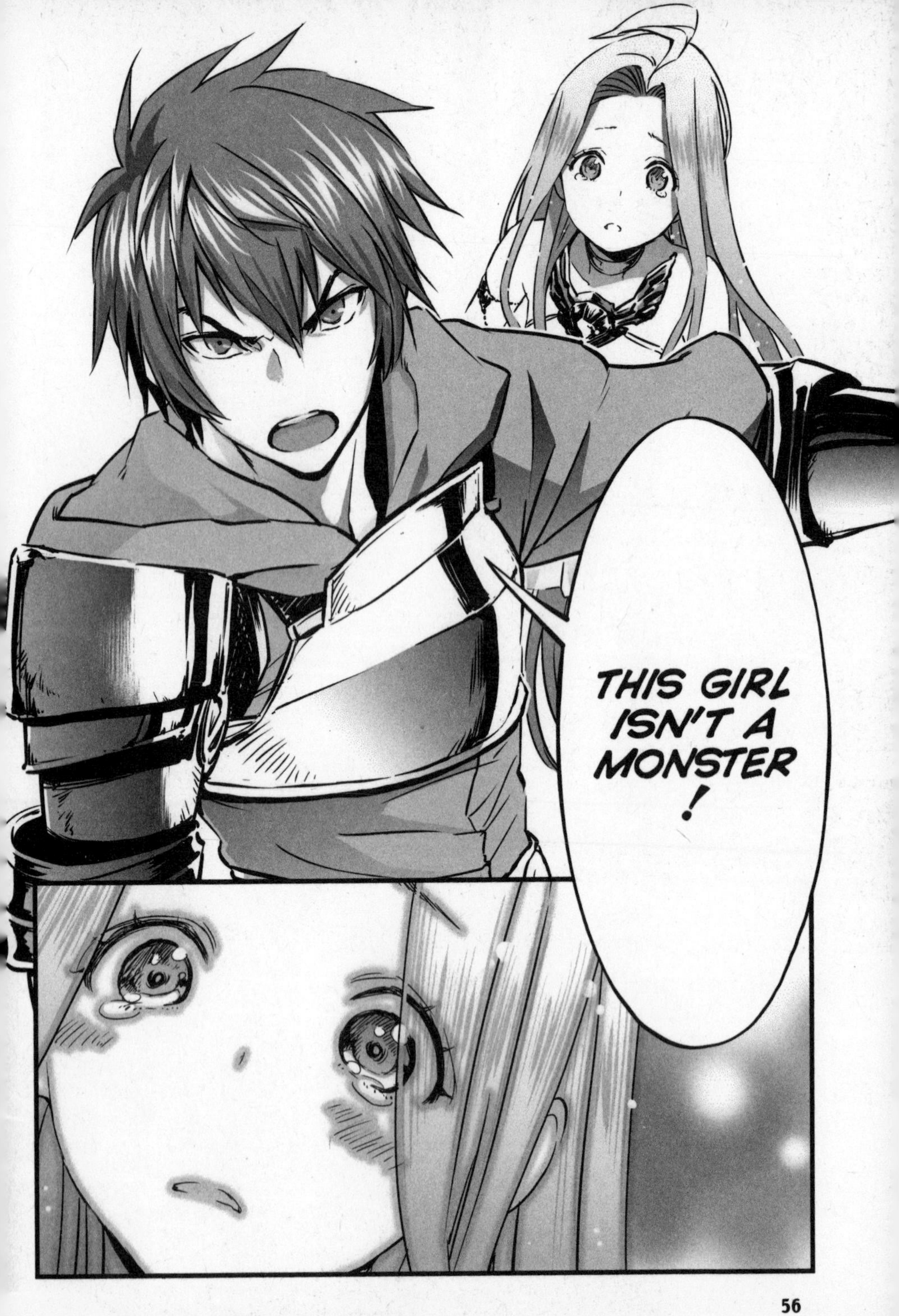
THIS GIRL ISN'T A MONSTER!

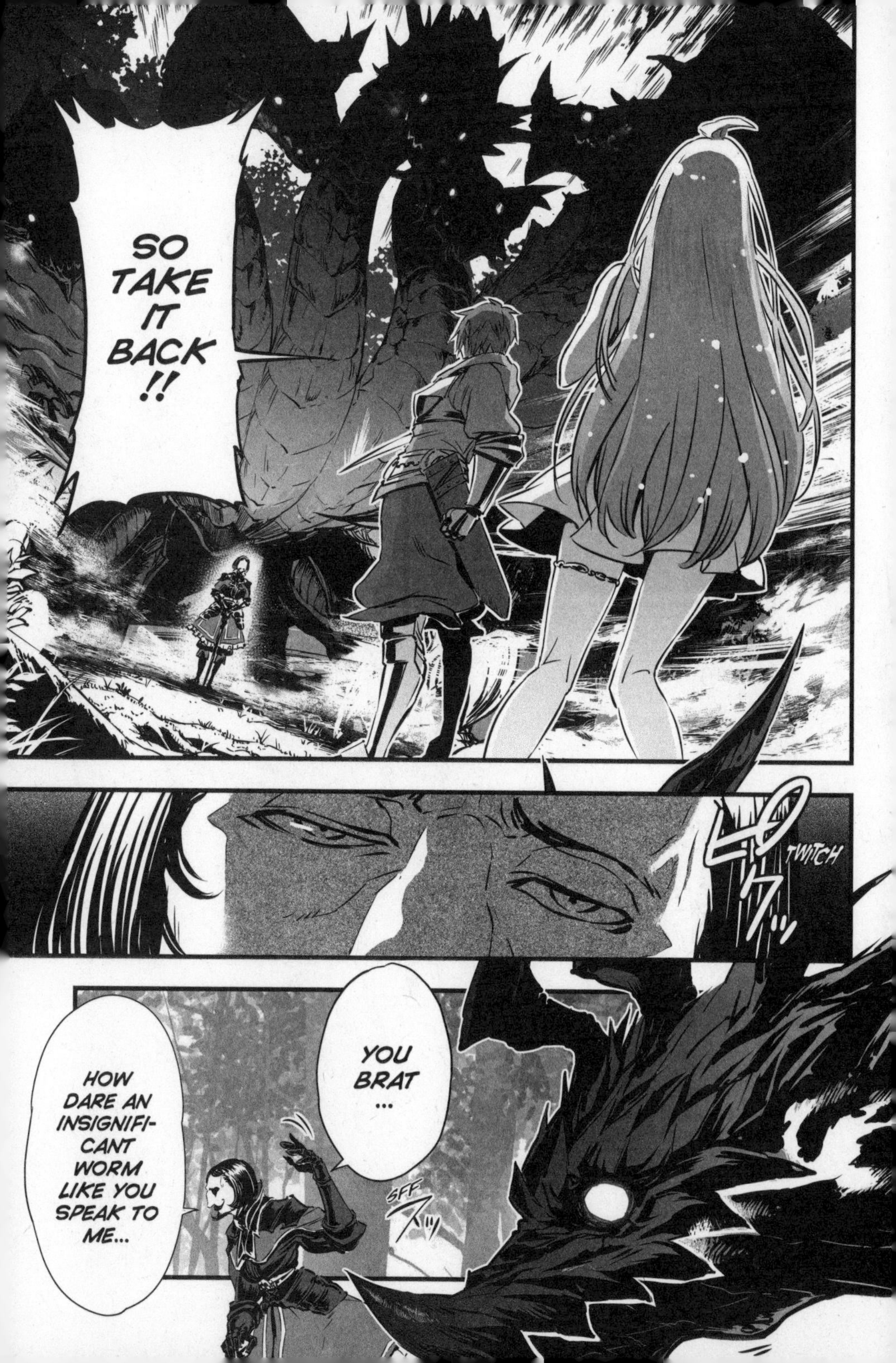
SO TAKE IT BACK!!
TWITCH
YOU BRAT ...
HOW DARE AN INSIGNIFI-CANT WORM LIKE YOU SPEAK TO ME...
SFF

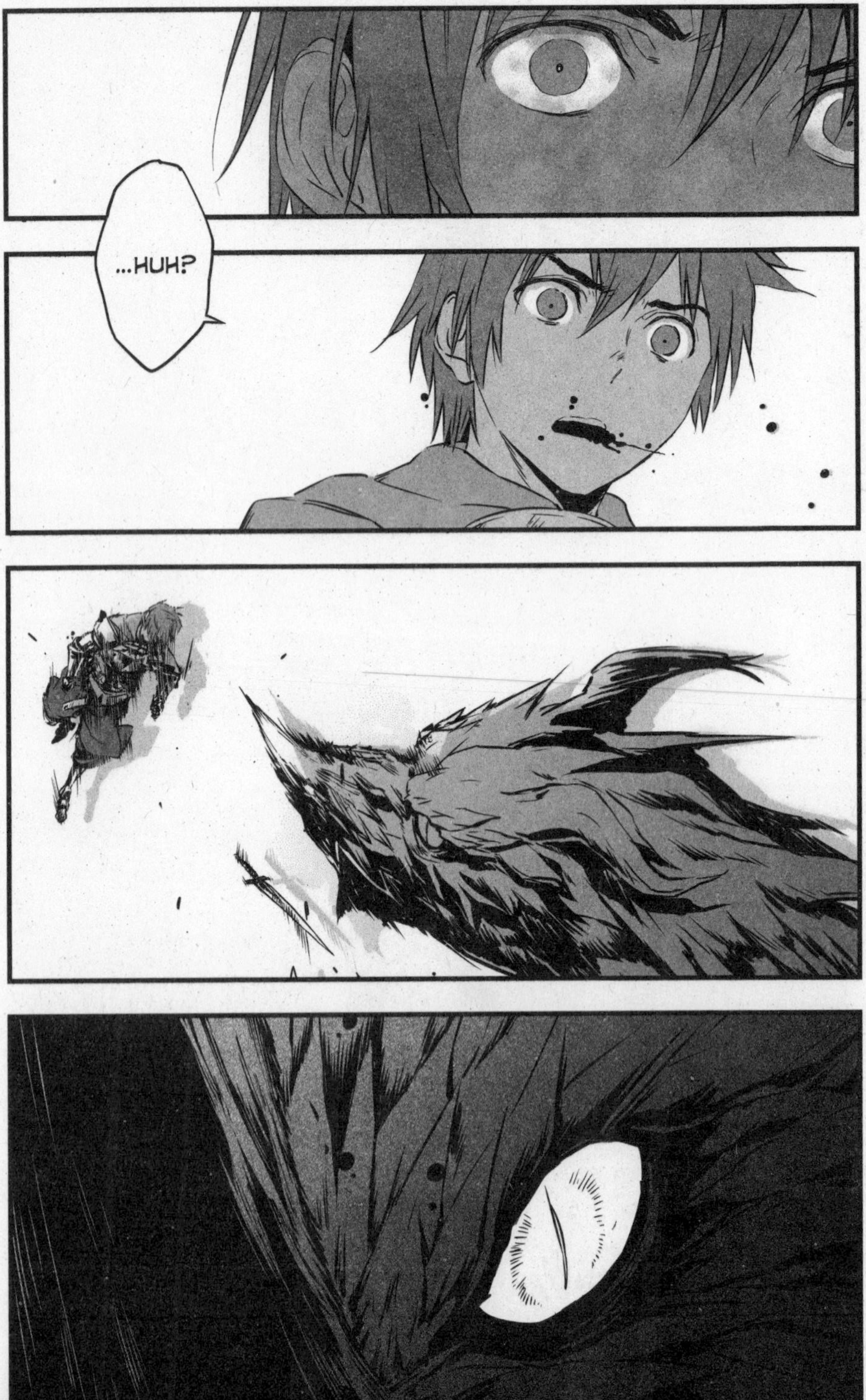
...HUH?

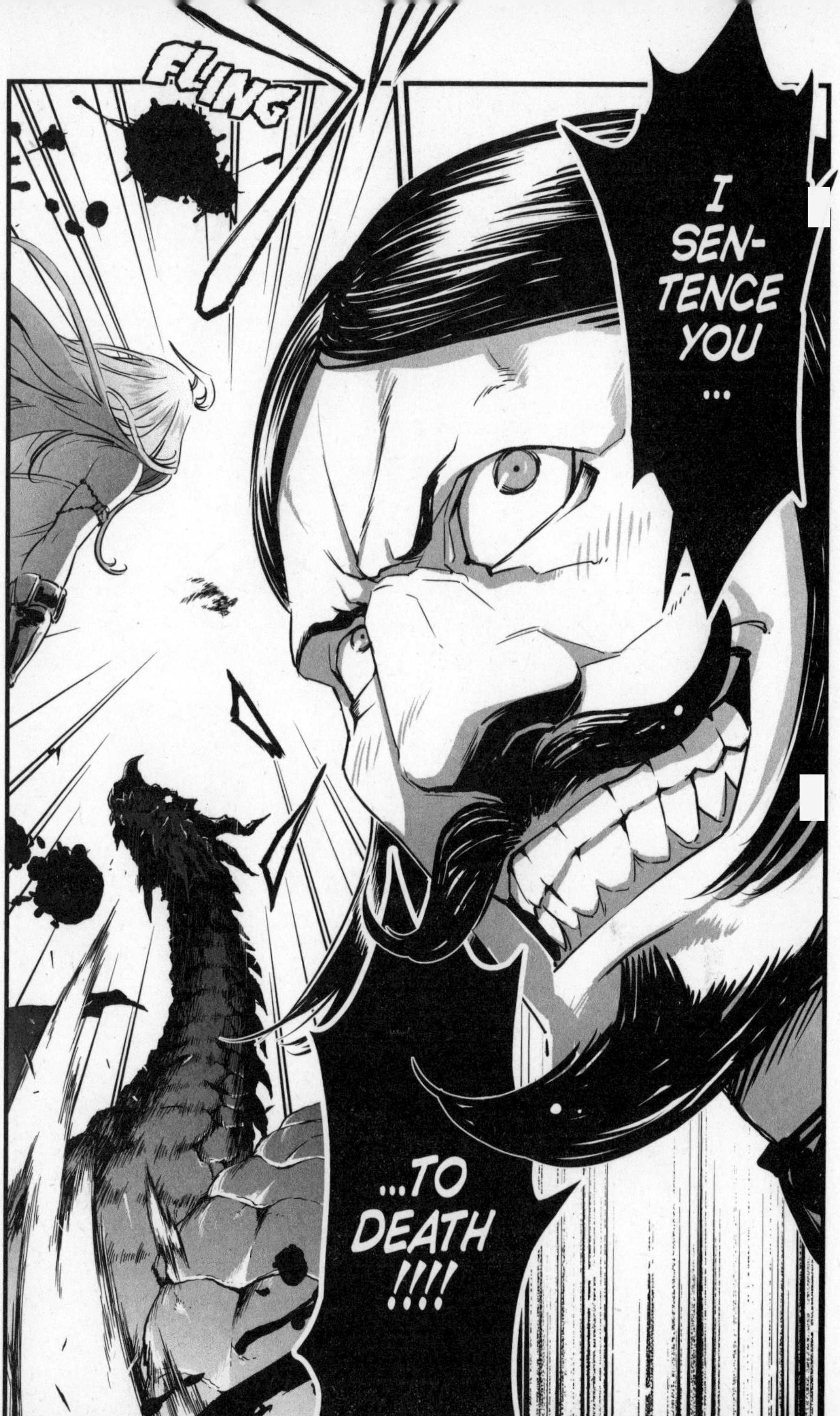
I SENTENCE YOU...
FLING
...TO DEATH!!!!

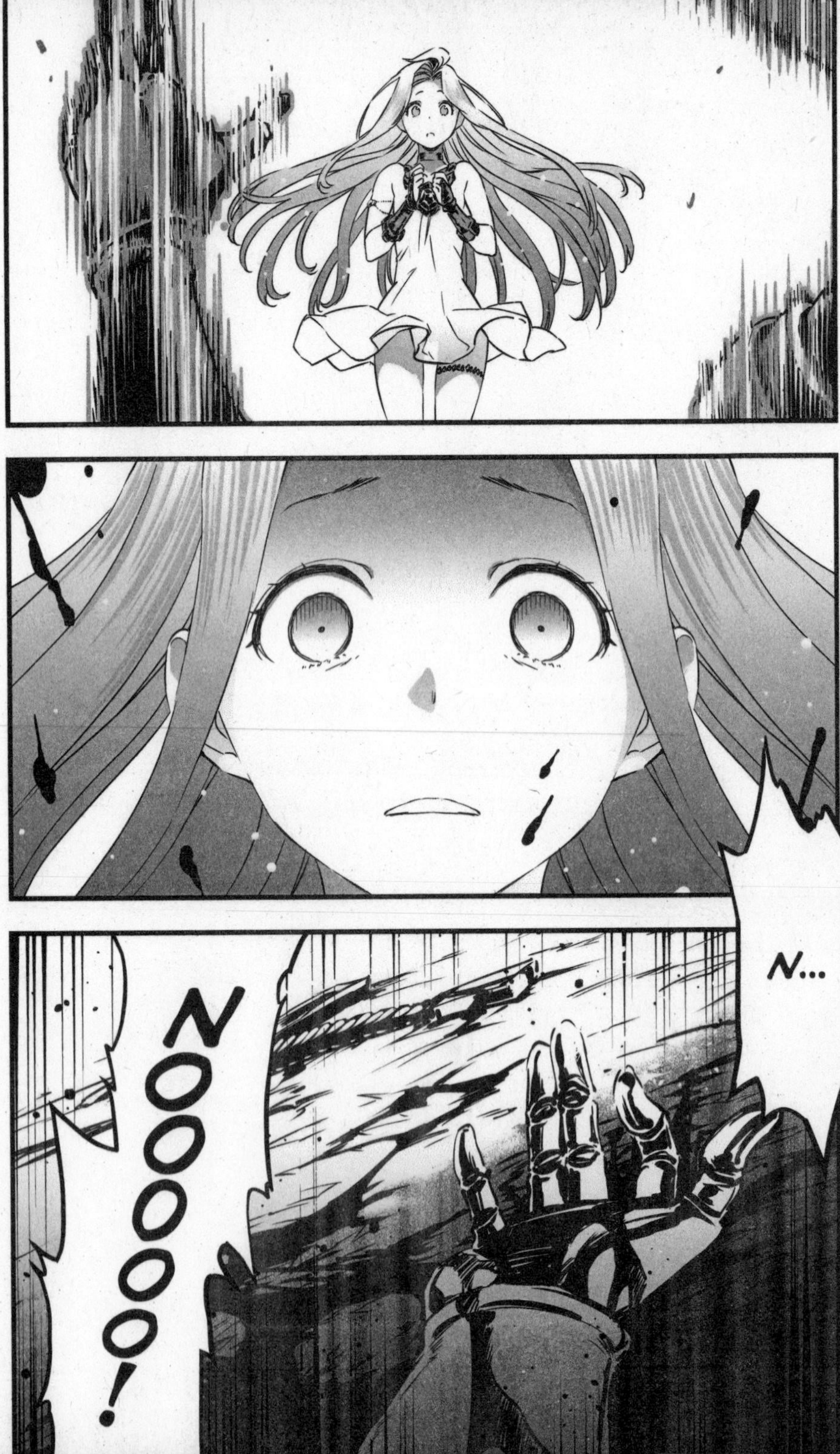
N...
NOOOOOO!

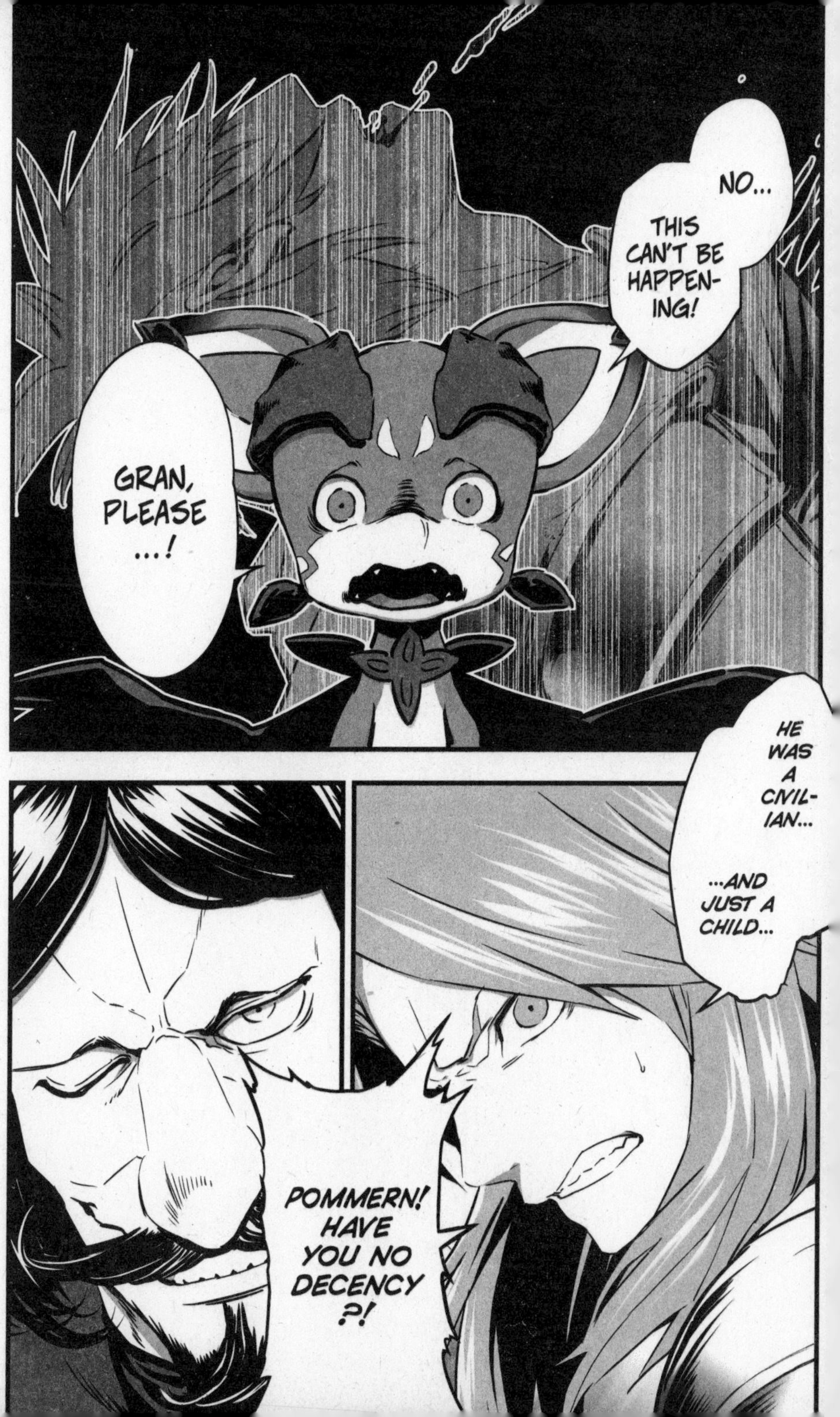
NO...
THIS CAN'T BE HAPPEN-ING!
GRAN, PLEASE ...!
HE WAS A CIVIL-IAN...
...AND JUST A CHILD...
POMMERN! HAVE YOU NO DECENCY ?!

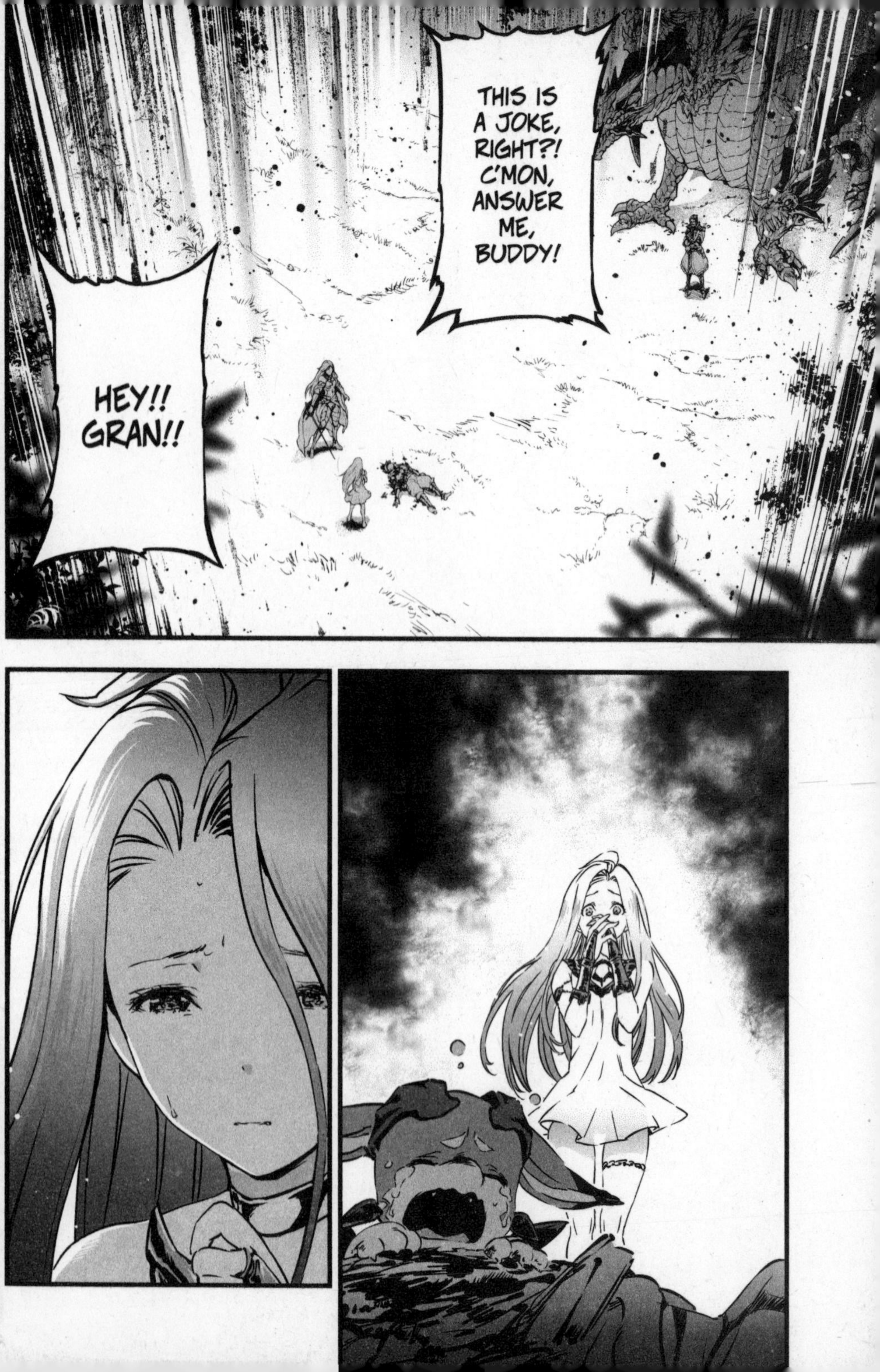
THIS IS A JOKE, RIGHT?! C'MON, ANSWER ME, BUDDY!
HEY!! GRAN!!

CHAPTER 3: Prologue (3)

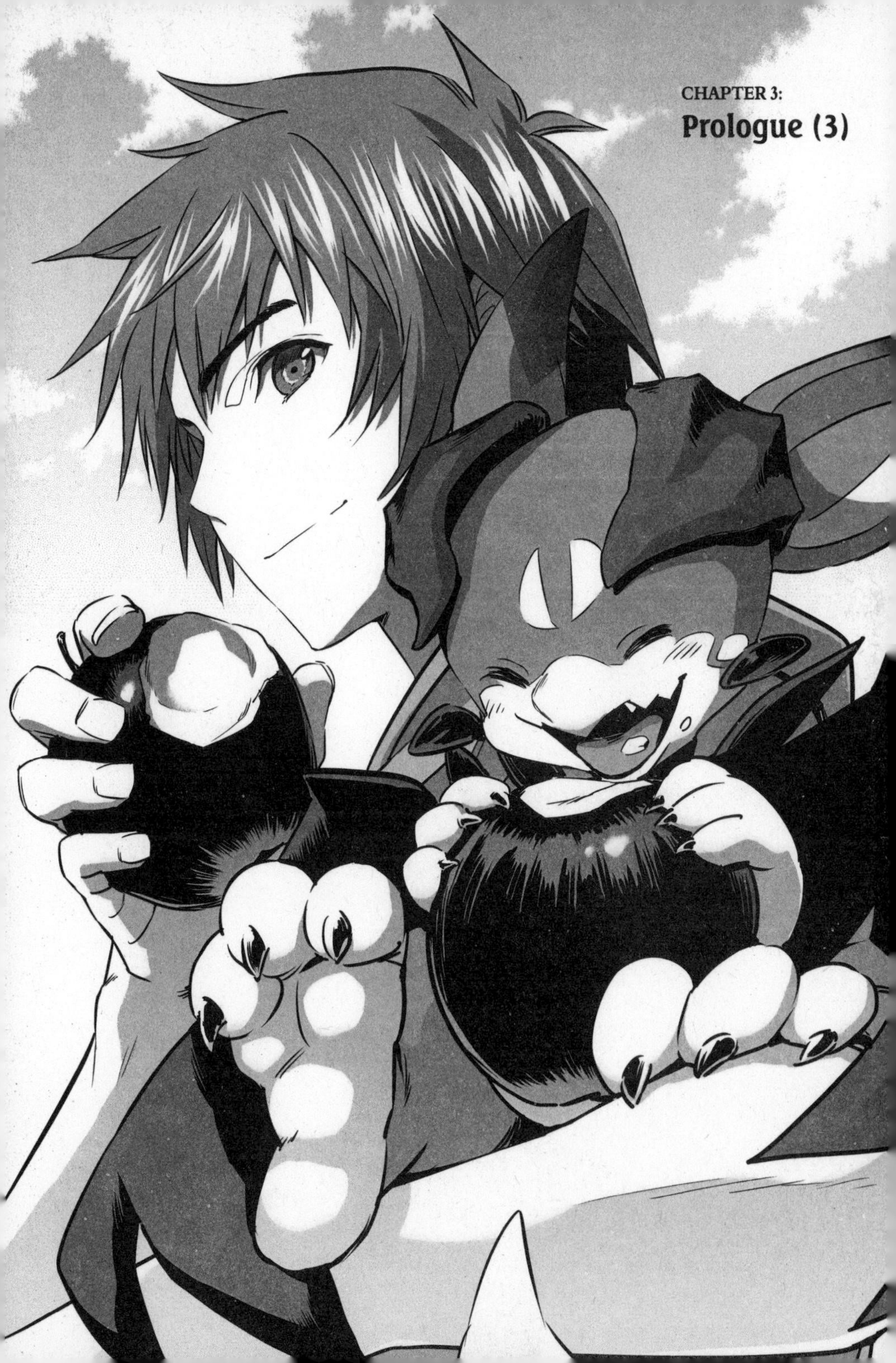

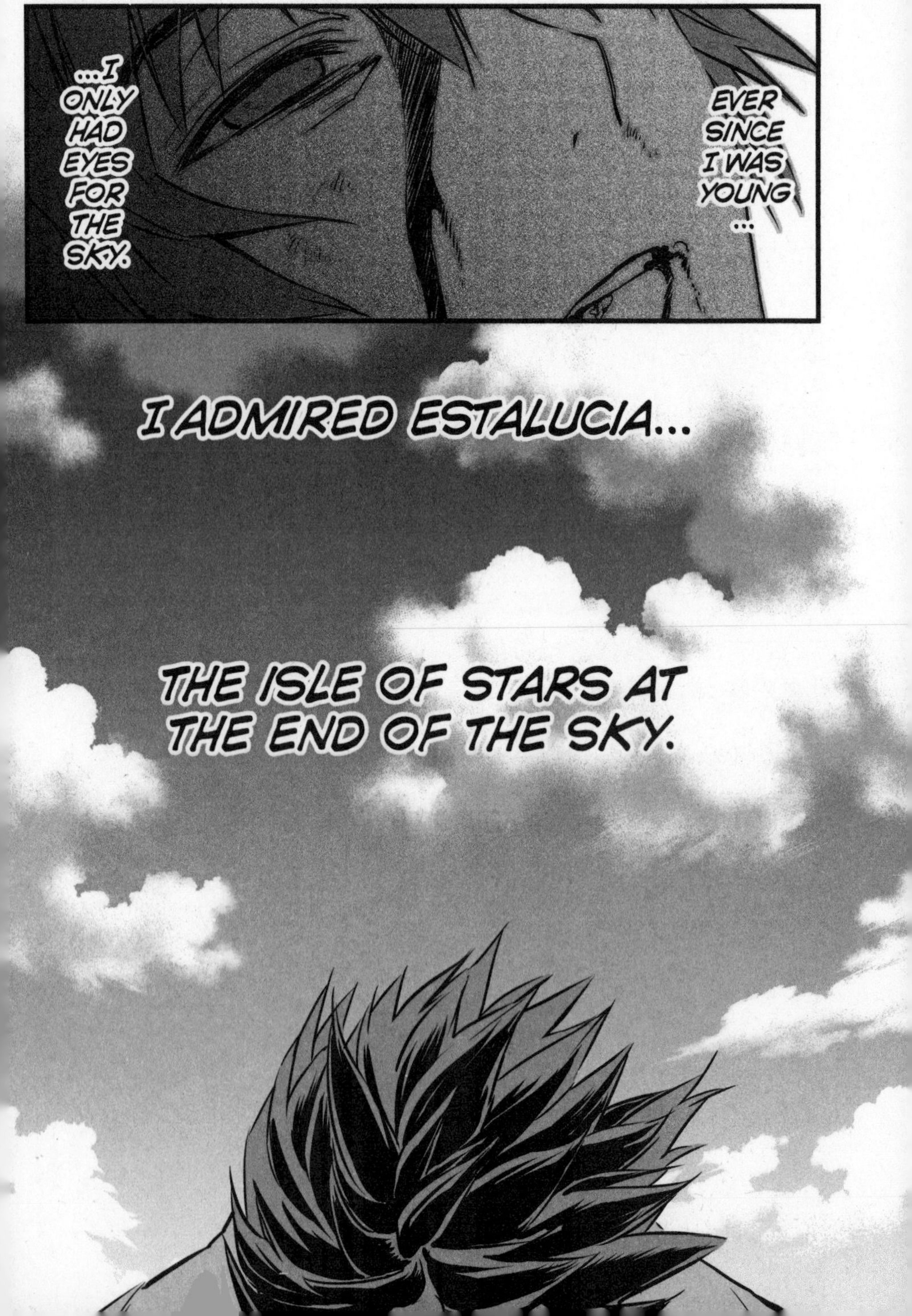
EVER SINCE I WAS YOUNG...
...I ONLY HAD EYES FOR THE SKY.
I ADMIRED ESTALUCIA...
THE ISLE OF STARS AT THE END OF THE SKY.

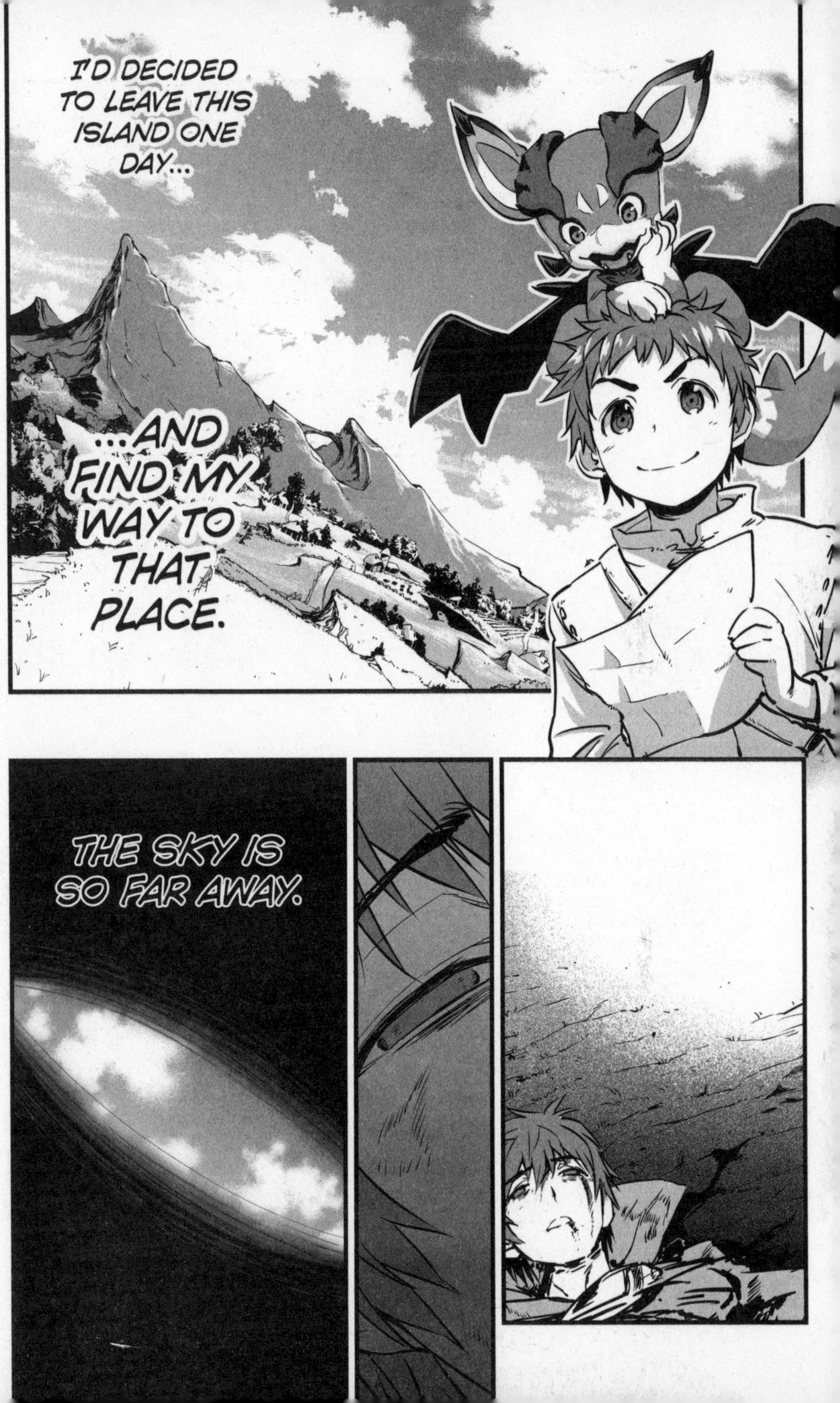
I'D DECIDED TO LEAVE THIS ISLAND ONE DAY...
...AND FIND MY WAY TO THAT PLACE.
THE SKY IS SO FAR AWAY.

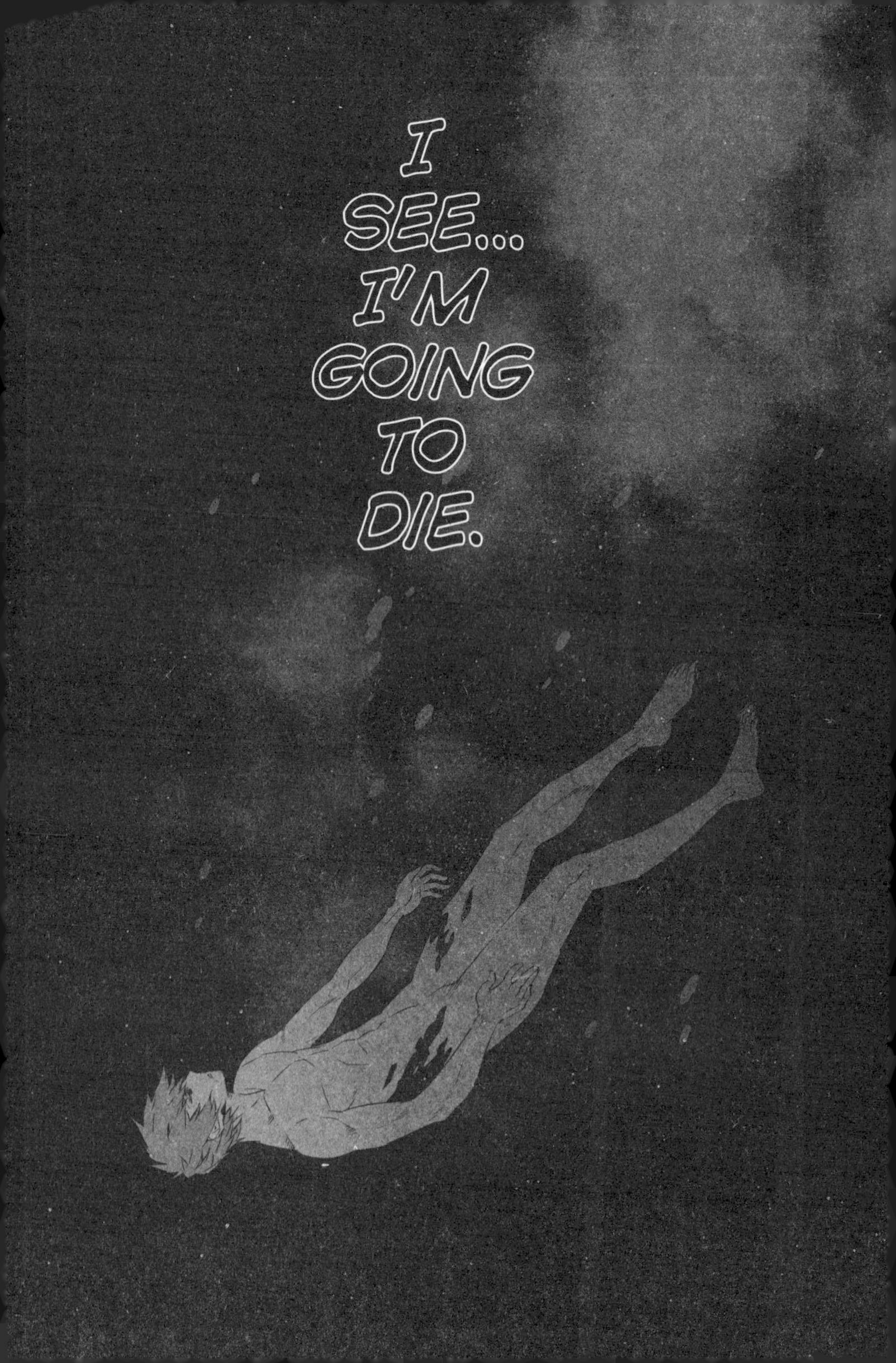
I SEE... I'M GOING TO DIE.

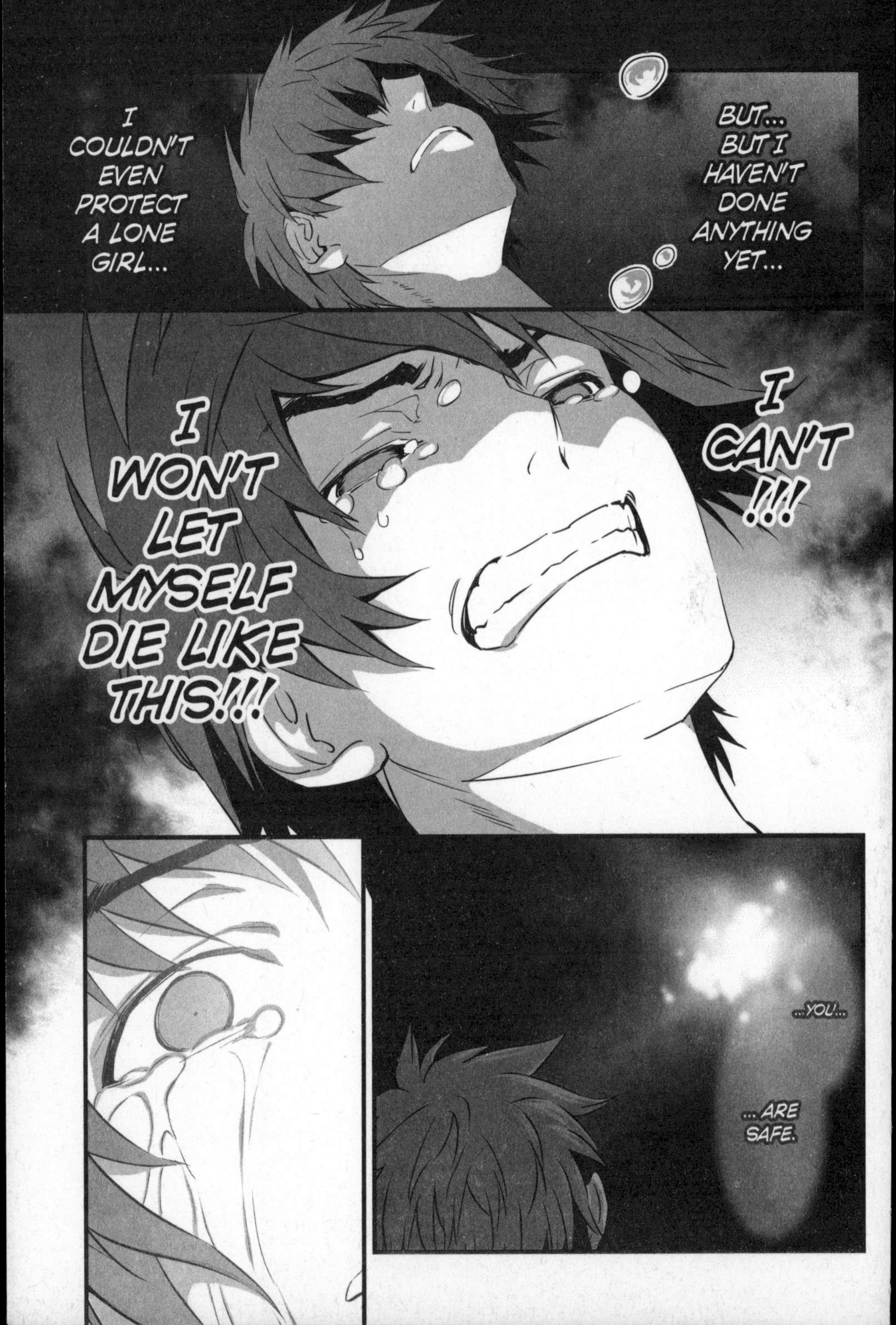
BUT... BUT I HAVEN'T DONE ANYTHING YET...
I COULDN'T EVEN PROTECT A LONE GIRL...
I CAN'T!!!
I WON'T LET MYSELF DIE LIKE THIS!!!
...YOU...
...ARE SAFE.

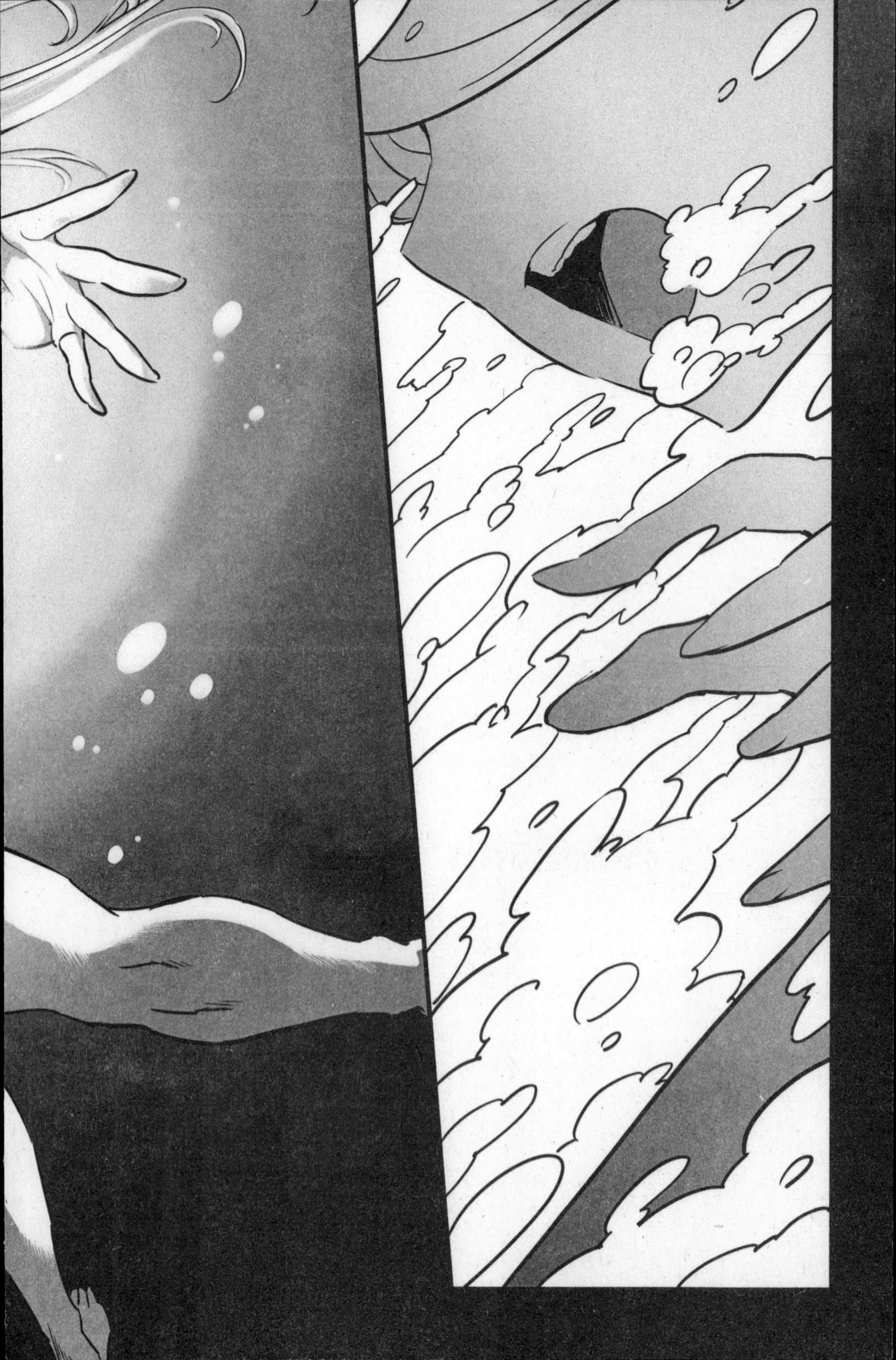

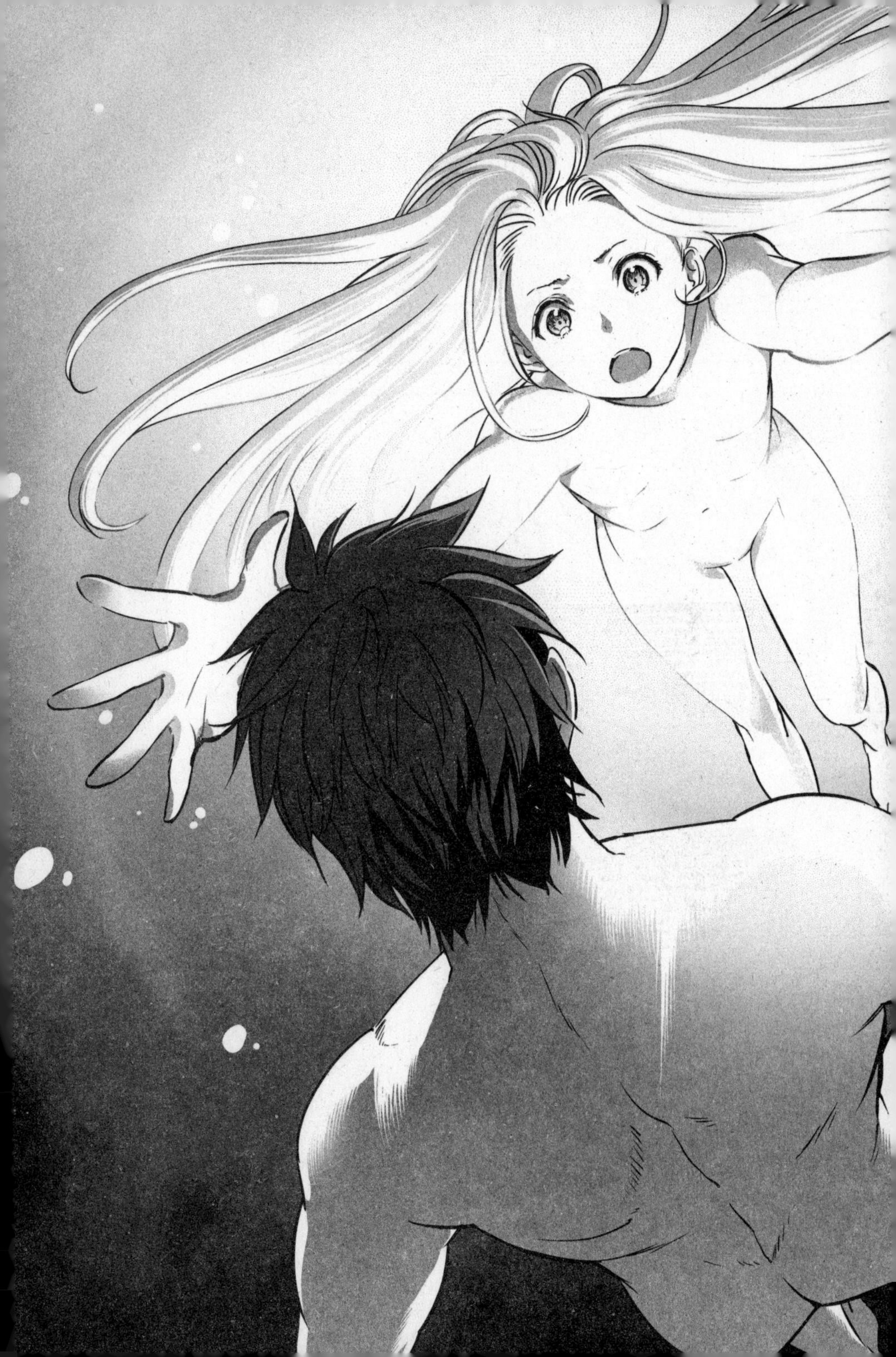

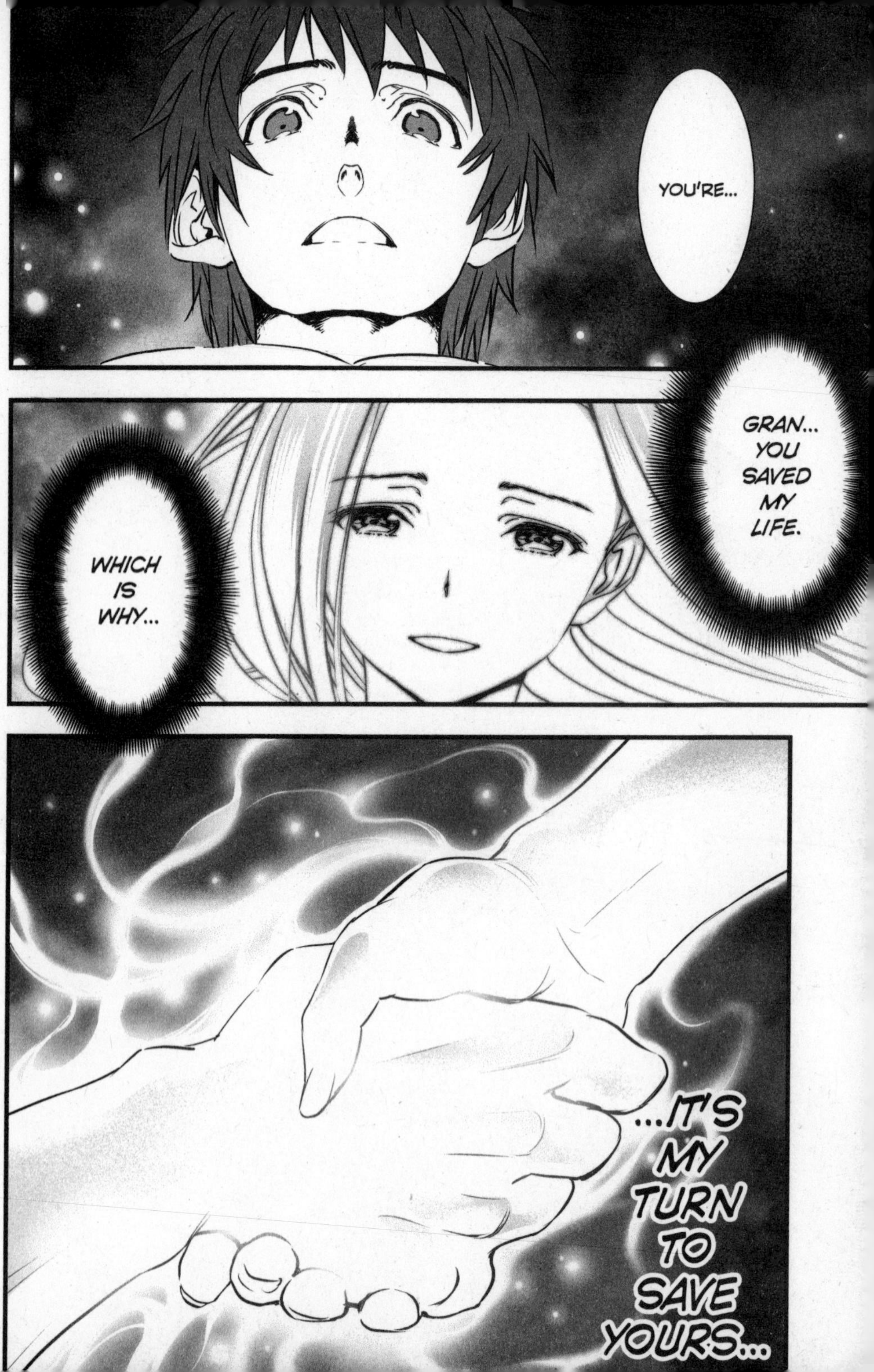
YOU'RE...
GRAN... YOU SAVED MY LIFE.
WHICH IS WHY...
...IT'S MY TURN TO SAVE YOURS...

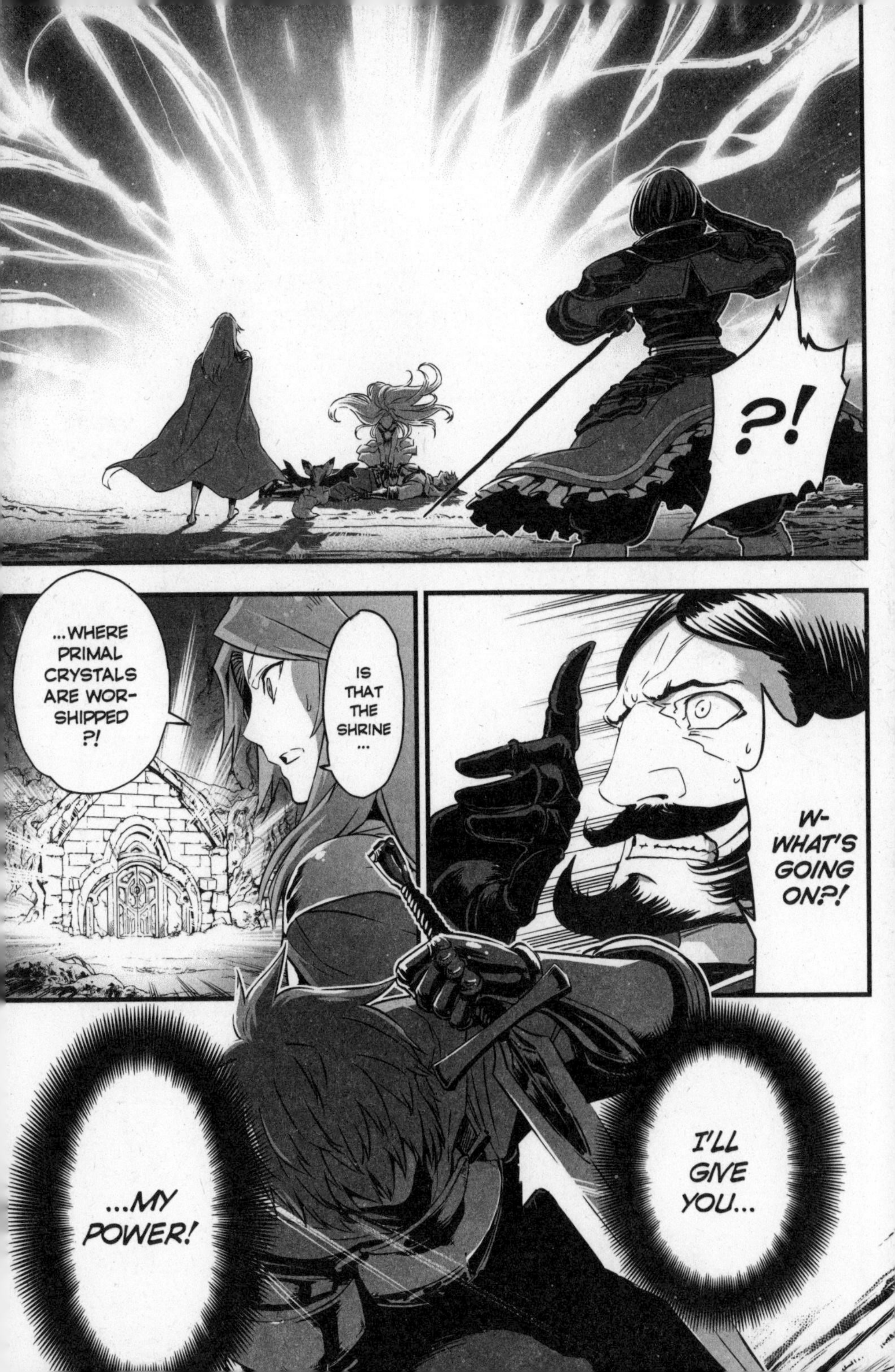
?!
W-WHAT'S GOING ON?!
IS THAT THE SHRINE...
...WHERE PRIMAL CRYSTALS ARE WOR-SHIPPED?!
I'LL GIVE YOU...
...MY POWER!

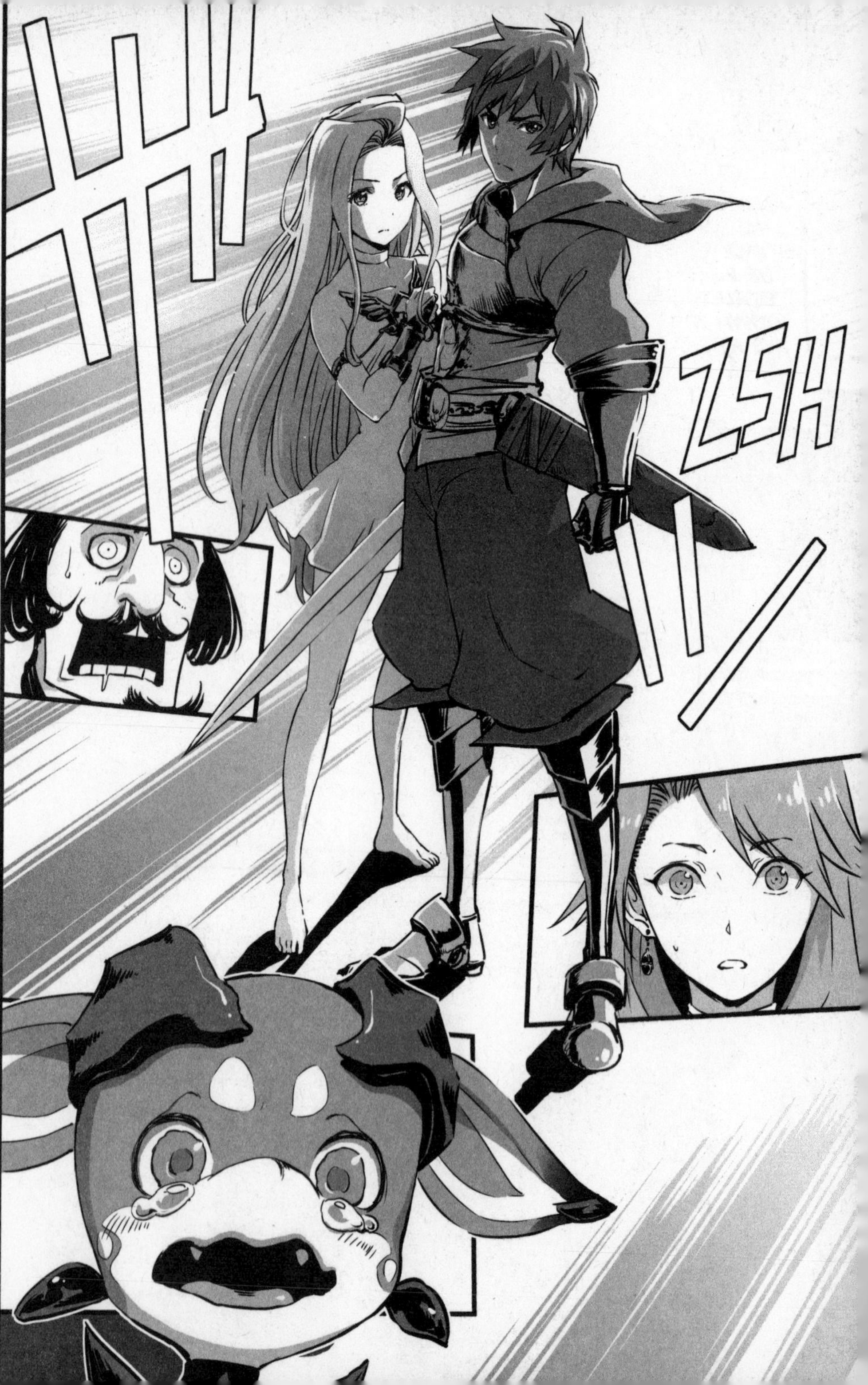
ZSH

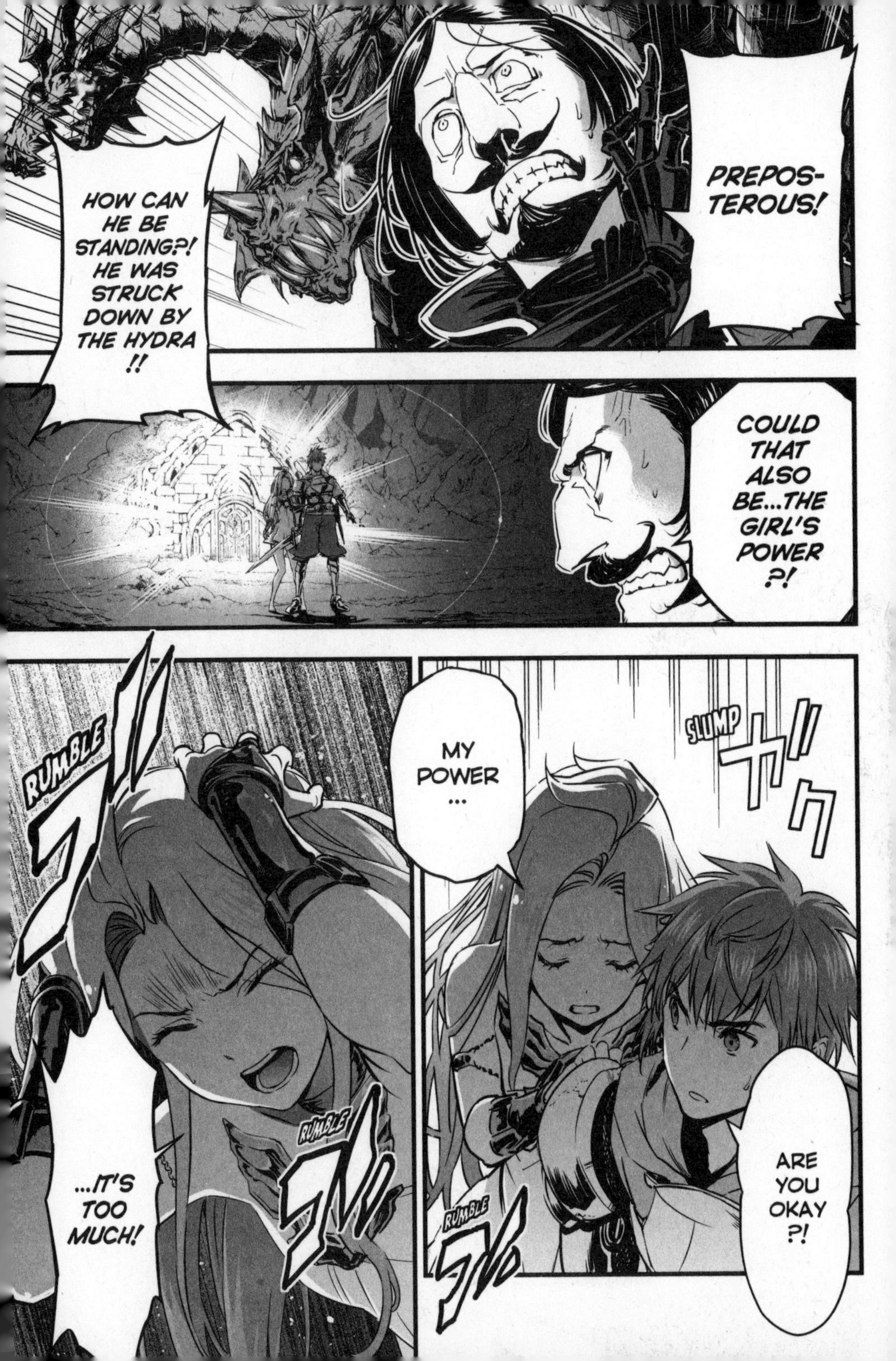
PREPOS-TEROUS!
HOW CAN HE BE STANDING?! HE WAS STRUCK DOWN BY THE HYDRA!!
COULD THAT ALSO BE...THE GIRL'S POWER?!
SLUMP
MY POWER ...
RUMBLE
ARE YOU OKAY?!
RUMBLE
RUMBLE
...IT'S TOO MUCH!

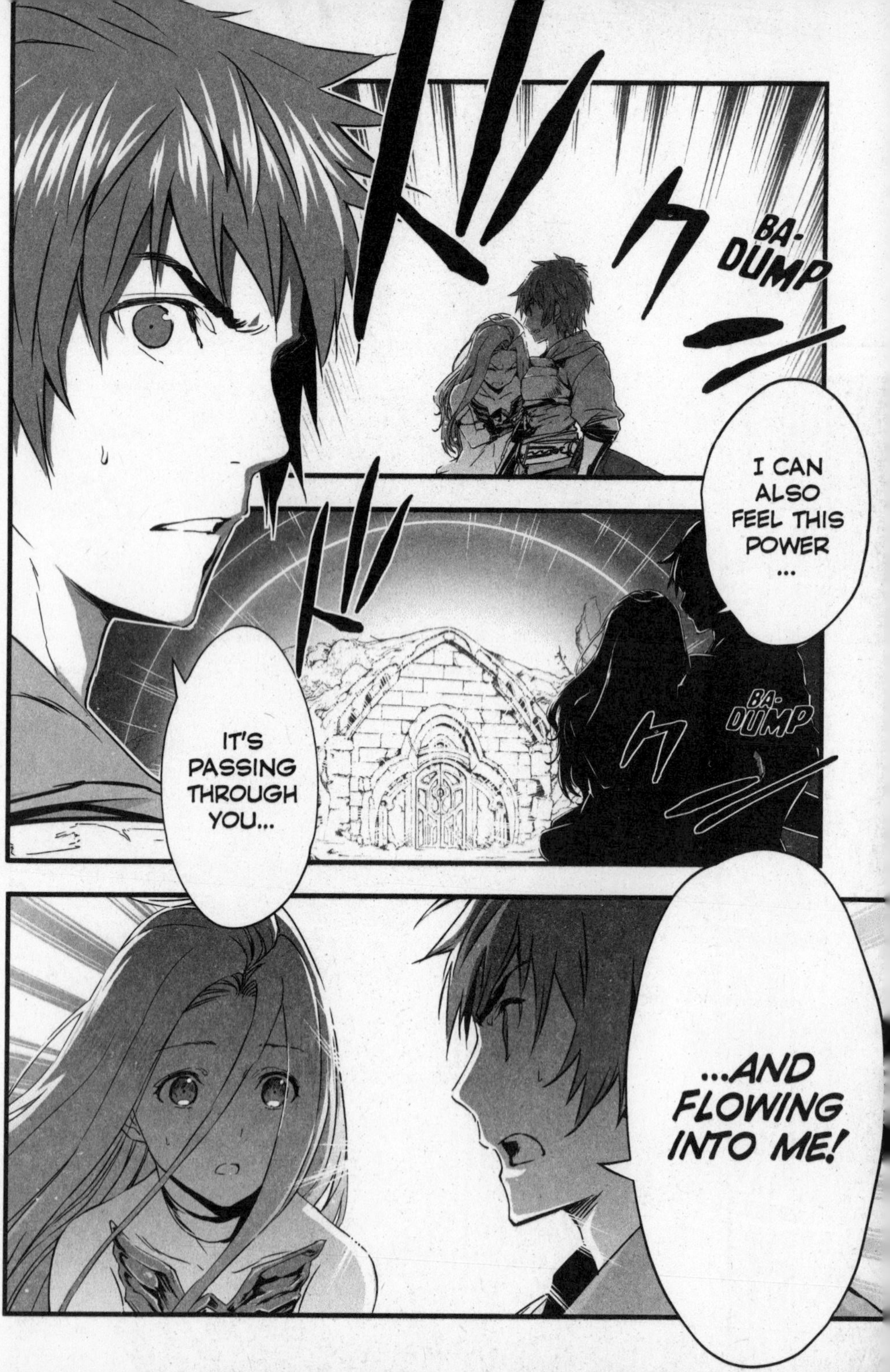
BA-DUMP
I CAN ALSO FEEL THIS POWER ...
BA-DUMP
IT'S PASSING THROUGH YOU...
...AND FLOWING INTO ME!

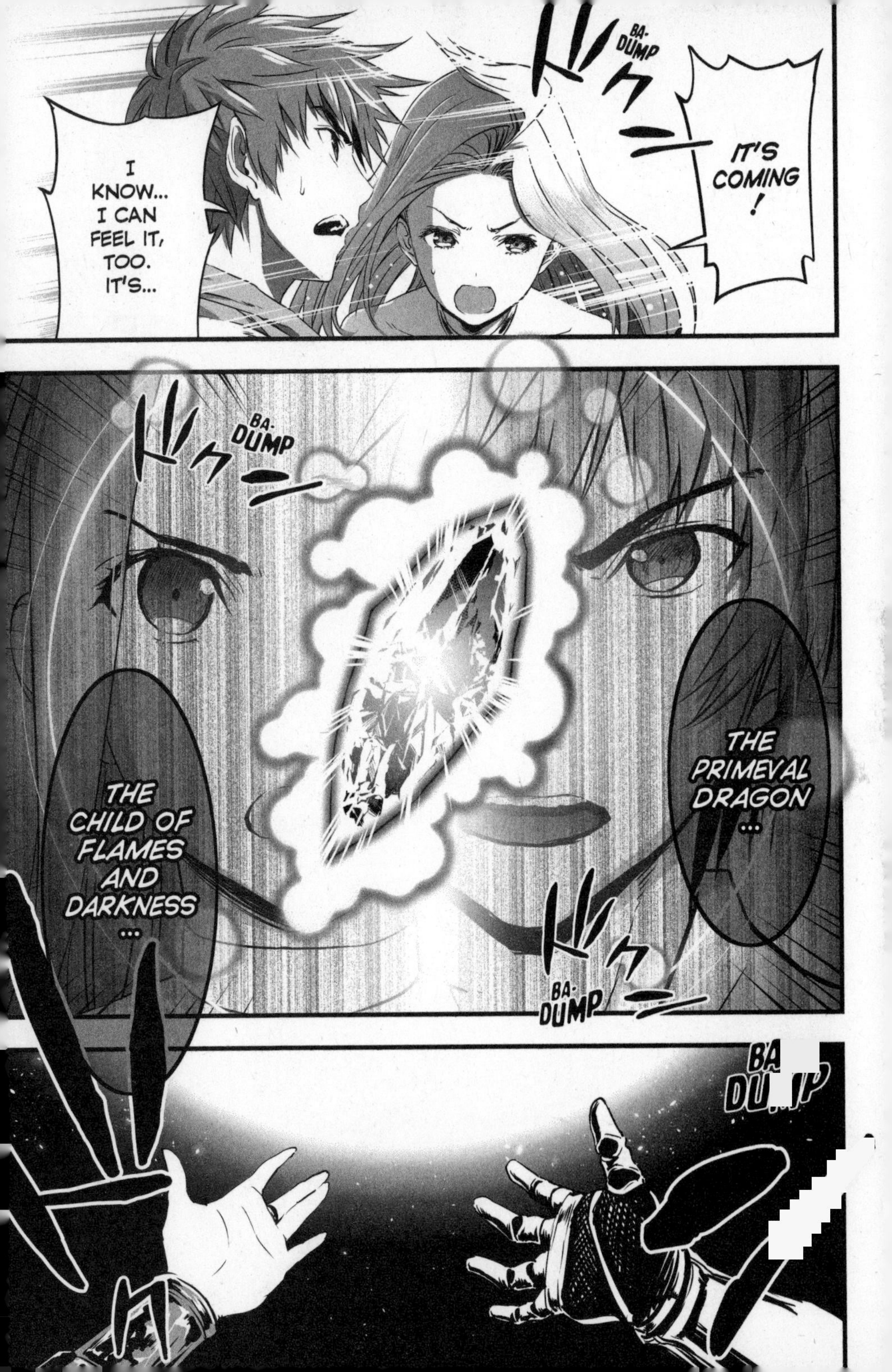
BA-DUMP
IT'S COMING!
I KNOW... I CAN FEEL IT, TOO. IT'S...
BA-DUMP
THE PRIMEVAL DRAGON...
THE CHILD OF FLAMES AND DARKNESS...
BA-DUMP

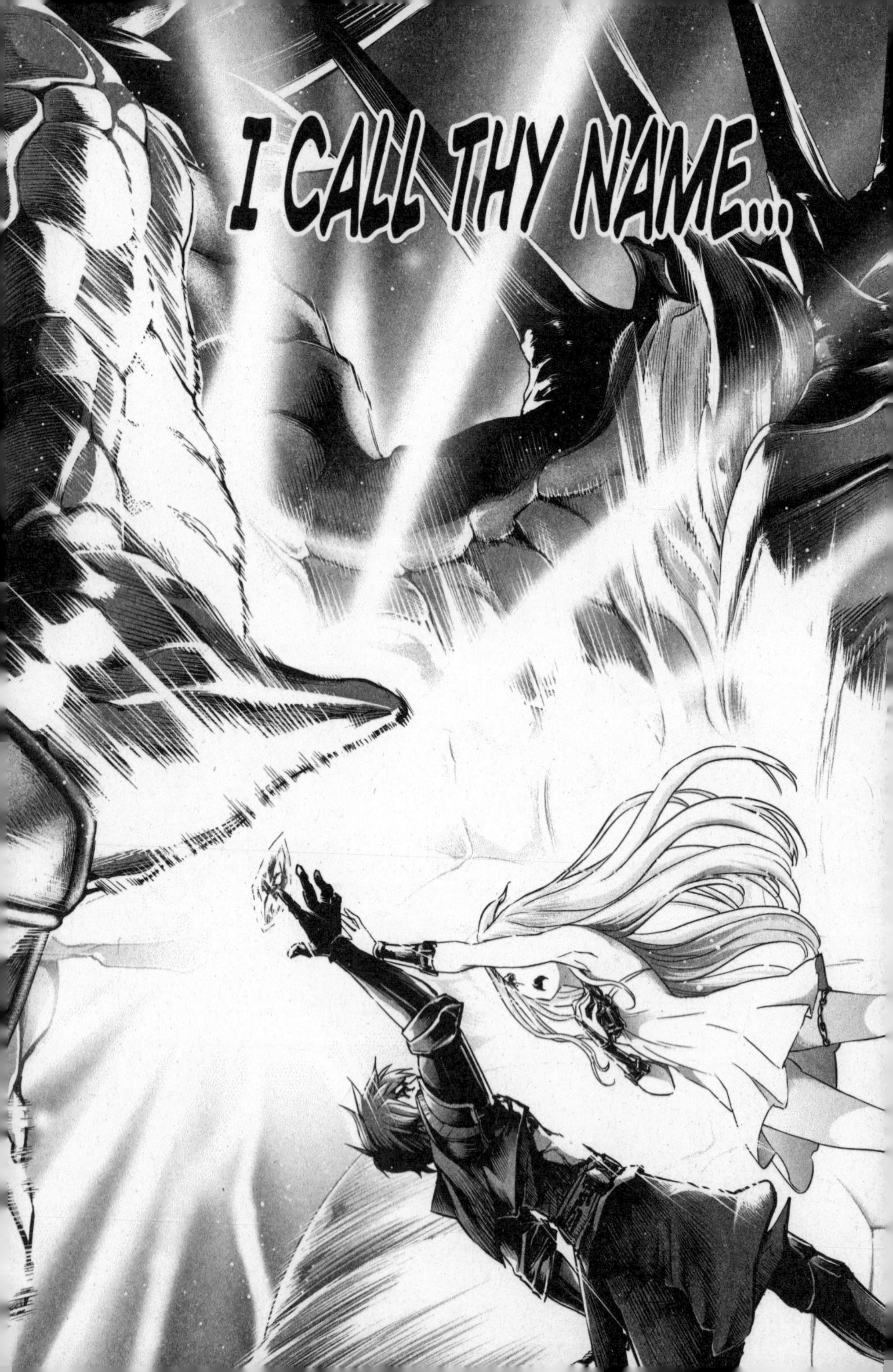
I CALL THY NAME...

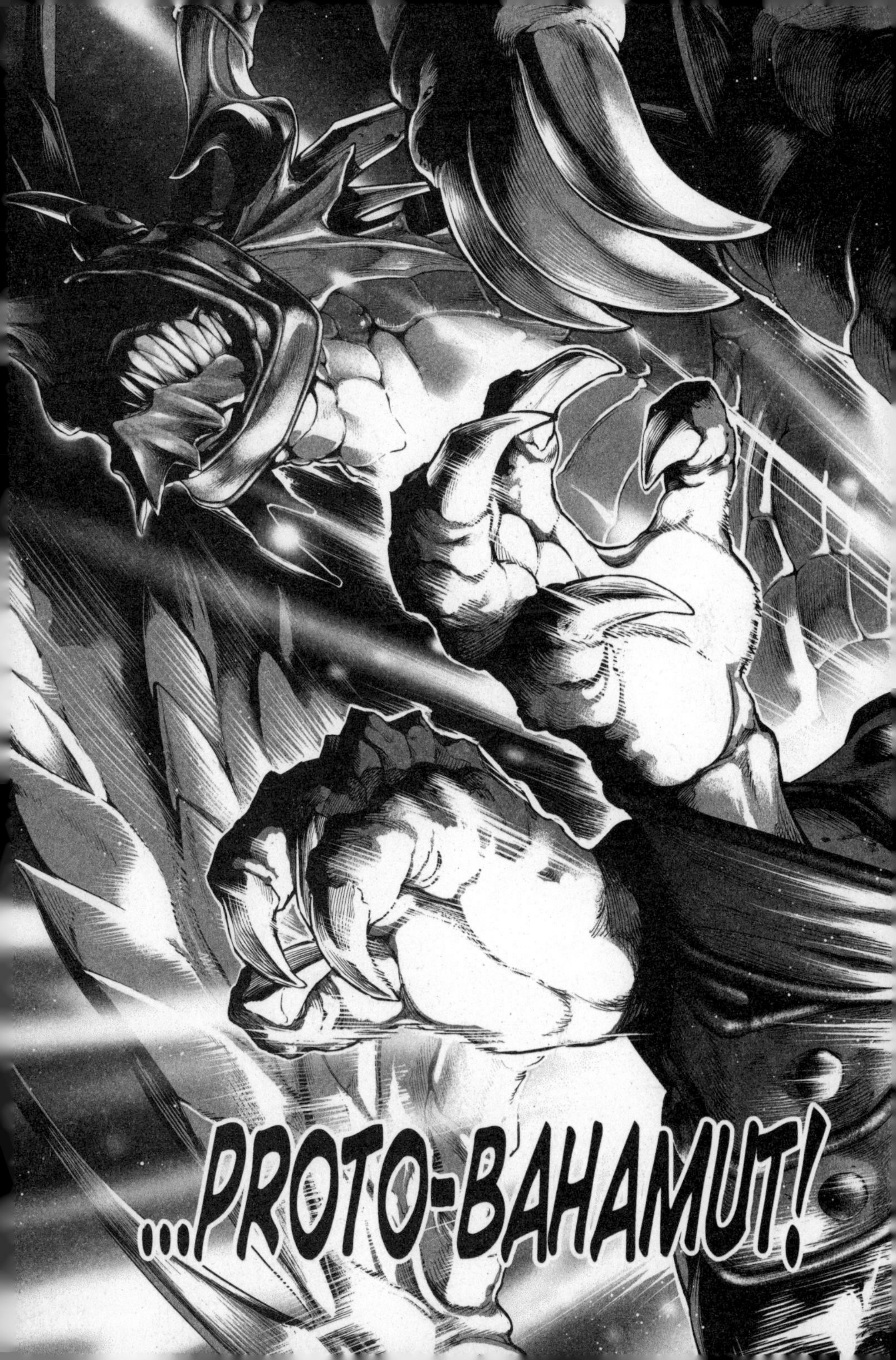
...PROTO-BAHAMUT!

CHAPTER 4:

Prologue (4)

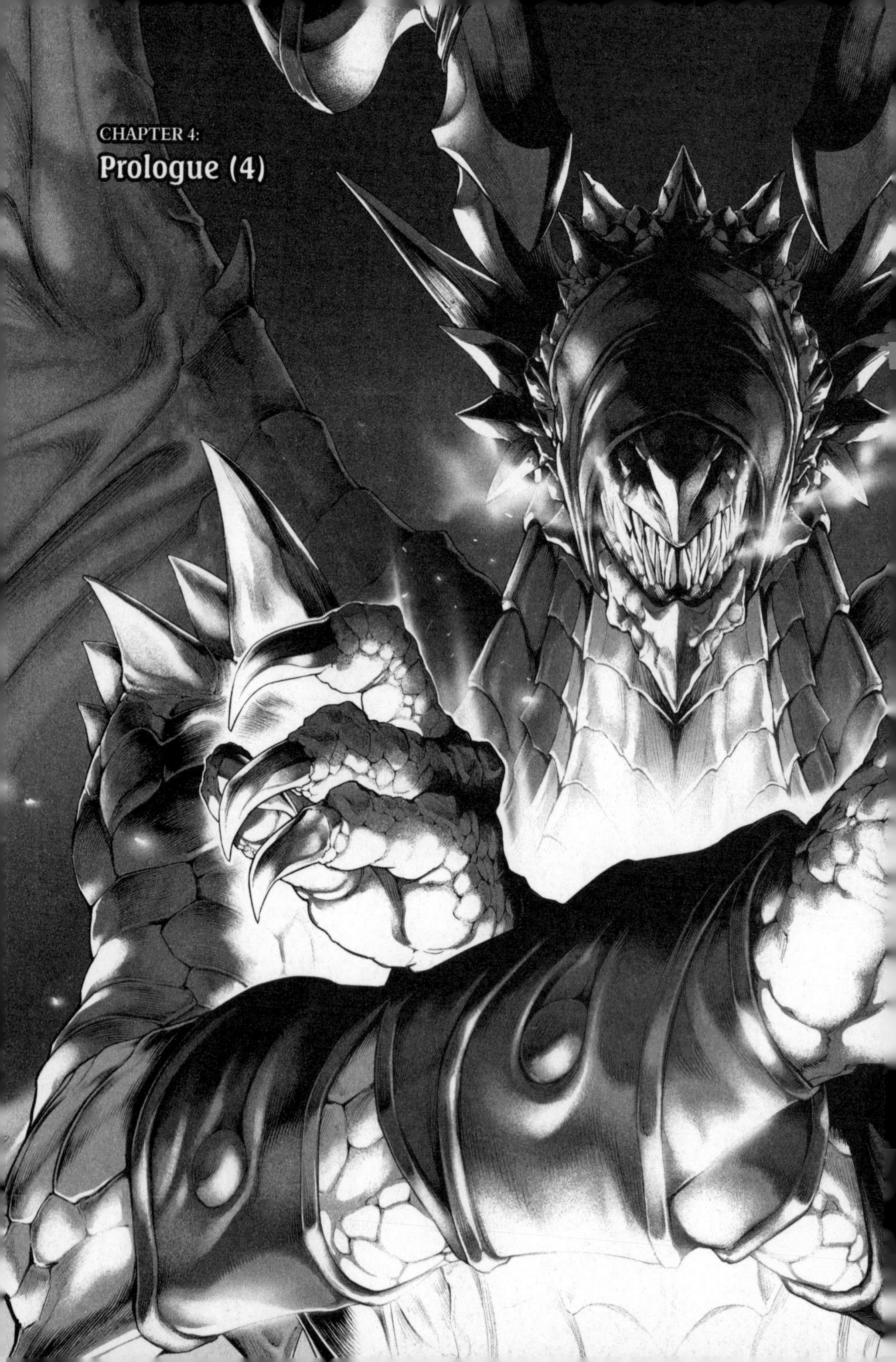

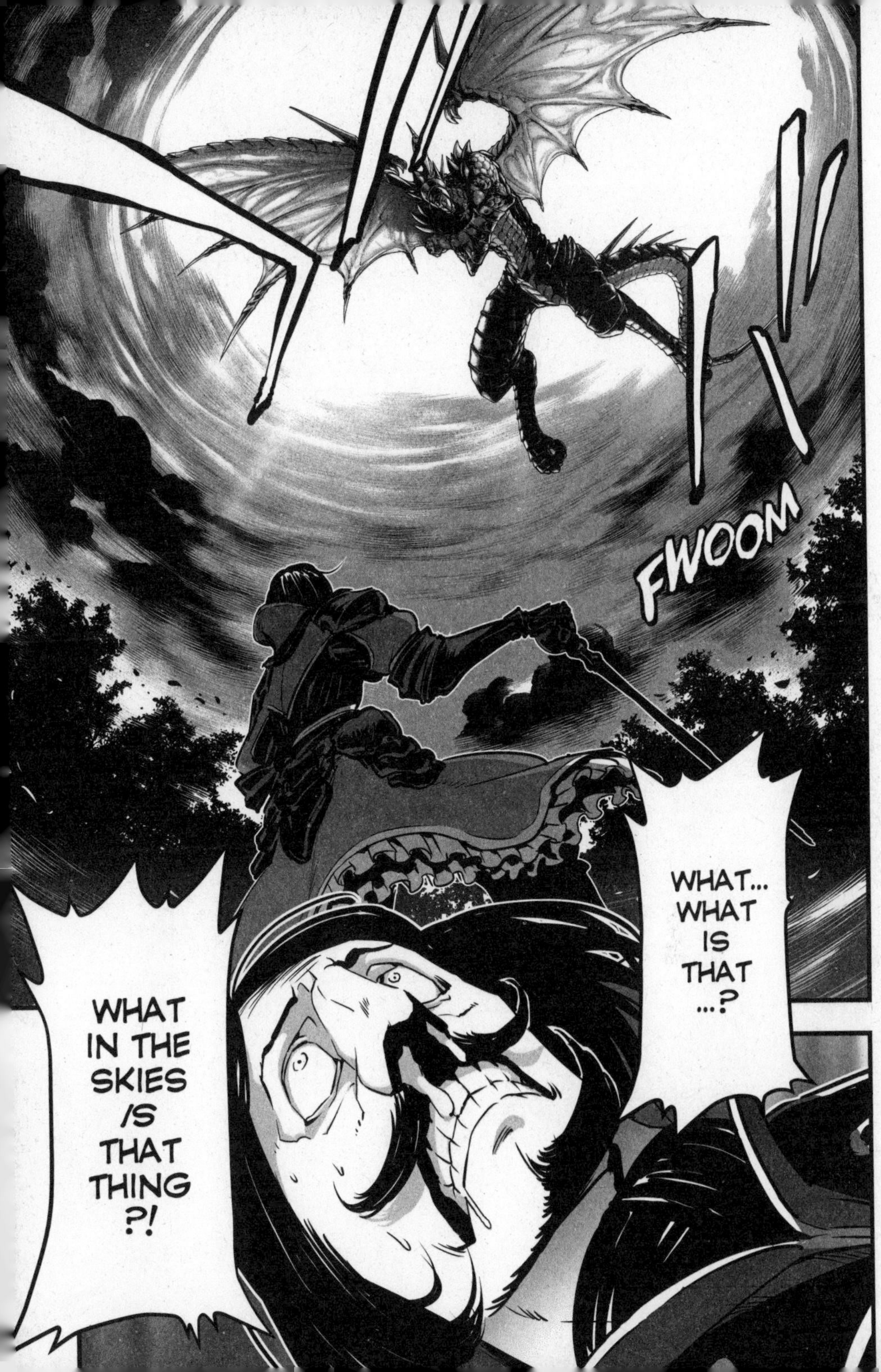
FWOOM
WHAT... WHAT IS THAT ...?
WHAT IN THE SKIES IS THAT THING?!

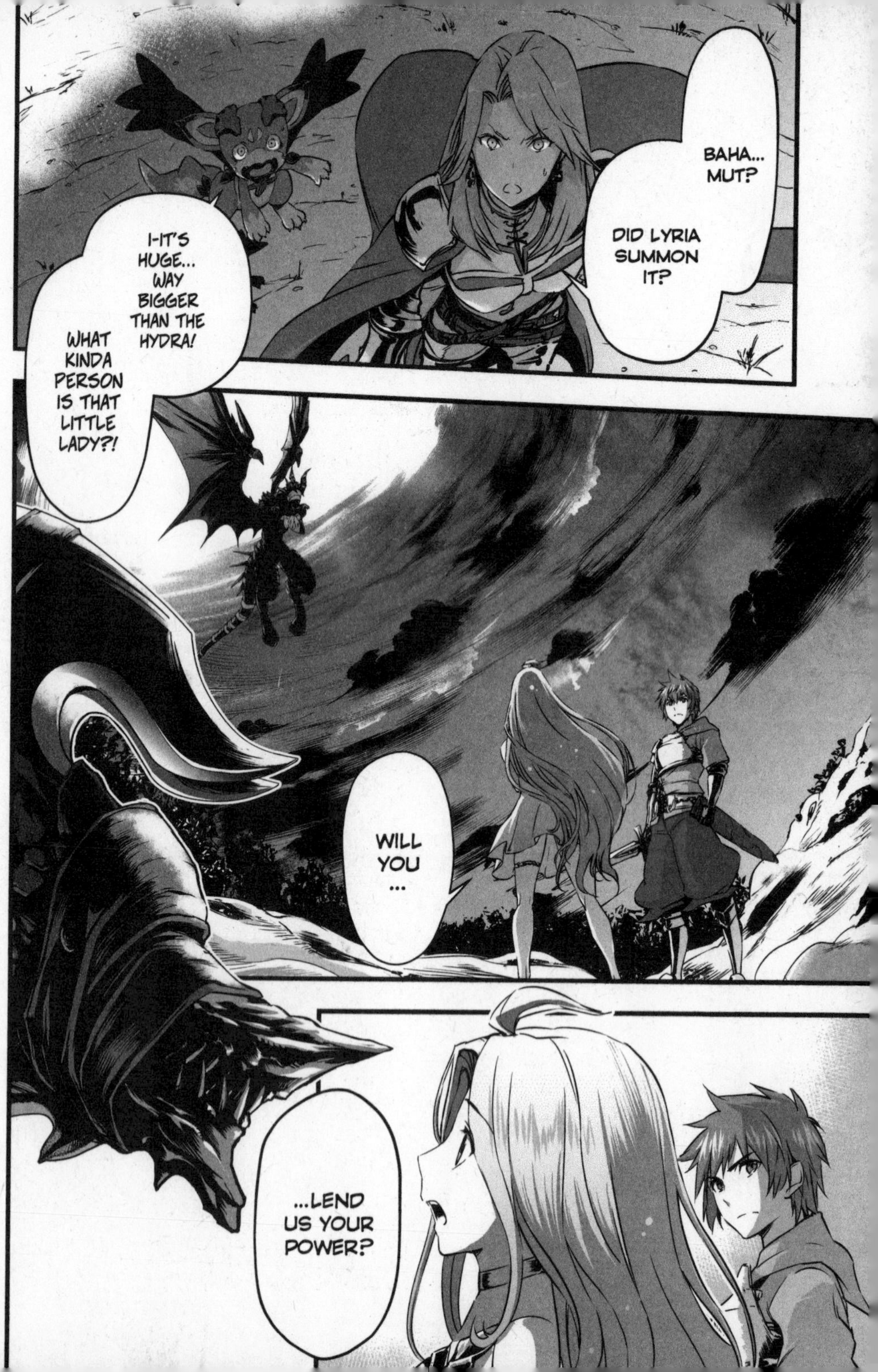
BAHA... MUT?
DID LYRIA SUMMON IT?
I-IT'S HUGE... WAY BIGGER THAN THE HYDRA!
WHAT KINDA PERSON IS THAT LITTLE LADY?!
WILL YOU ...
...LEND US YOUR POWER?

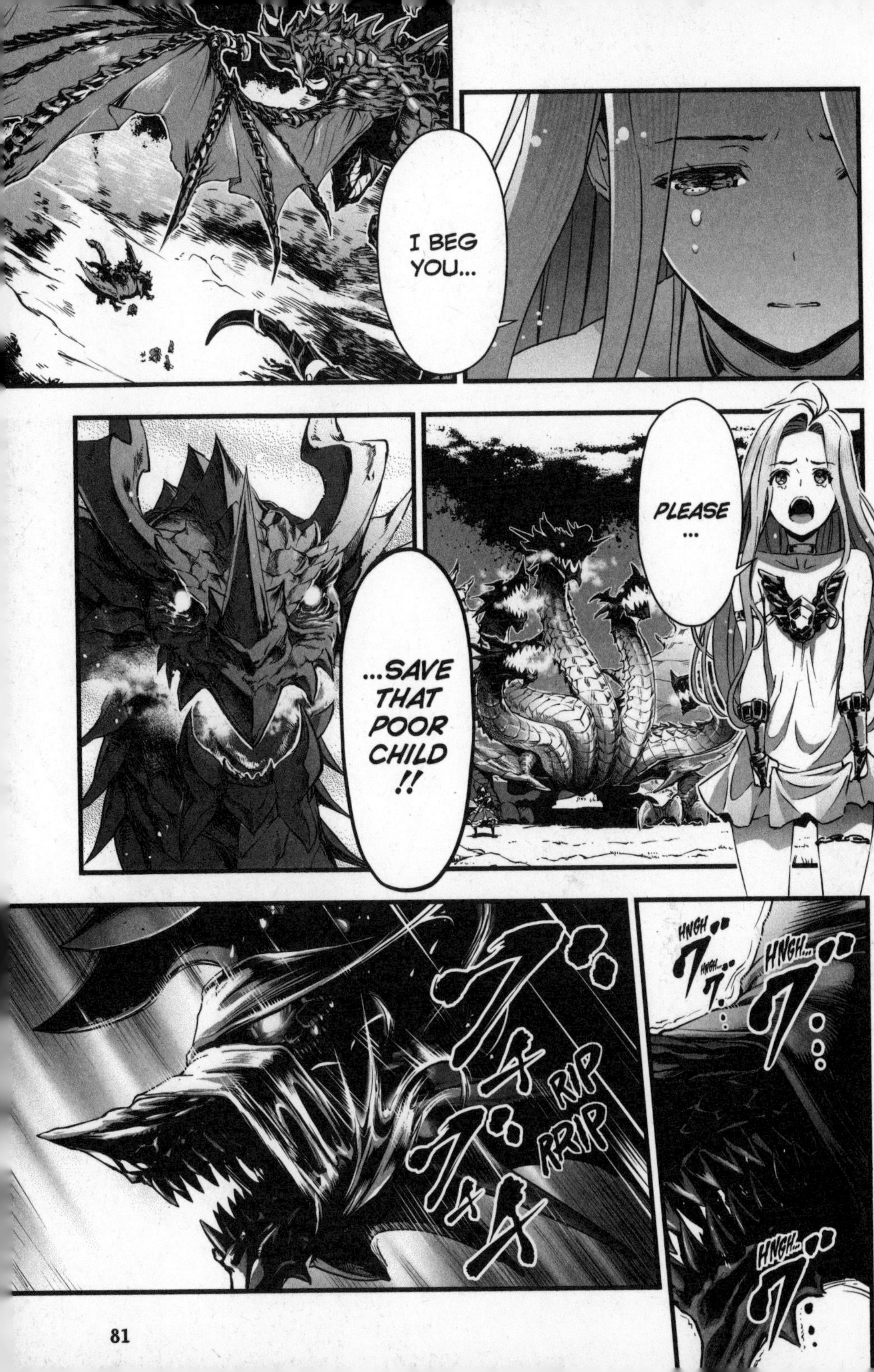
I BEG YOU...
PLEASE ...
...SAVE THAT POOR CHILD !!
HNGH
HNGH...
HNGH...
HNGH...
HNGH...
RIP RRIP

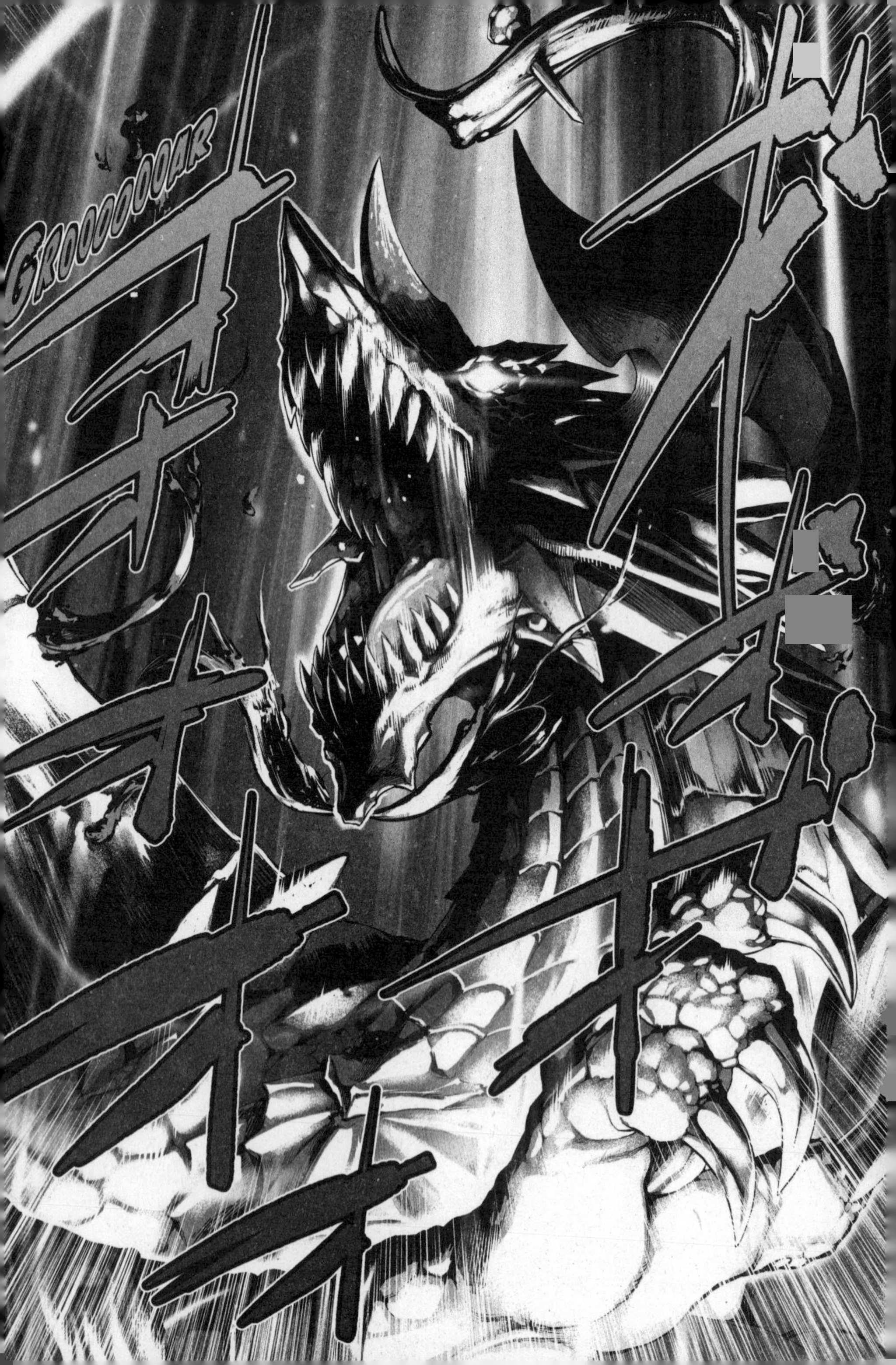
GROOOOOOAR

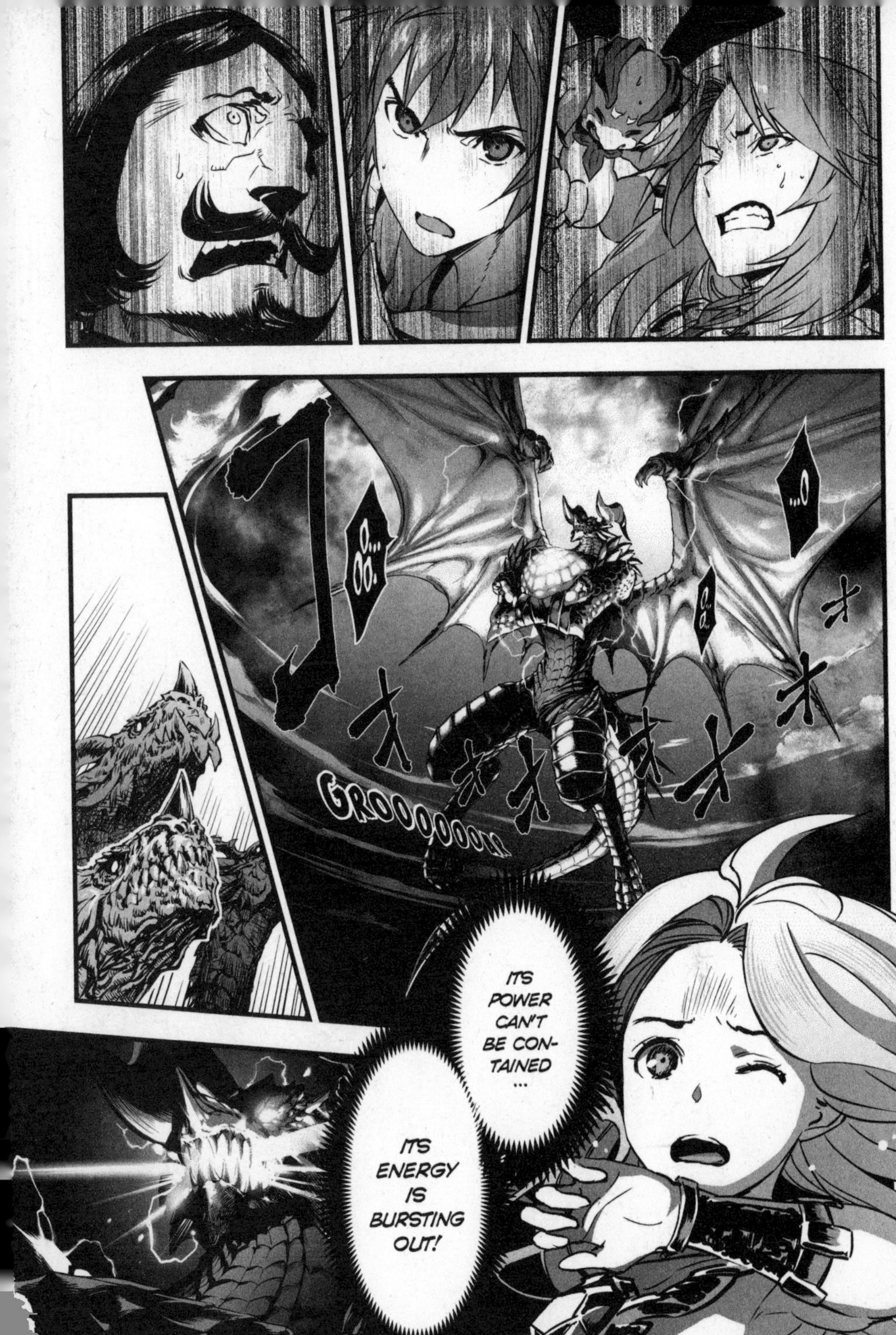
O...
O... O...
O... OO...
GROOOOOOR!
ITS POWER CAN'T BE CON-TAINED ...
ITS ENERGY IS BURSTING OUT!

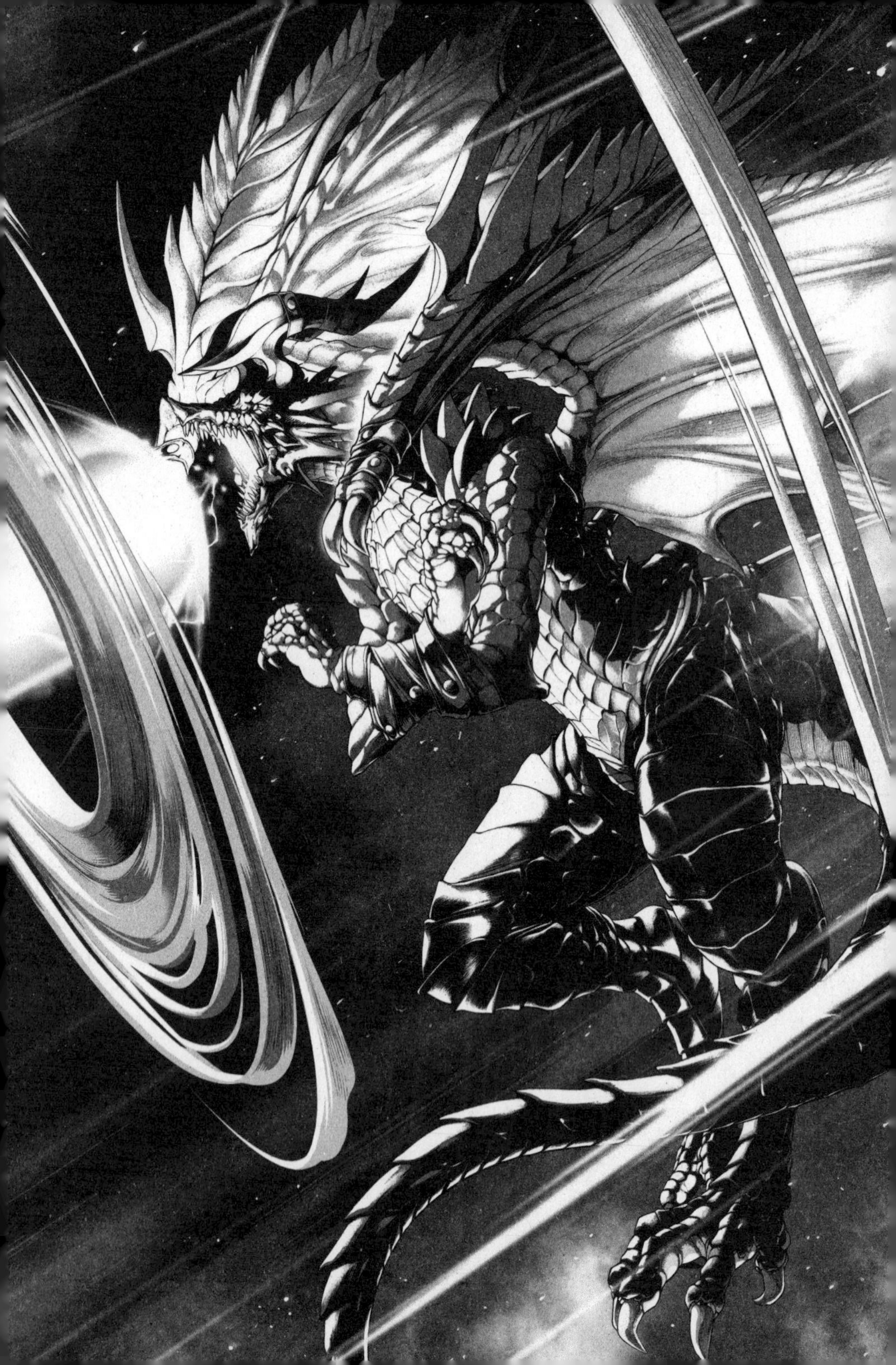

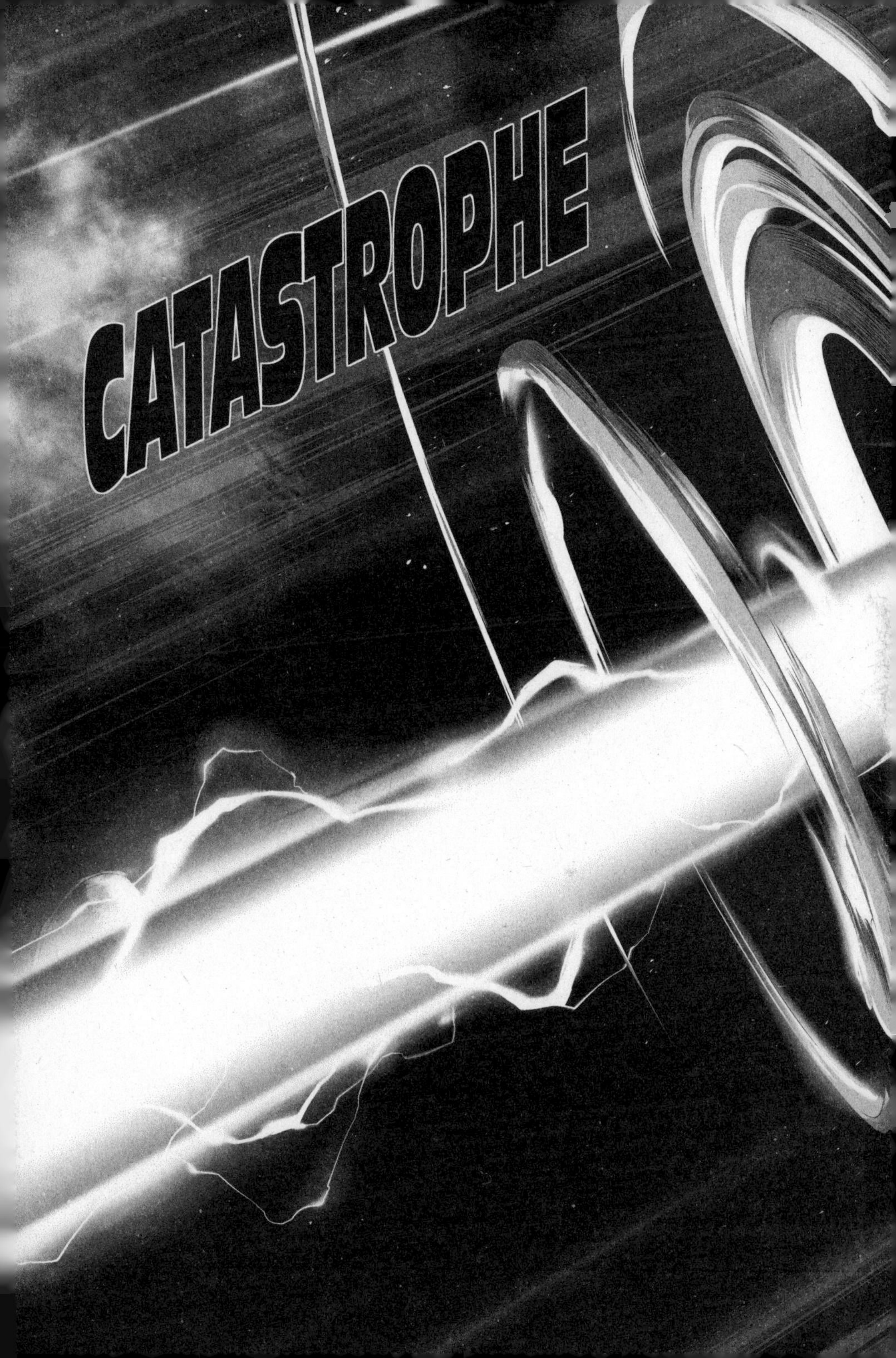
CATASTROPHE

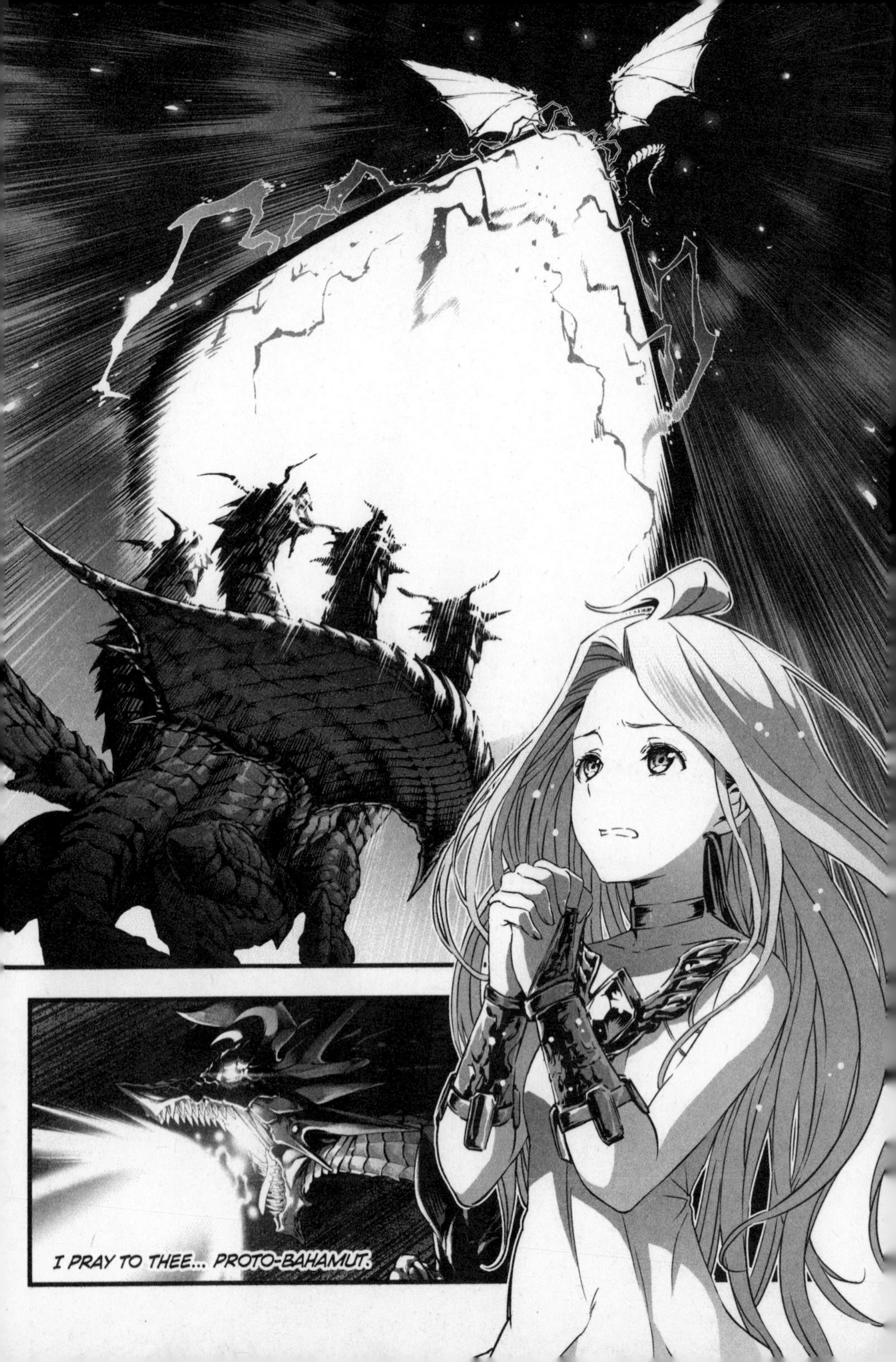
I PRAY TO THEE... PROTO-BAHAMUT.

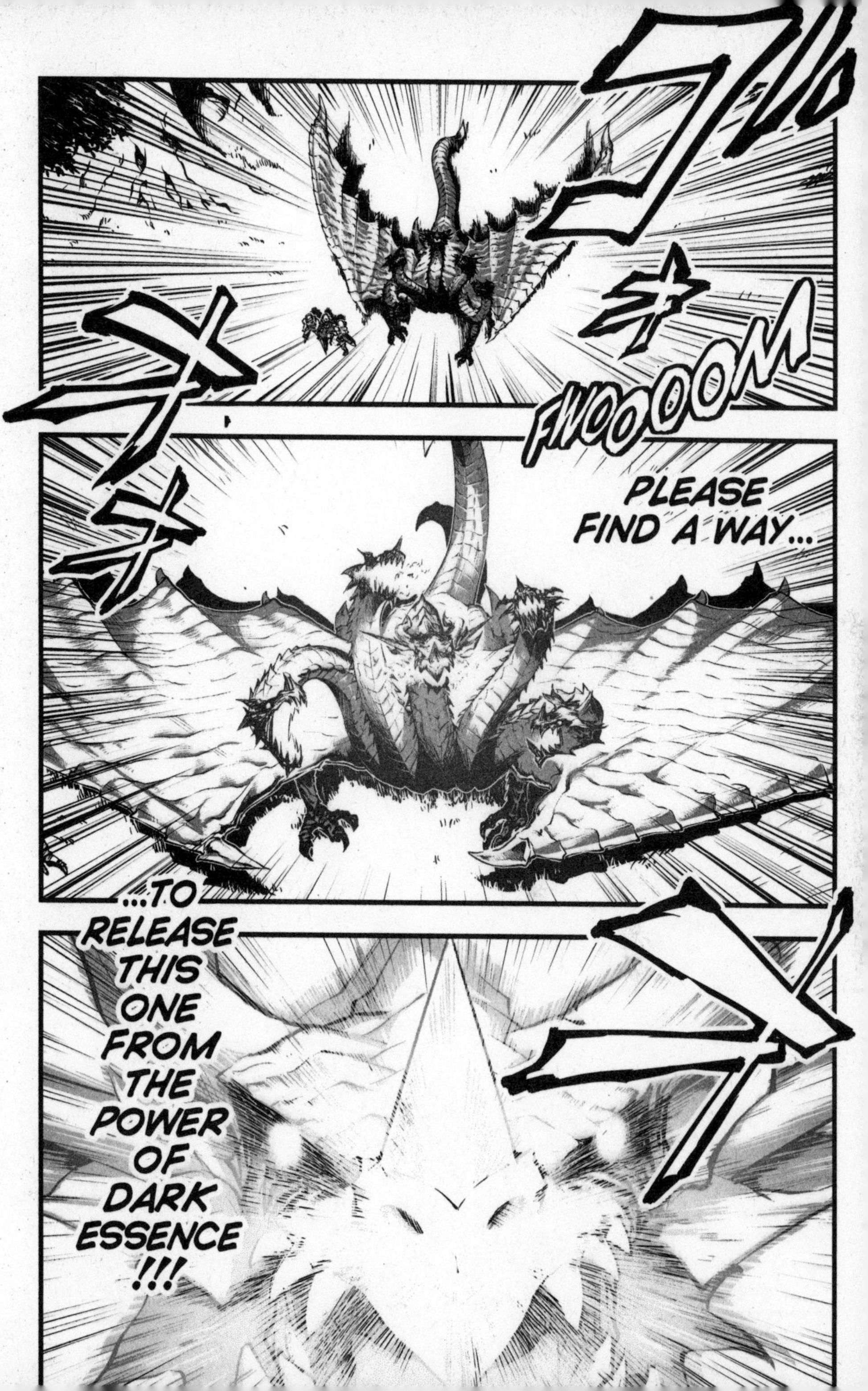
FWOOOOOM
PLEASE FIND A WAY...
...TO RELEASE THIS ONE FROM THE POWER OF DARK ESSENCE!!!

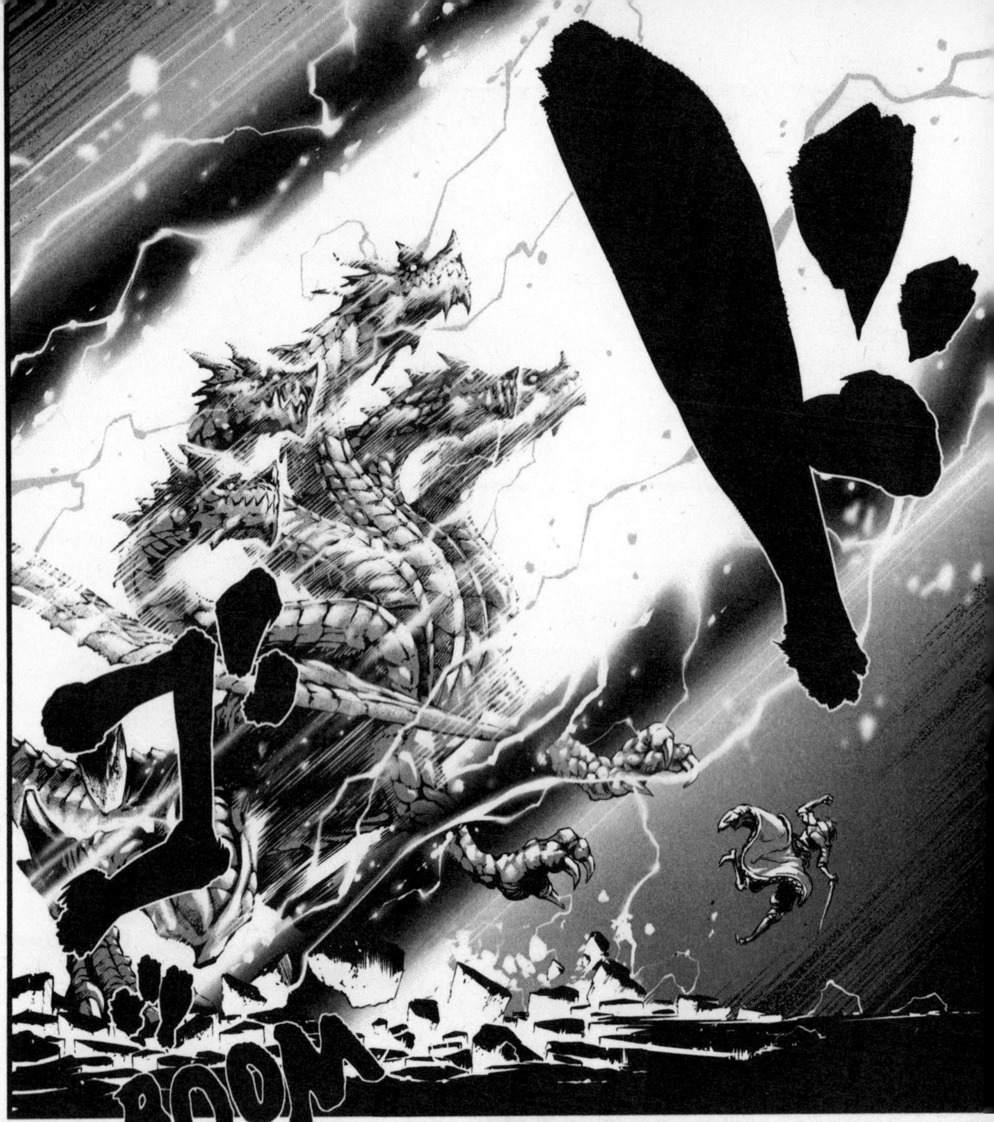
BOOM

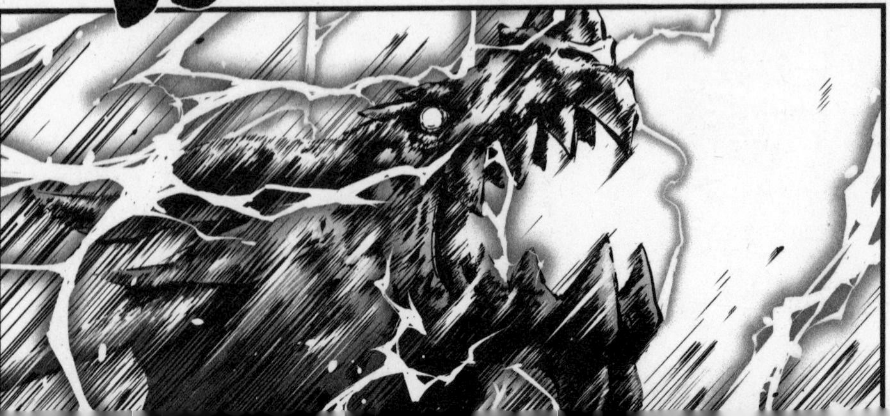

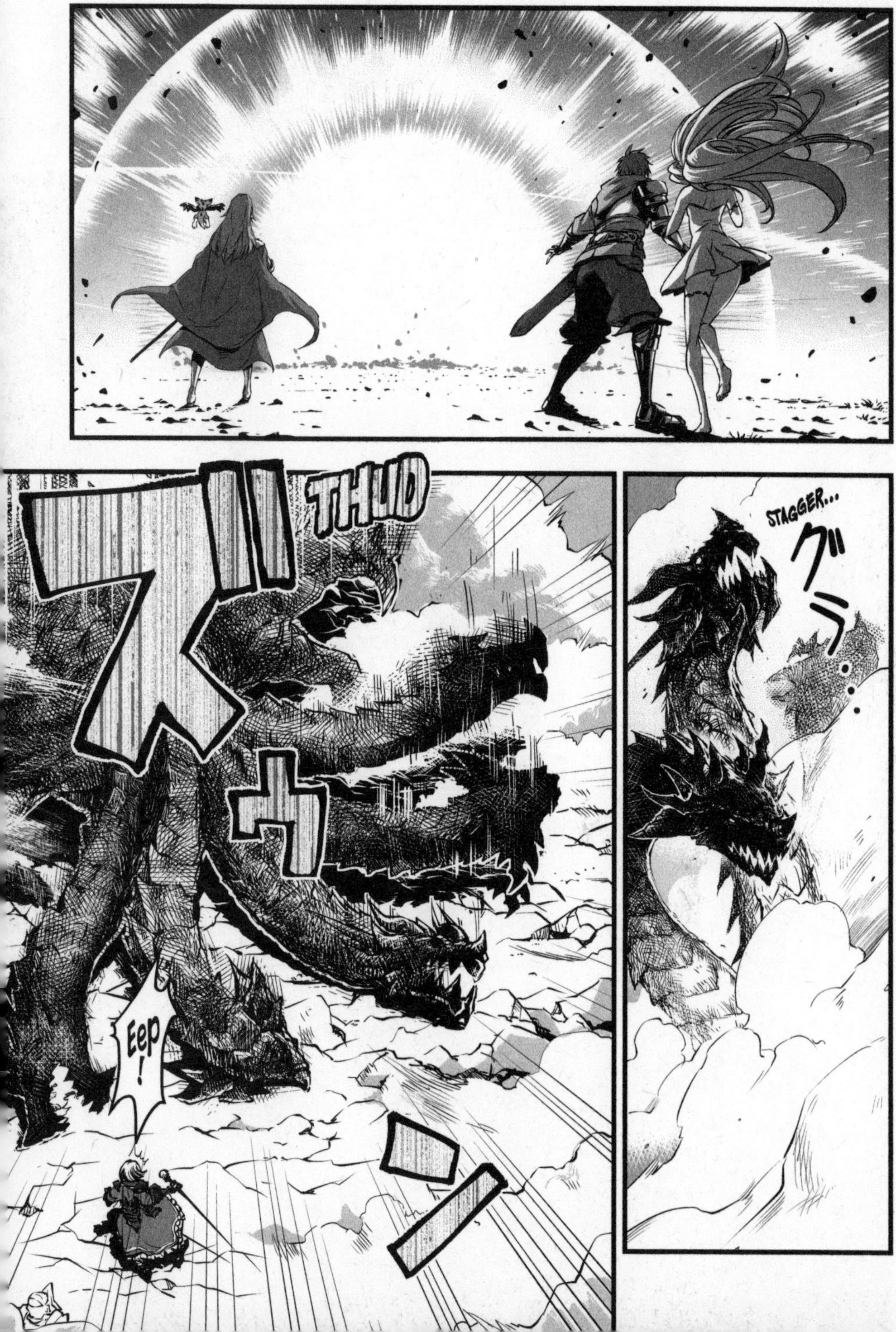
STAGGER...
THUD
Eep!

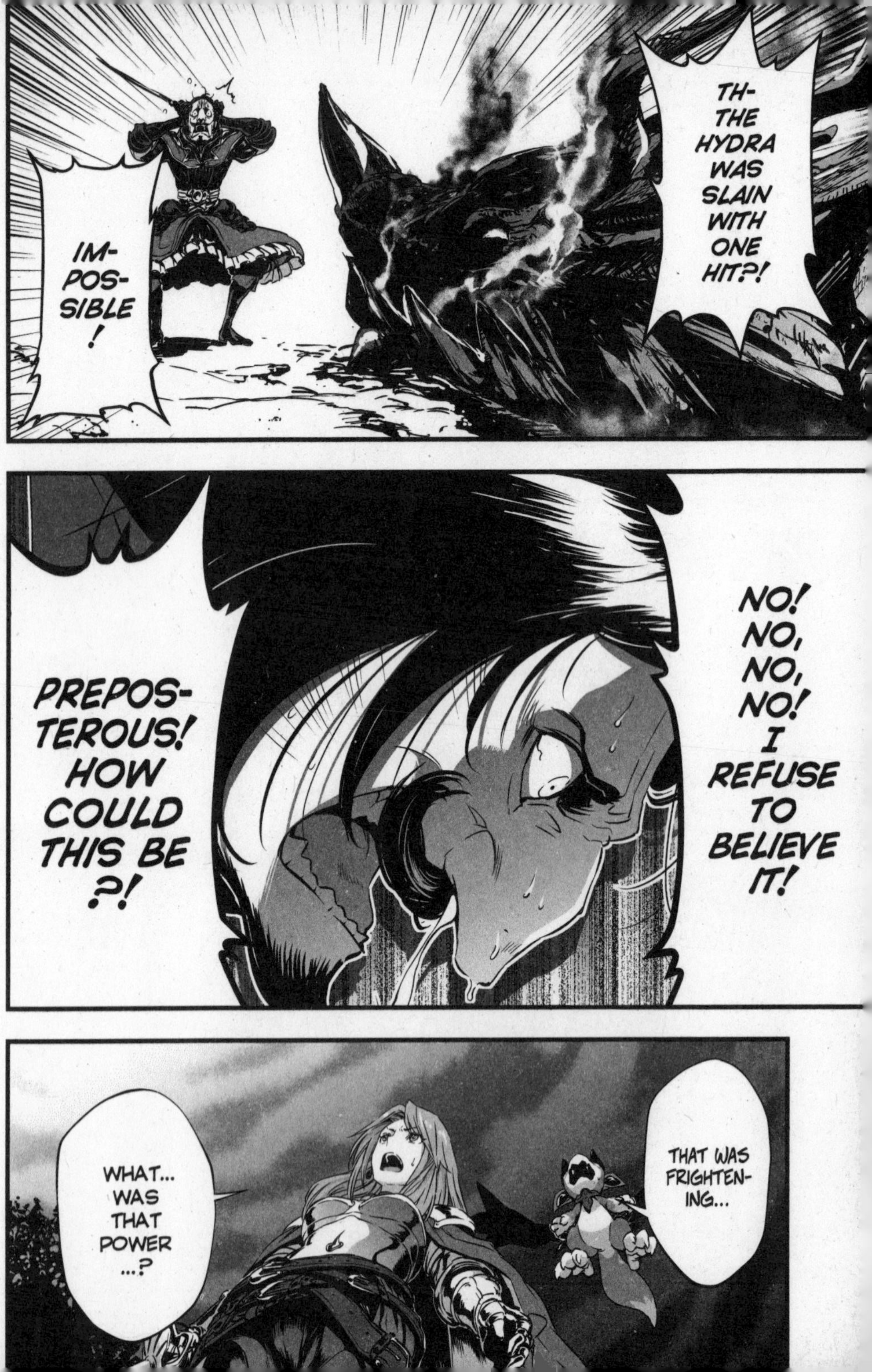
TH-THE HYDRA WAS SLAIN WITH ONE HIT?!
IMPOSSIBLE!
NO! NO, NO, NO! I REFUSE TO BELIEVE IT!
PREPOSTEROUS! HOW COULD THIS BE?!
THAT WAS FRIGHTENING...
WHAT... WAS THAT POWER...?

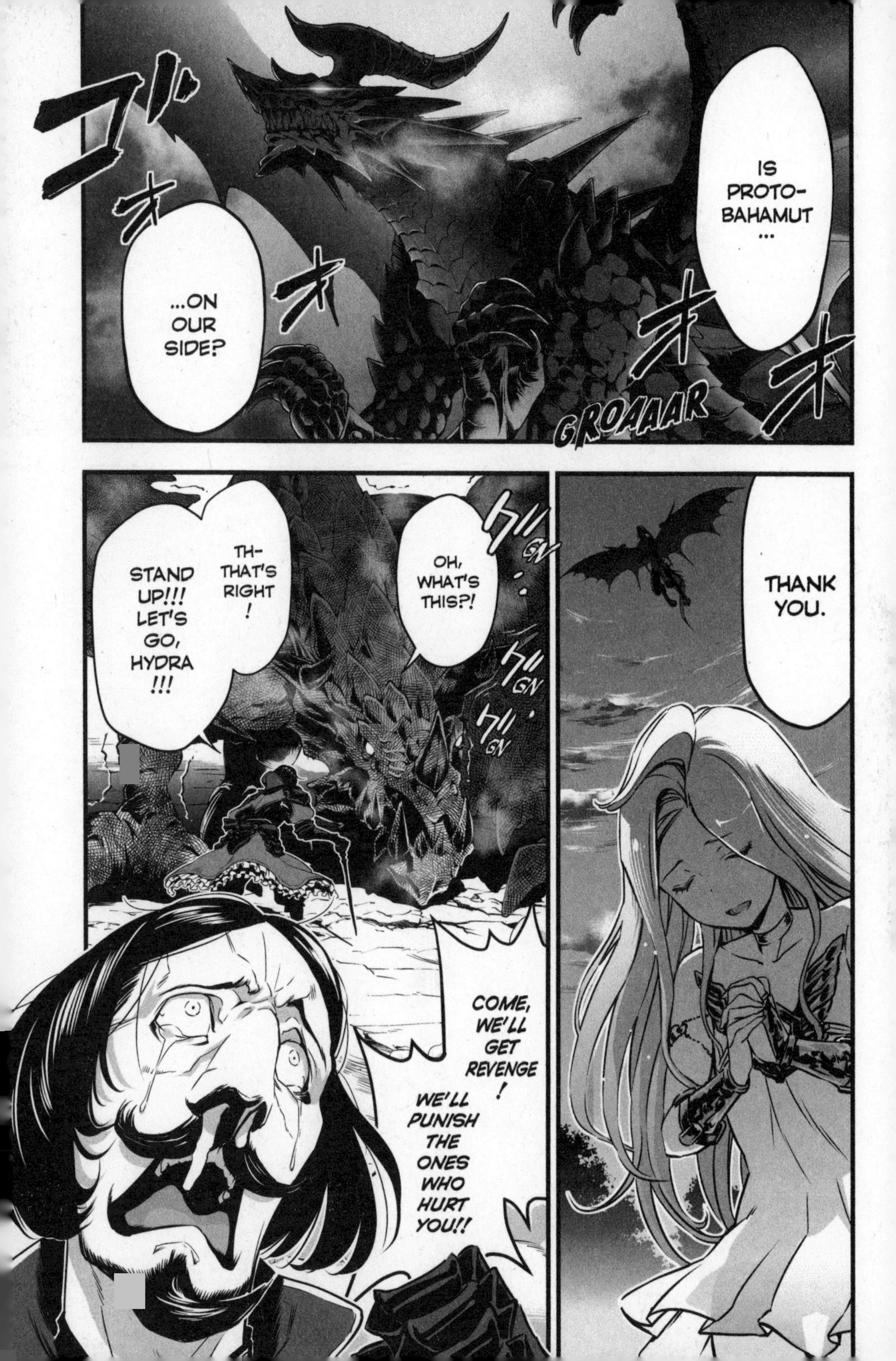
IS PROTO-BAHAMUT...
...ON OUR SIDE?
GROAAAR
THANK YOU.
OH, WHAT'S THIS?!
GN
GN
GN
TH-THAT'S RIGHT!
STAND UP!!! LET'S GO, HYDRA!!!
COME, WE'LL GET REVENGE!
WE'LL PUNISH THE ONES WHO HURT YOU!!

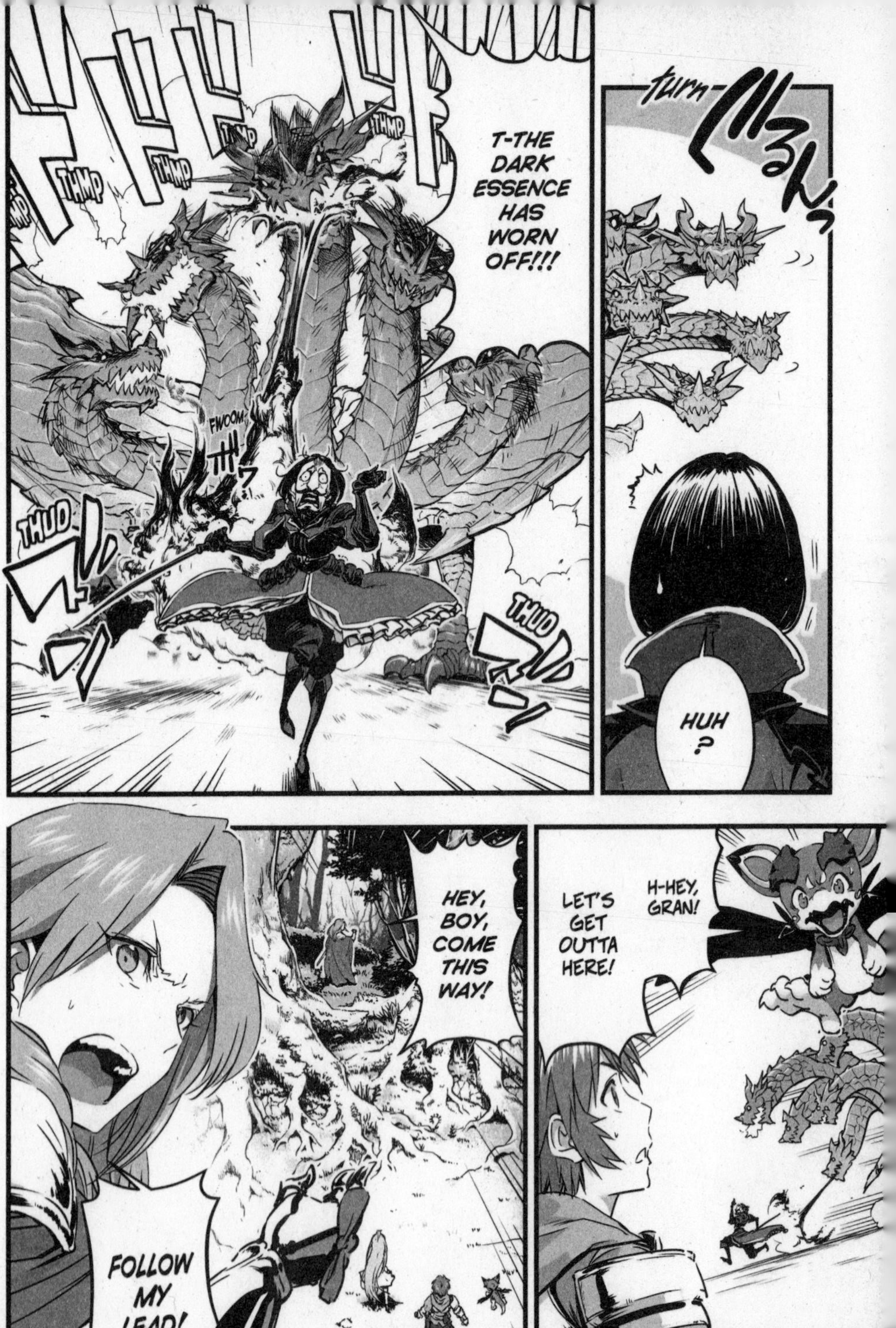
turn
HUH?
THMP
THMP
THMP
THMP
THMP
T-THE DARK ESSENCE HAS WORN OFF!!!
FWOOM
THUD
THUD
H-HEY, GRAN!
LET'S GET OUTTA HERE!
HEY, BOY, COME THIS WAY!
FOLLOW MY LEAD!

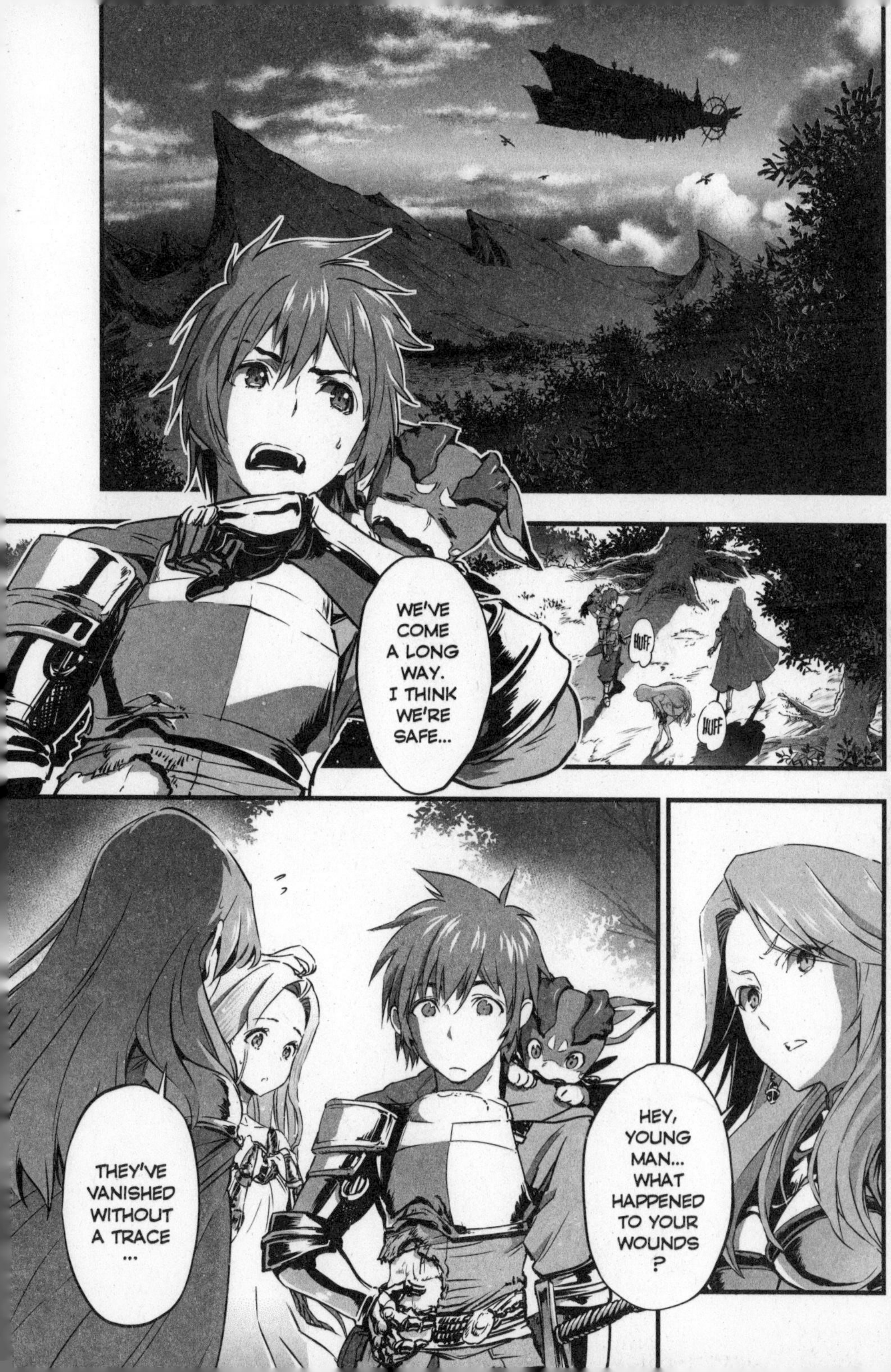
WE'VE COME A LONG WAY. I THINK WE'RE SAFE...
HUFF
HUFF
HEY, YOUNG MAN... WHAT HAPPENED TO YOUR WOUNDS?
THEY'VE VANISHED WITHOUT A TRACE...

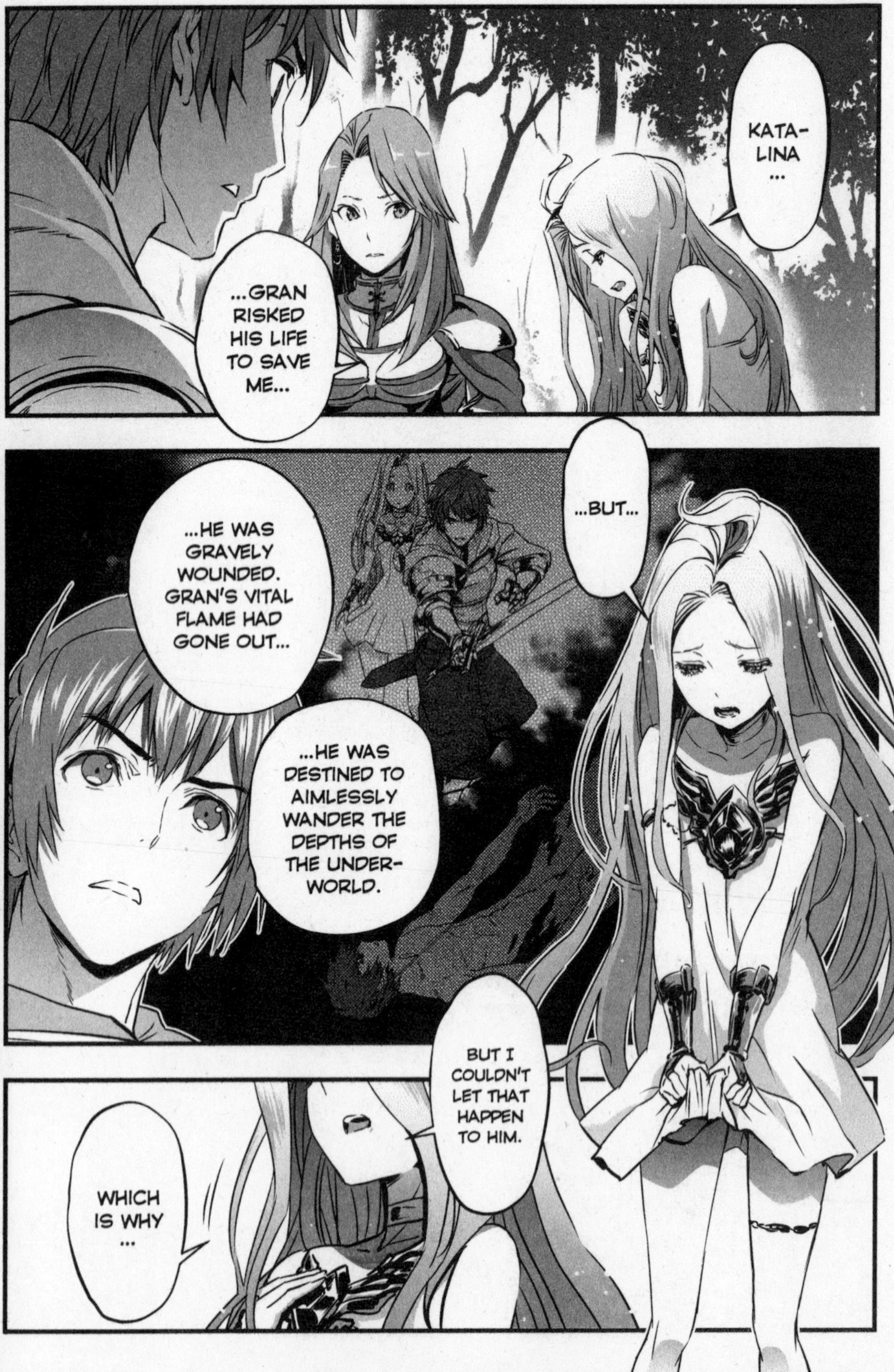
KATA-LINA ...
...GRAN RISKED HIS LIFE TO SAVE ME...
...BUT...
...HE WAS GRAVELY WOUNDED. GRAN'S VITAL FLAME HAD GONE OUT...
...HE WAS DESTINED TO AIMLESSLY WANDER THE DEPTHS OF THE UNDER-WORLD.
BUT I COULDN'T LET THAT HAPPEN TO HIM.
WHICH IS WHY ...

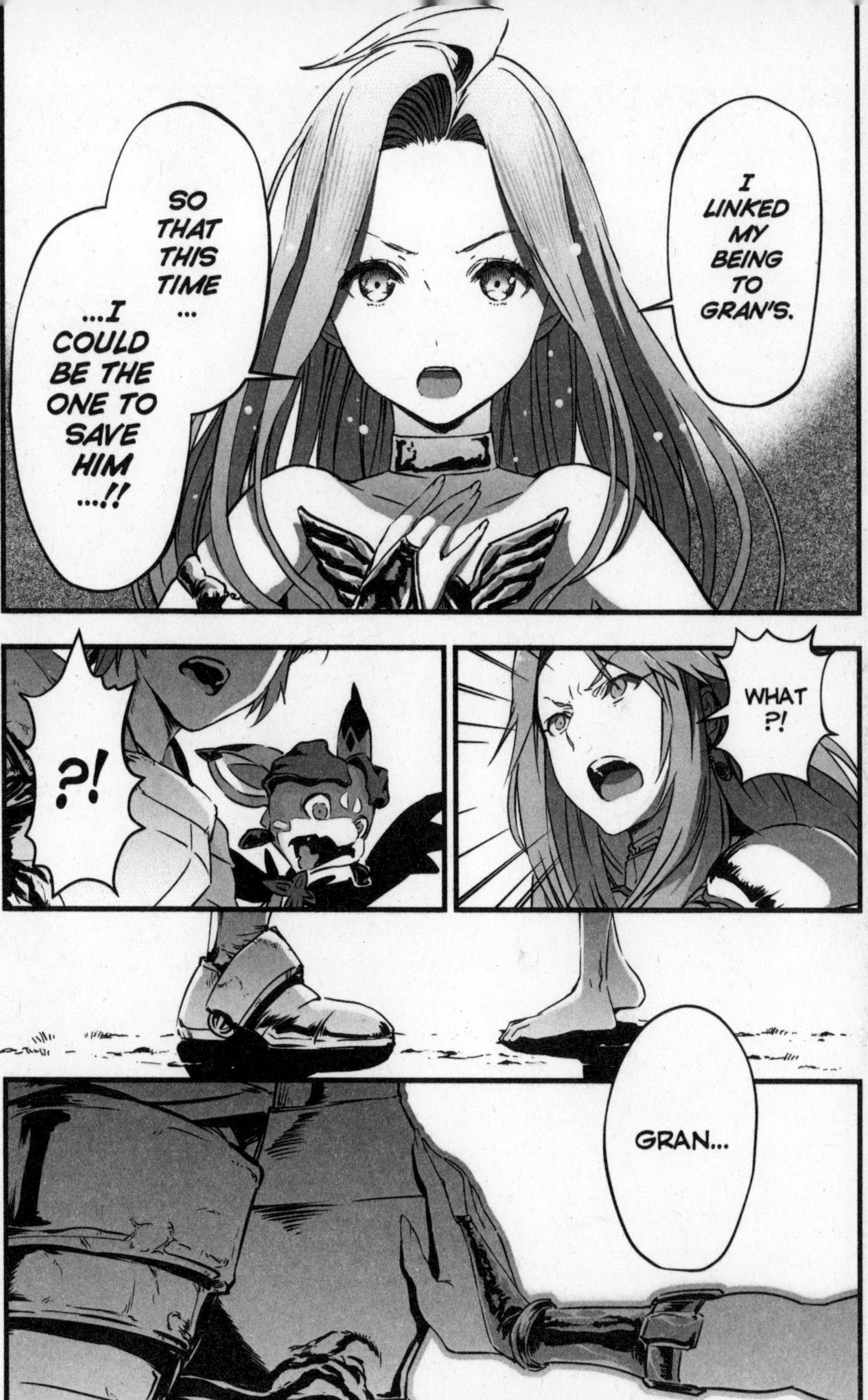
I LINKED MY BEING TO GRAN'S.
SO THAT THIS TIME...
...I COULD BE THE ONE TO SAVE HIM...!!
WHAT?!
?!
GRAN...

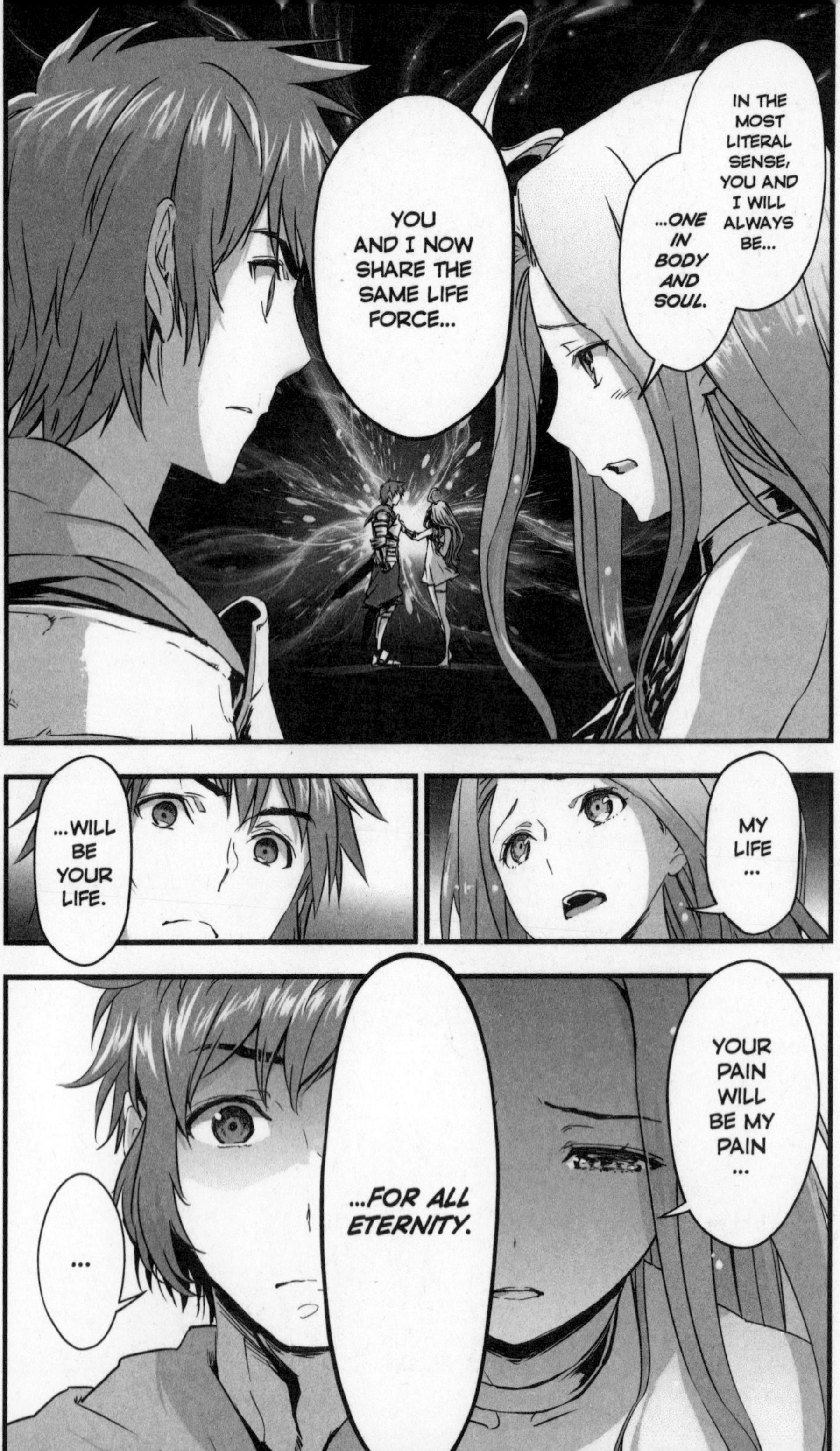
IN THE MOST LITERAL SENSE, YOU AND I WILL ALWAYS BE...
...ONE IN BODY AND SOUL.
YOU AND I NOW SHARE THE SAME LIFE FORCE...
MY LIFE ...
...WILL BE YOUR LIFE.
YOUR PAIN WILL BE MY PAIN ...
...FOR ALL ETERNITY.
...

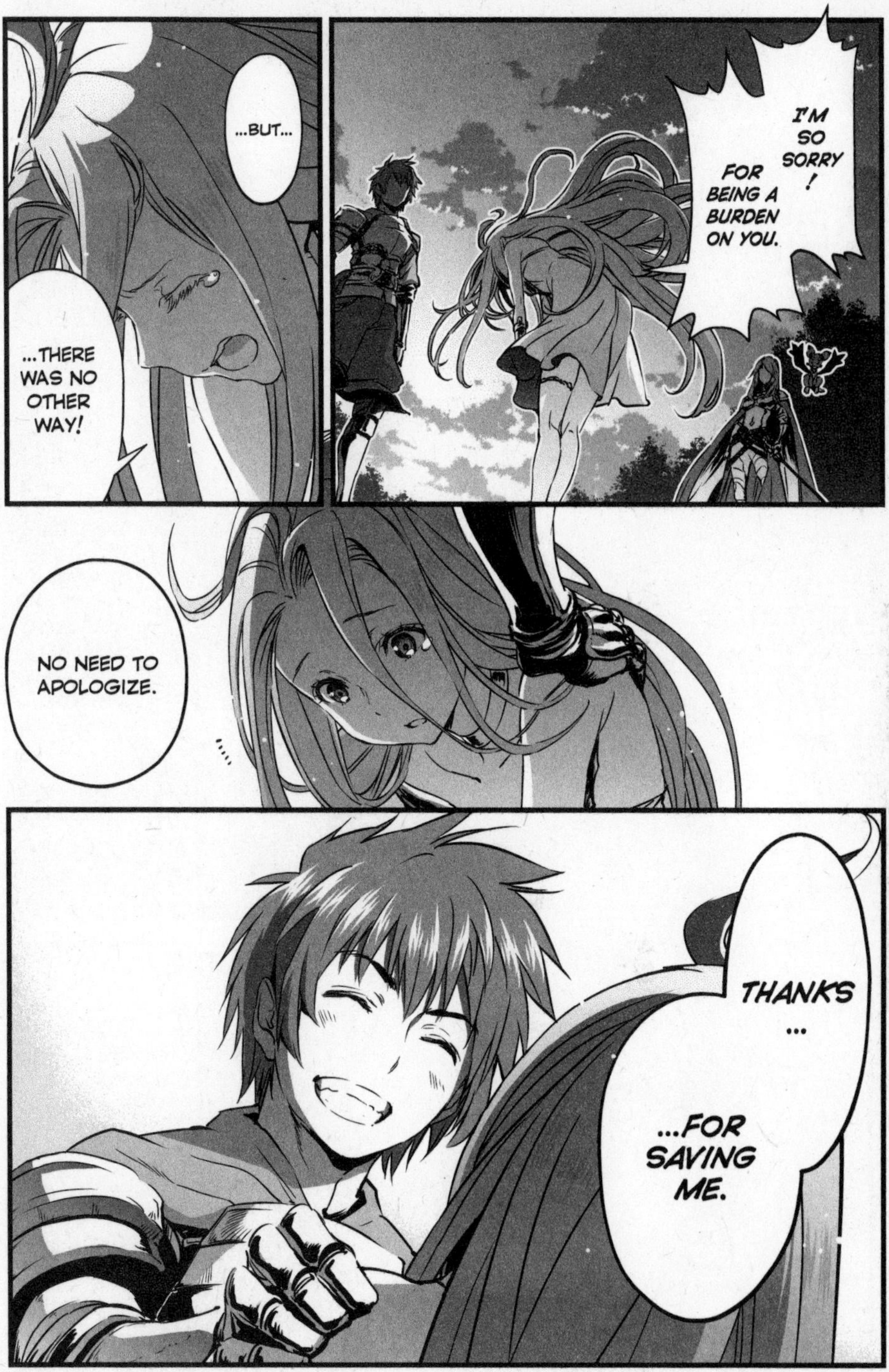
I'M SO SORRY!
FOR BEING A BURDEN ON YOU.
...BUT...
...THERE WAS NO OTHER WAY!
NO NEED TO APOLOGIZE.
THANKS...
...FOR SAVING ME.

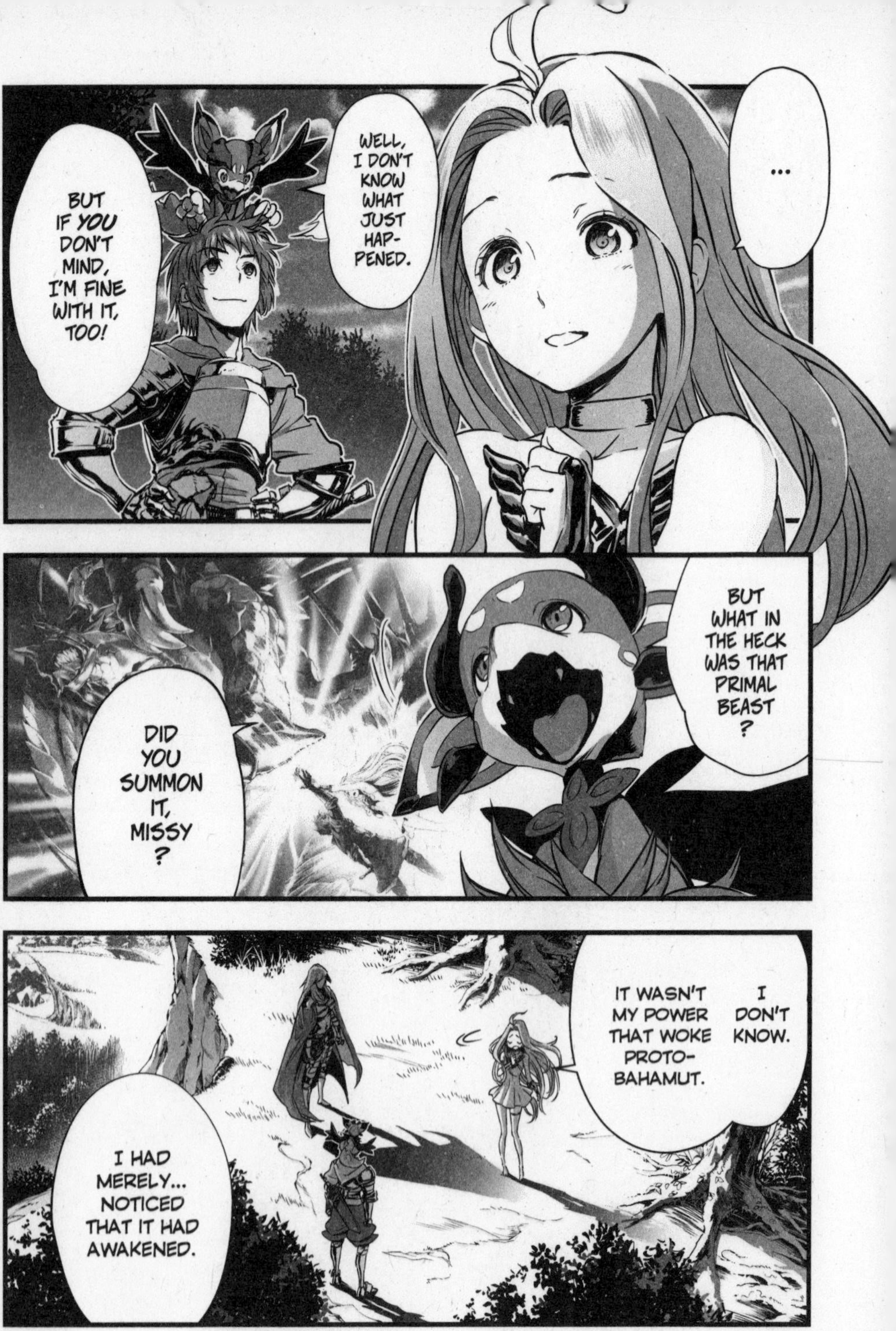
...
WELL, I DON'T KNOW WHAT JUST HAP-PENED.
BUT IF YOU DON'T MIND, I'M FINE WITH IT, TOO!
BUT WHAT IN THE HECK WAS THAT PRIMAL BEAST?
DID YOU SUMMON IT, MISSY?
I DON'T KNOW.
IT WASN'T MY POWER THAT WOKE PROTO-BAHAMUT.
I HAD MERELY... NOTICED THAT IT HAD AWAKENED.

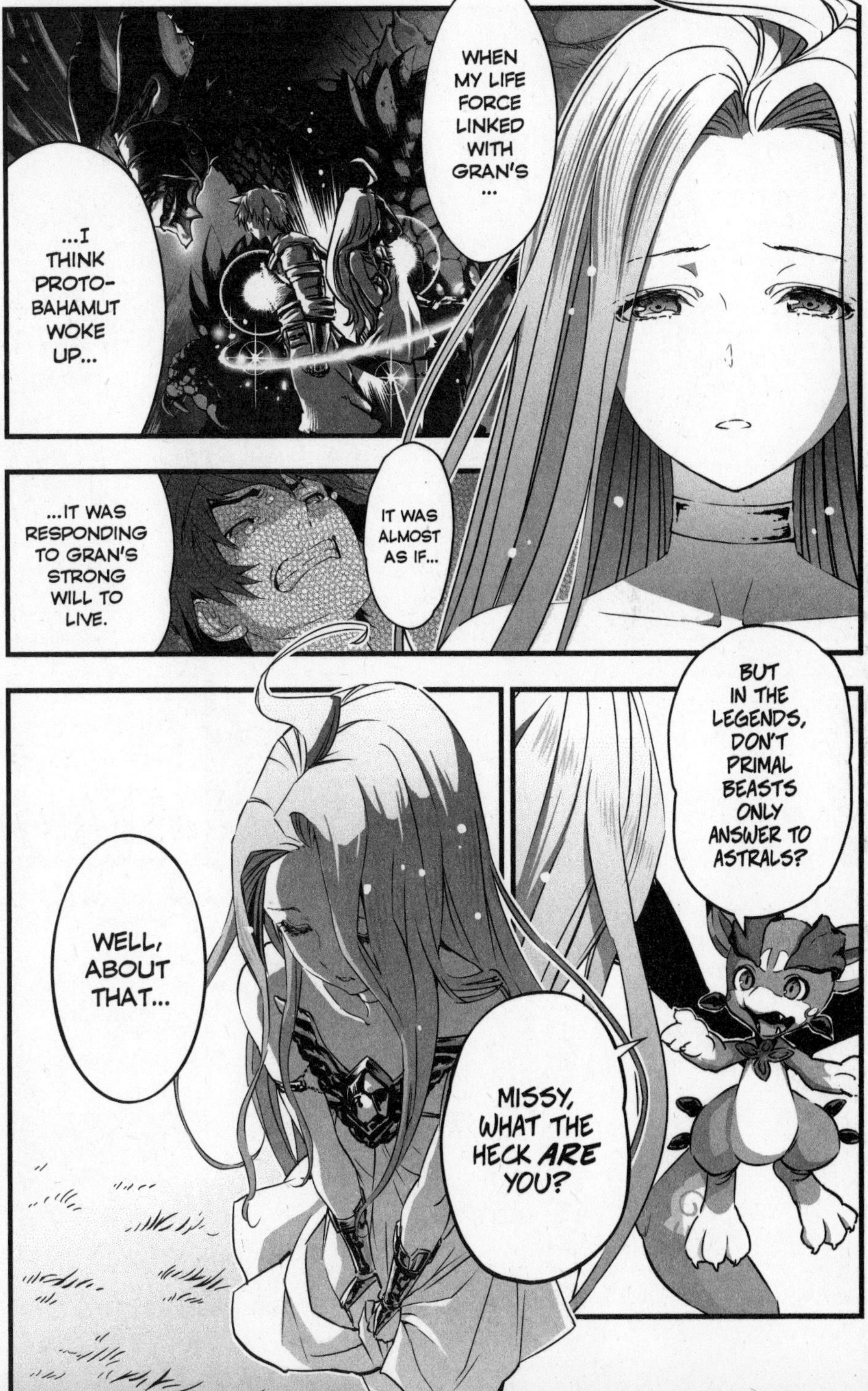
WHEN MY LIFE FORCE LINKED WITH GRAN'S...
...I THINK PROTO-BAHAMUT WOKE UP...
IT WAS ALMOST AS IF...
...IT WAS RESPONDING TO GRAN'S STRONG WILL TO LIVE.
BUT IN THE LEGENDS, DON'T PRIMAL BEASTS ONLY ANSWER TO ASTRALS?
MISSY, WHAT THE HECK *ARE* YOU?
WELL, ABOUT THAT...

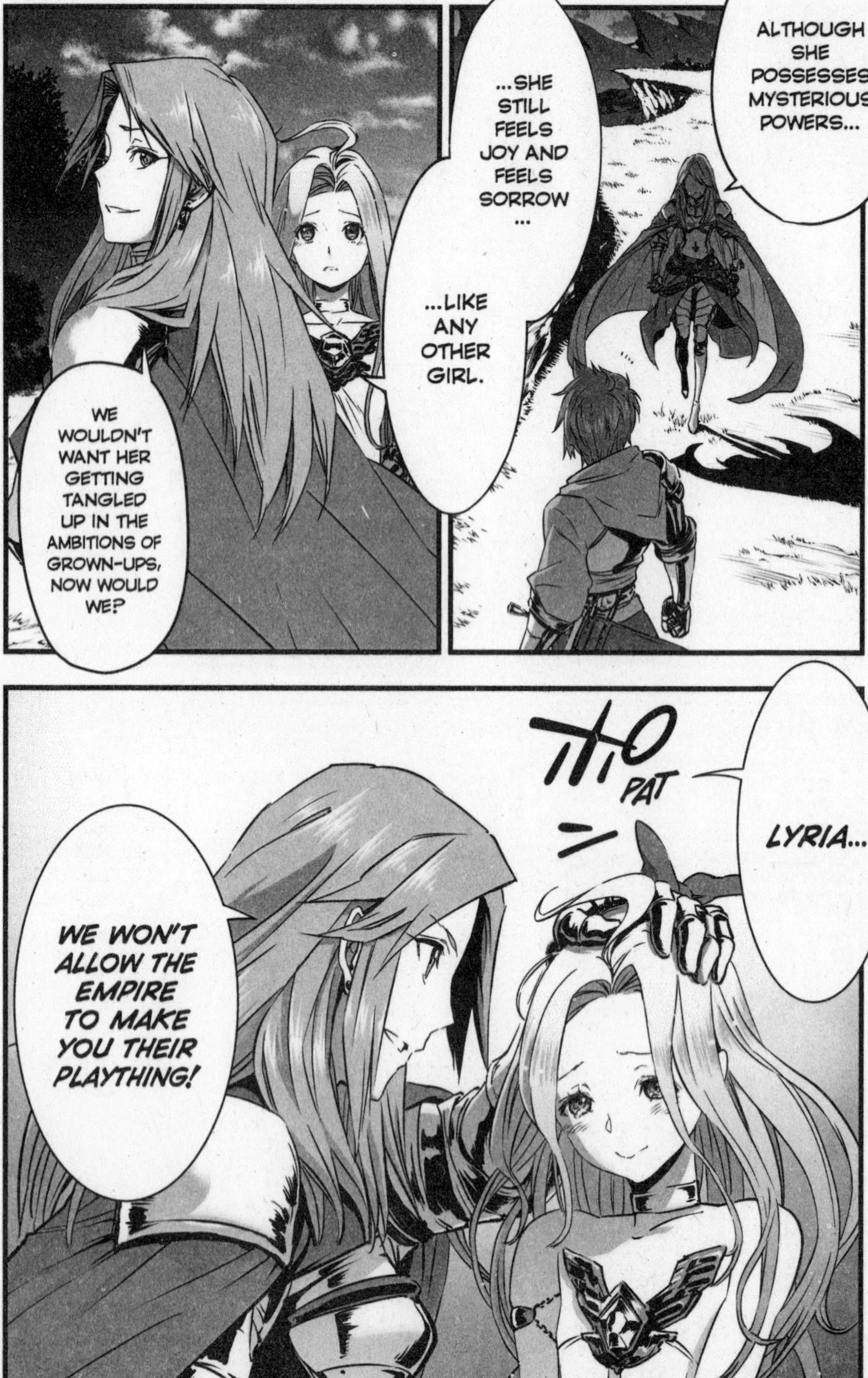
ALTHOUGH SHE POSSESSES MYSTERIOUS POWERS...
...SHE STILL FEELS JOY AND FEELS SORROW ...
...LIKE ANY OTHER GIRL.
WE WOULDN'T WANT HER GETTING TANGLED UP IN THE AMBITIONS OF GROWN-UPS, NOW WOULD WE?
LYRIA...
PAT
WE WON'T ALLOW THE EMPIRE TO MAKE YOU THEIR PLAYTHING!

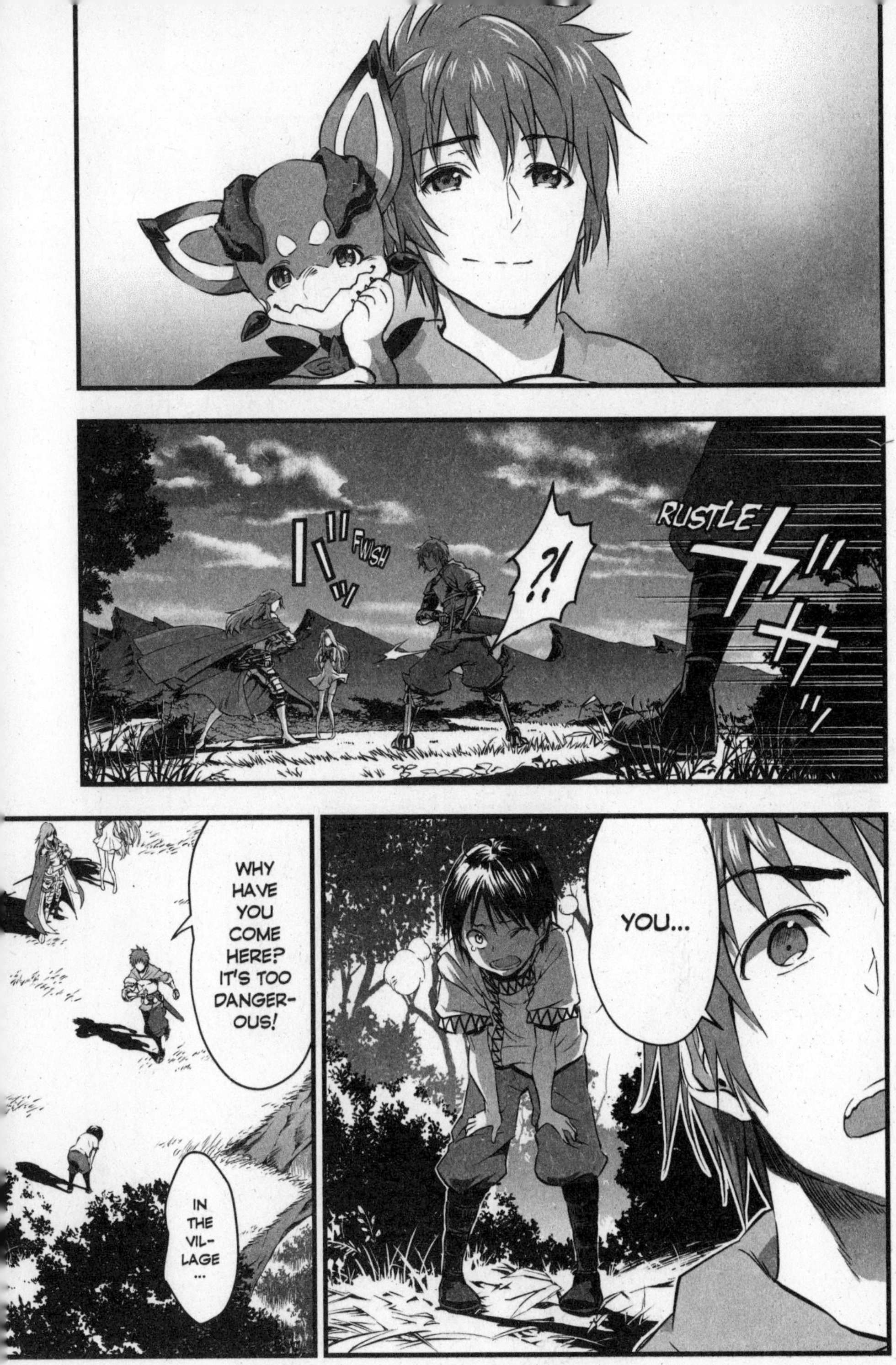

RUSTLE
?!
FWISH
YOU...
WHY HAVE YOU COME HERE? IT'S TOO DANGER-OUS!
IN THE VIL-LAGE ...

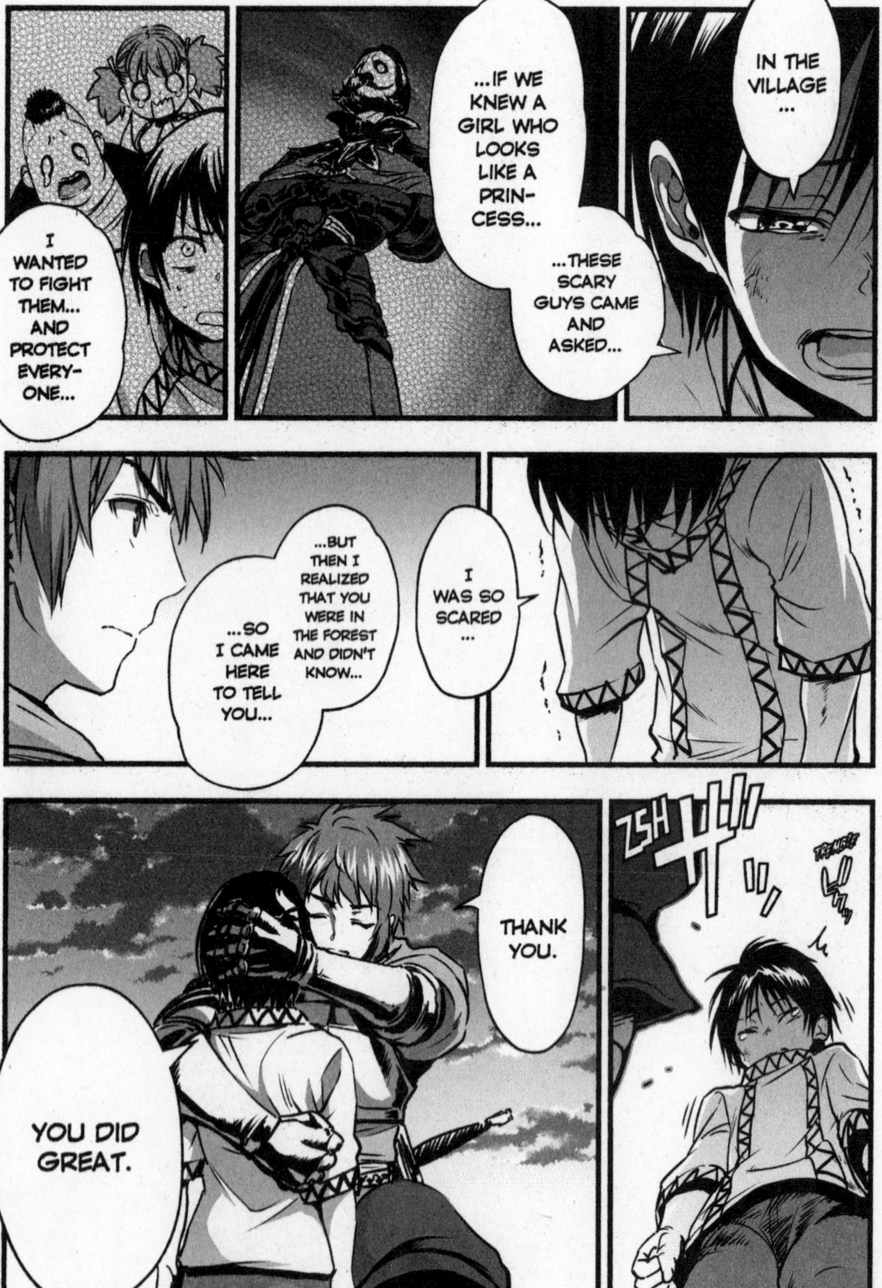
IN THE VILLAGE ...
...THESE SCARY GUYS CAME AND ASKED...
...IF WE KNEW A GIRL WHO LOOKS LIKE A PRINCESS...
I WANTED TO FIGHT THEM... AND PROTECT EVERYONE...
I WAS SO SCARED ...
...BUT THEN I REALIZED THAT YOU WERE IN THE FOREST AND DIDN'T KNOW...
...SO I CAME HERE TO TELL YOU...
ZSH
TREMBLE
THANK YOU.
YOU DID GREAT.

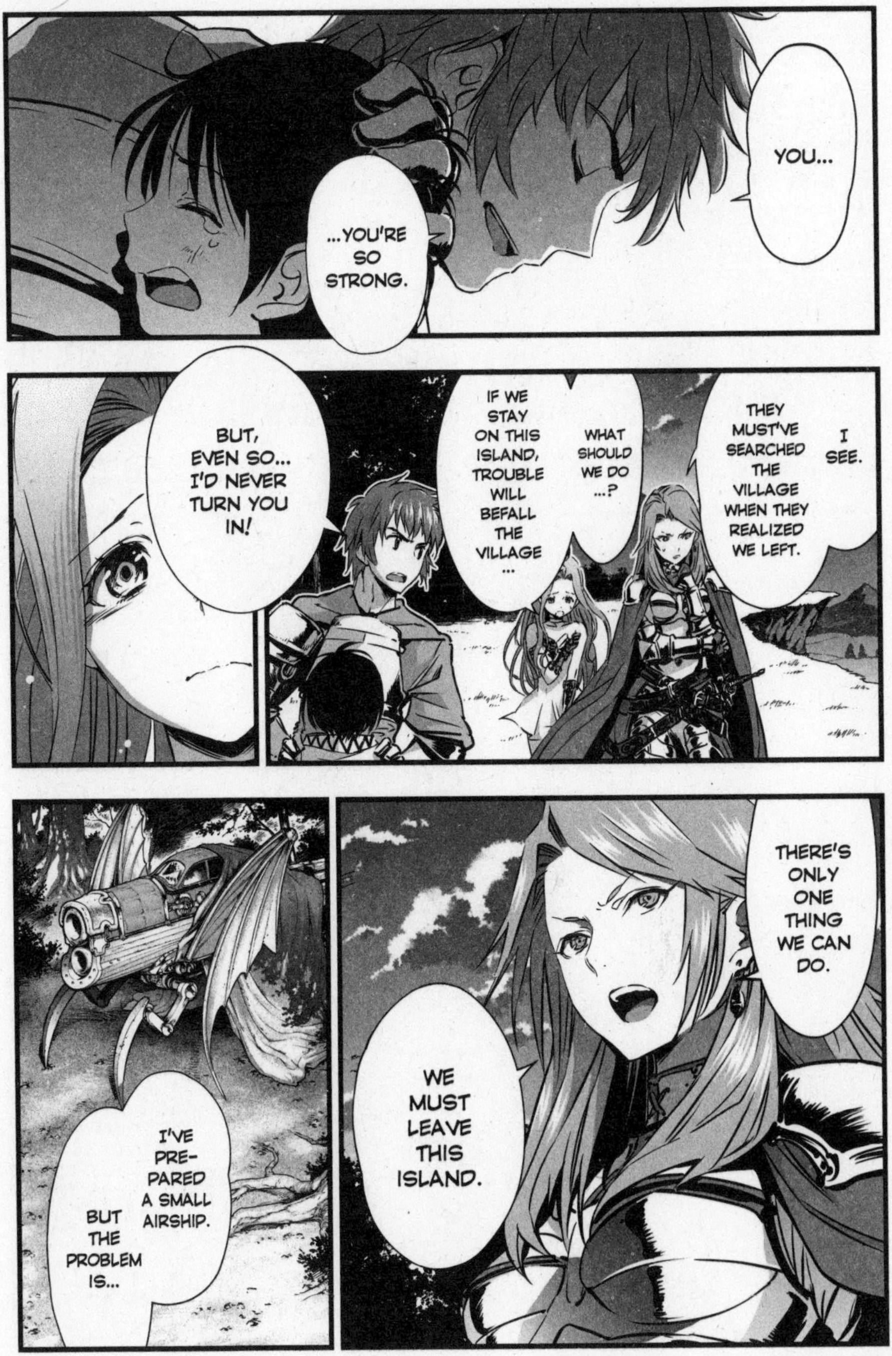
YOU...
...YOU'RE SO STRONG.
I SEE.
THEY MUST'VE SEARCHED THE VILLAGE WHEN THEY REALIZED WE LEFT.
WHAT SHOULD WE DO ...?
IF WE STAY ON THIS ISLAND, TROUBLE WILL BEFALL THE VILLAGE ...
BUT, EVEN SO... I'D NEVER TURN YOU IN!
THERE'S ONLY ONE THING WE CAN DO.
WE MUST LEAVE THIS ISLAND.
I'VE PRE-PARED A SMALL AIRSHIP.
BUT THE PROBLEM IS...

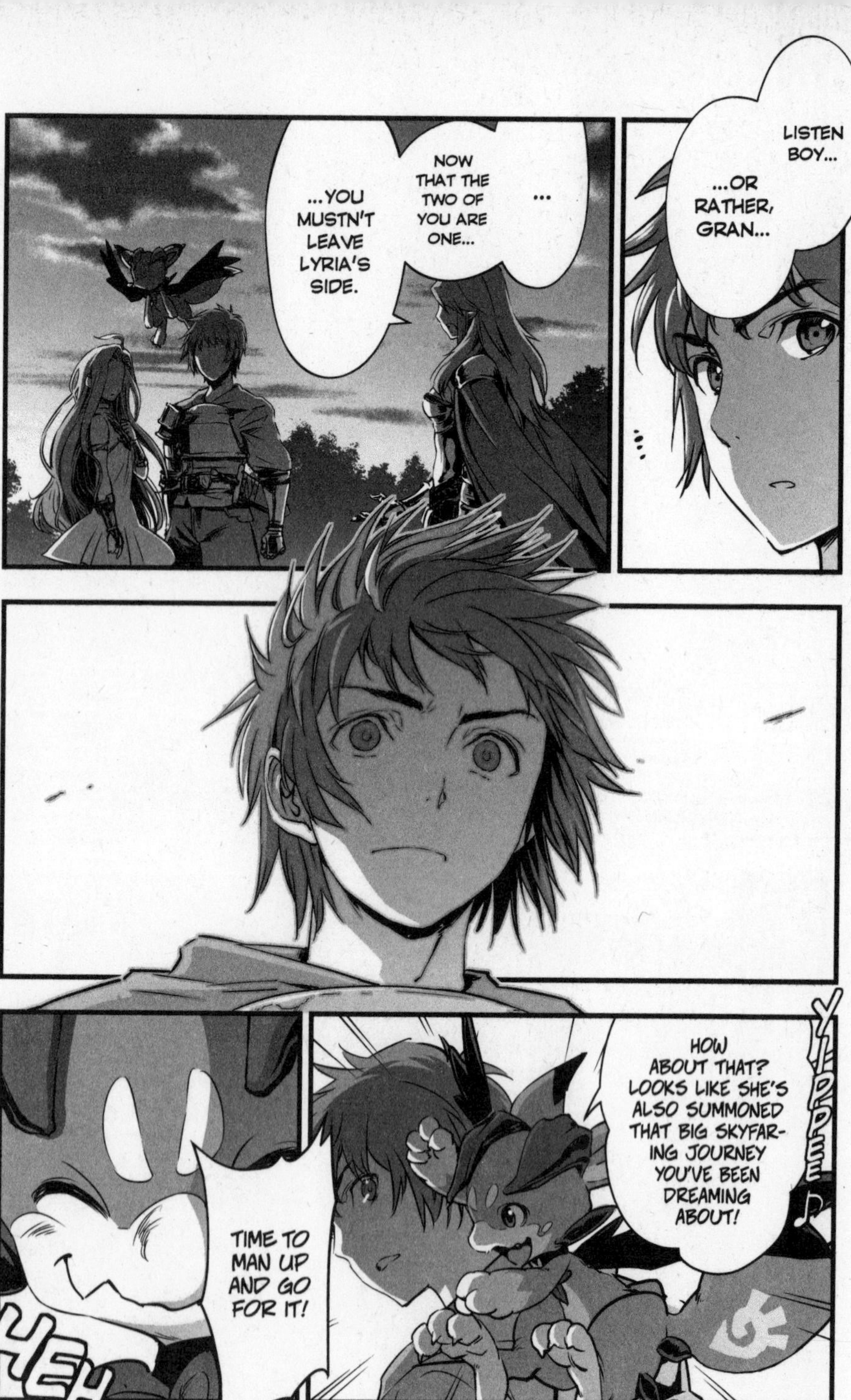
LISTEN BOY...
...OR RATHER, GRAN...
...
NOW THAT THE TWO OF YOU ARE ONE...
...YOU MUSTN'T LEAVE LYRIA'S SIDE.
YIPPEE♪
HOW ABOUT THAT? LOOKS LIKE SHE'S ALSO SUMMONED THAT BIG SKYFARING JOURNEY YOU'VE BEEN DREAMING ABOUT!
TIME TO MAN UP AND GO FOR IT!
HEH

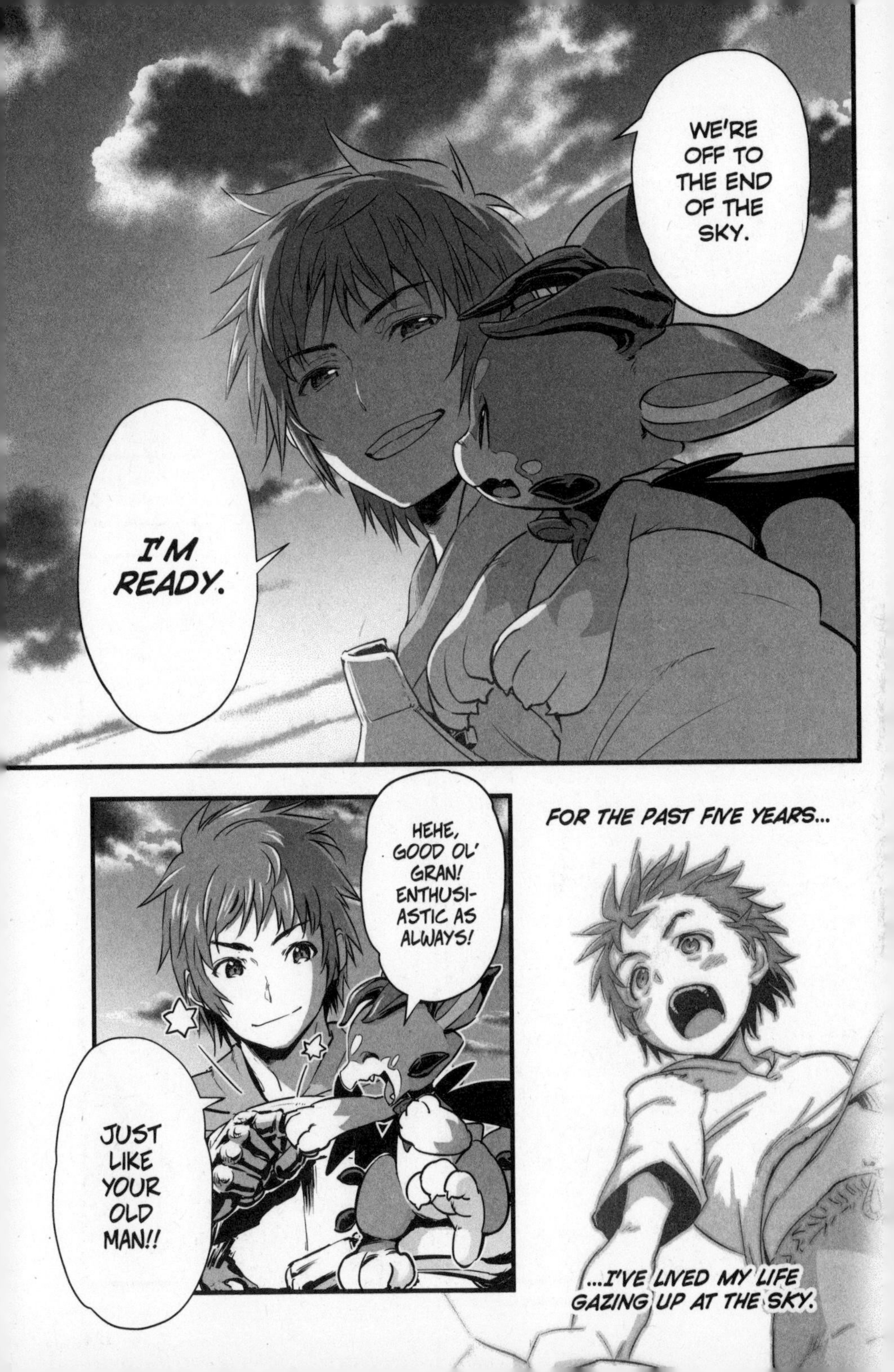
WE'RE OFF TO THE END OF THE SKY.
I'M READY.
FOR THE PAST FIVE YEARS...
...I'VE LIVED MY LIFE GAZING UP AT THE SKY.
HEHE, GOOD OL' GRAN! ENTHUSI-ASTIC AS ALWAYS!
JUST LIKE YOUR OLD MAN!!

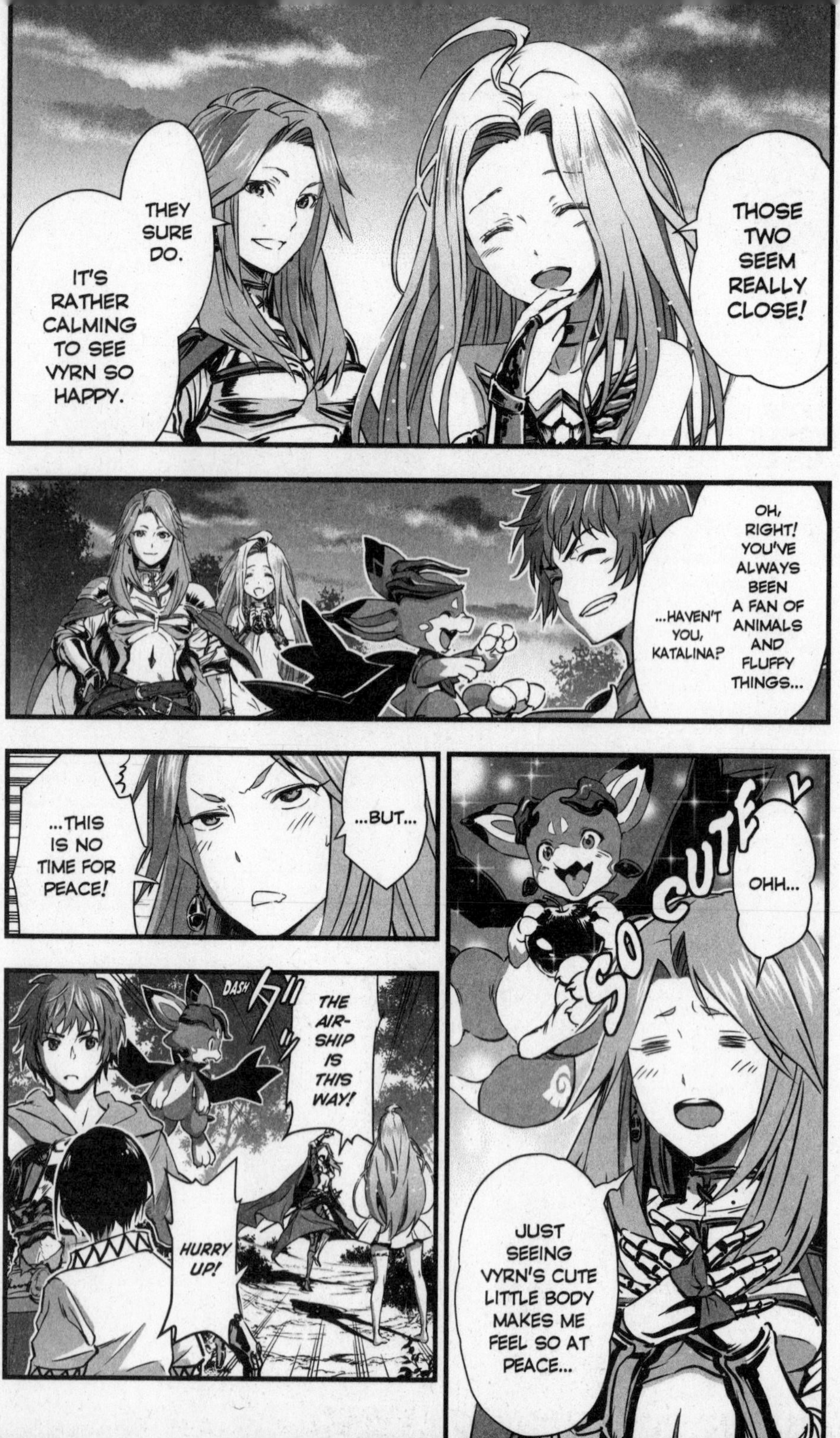
THOSE TWO SEEM REALLY CLOSE!
THEY SURE DO.
IT'S RATHER CALMING TO SEE VYRN SO HAPPY.
OH, RIGHT! YOU'VE ALWAYS BEEN A FAN OF ANIMALS AND FLUFFY THINGS...
...HAVEN'T YOU, KATALINA?
SO CUTE ♥
OHH...
JUST SEEING VYRN'S CUTE LITTLE BODY MAKES ME FEEL SO AT PEACE...
...BUT...
...THIS IS NO TIME FOR PEACE!
DASH
THE AIR-SHIP IS THIS WAY!
HURRY UP!

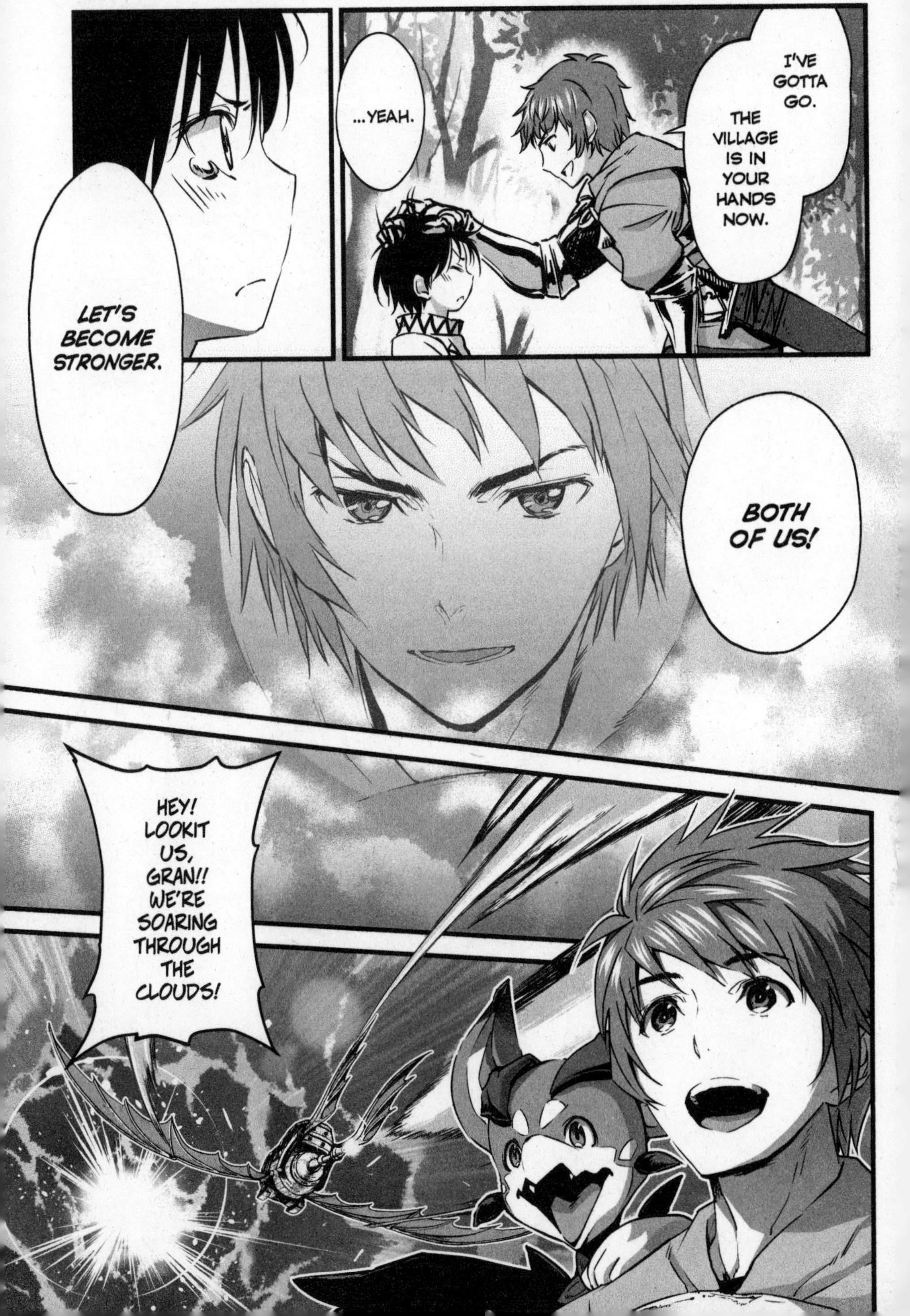
I'VE GOTTA GO. THE VILLAGE IS IN YOUR HANDS NOW.
...YEAH.
LET'S BECOME STRONGER.
BOTH OF US!
HEY! LOOKIT US, GRAN!! WE'RE SOARING THROUGH THE CLOUDS!

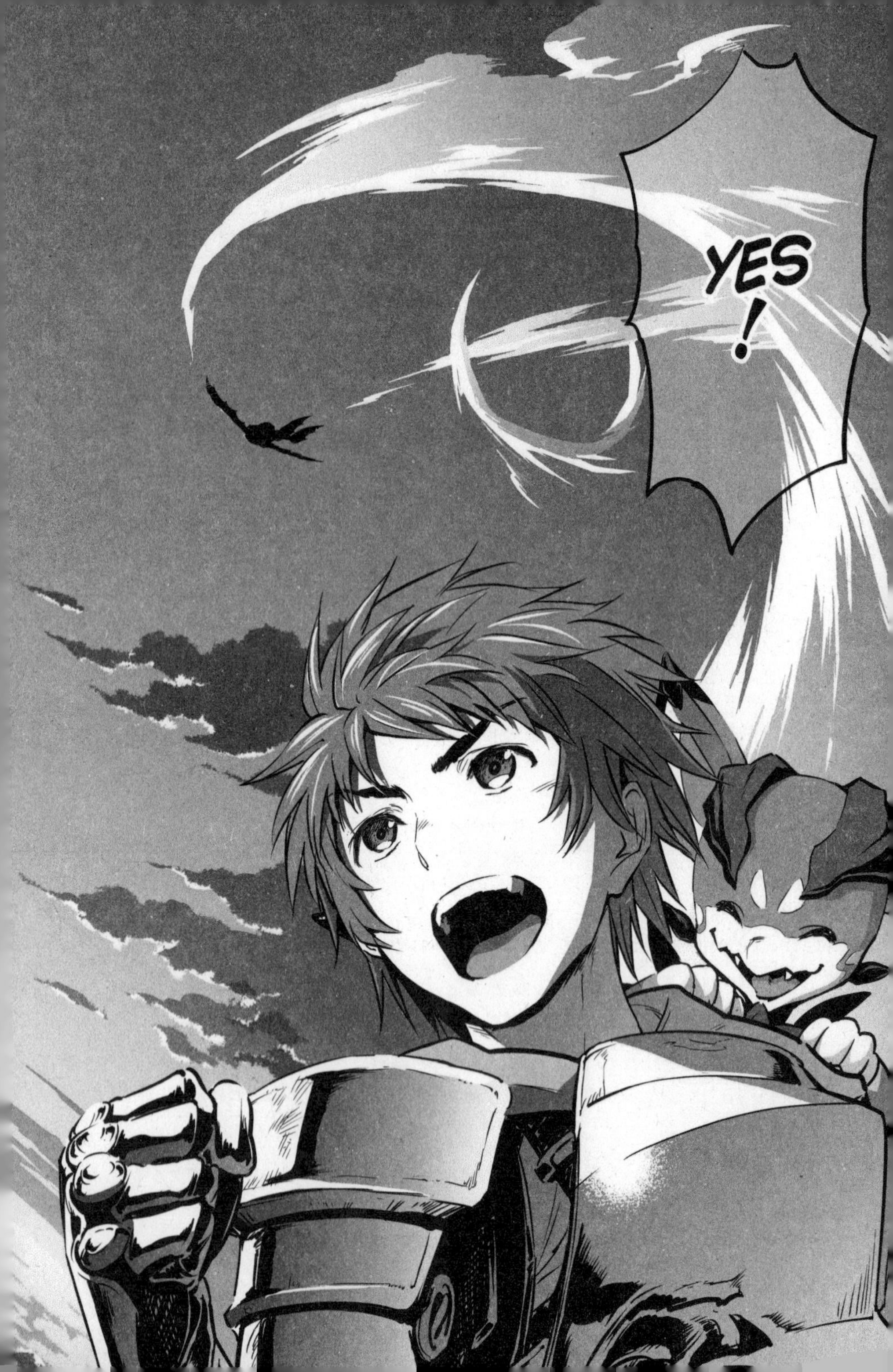
YES!

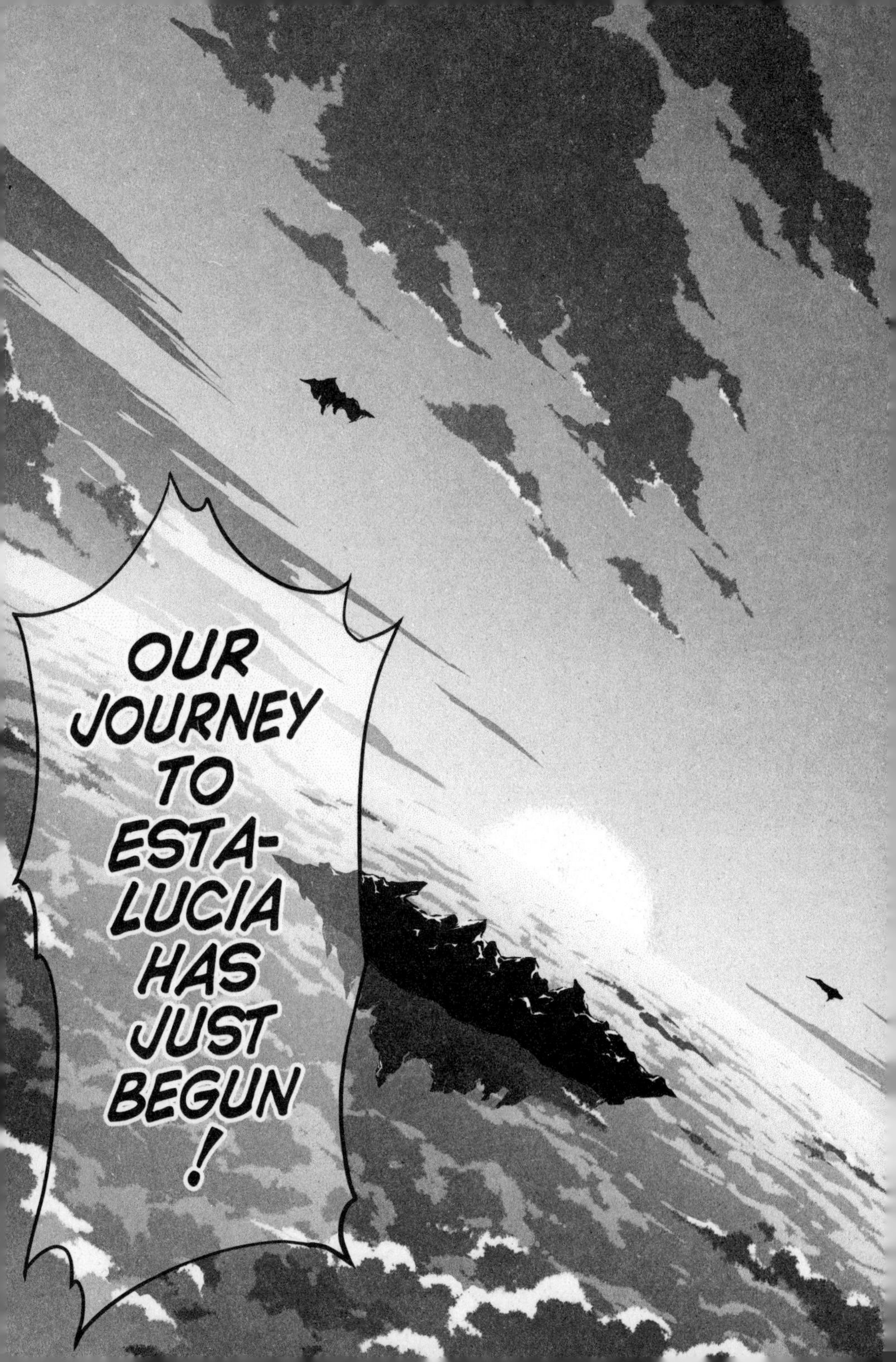
OUR JOURNEY TO ESTA-LUCIA HAS JUST BEGUN!

GRANBLUE FANTASY
グランブルーファンタジー

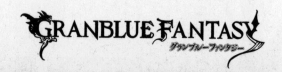

CHAPTER 5: Port Breeze Archipelago (1)

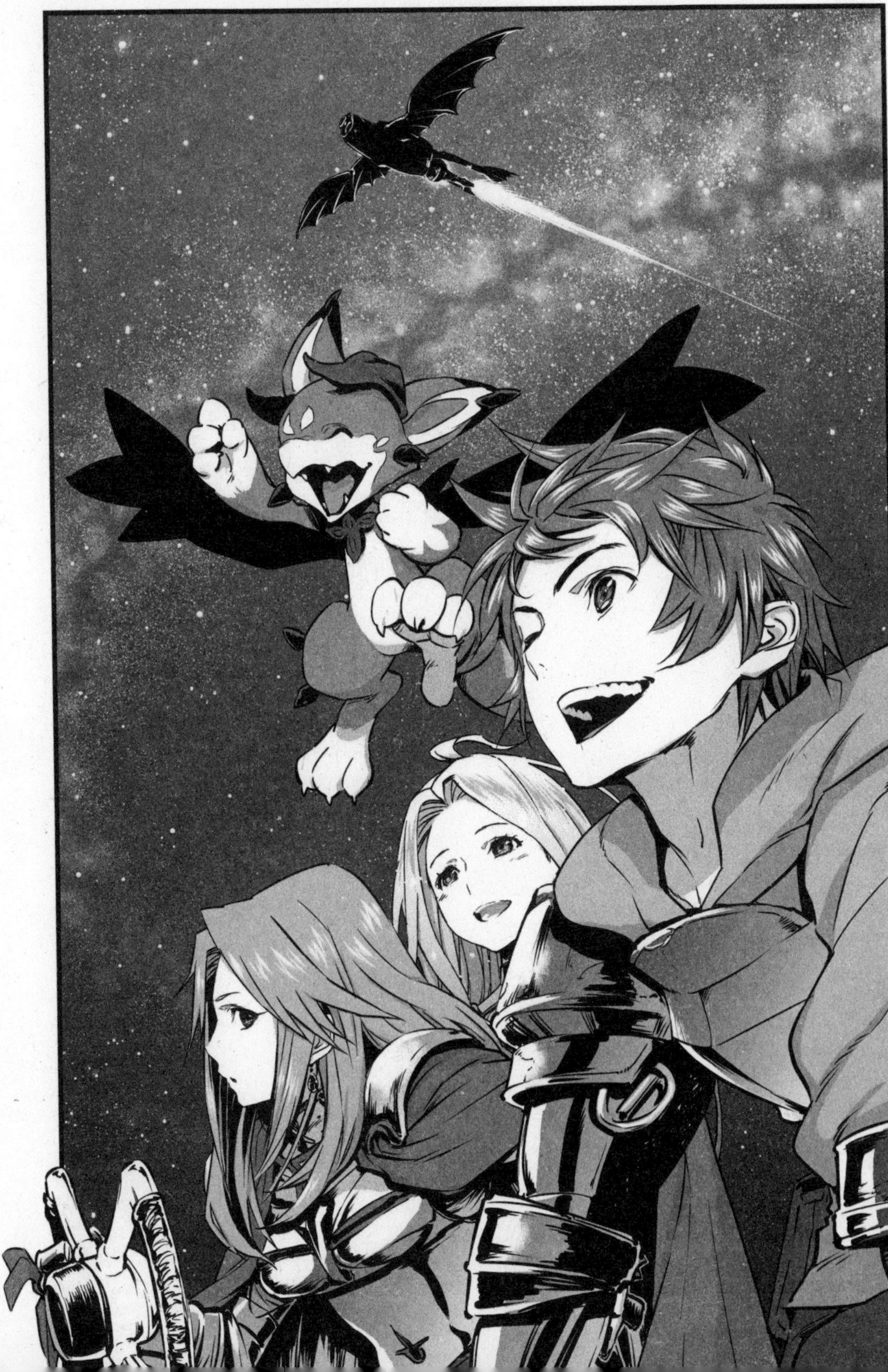

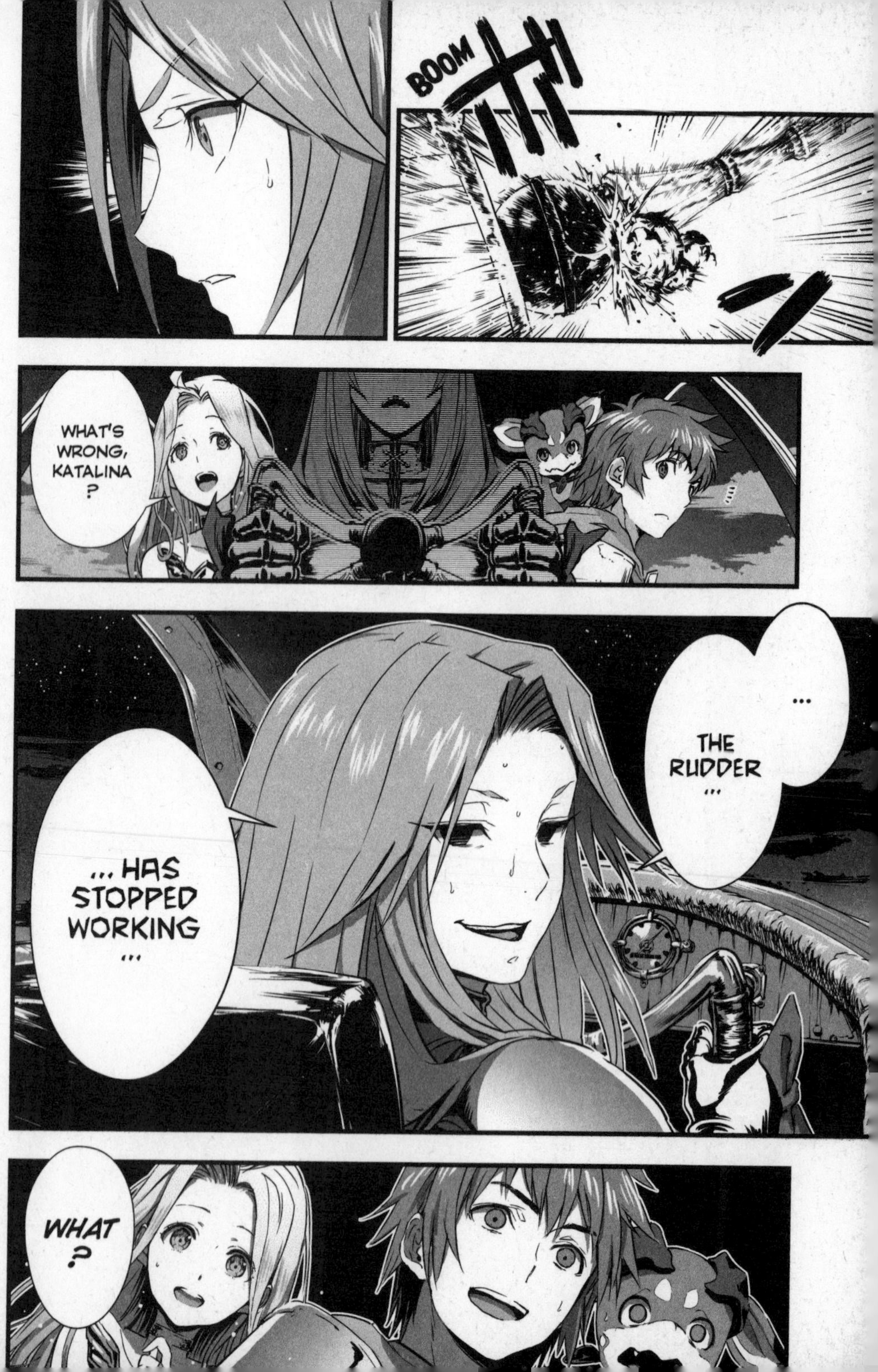
BOOM
WHAT'S WRONG, KATALINA?
...
THE RUDDER ...
... HAS STOPPED WORKING ...
WHAT?

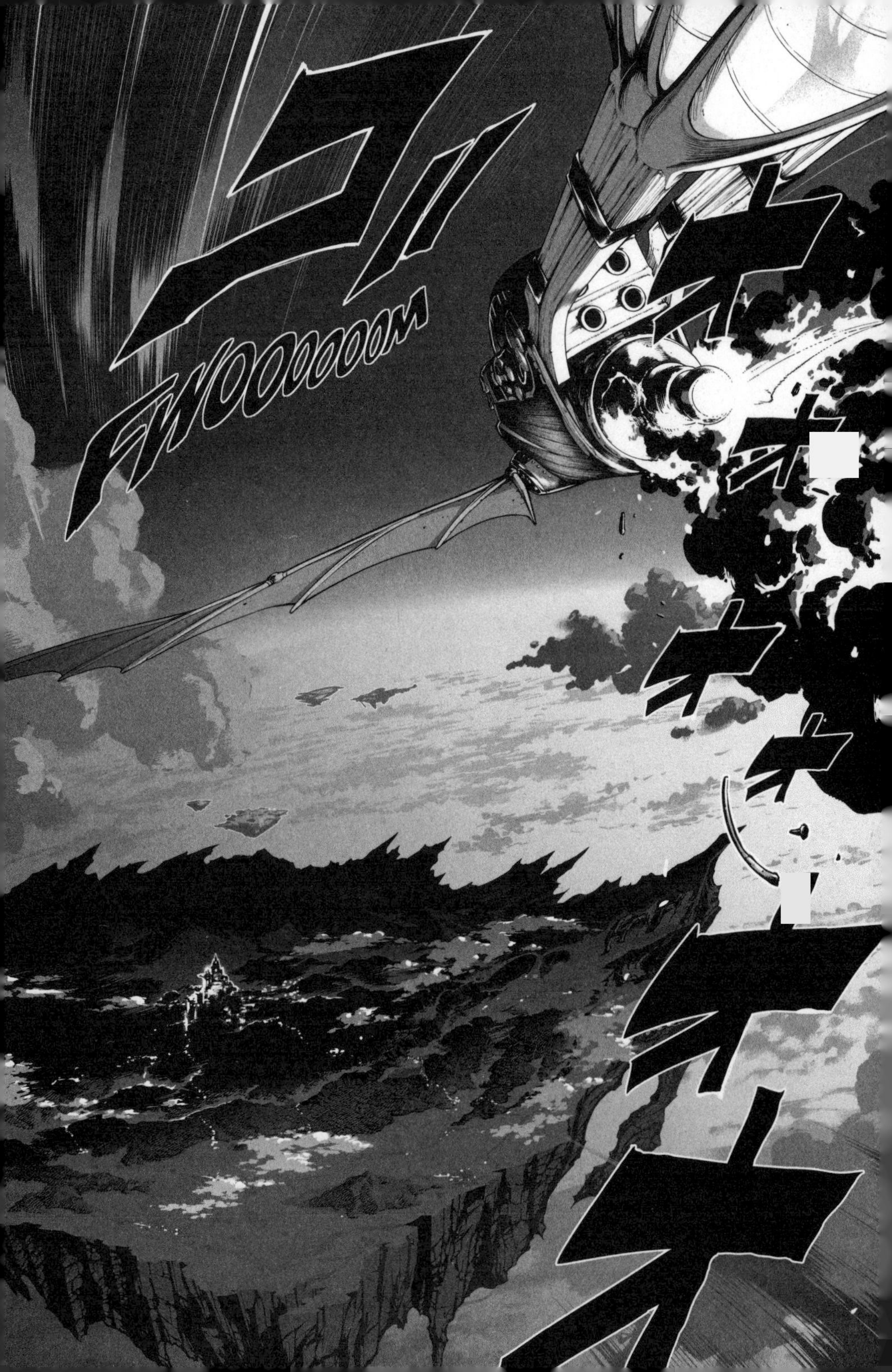
FWOOOOOOM

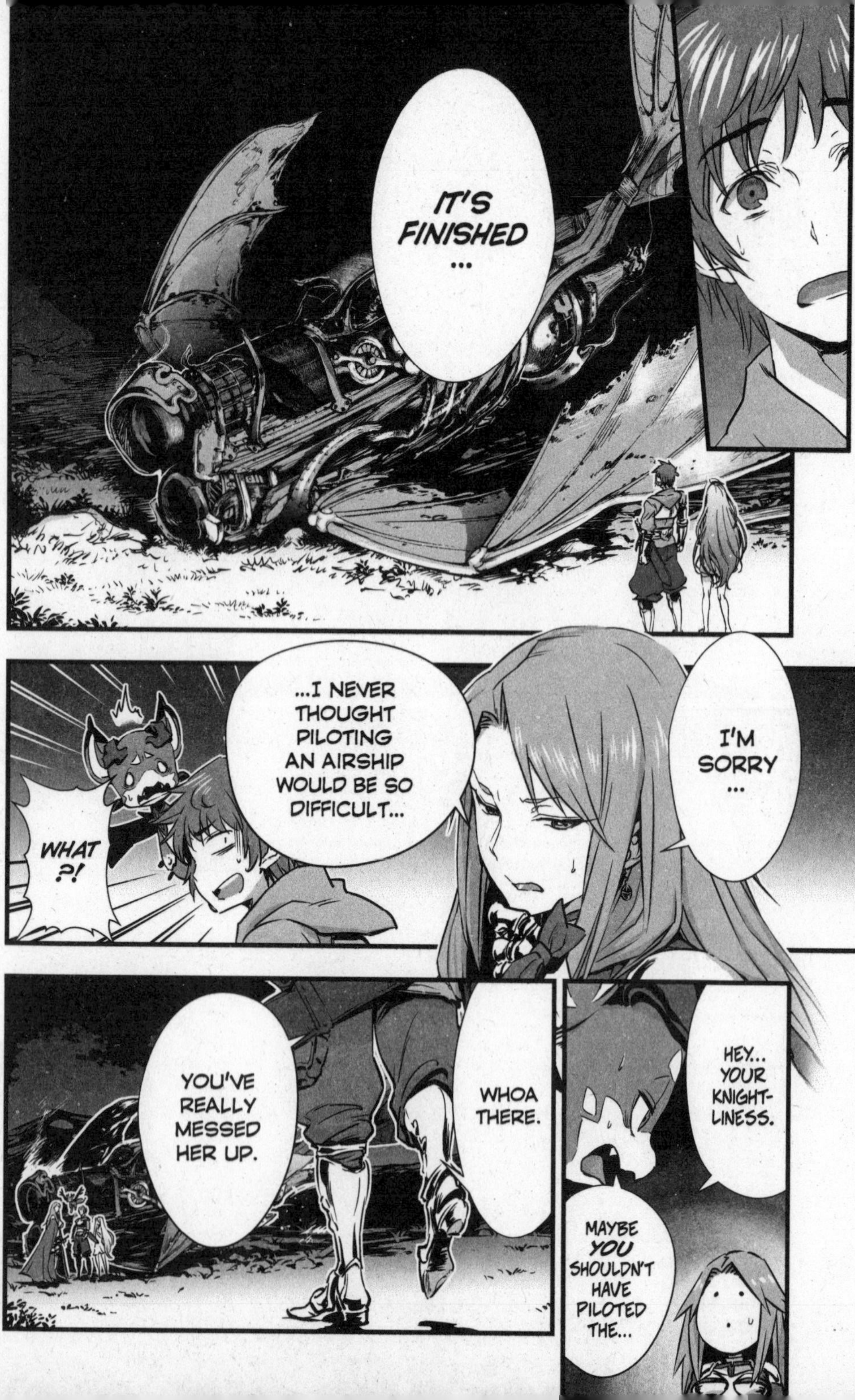
IT'S FINISHED...
I'M SORRY...
...I NEVER THOUGHT PILOTING AN AIRSHIP WOULD BE SO DIFFICULT...
WHAT?!
HEY... YOUR KNIGHT-LINESS.
MAYBE YOU SHOULDN'T HAVE PILOTED THE...
WHOA THERE.
YOU'VE REALLY MESSED HER UP.

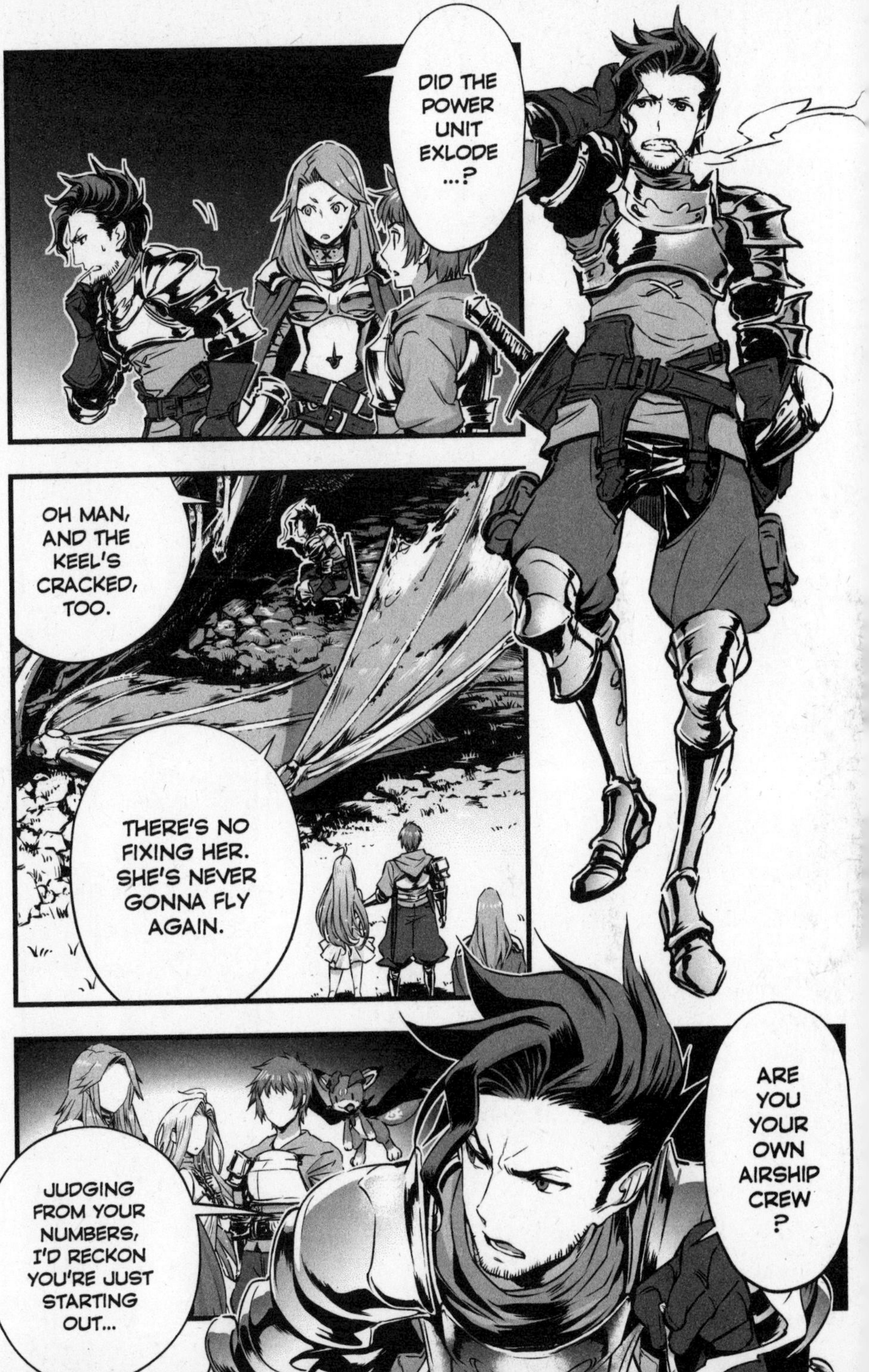
DID THE POWER UNIT EXLODE ...?
OH MAN, AND THE KEEL'S CRACKED, TOO.
THERE'S NO FIXING HER. SHE'S NEVER GONNA FLY AGAIN.
ARE YOU YOUR OWN AIRSHIP CREW ?
JUDGING FROM YOUR NUMBERS, I'D RECKON YOU'RE JUST STARTING OUT...

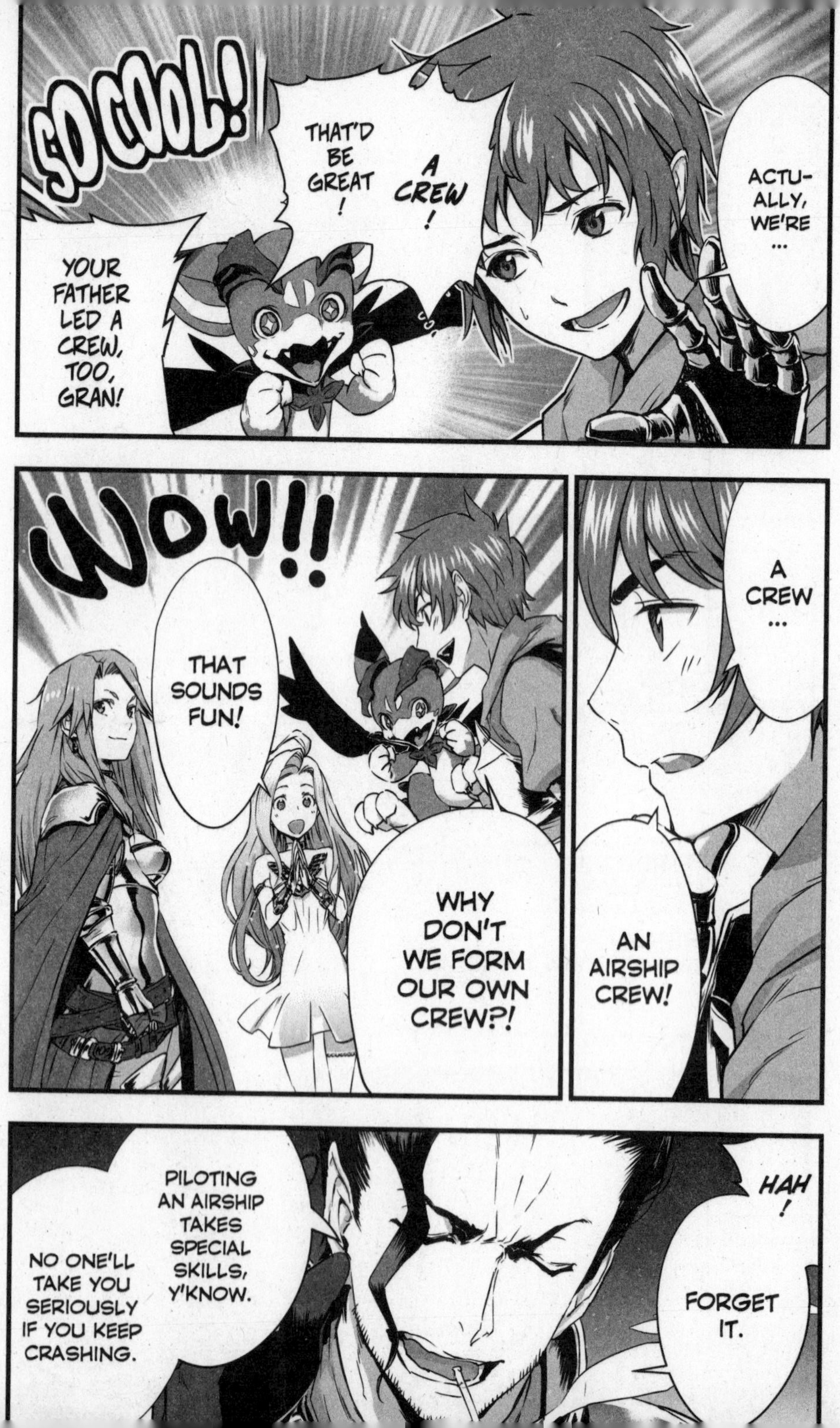
ACTU-ALLY, WE'RE ...
A CREW!
THAT'D BE GREAT!
SO COOL!
YOUR FATHER LED A CREW, TOO, GRAN!
A CREW ...
AN AIRSHIP CREW!
WOW!!
THAT SOUNDS FUN!
WHY DON'T WE FORM OUR OWN CREW?!
HAH!
FORGET IT.
PILOTING AN AIRSHIP TAKES SPECIAL SKILLS, Y'KNOW.
NO ONE'LL TAKE YOU SERIOUSLY IF YOU KEEP CRASHING.

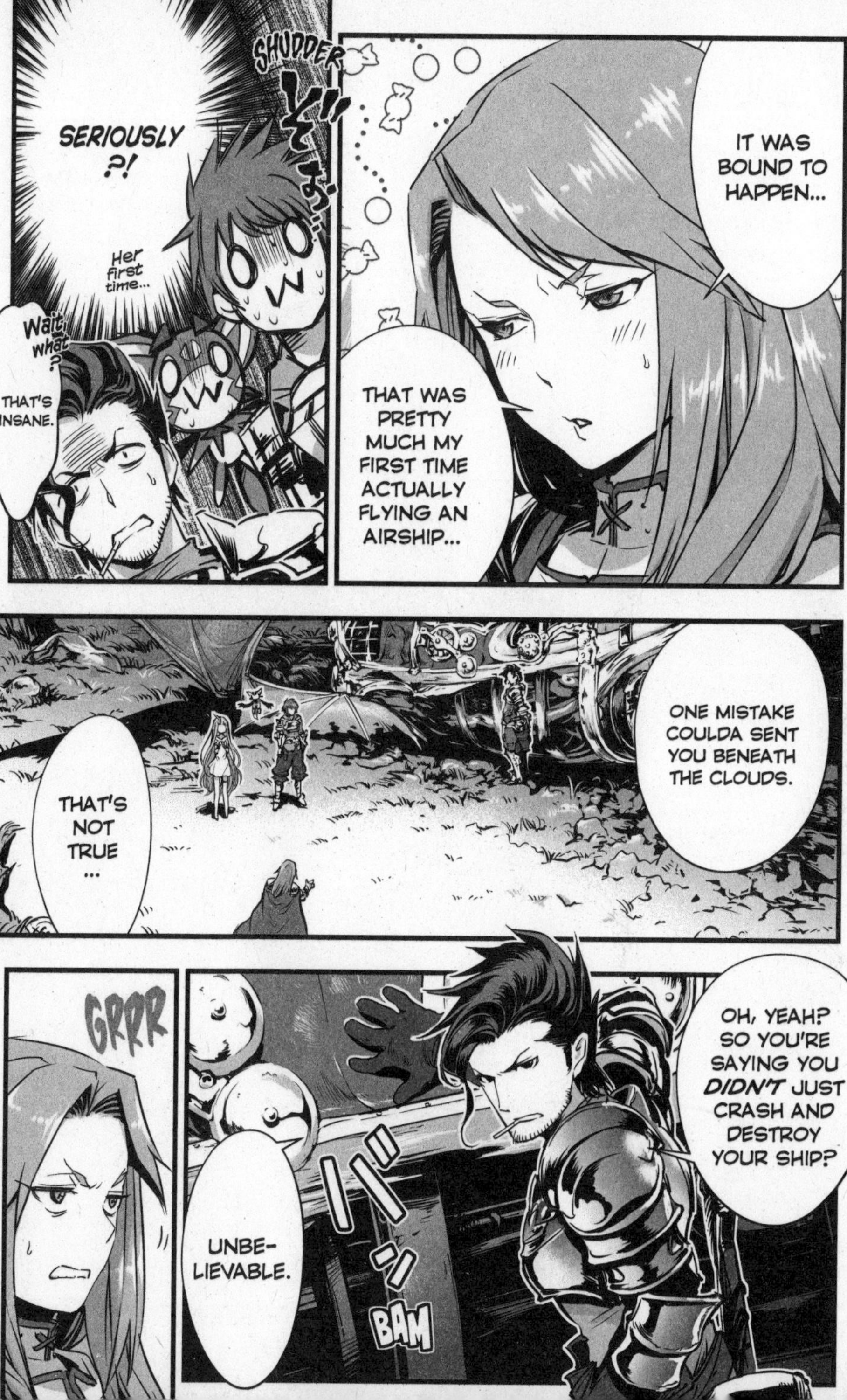
IT WAS BOUND TO HAPPEN...
THAT WAS PRETTY MUCH MY FIRST TIME ACTUALLY FLYING AN AIRSHIP...
SHUDDER
SERIOUSLY ?!
Her first time...
Wait, what?
THAT'S INSANE.
ONE MISTAKE COULDA SENT YOU BENEATH THE CLOUDS.
THAT'S NOT TRUE ...
OH, YEAH? SO YOU'RE SAYING YOU *DIDN'T* JUST CRASH AND DESTROY YOUR SHIP?
BAM
UNBE-LIEVABLE.
GRRR

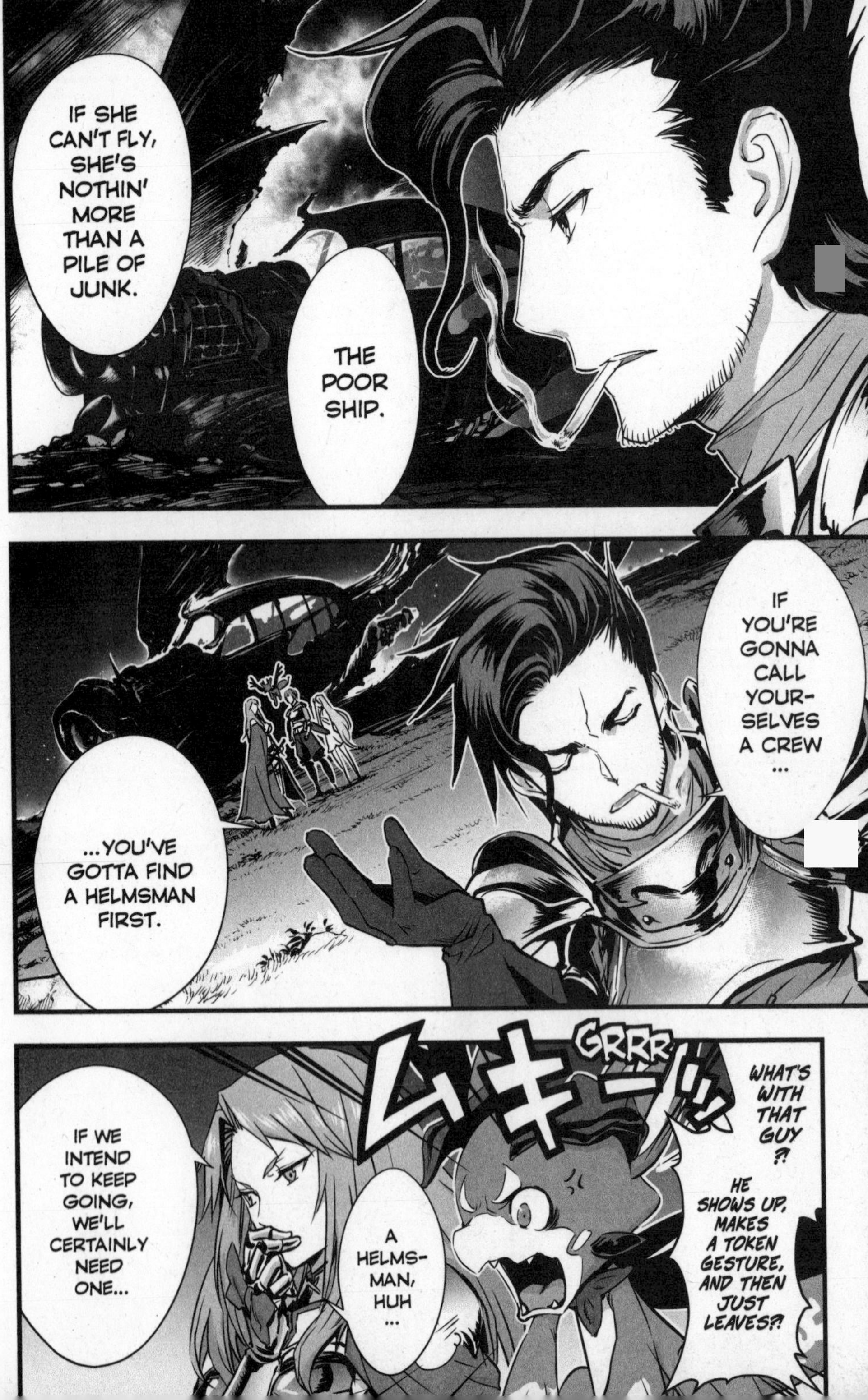
THE POOR SHIP.
IF SHE CAN'T FLY, SHE'S NOTHIN' MORE THAN A PILE OF JUNK.
IF YOU'RE GONNA CALL YOUR-SELVES A CREW ...
...YOU'VE GOTTA FIND A HELMSMAN FIRST.
ムキーッ!!
GRRR
WHAT'S WITH THAT GUY?!
HE SHOWS UP, MAKES A TOKEN GESTURE, AND THEN JUST LEAVES?!
A HELMS-MAN, HUH ...
IF WE INTEND TO KEEP GOING, WE'LL CERTAINLY NEED ONE...

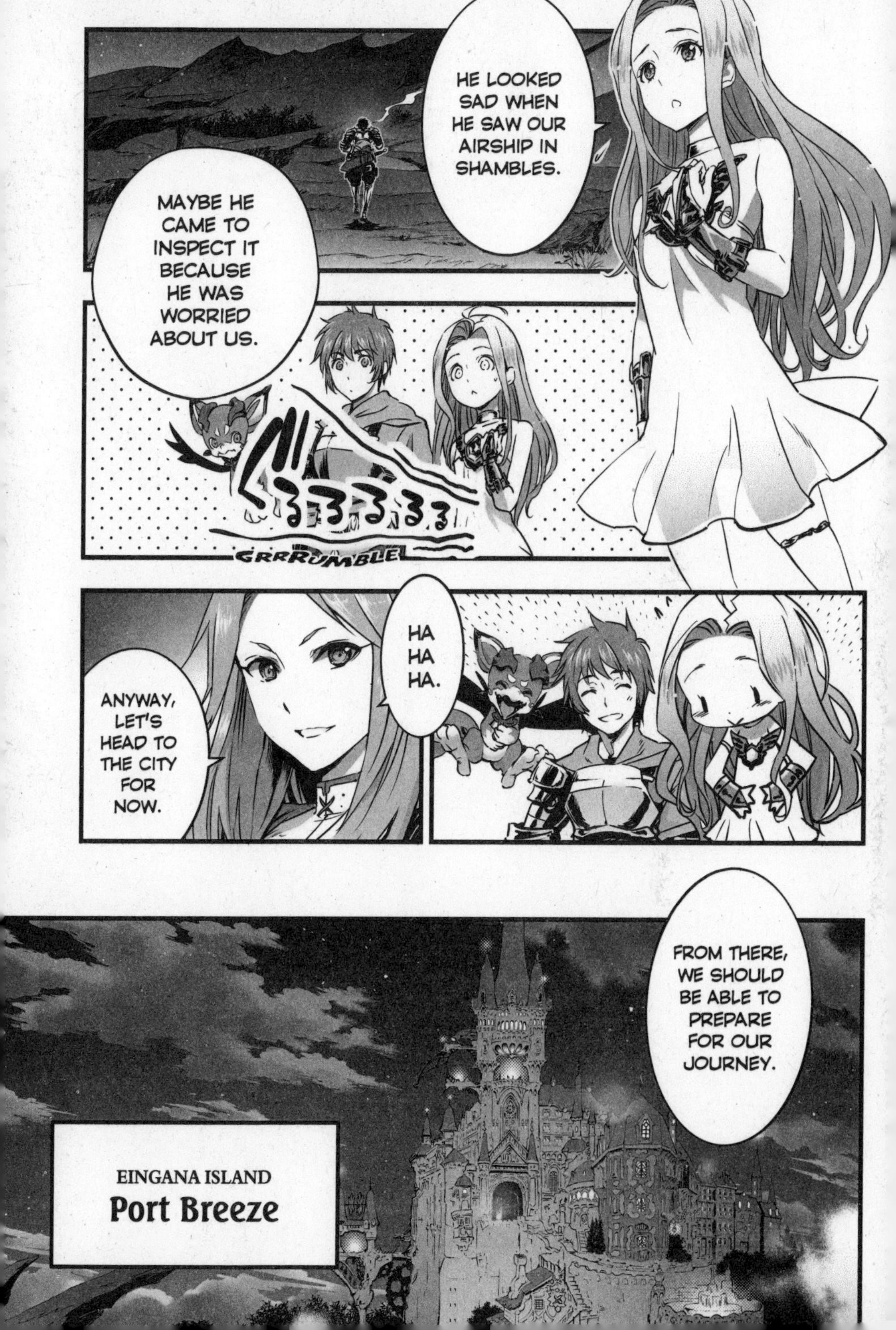
HE LOOKED SAD WHEN HE SAW OUR AIRSHIP IN SHAMBLES.
MAYBE HE CAME TO INSPECT IT BECAUSE HE WAS WORRIED ABOUT US.
ぐるるるるる
GRRRUMBLE
HA HA HA.
ANYWAY, LET'S HEAD TO THE CITY FOR NOW.
FROM THERE, WE SHOULD BE ABLE TO PREPARE FOR OUR JOURNEY.
EINGANA ISLAND
Port Breeze

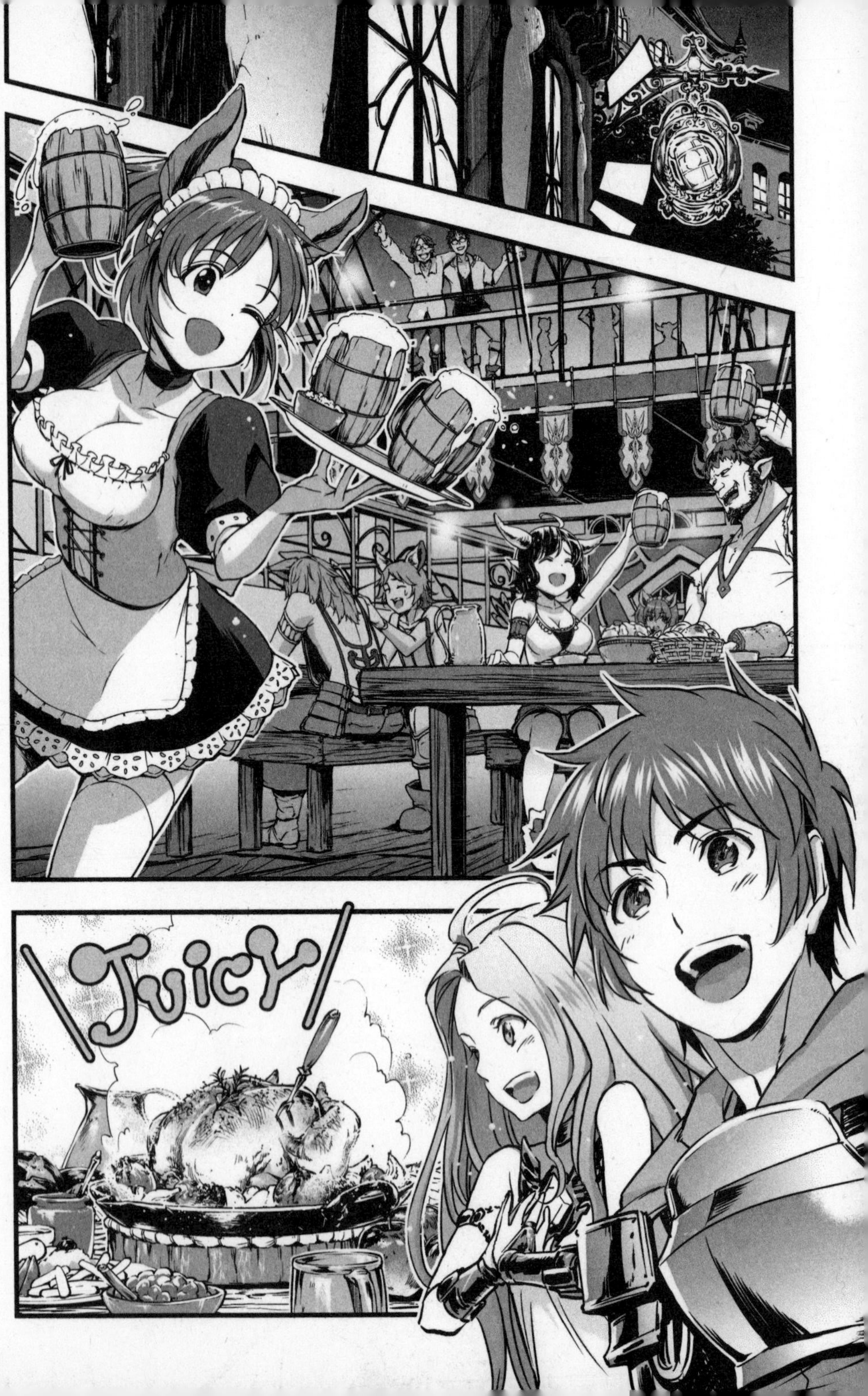
JUICY

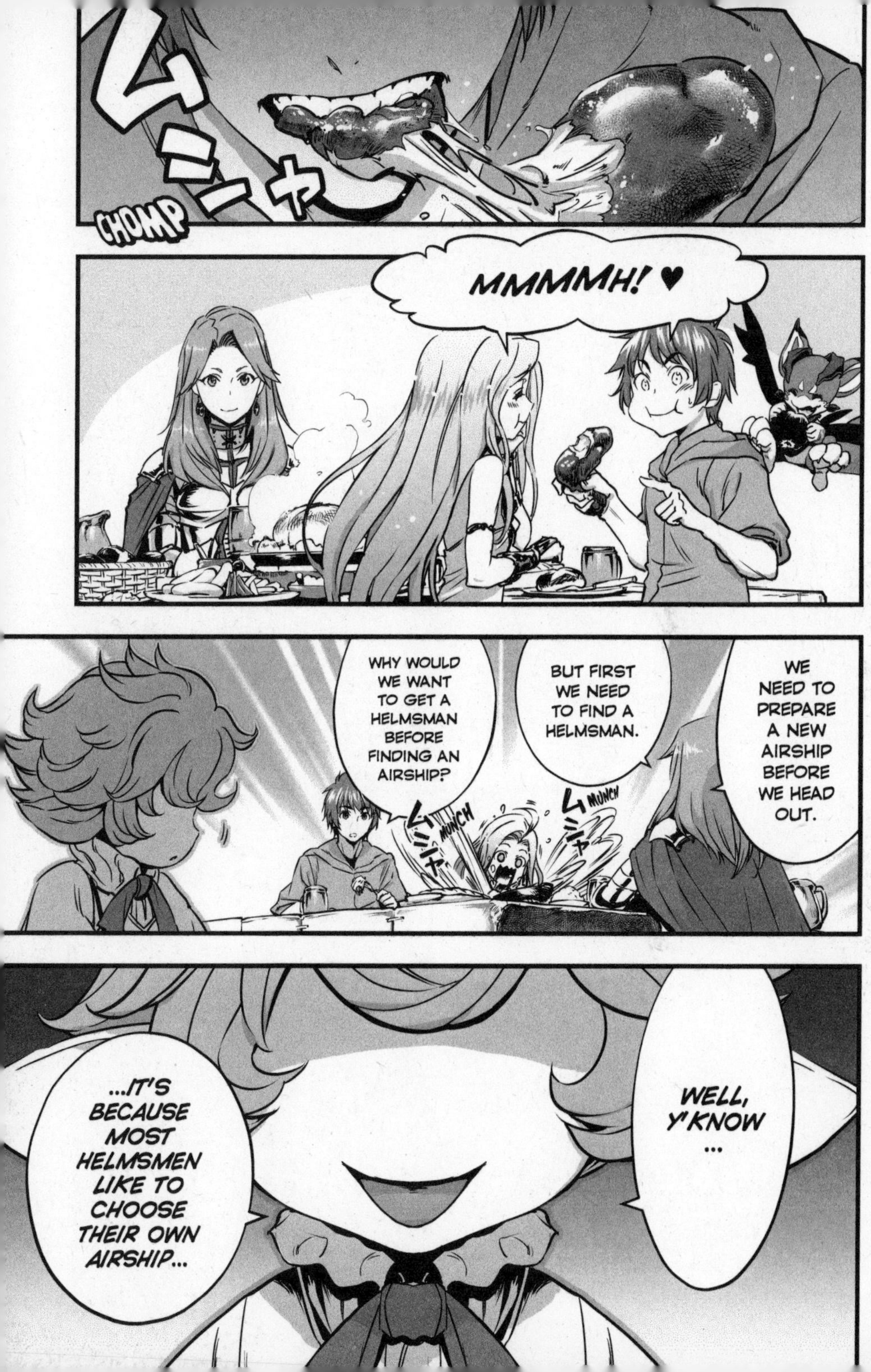
ムシャ
CHOMP
MMMMH! ♥
WE NEED TO PREPARE A NEW AIRSHIP BEFORE WE HEAD OUT.
BUT FIRST WE NEED TO FIND A HELMSMAN.
WHY WOULD WE WANT TO GET A HELMSMAN BEFORE FINDING AN AIRSHIP?
ムシャ MUNCH
ムシャ MUNCH
WELL, Y'KNOW ...
...IT'S BECAUSE MOST HELMSMEN LIKE TO CHOOSE THEIR OWN AIRSHIP...

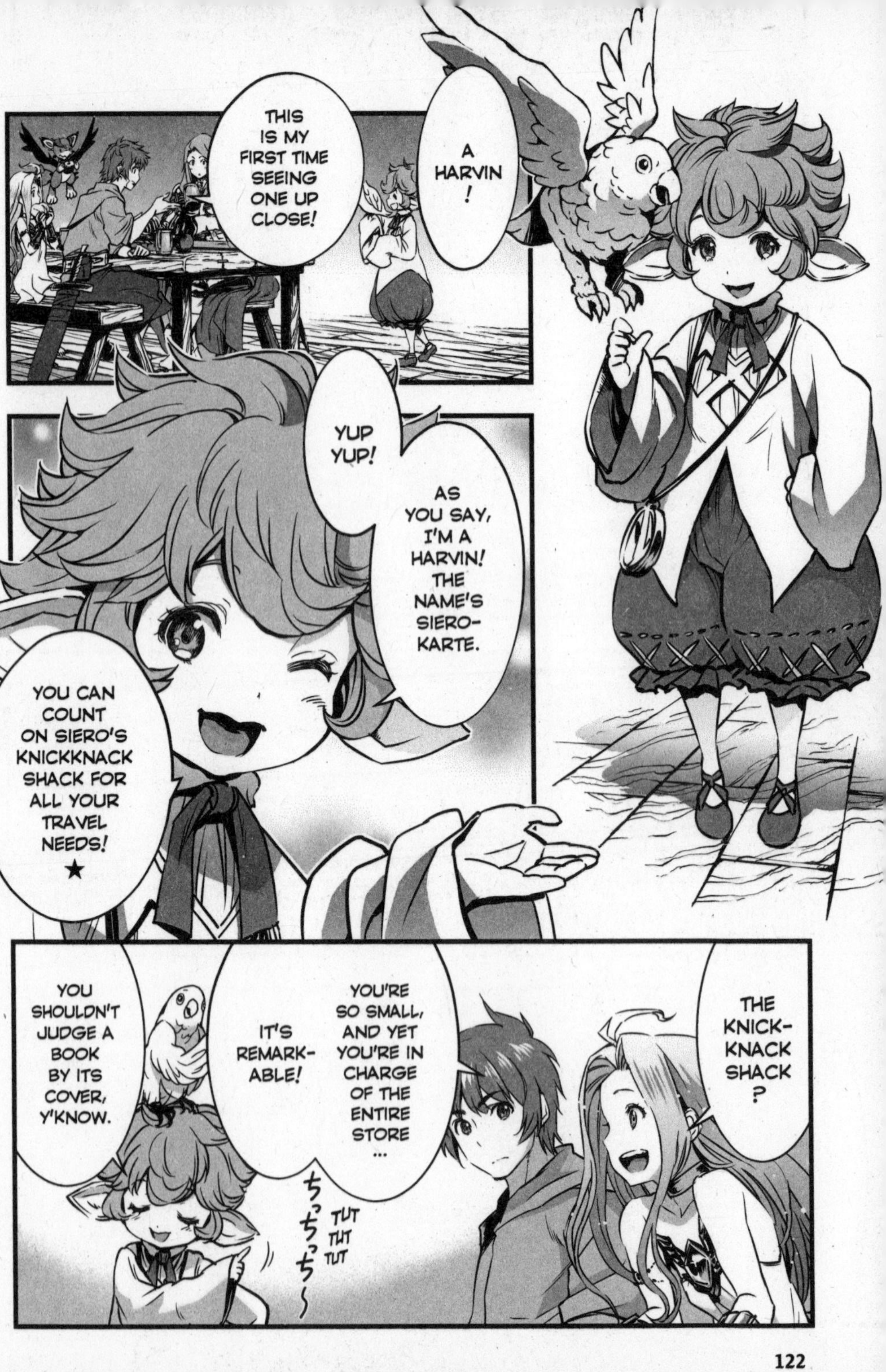
A HARVIN!
THIS IS MY FIRST TIME SEEING ONE UP CLOSE!
YUP YUP!
AS YOU SAY, I'M A HARVIN! THE NAME'S SIERO-KARTE.
YOU CAN COUNT ON SIERO'S KNICKKNACK SHACK FOR ALL YOUR TRAVEL NEEDS! ★
THE KNICK-KNACK SHACK?
YOU'RE SO SMALL, AND YET YOU'RE IN CHARGE OF THE ENTIRE STORE ...
IT'S REMARKABLE!
ちっちっち～
TUT TUT TUT
YOU SHOULDN'T JUDGE A BOOK BY ITS COVER, Y'KNOW.

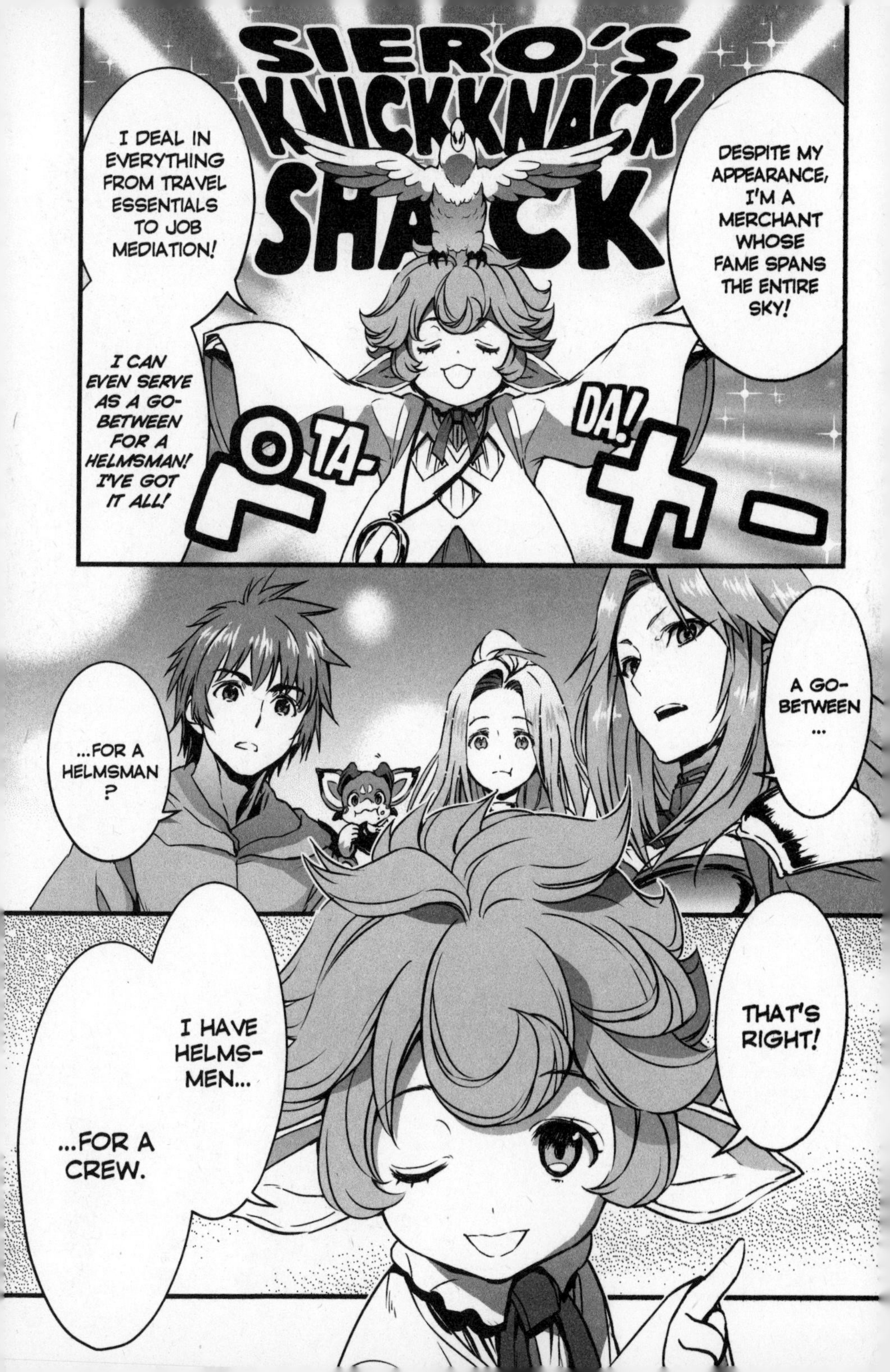
SIERO'S KNICKKNACK SHACK
DESPITE MY APPEARANCE, I'M A MERCHANT WHOSE FAME SPANS THE ENTIRE SKY!
I DEAL IN EVERYTHING FROM TRAVEL ESSENTIALS TO JOB MEDIATION!
I CAN EVEN SERVE AS A GO-BETWEEN FOR A HELMSMAN! I'VE GOT IT ALL!
TA-
DA!
A GO-BETWEEN...
...FOR A HELMSMAN?
THAT'S RIGHT!
I HAVE HELMS-MEN...
...FOR A CREW.

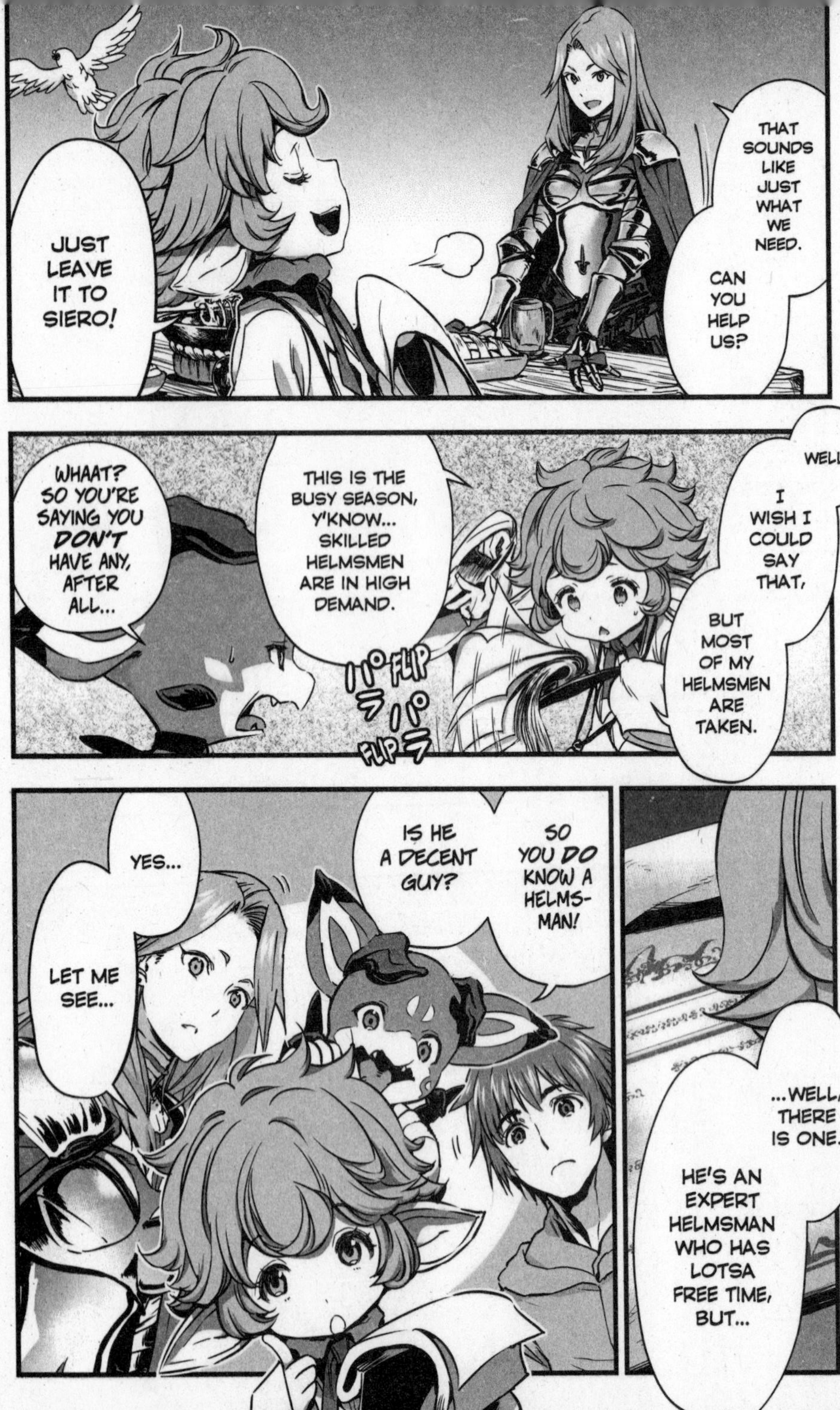
THAT SOUNDS LIKE JUST WHAT WE NEED.
CAN YOU HELP US?
JUST LEAVE IT TO SIERO!
WELL,
I WISH I COULD SAY THAT,
BUT MOST OF MY HELMSMEN ARE TAKEN.
THIS IS THE BUSY SEASON, Y'KNOW... SKILLED HELMSMEN ARE IN HIGH DEMAND.
FLIP FLIP
WHAAT? SO YOU'RE SAYING YOU *DON'T* HAVE ANY, AFTER ALL...
...WELL, THERE IS ONE.
HE'S AN EXPERT HELMSMAN WHO HAS LOTSA FREE TIME, BUT...
SO YOU *DO* KNOW A HELMS-MAN!
IS HE A DECENT GUY?
YES...
LET ME SEE...

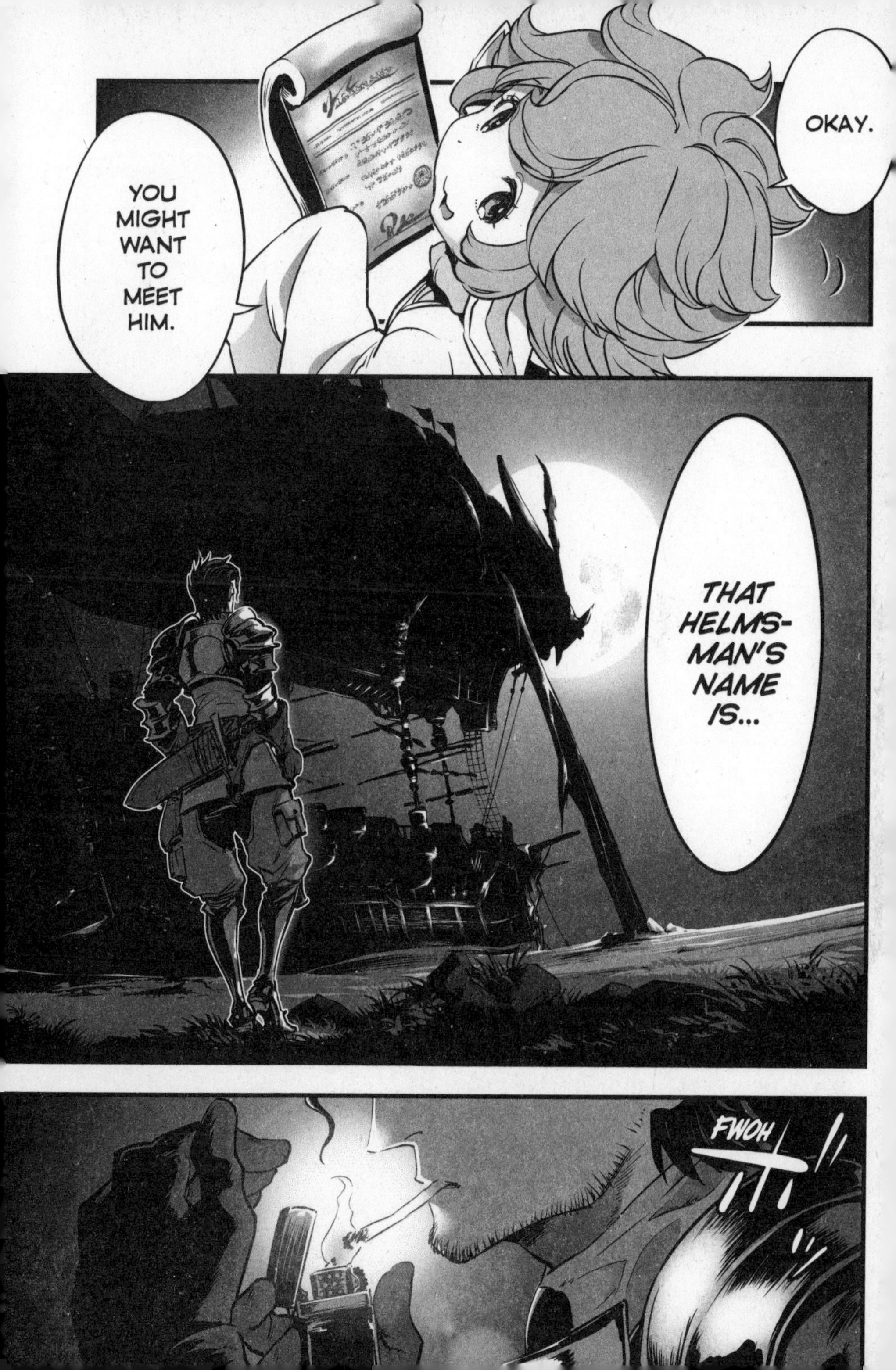
OKAY.
YOU MIGHT WANT TO MEET HIM.
THAT HELMS-MAN'S NAME IS...
FWOH

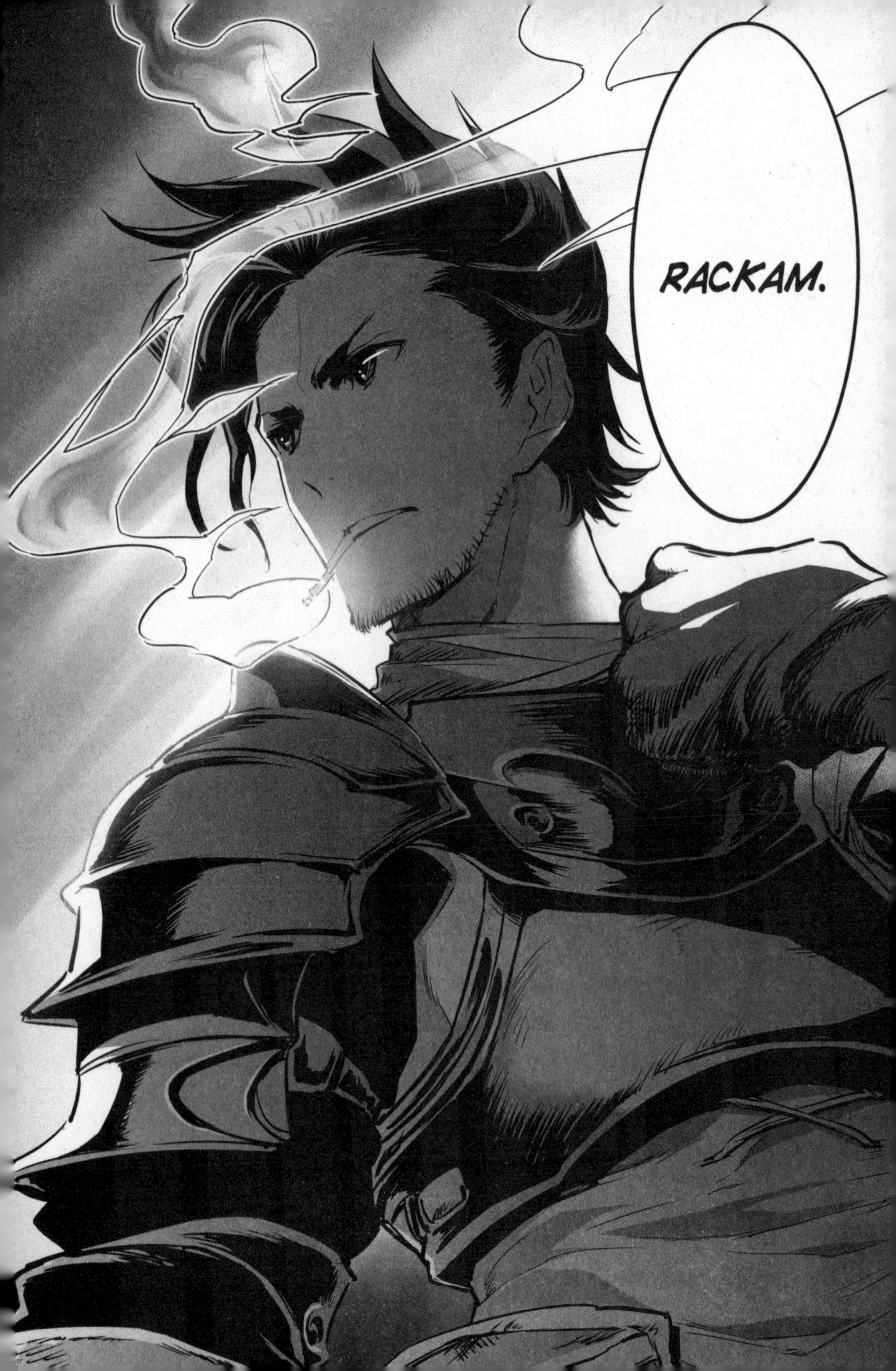
RACKAM.

CHAPTER 6:

Port Breeze Archipelago (2)

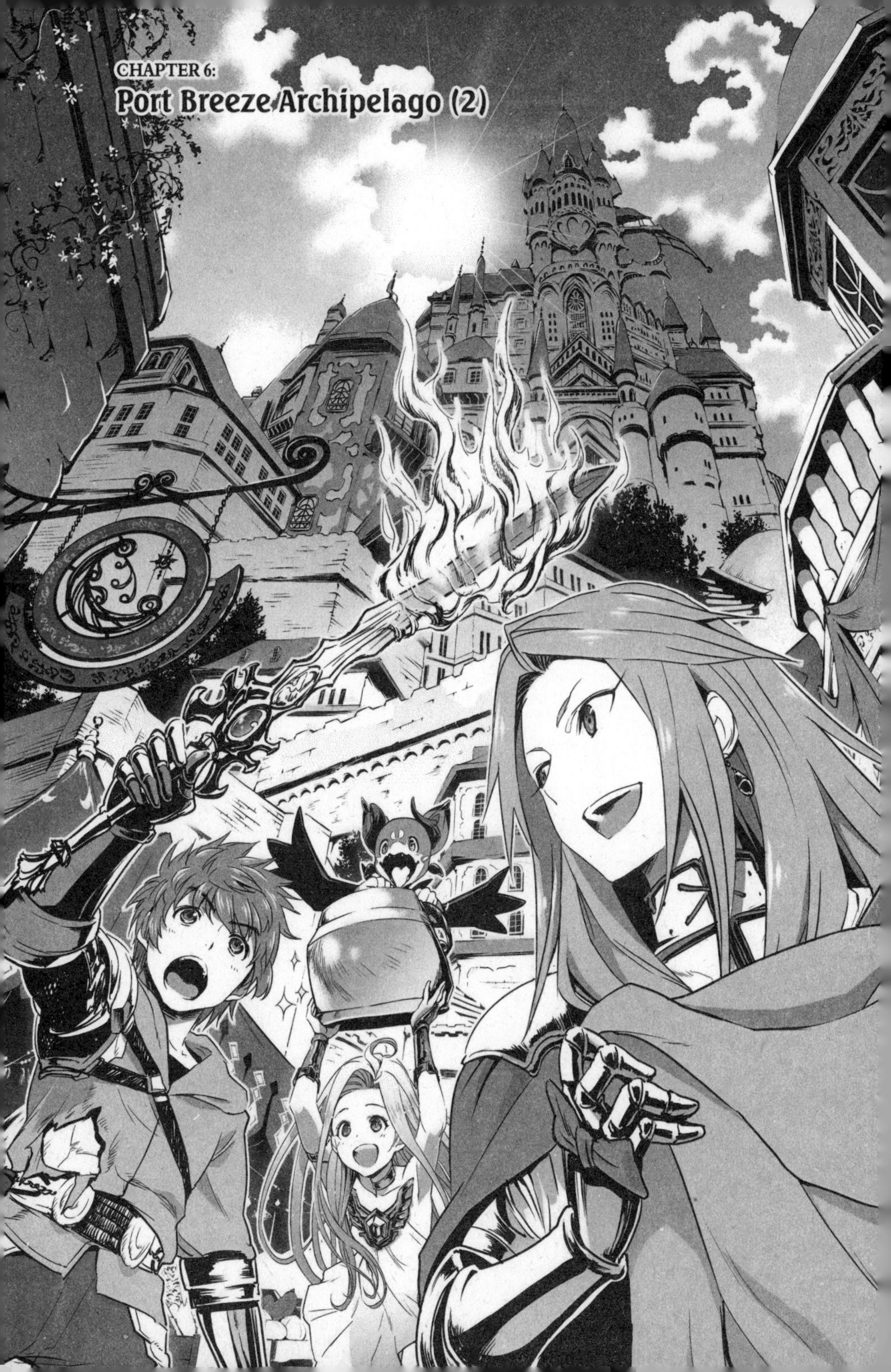

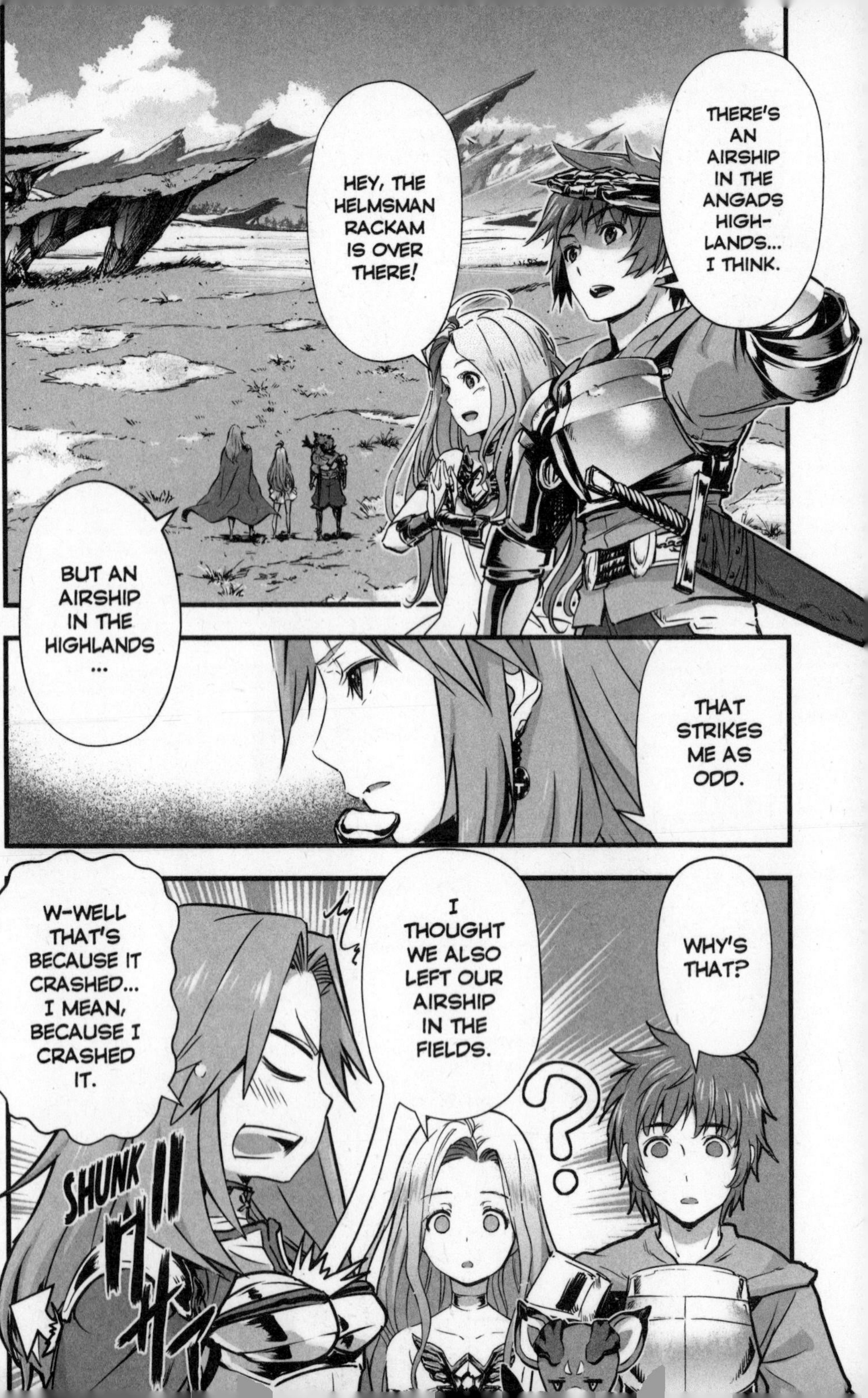
THERE'S AN AIRSHIP IN THE ANGADS HIGH-LANDS... I THINK.
HEY, THE HELMSMAN RACKAM IS OVER THERE!
BUT AN AIRSHIP IN THE HIGHLANDS ...
THAT STRIKES ME AS ODD.
WHY'S THAT?
I THOUGHT WE ALSO LEFT OUR AIRSHIP IN THE FIELDS.
W-WELL THAT'S BECAUSE IT CRASHED... I MEAN, BECAUSE I CRASHED IT.
SHUNK

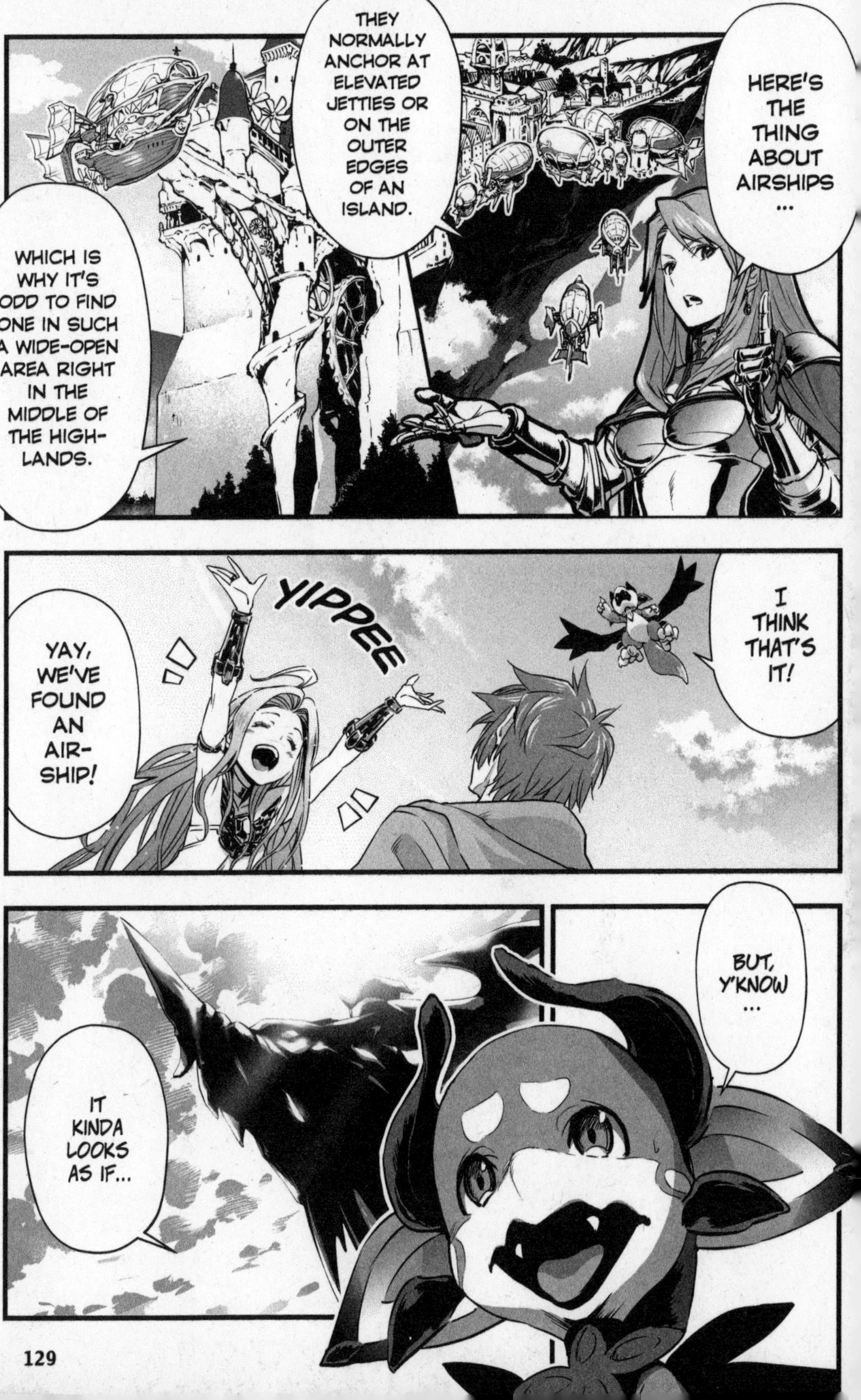
HERE'S THE THING ABOUT AIRSHIPS ...
THEY NORMALLY ANCHOR AT ELEVATED JETTIES OR ON THE OUTER EDGES OF AN ISLAND.
WHICH IS WHY IT'S ODD TO FIND ONE IN SUCH A WIDE-OPEN AREA RIGHT IN THE MIDDLE OF THE HIGH-LANDS.
I THINK THAT'S IT!
YIPPEE
YAY, WE'VE FOUND AN AIR-SHIP!
BUT, Y'KNOW ...
IT KINDA LOOKS AS IF...

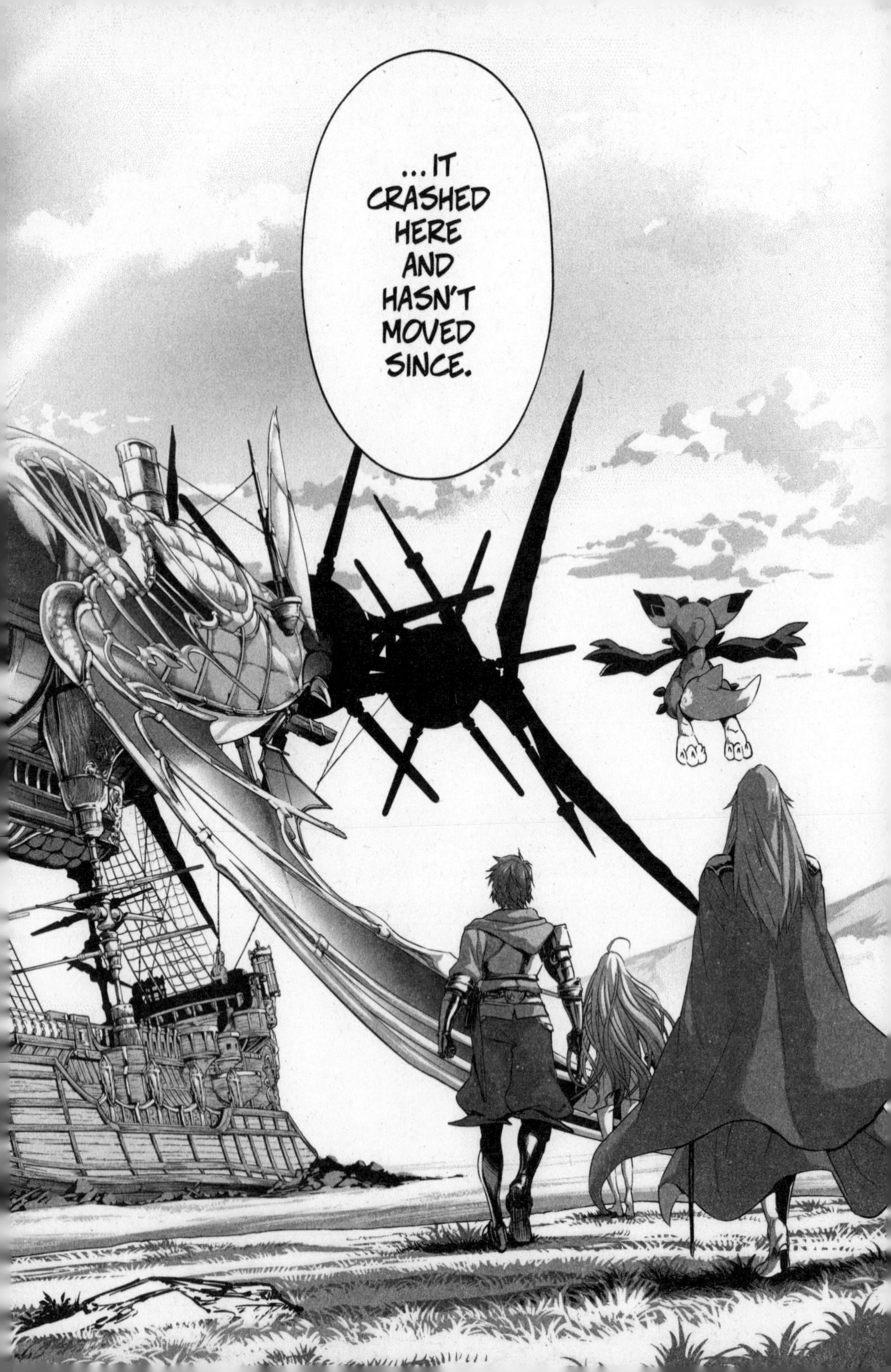
...IT CRASHED HERE AND HASN'T MOVED SINCE.

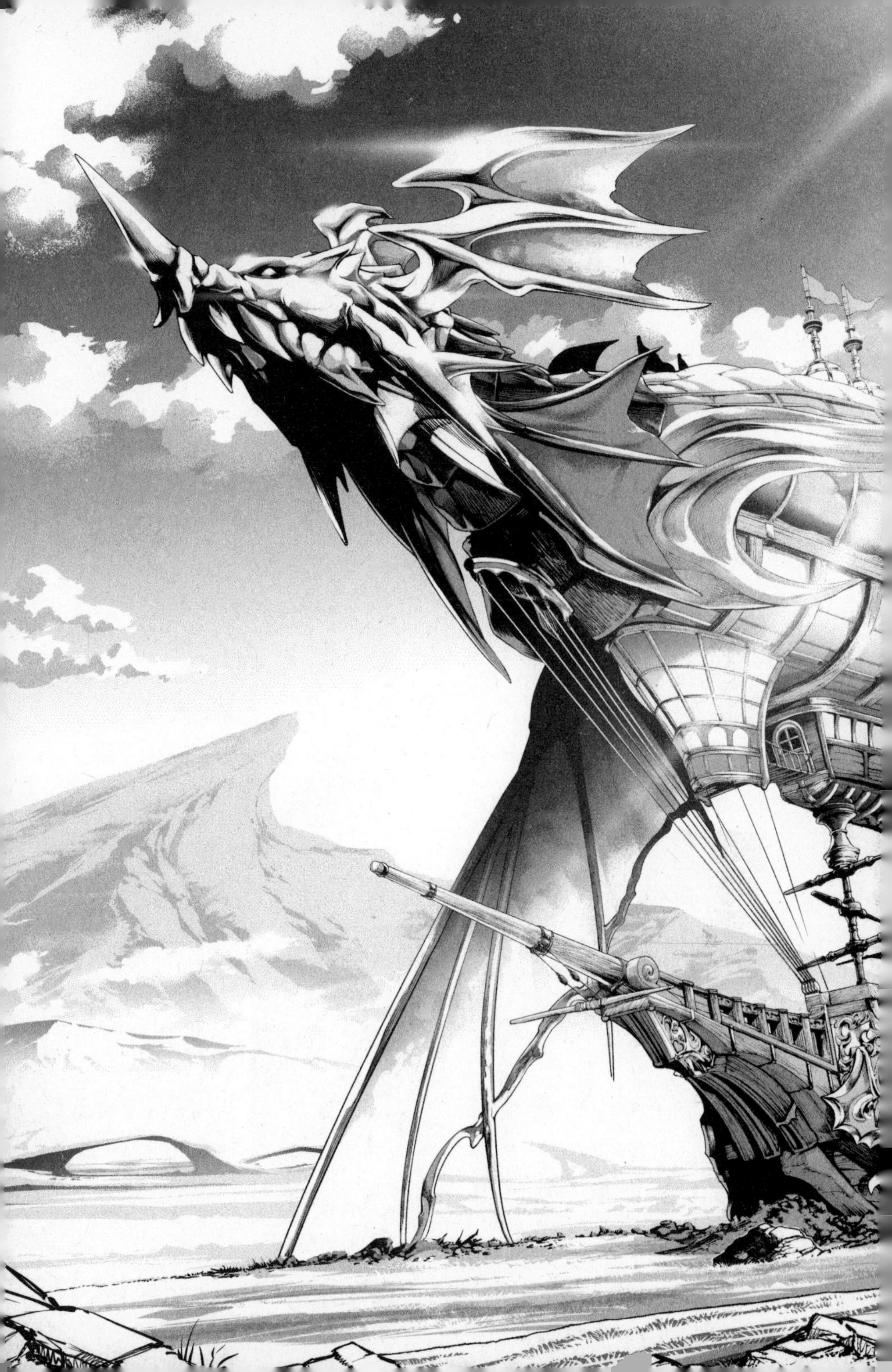

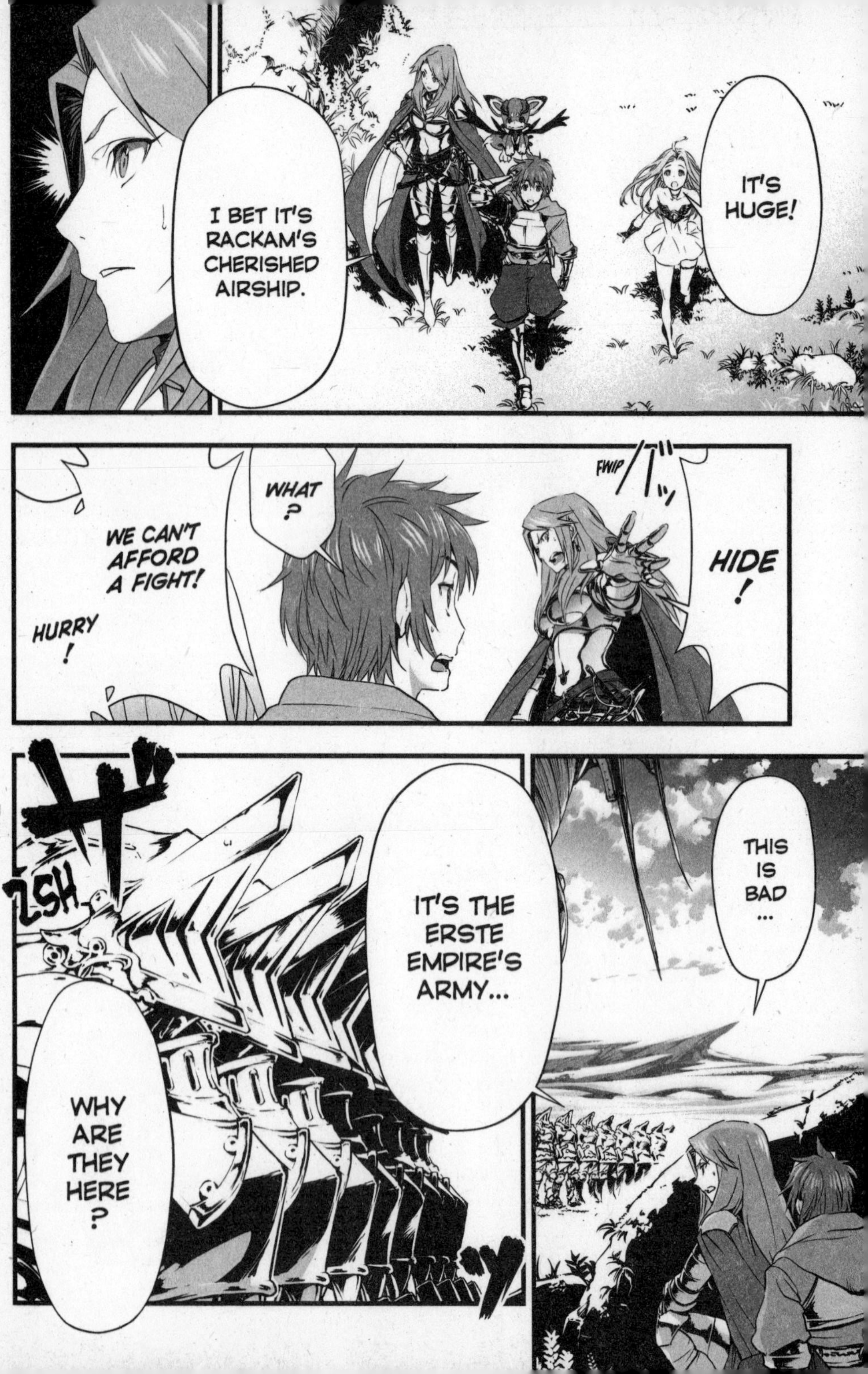
IT'S HUGE!
I BET IT'S RACKAM'S CHERISHED AIRSHIP.
FWIP
HIDE!
WHAT?
WE CAN'T AFFORD A FIGHT!
HURRY!
THIS IS BAD...
ZSH
IT'S THE ERSTE EMPIRE'S ARMY...
WHY ARE THEY HERE?

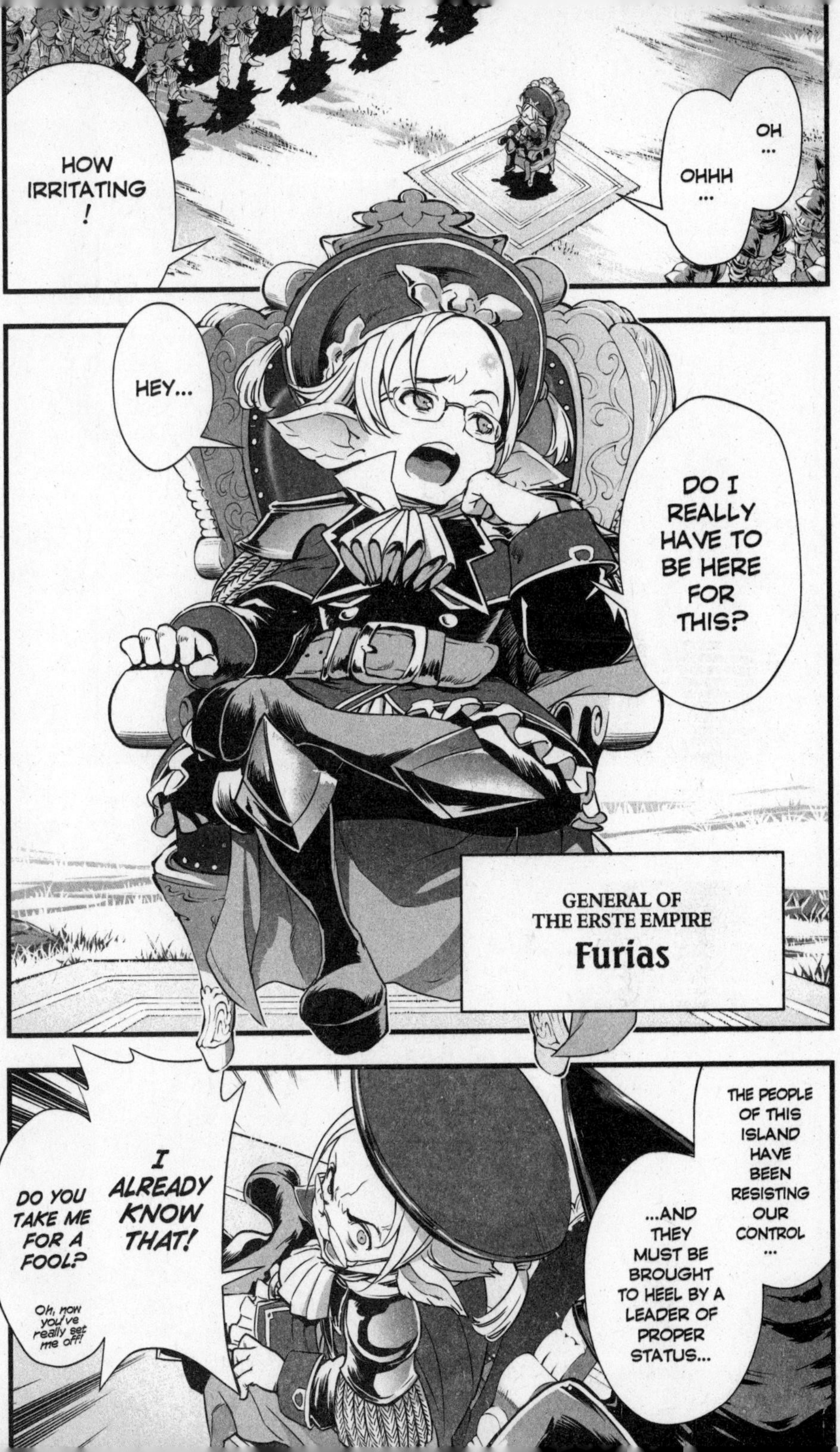
OH... OHHH...
HOW IRRITATING!
HEY...
DO I REALLY HAVE TO BE HERE FOR THIS?
GENERAL OF THE ERSTE EMPIRE
Furias
THE PEOPLE OF THIS ISLAND HAVE BEEN RESISTING OUR CONTROL...
...AND THEY MUST BE BROUGHT TO HEEL BY A LEADER OF PROPER STATUS...
I ALREADY KNOW THAT!
DO YOU TAKE ME FOR A FOOL?
Oh, now you've really set me off!

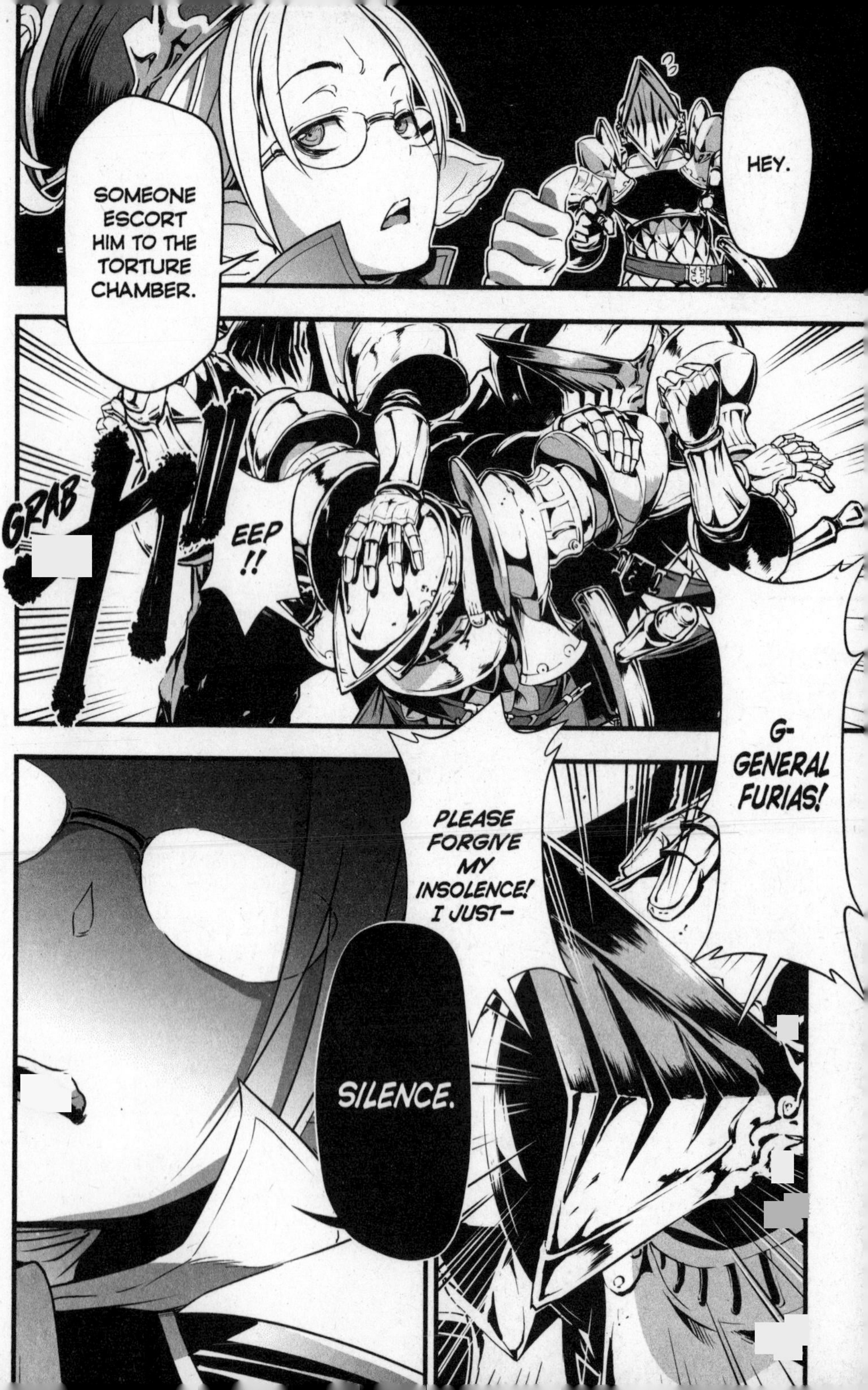
HEY.
SOMEONE ESCORT HIM TO THE TORTURE CHAMBER.
GRAB
EEP!!
G-GENERAL FURIAS!
PLEASE FORGIVE MY INSOLENCE! I JUST–
SILENCE.

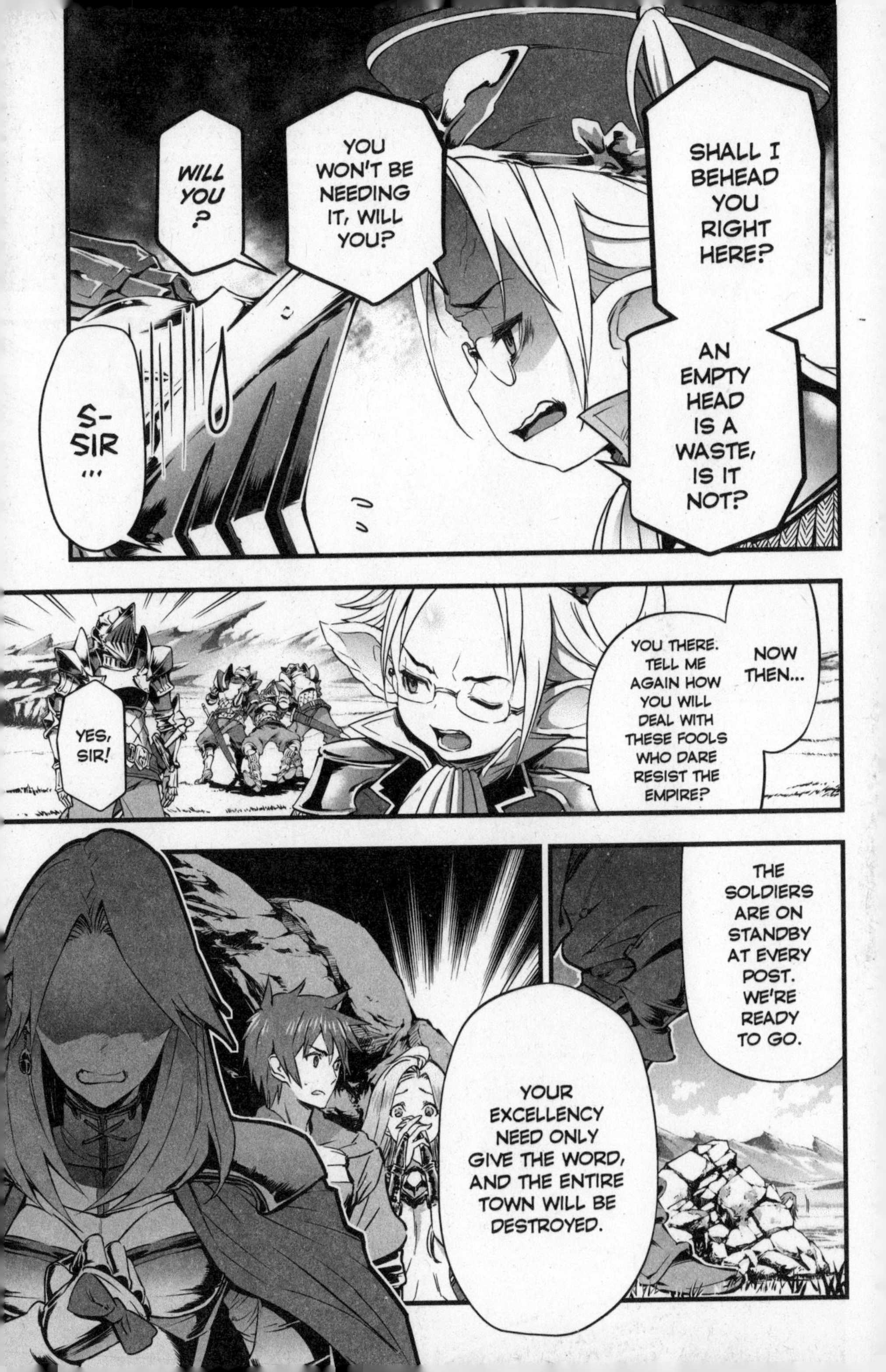
SHALL I BEHEAD YOU RIGHT HERE?
AN EMPTY HEAD IS A WASTE, IS IT NOT?
YOU WON'T BE NEEDING IT, WILL YOU?
WILL YOU?
S-SIR...
NOW THEN...
YOU THERE. TELL ME AGAIN HOW YOU WILL DEAL WITH THESE FOOLS WHO DARE RESIST THE EMPIRE?
YES, SIR!
THE SOLDIERS ARE ON STANDBY AT EVERY POST. WE'RE READY TO GO.
YOUR EXCELLENCY NEED ONLY GIVE THE WORD, AND THE ENTIRE TOWN WILL BE DESTROYED.

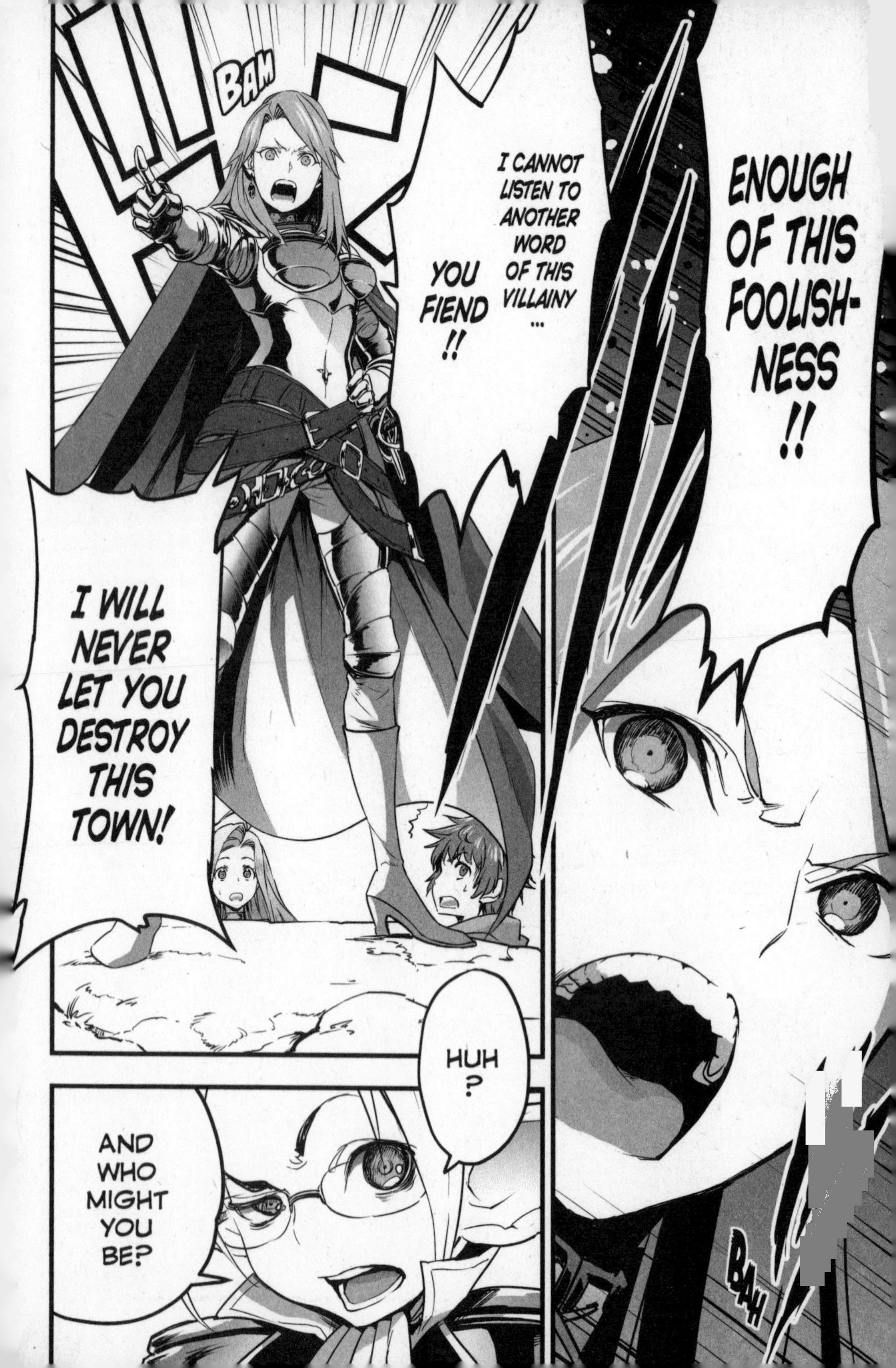
ENOUGH OF THIS FOOLISH-NESS!!
BAH
I CANNOT LISTEN TO ANOTHER WORD OF THIS VILLAINY...
YOU FIEND!!
BAM
I WILL NEVER LET YOU DESTROY THIS TOWN!
HUH?
AND WHO MIGHT YOU BE?

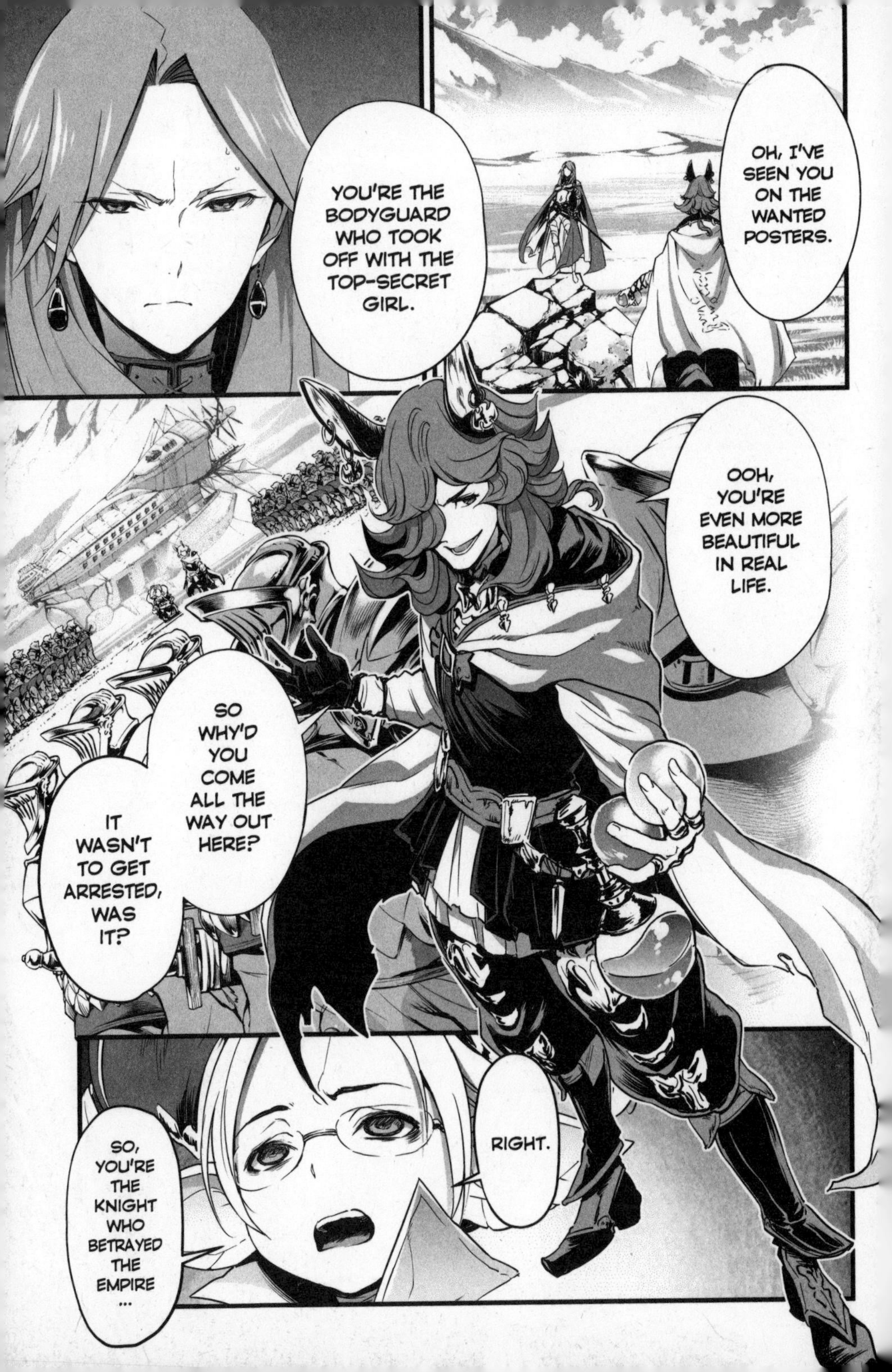
OH, I'VE SEEN YOU ON THE WANTED POSTERS.
YOU'RE THE BODYGUARD WHO TOOK OFF WITH THE TOP-SECRET GIRL.
OOH, YOU'RE EVEN MORE BEAUTIFUL IN REAL LIFE.
SO WHY'D YOU COME ALL THE WAY OUT HERE?
IT WASN'T TO GET ARRESTED, WAS IT?
RIGHT.
SO, YOU'RE THE KNIGHT WHO BETRAYED THE EMPIRE ...

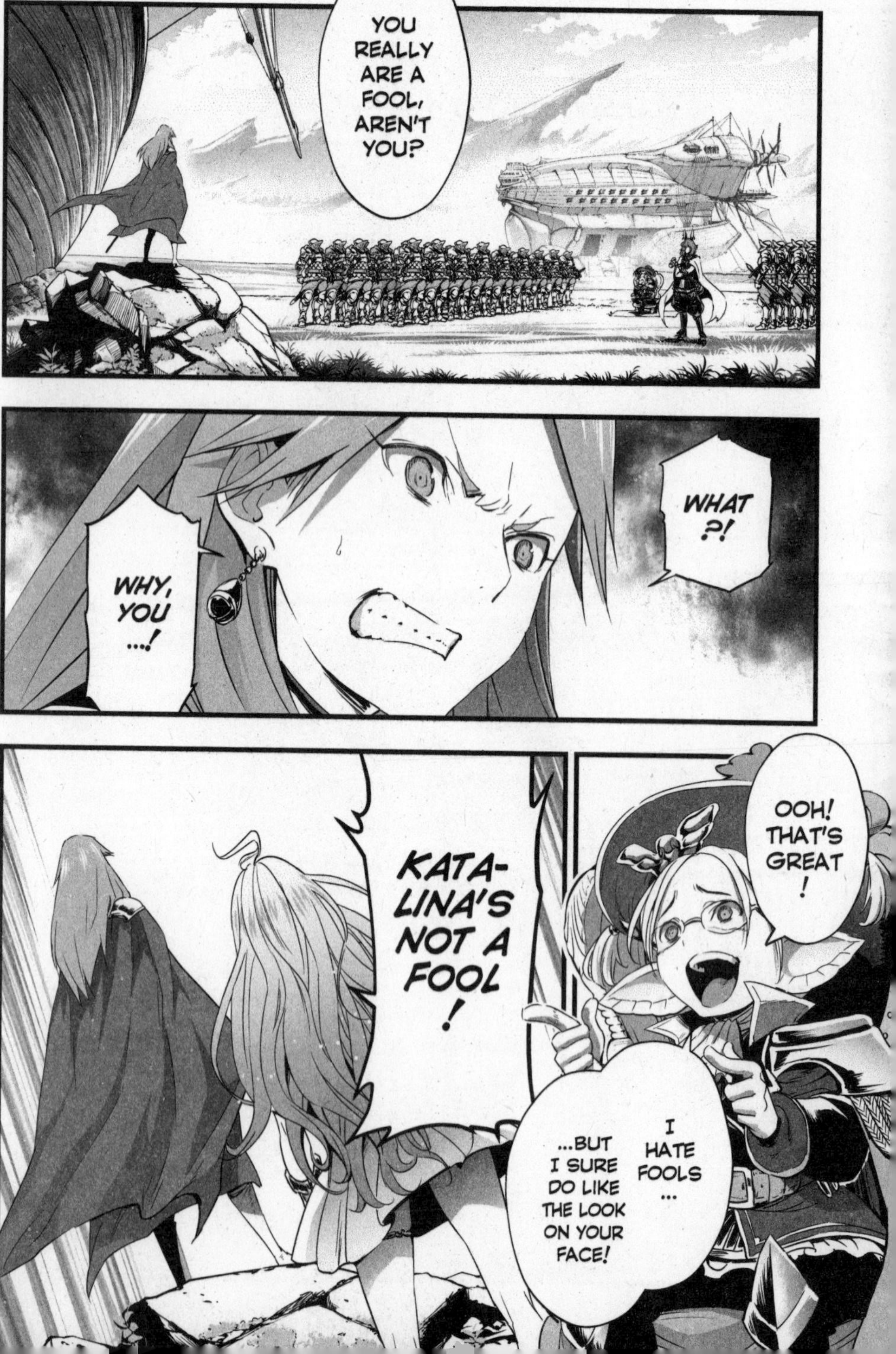
YOU REALLY ARE A FOOL, AREN'T YOU?
WHAT?!
WHY, YOU ...!
OOH! THAT'S GREAT!
I HATE FOOLS ...
...BUT I SURE DO LIKE THE LOOK ON YOUR FACE!
KATA-LINA'S NOT A FOOL!

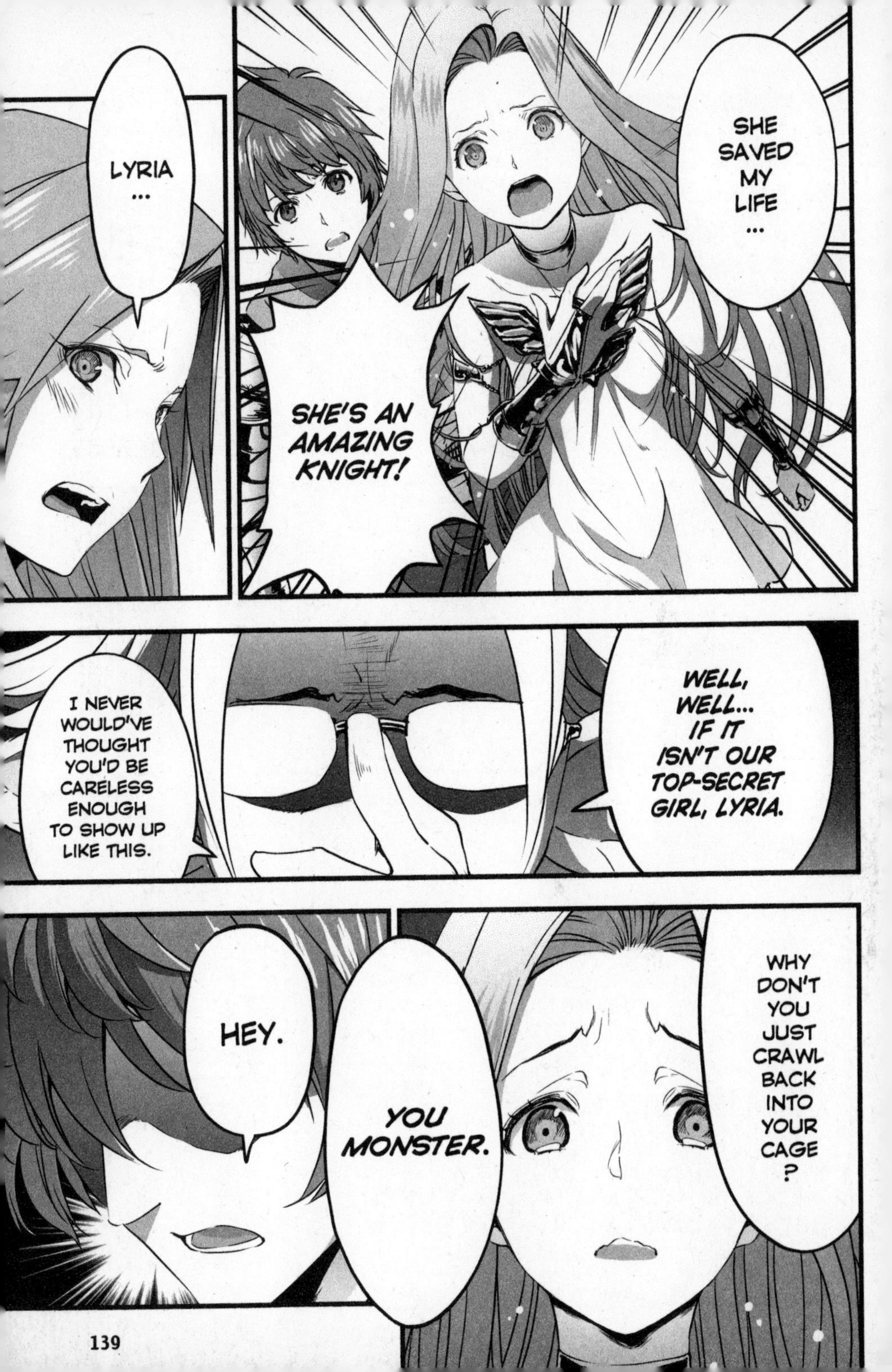
SHE SAVED MY LIFE ...
SHE'S AN AMAZING KNIGHT!
LYRIA ...
WELL, WELL... IF IT ISN'T OUR TOP-SECRET GIRL, LYRIA.
I NEVER WOULD'VE THOUGHT YOU'D BE CARELESS ENOUGH TO SHOW UP LIKE THIS.
WHY DON'T YOU JUST CRAWL BACK INTO YOUR CAGE ?
YOU MONSTER.
HEY.

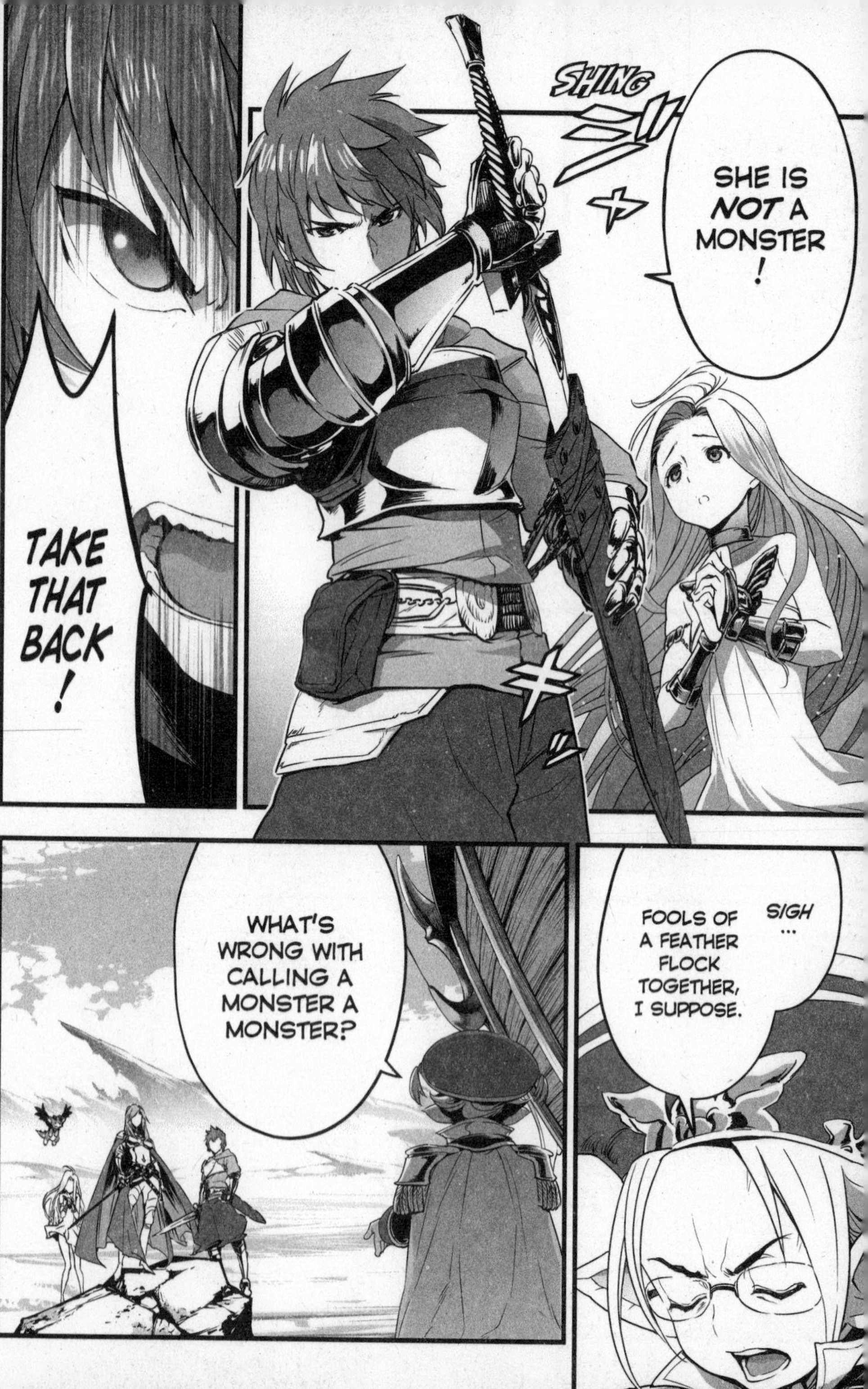
SHING
SHE IS NOT A MONSTER!
TAKE THAT BACK!
SIGH...
FOOLS OF A FEATHER FLOCK TOGETHER, I SUPPOSE.
WHAT'S WRONG WITH CALLING A MONSTER A MONSTER?

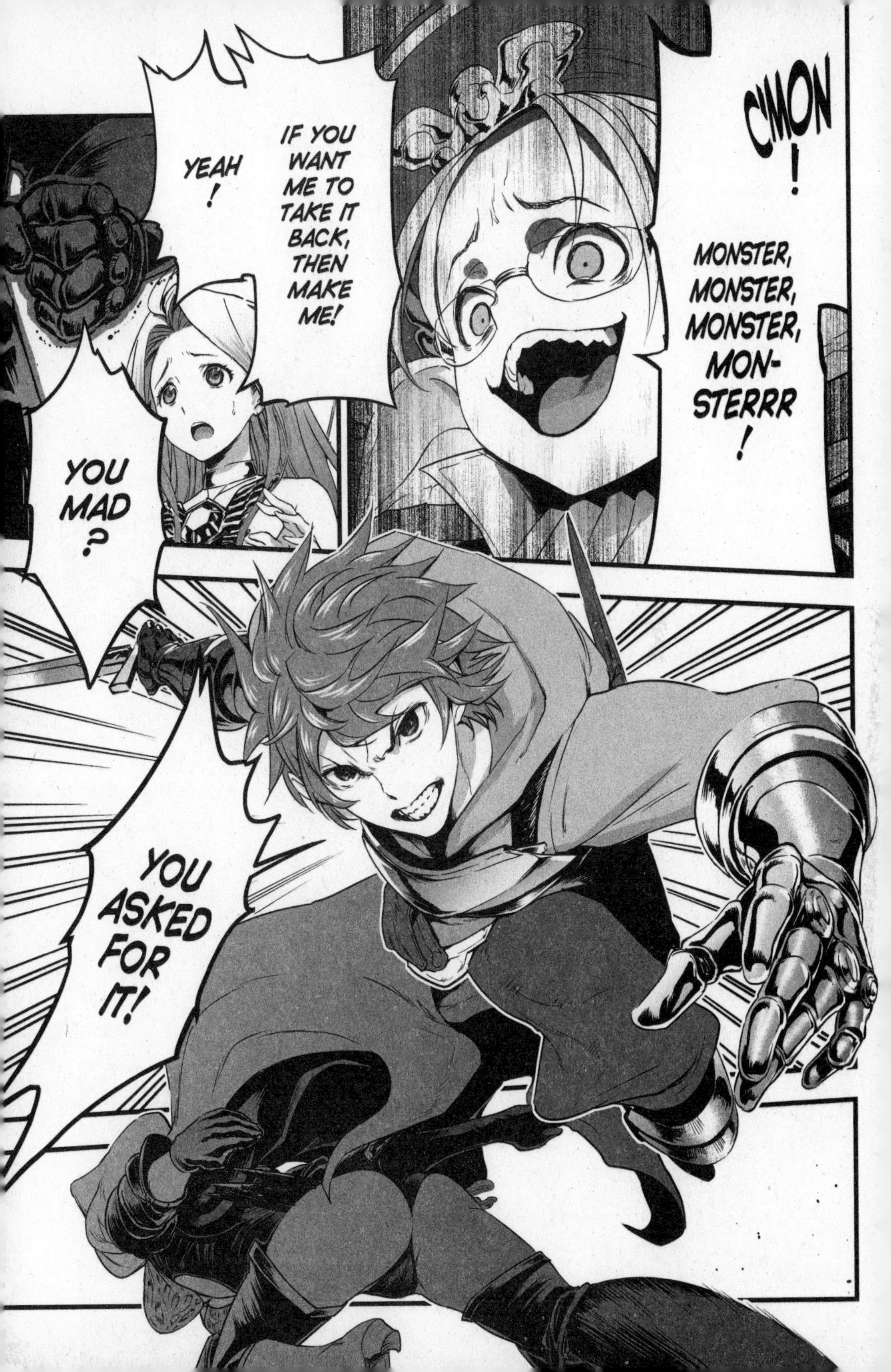
C'MON!
MONSTER, MONSTER, MONSTER, MON-STERRR!
YEAH! IF YOU WANT ME TO TAKE IT BACK, THEN MAKE ME!
YOU MAD?
YOU ASKED FOR IT!

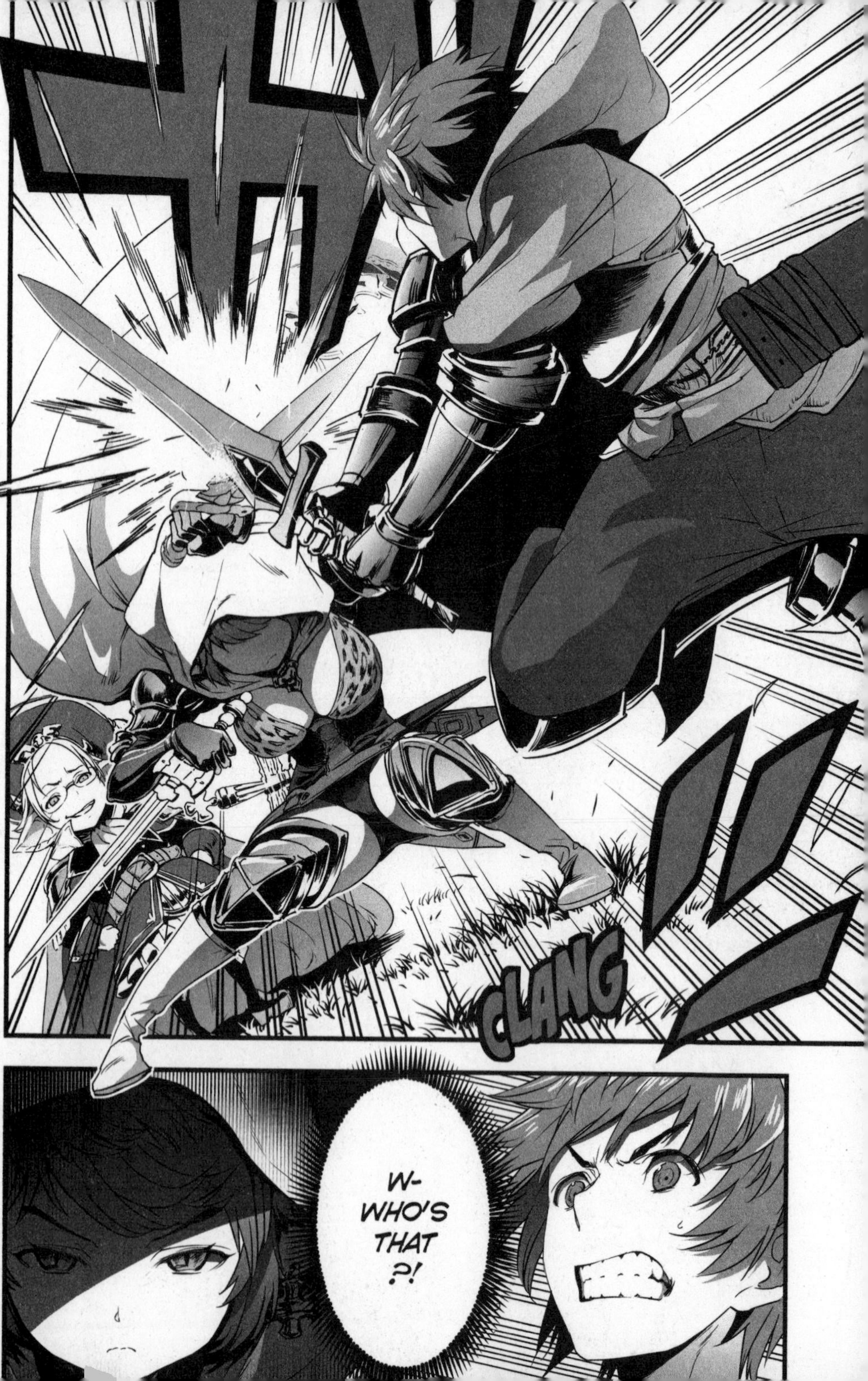
CLANG
W-WHO'S THAT?!

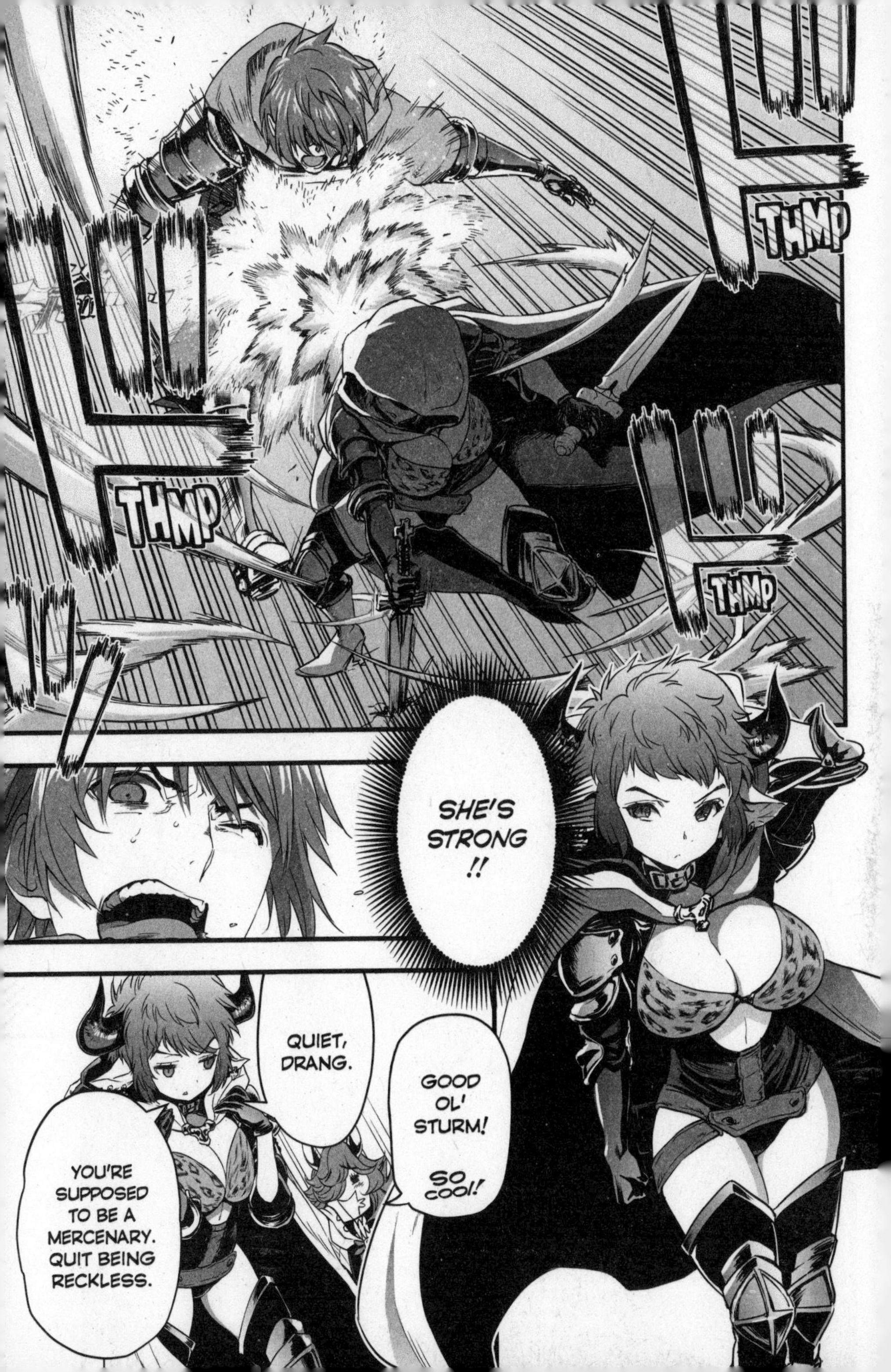
THMP
THMP
THMP
SHE'S STRONG !!
GOOD OL' STURM!
SO COOL!
QUIET, DRANG.
YOU'RE SUPPOSED TO BE A MERCENARY. QUIT BEING RECKLESS.

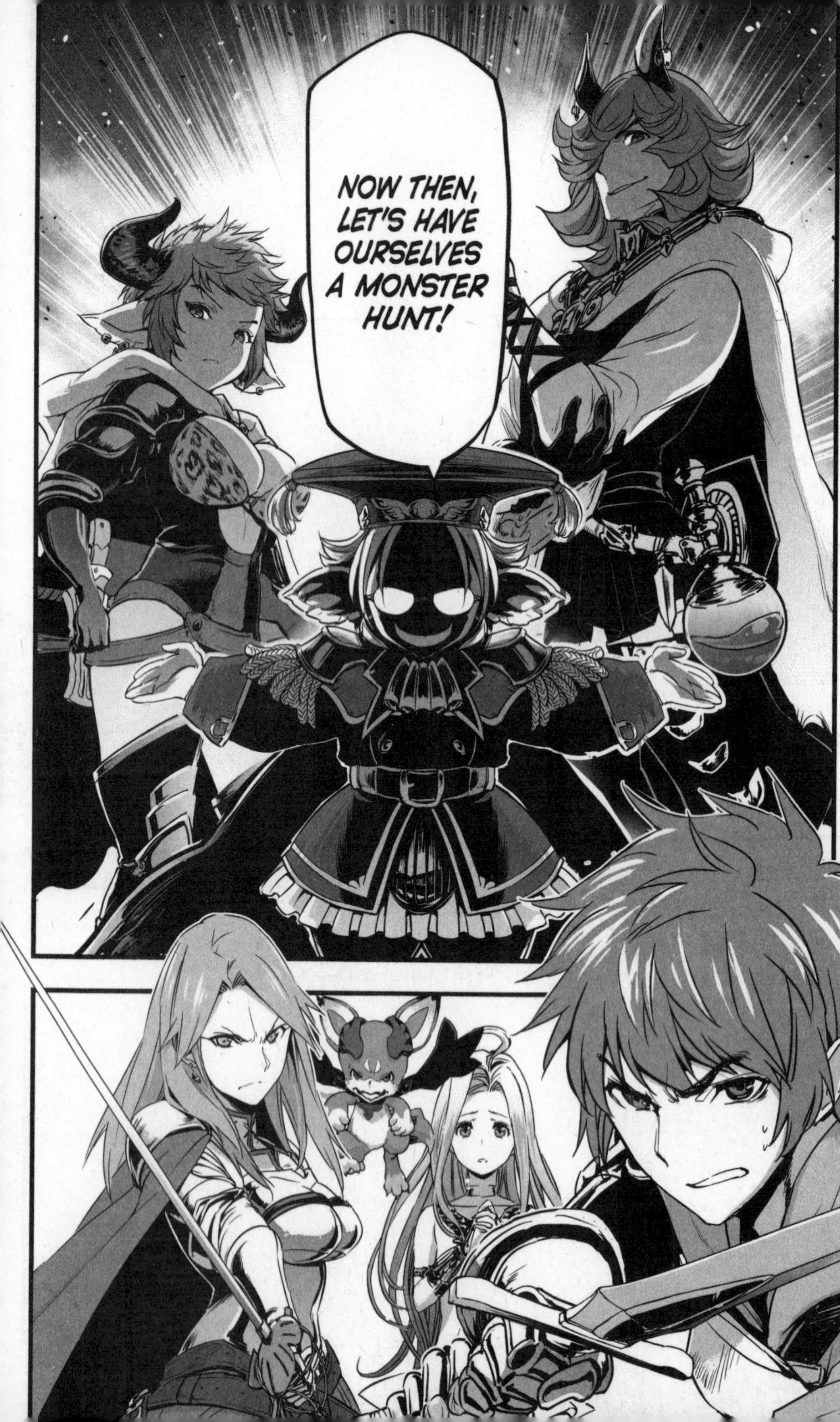
NOW THEN, LET'S HAVE OURSELVES A MONSTER HUNT!

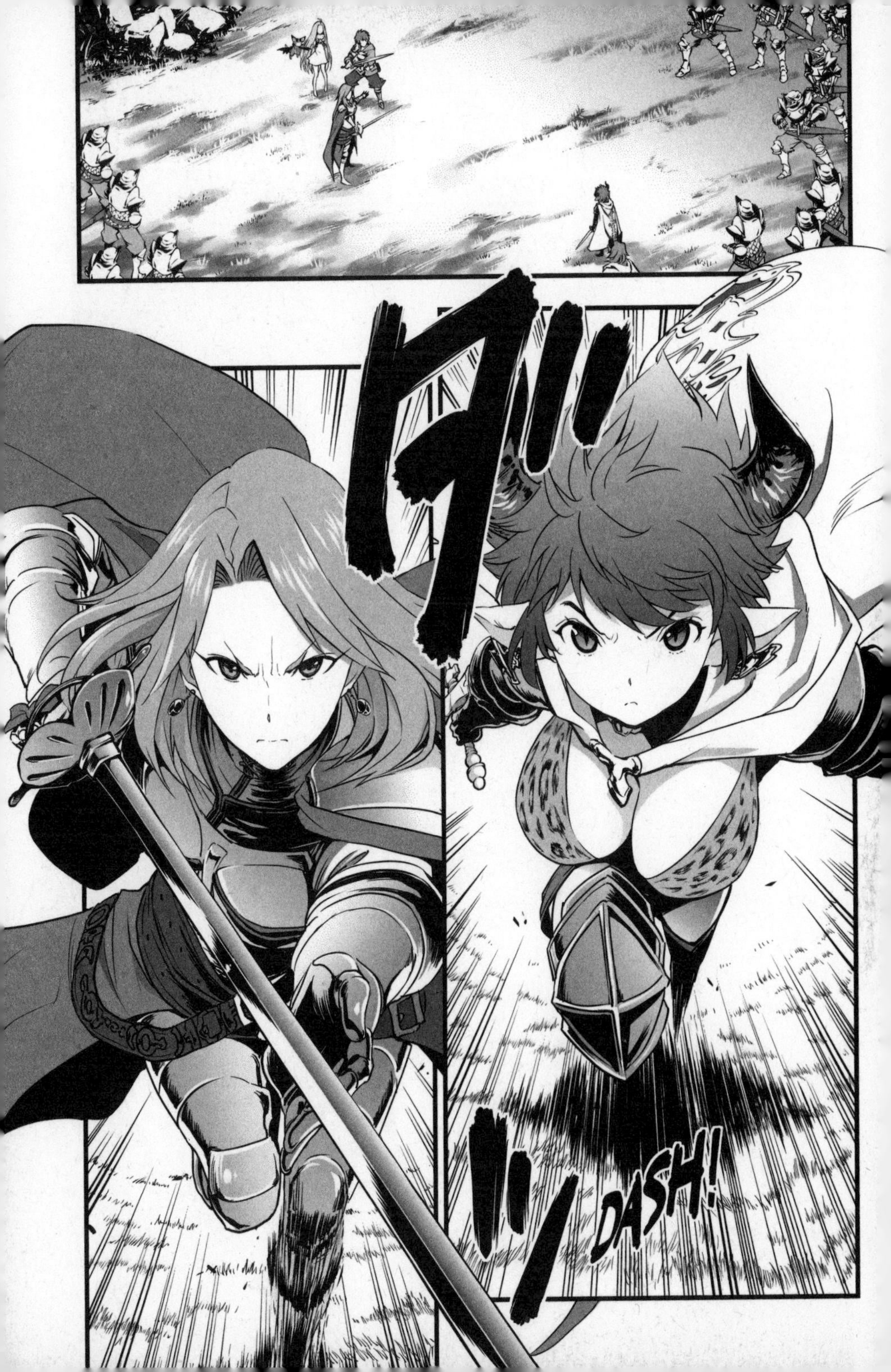
DASH!

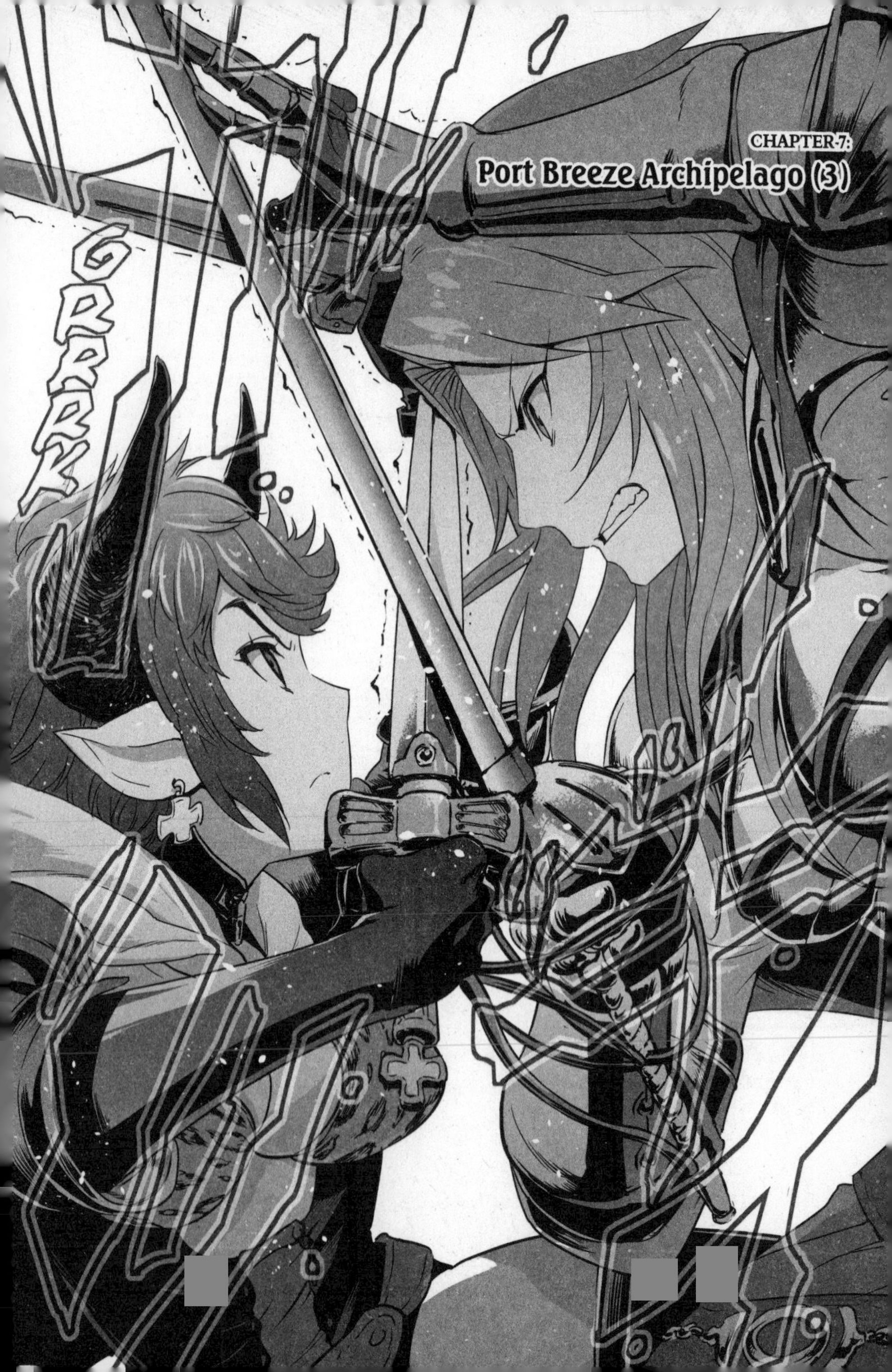
CHAPTER 7:
Port Breeze Archipelago (3)
GRRRK

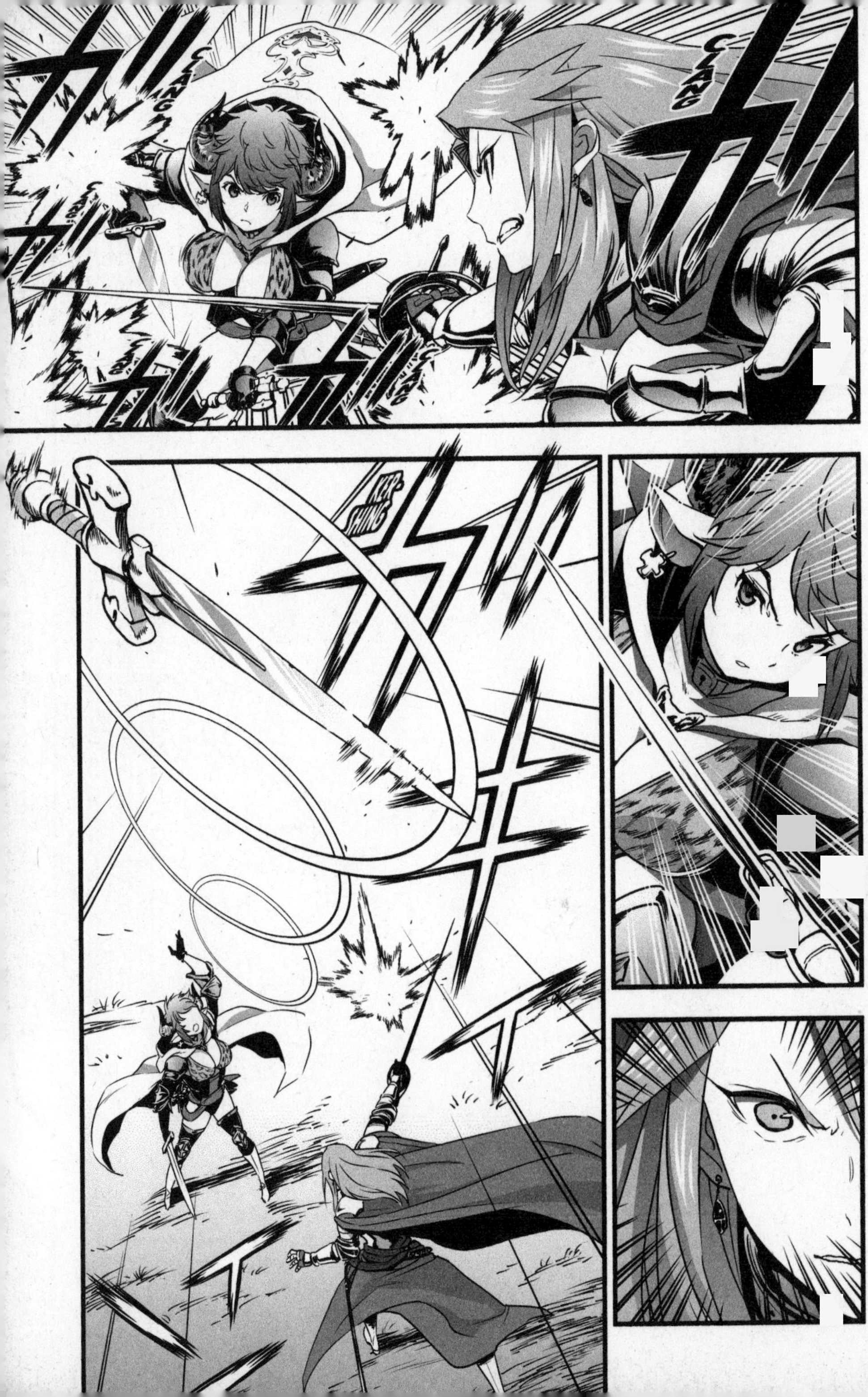
CLANG
CLANG
CLANG
KER-SHING

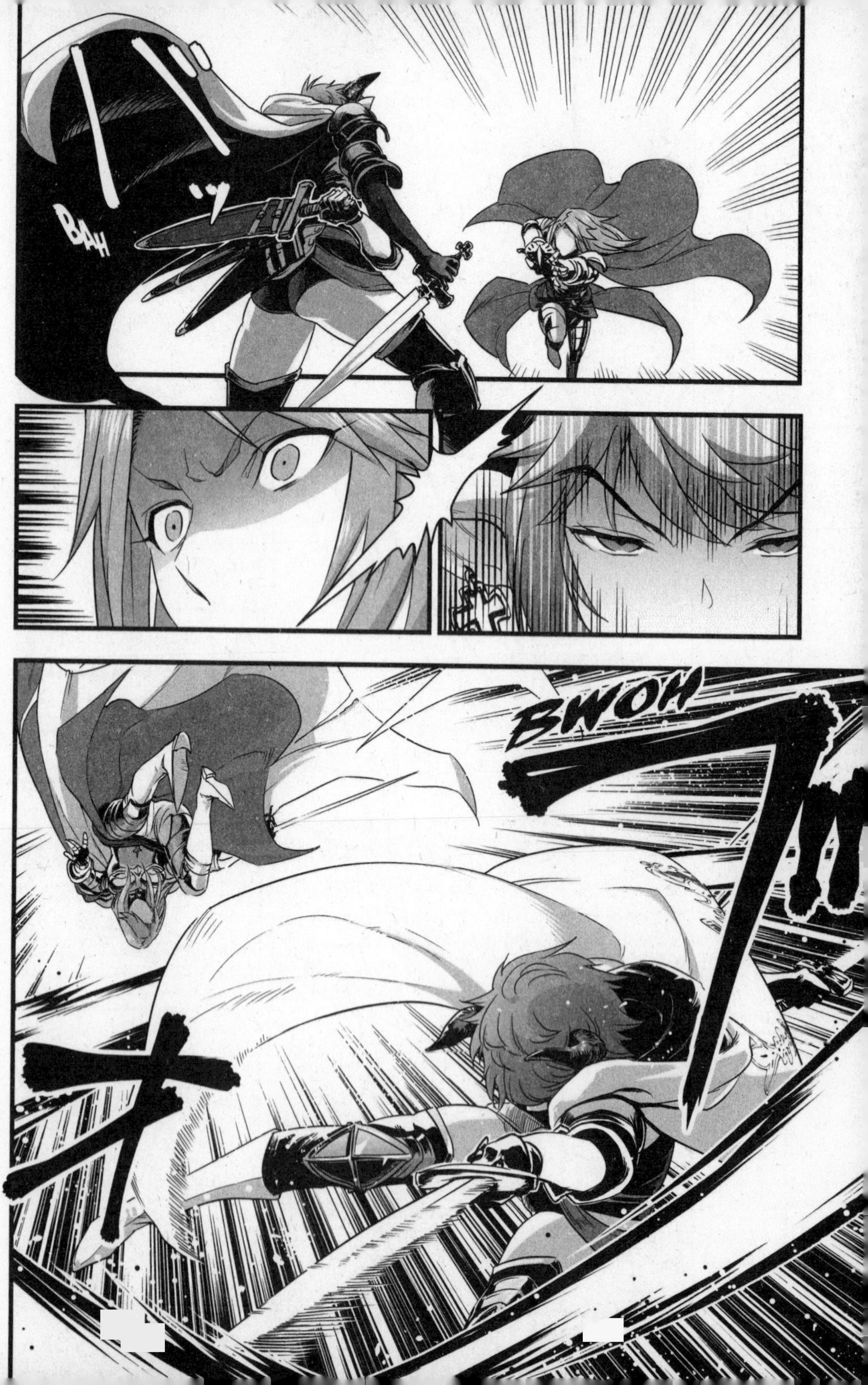
BAH
BWOH

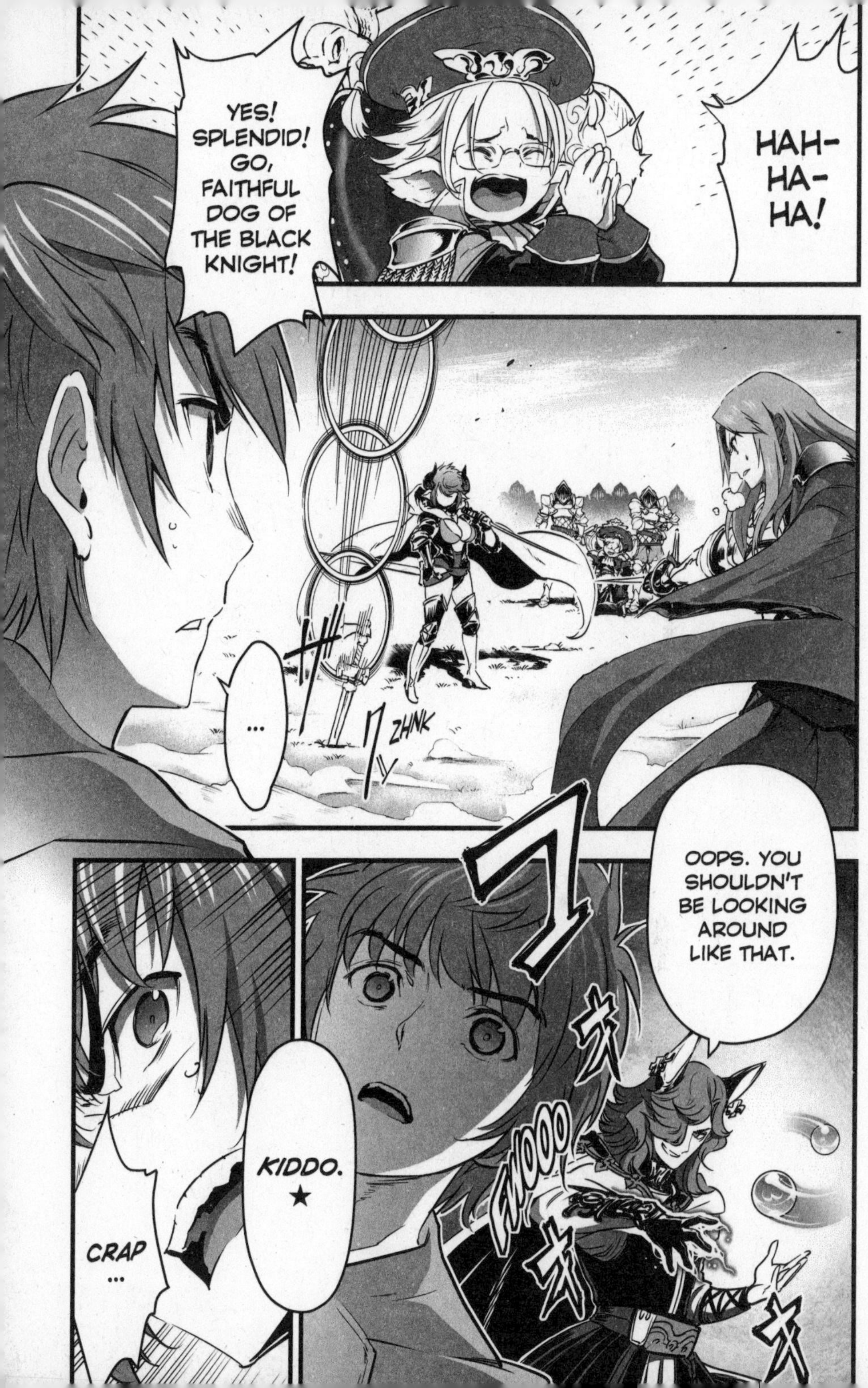
HAH-HA-HA!
YES! SPLENDID! GO, FAITHFUL DOG OF THE BLACK KNIGHT!
ZHNK
...
OOPS. YOU SHOULDN'T BE LOOKING AROUND LIKE THAT.
KIDDO. ★
FWOOO
CRAP ...

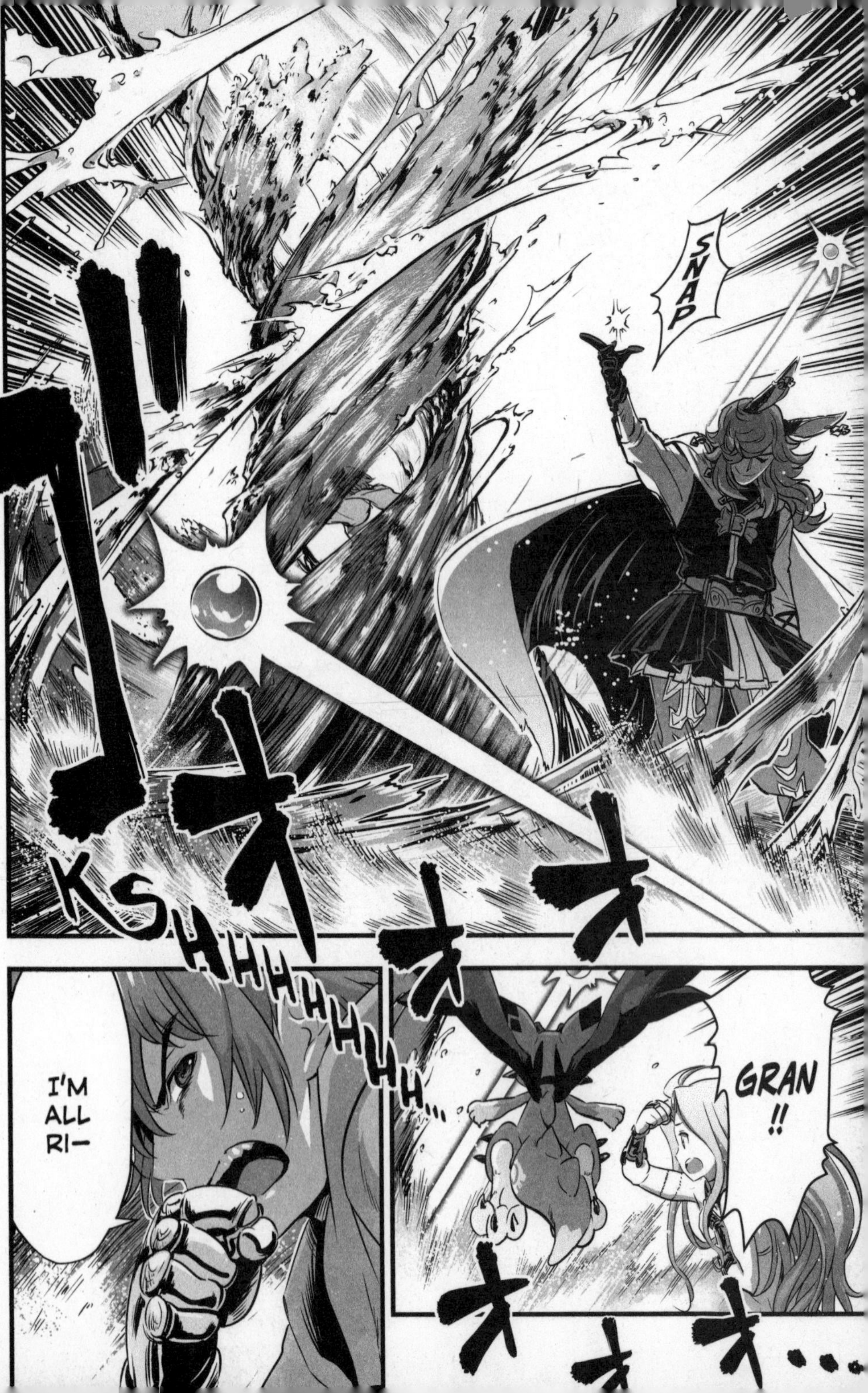
SNAP
KSHHHHHHHHH...
GRAN!!
I'M ALL RI—

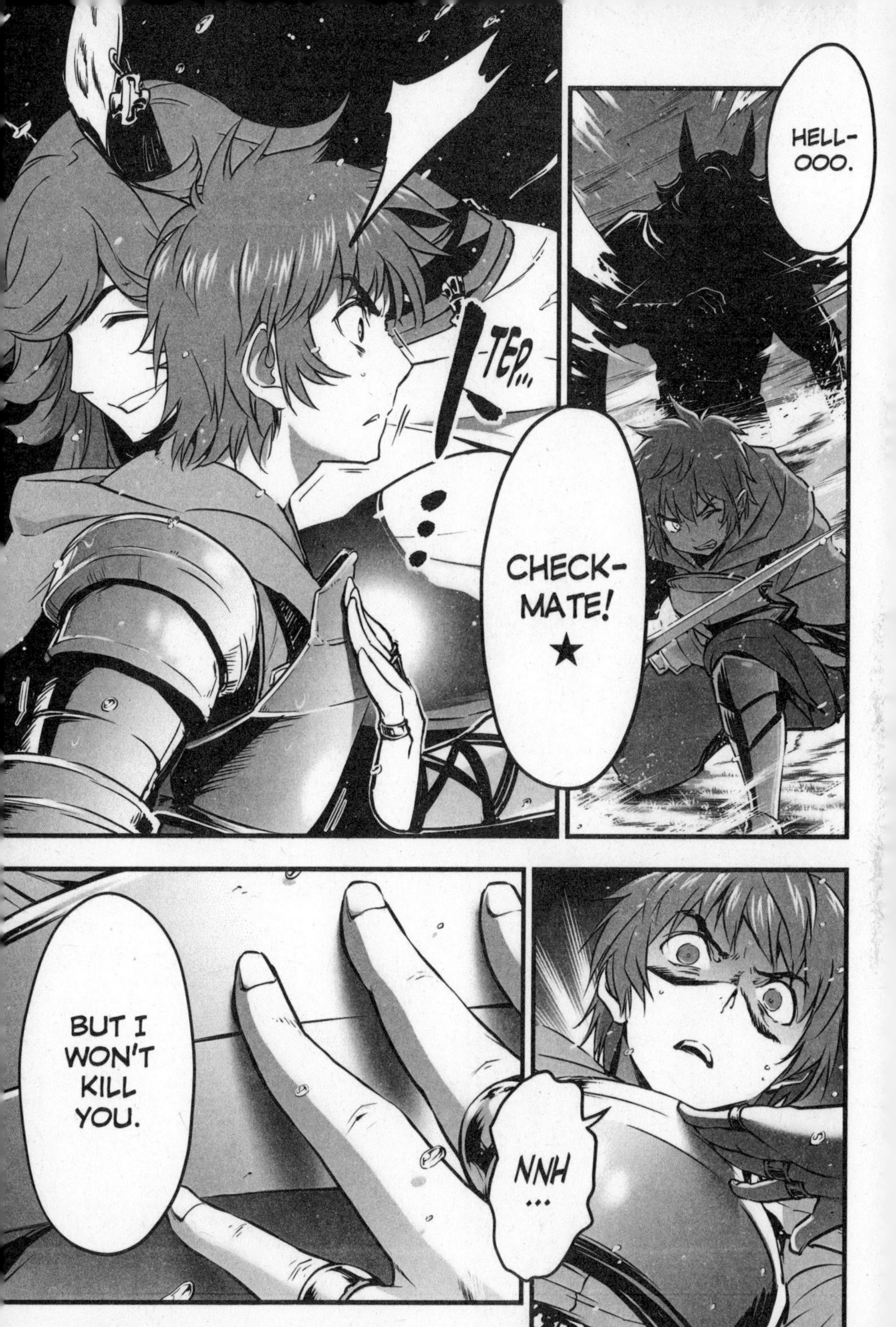
HELL-OOO.
CHECK-MATE! ★
-TEP...
...
NNH...
BUT I WON'T KILL YOU.

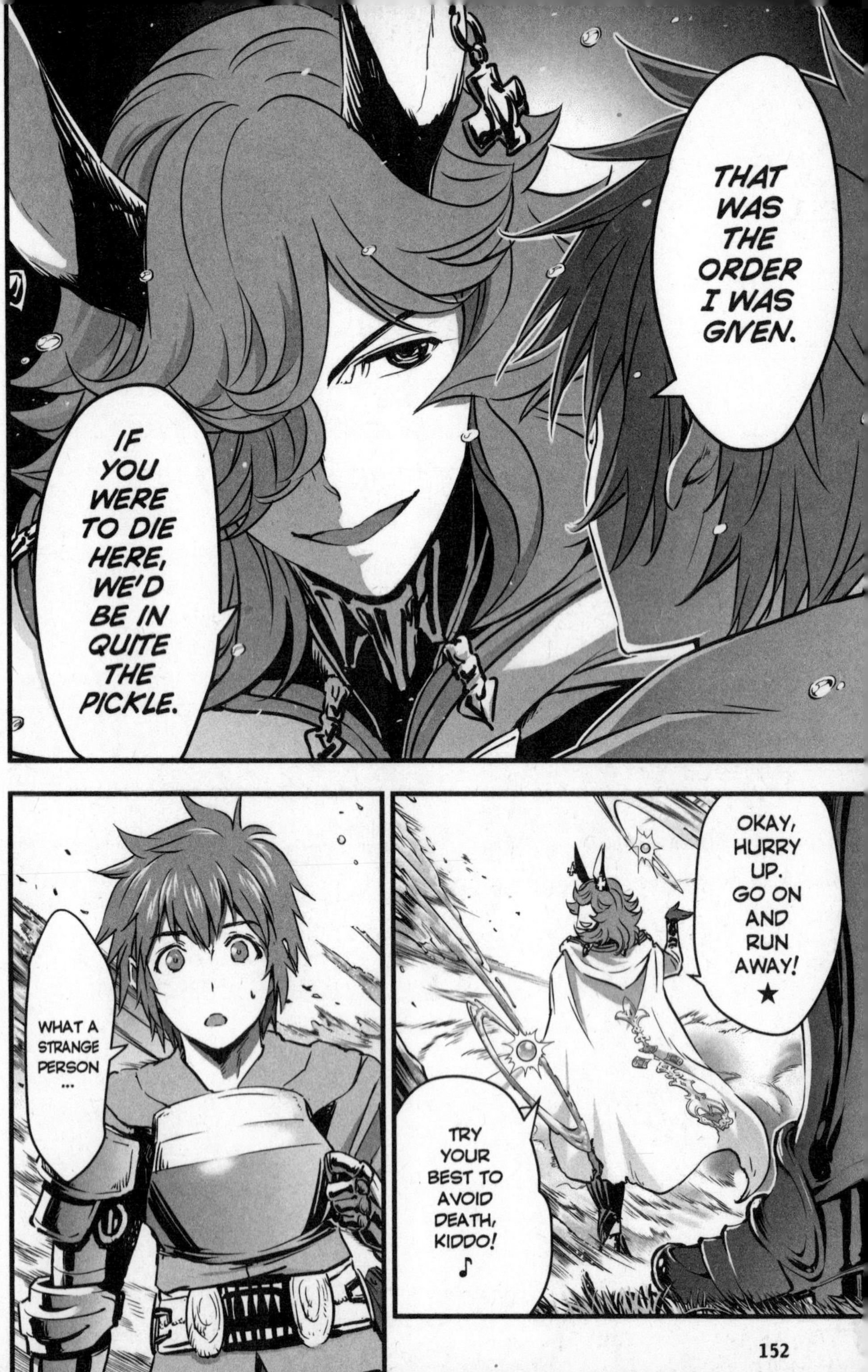
THAT WAS THE ORDER I WAS GIVEN.
IF YOU WERE TO DIE HERE, WE'D BE IN QUITE THE PICKLE.
OKAY, HURRY UP. GO ON AND RUN AWAY! ★
TRY YOUR BEST TO AVOID DEATH, KIDDO! ♪
WHAT A STRANGE PERSON...

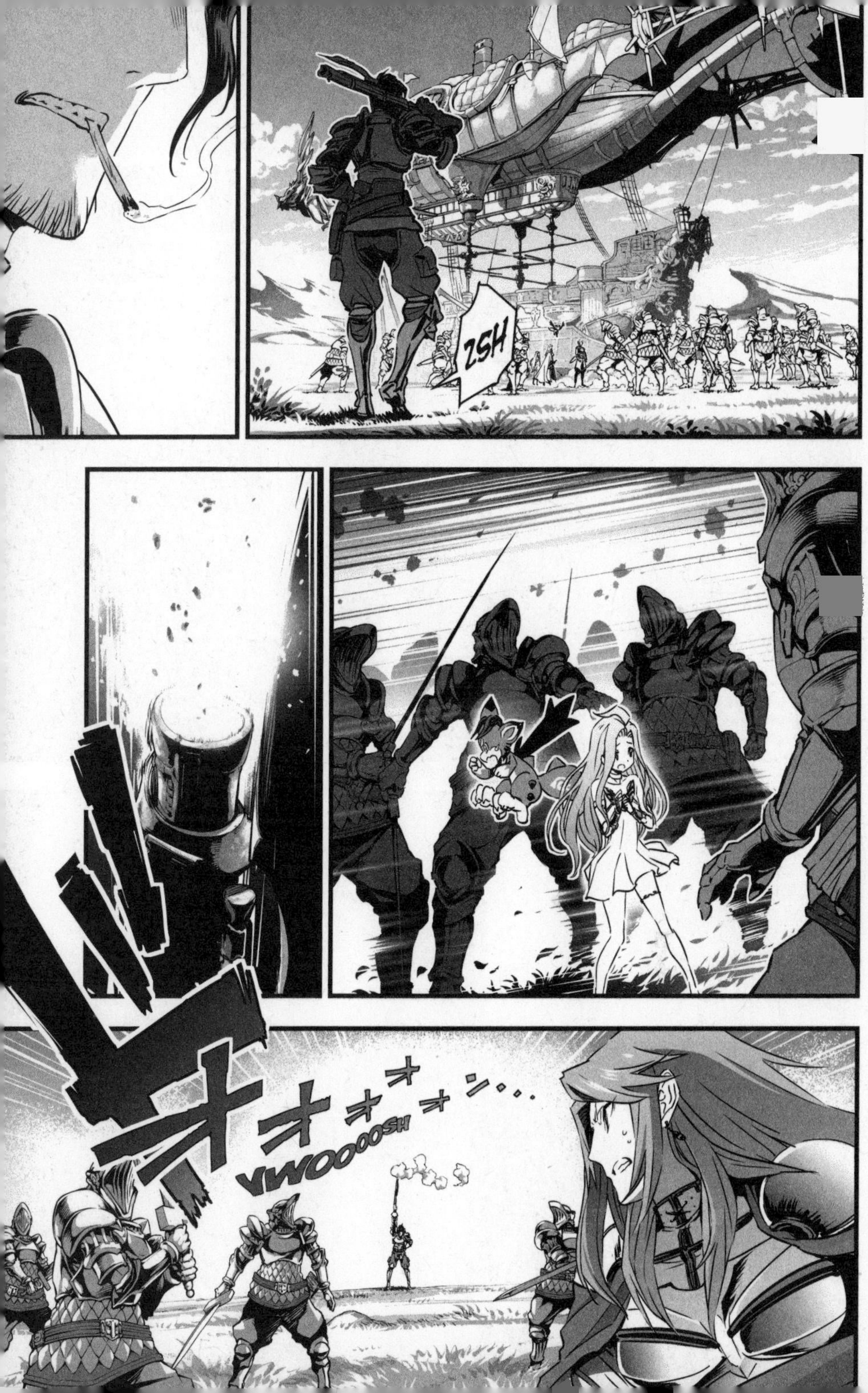
ZSH
ドオオオオオン。。。
VWOOOOOSH

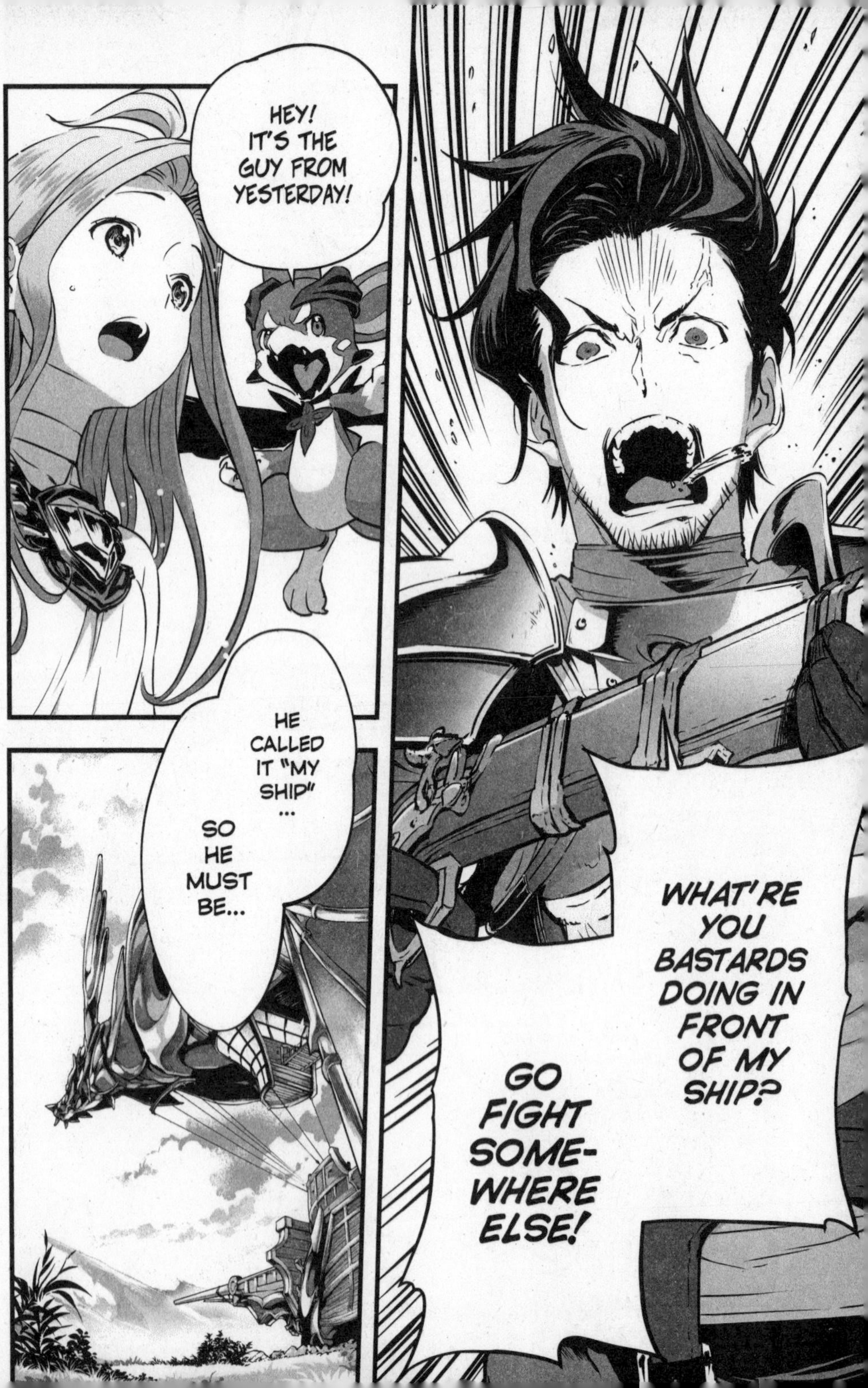
WHAT'RE YOU BASTARDS DOING IN FRONT OF MY SHIP?
GO FIGHT SOME-WHERE ELSE!
HEY! IT'S THE GUY FROM YESTERDAY!
HE CALLED IT "MY SHIP"...
SO HE MUST BE...

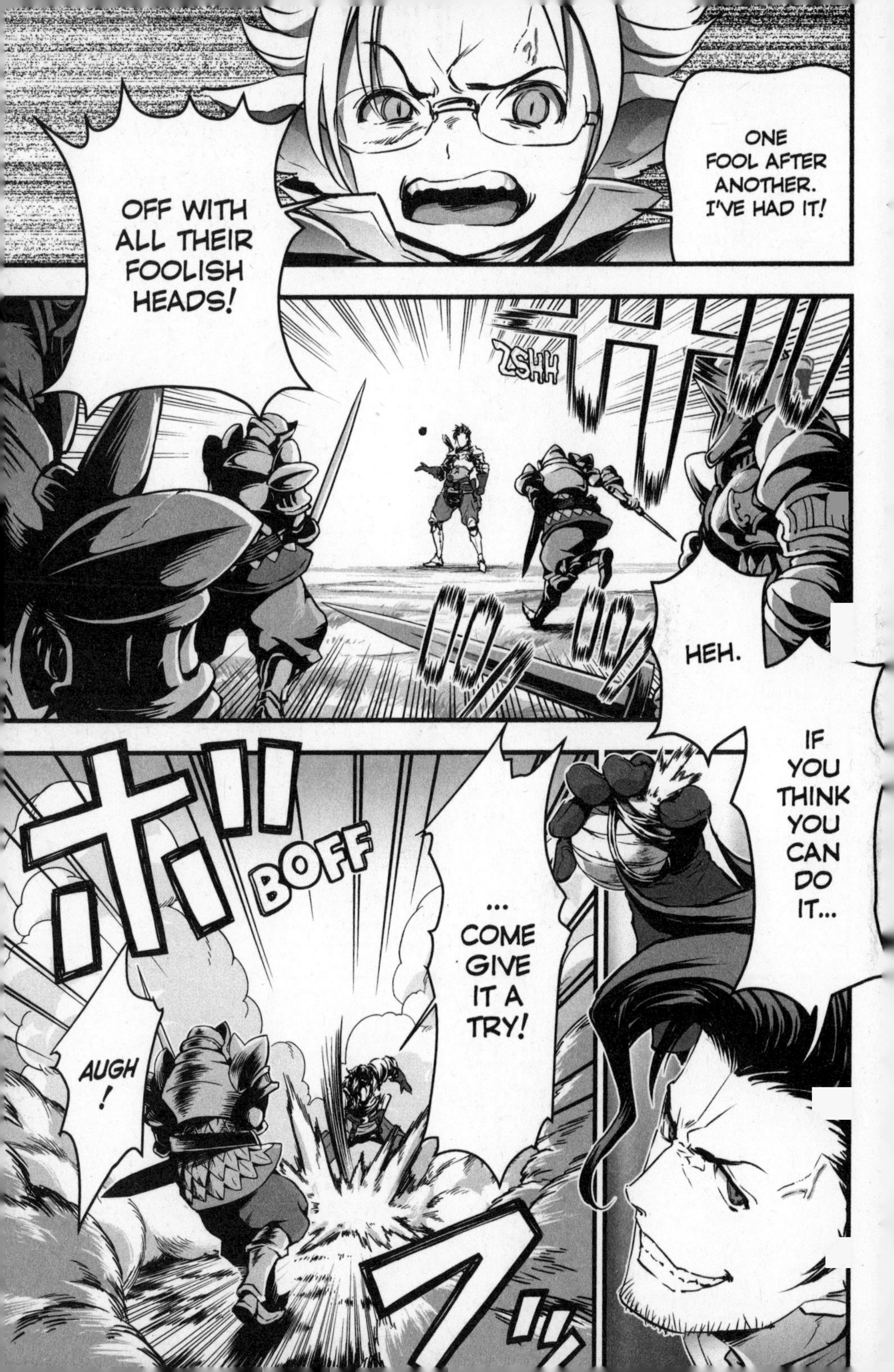
ONE FOOL AFTER ANOTHER. I'VE HAD IT!
OFF WITH ALL THEIR FOOLISH HEADS!
ZSHH
HEH.
IF YOU THINK YOU CAN DO IT...
... COME GIVE IT A TRY!
BOFF
AUGH!

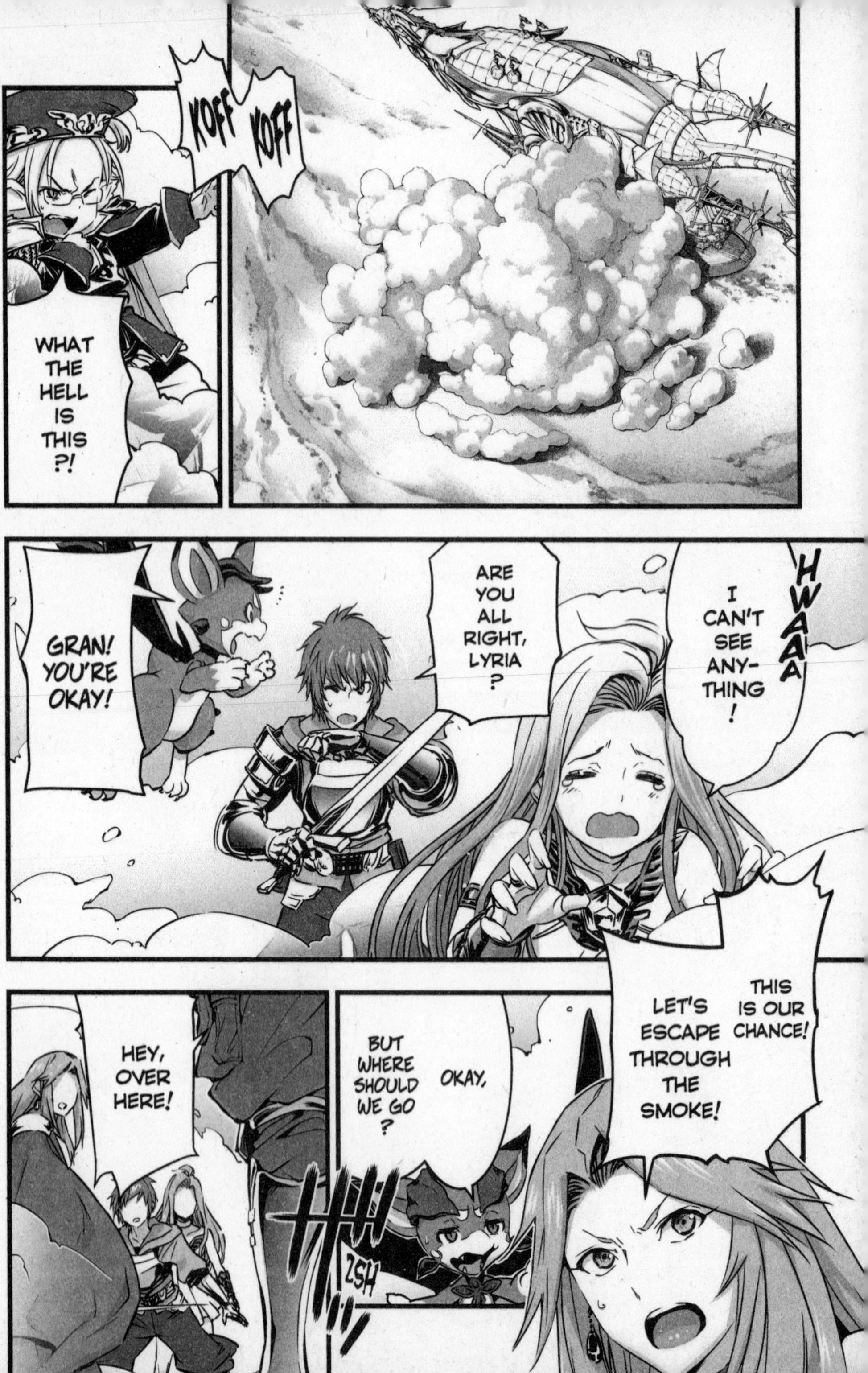
KOFF
KOFF
WHAT THE HELL IS THIS?!
HWAAAA
I CAN'T SEE ANYTHING!
ARE YOU ALL RIGHT, LYRIA?
GRAN! YOU'RE OKAY!
THIS IS OUR CHANCE!
LET'S ESCAPE THROUGH THE SMOKE!
OKAY,
BUT WHERE SHOULD WE GO?
ZSH
HEY, OVER HERE!

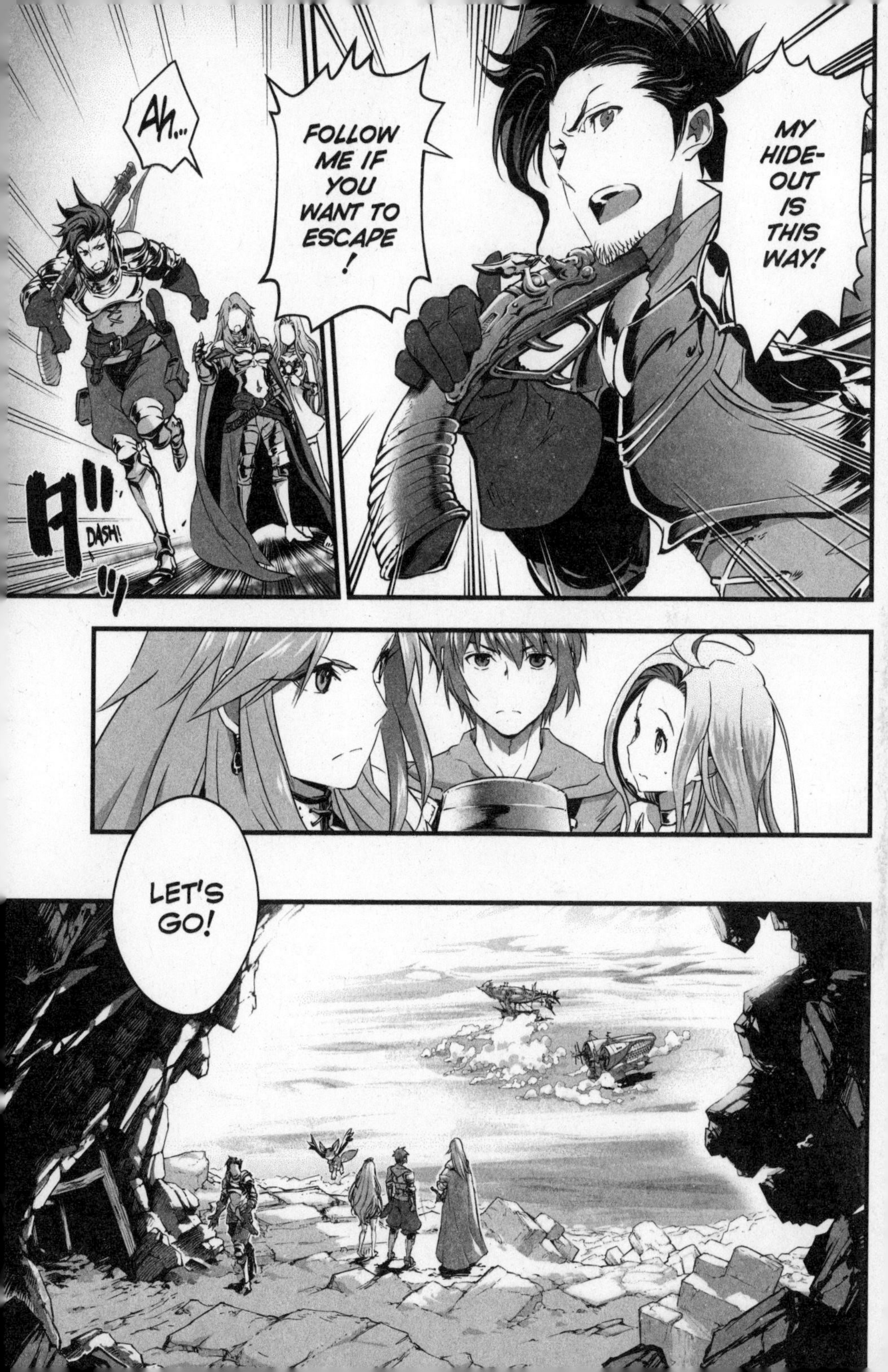
MY HIDE-OUT IS THIS WAY!
FOLLOW ME IF YOU WANT TO ESCAPE!
Ah...
DASH!
LET'S GO!

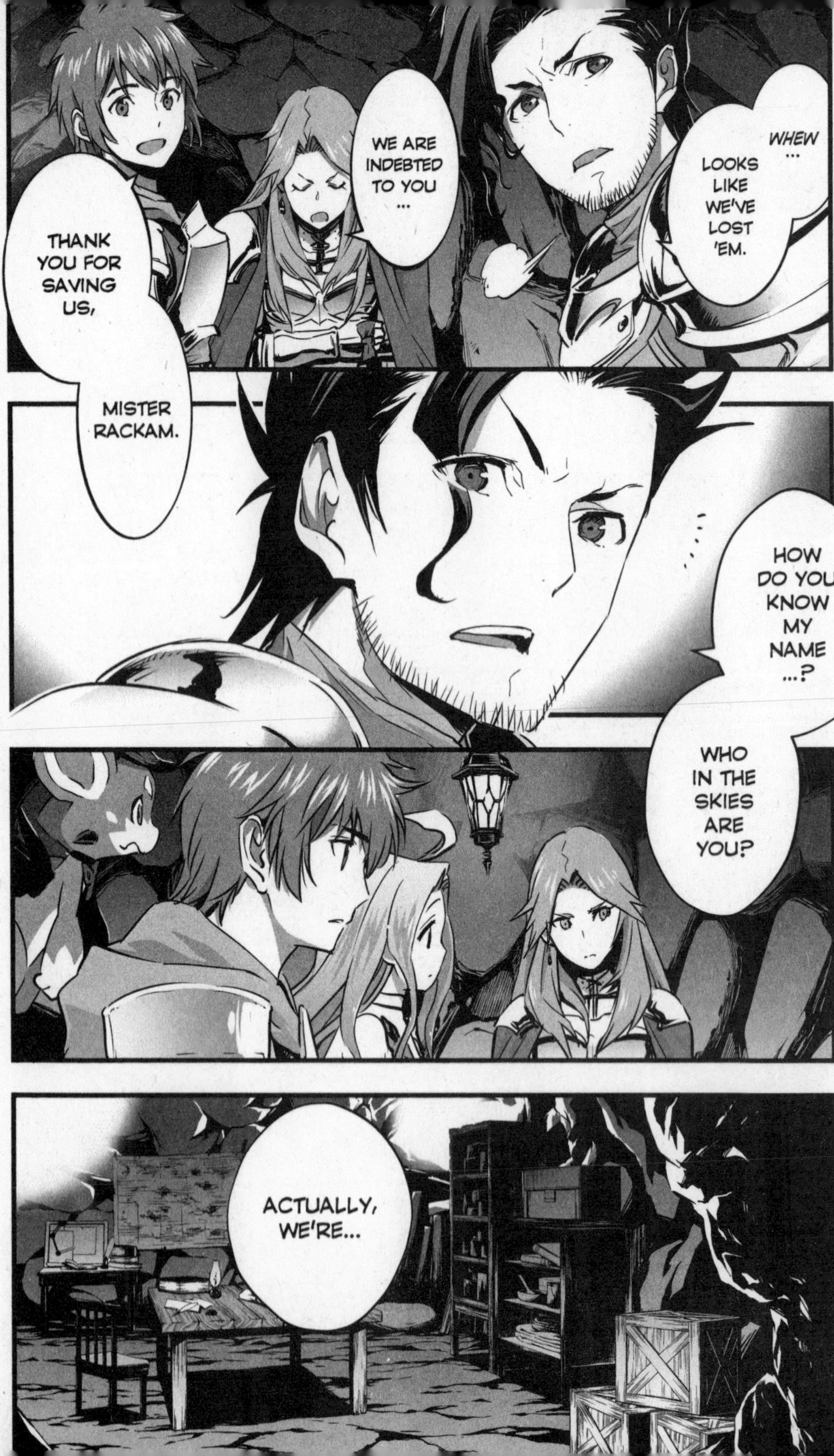
WHEW... LOOKS LIKE WE'VE LOST 'EM.
WE ARE INDEBTED TO YOU...
THANK YOU FOR SAVING US,
MISTER RACKAM.
HOW DO YOU KNOW MY NAME...?
WHO IN THE SKIES ARE YOU?
ACTUALLY, WE'RE...

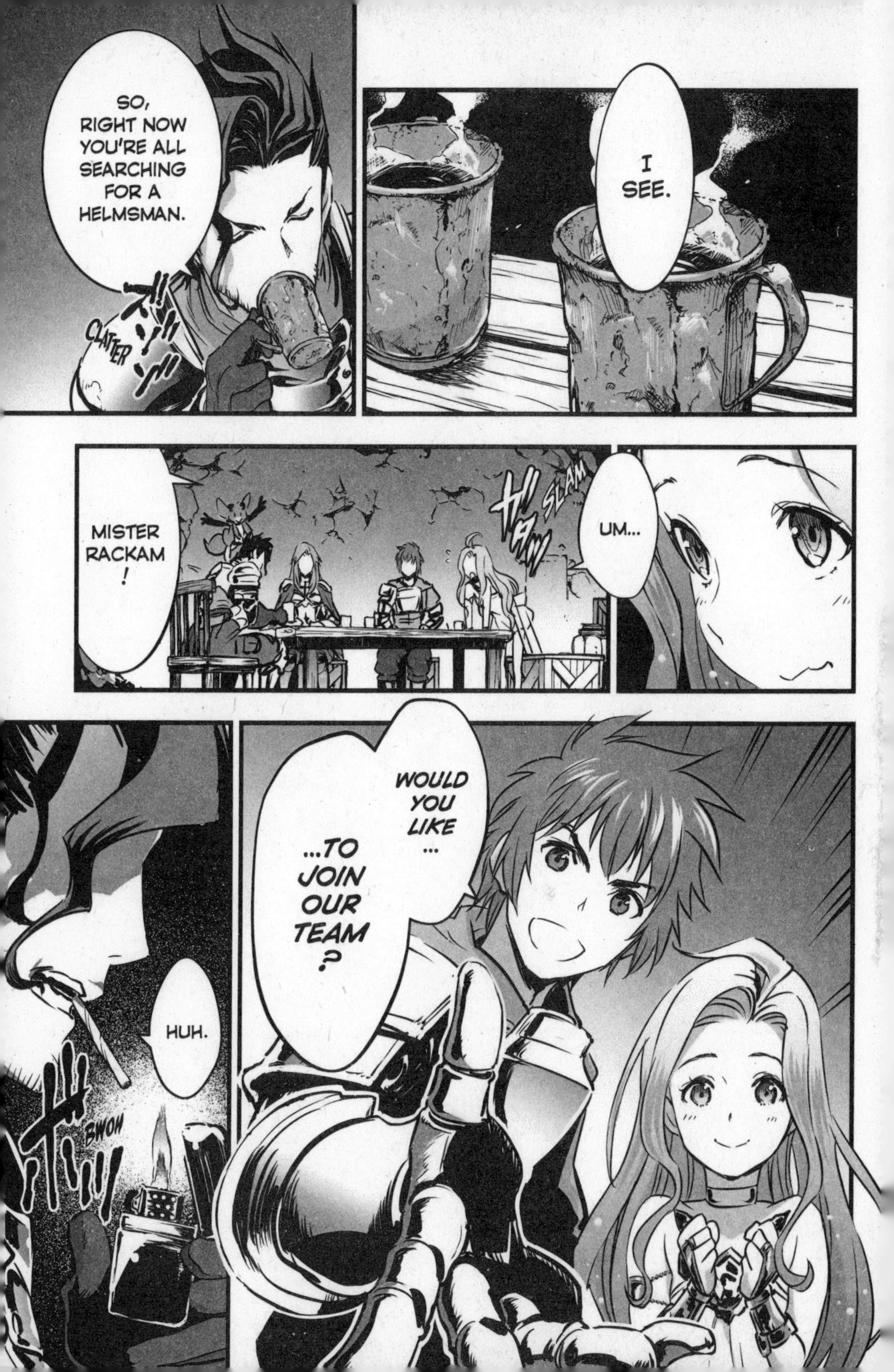
I SEE.
SO, RIGHT NOW YOU'RE ALL SEARCHING FOR A HELMSMAN.
CLATTER
UM...
SLAM
MISTER RACKAM!
WOULD YOU LIKE ...
...TO JOIN OUR TEAM?
HUH.
BWOH

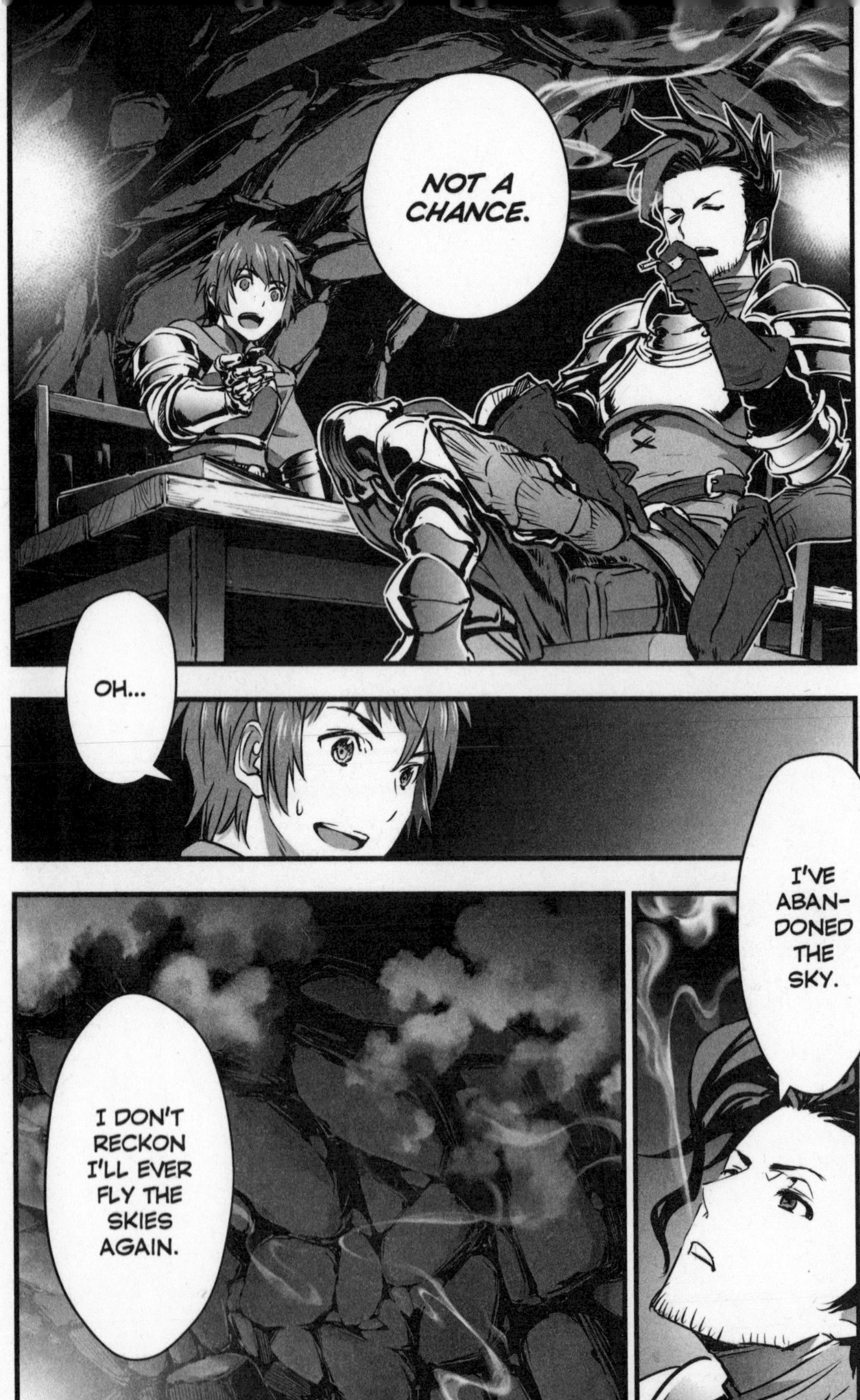
NOT A CHANCE.
OH...
I'VE ABAN-DONED THE SKY.
I DON'T RECKON I'LL EVER FLY THE SKIES AGAIN.

GRANBLUE FANTASY: END OF VOLUME ONE

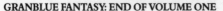

GRANBLUE FANTASY
グランブルーファンタジー

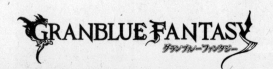

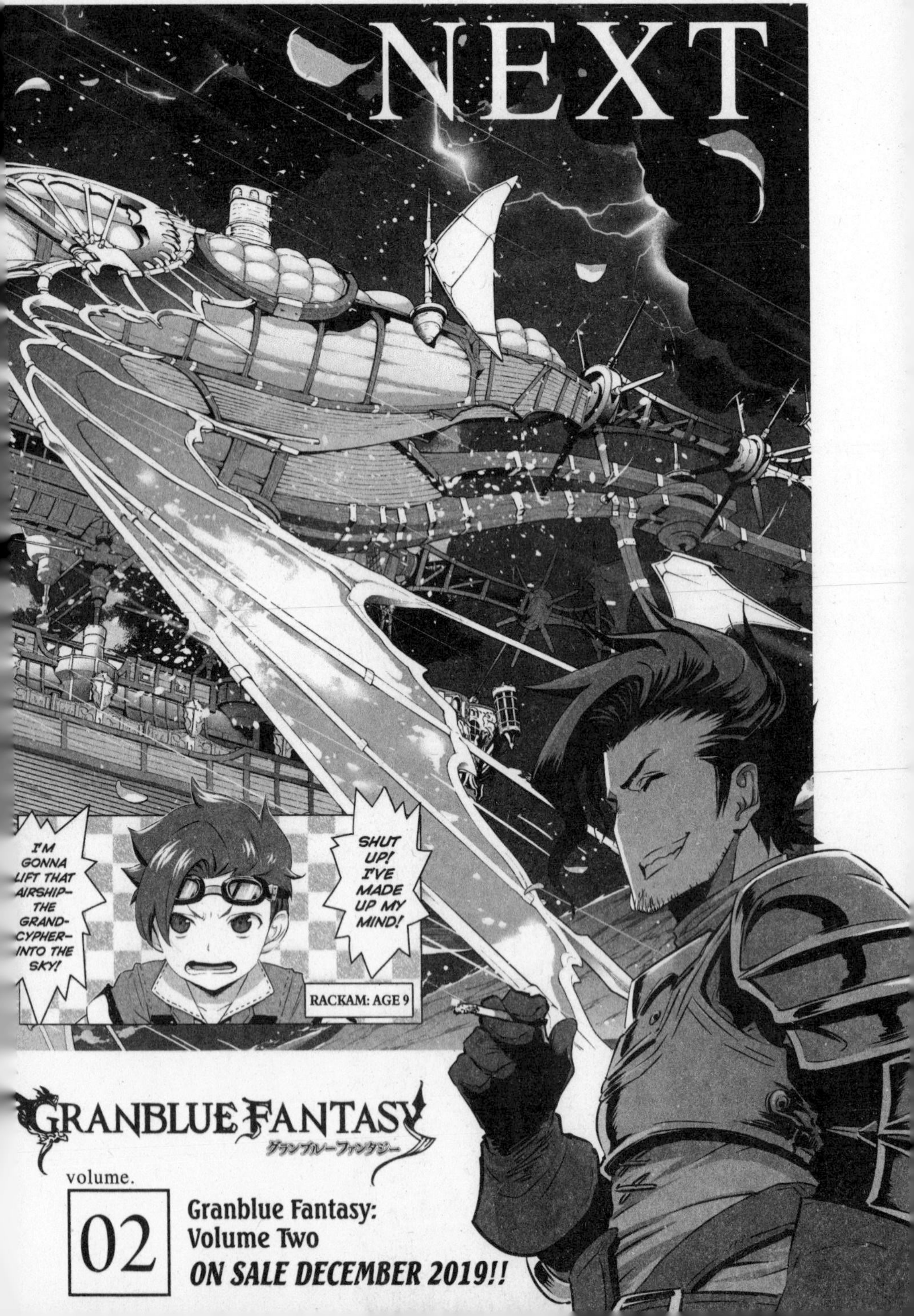
NEXT
SHUT UP! I'VE MADE UP MY MIND!
I'M GONNA LIFT THAT AIRSHIP—THE GRAND-CYPHER—INTO THE SKY!
RACKAM: AGE 9

GRANBLUE FANTASY
グランブルーファンタジー

volume.
02

Granblue Fantasy: Volume Two

ON SALE DECEMBER 2019!!

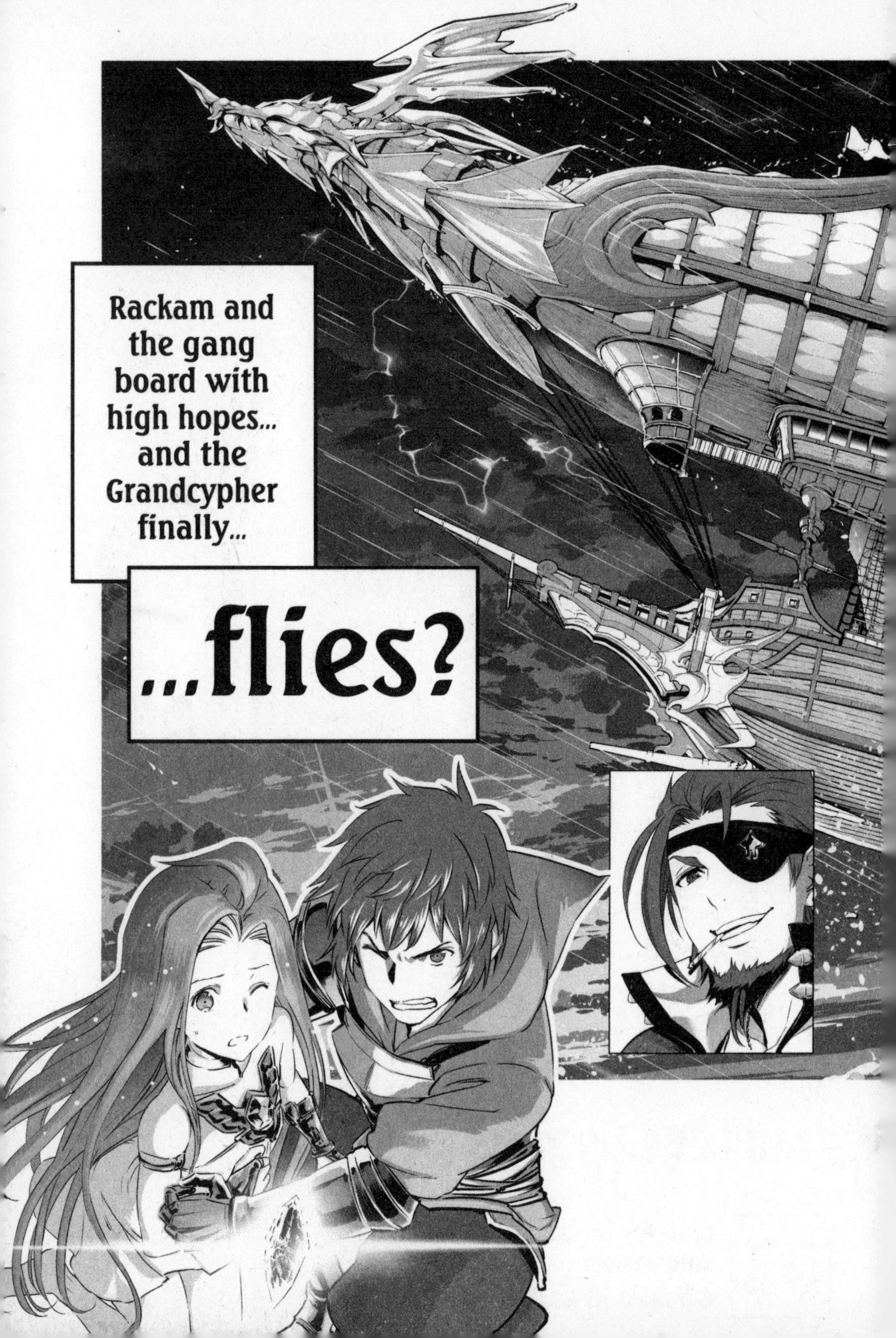
Rackam and the gang board with high hopes... and the Grandcypher finally...
...flies?

Granblue Fantasy Volume 1 is a work of fiction.
Names, characters, places, and incidents are the products of
the author's imagination or are used fictitiously.
Any resemblance to actual events, locales, or
persons, living or dead, is entirely coincidental.

A Kodansha Comics Trade Paperback Original
Granblue Fantasy Volume 1 copyright
© Cygames
© 2017 cocho
© 2017 Makoto Fugetsu

English translation copyright
© Cygames
© 2019 cocho
© 2019 Makoto Fugetsu

All rights reserved.

Published in the United States by Kodansha Comics, an imprint of
Kodansha USA Publishing, LLC, New York.

Publication rights for this English edition arranged through
Kodansha Ltd., Tokyo.

First published in Japan in 2017 by Kodansha Ltd., Tokyo,
as *Granblue Fantasy* Volume 1.

ISBN 978-1-63236-809-6

Printed in the United States of America.

www.kodanshacomics.com

9 8 7 6 5 4 3 2 1
Translation: Kristi Fernandez
Lettering: Evan Hayden
Kodansha Comics edition cover design by Phil Balsman